THE GATES OF HELL

SHARON K.   DEREK P.
GILBERT & GILBERT

Authors of *Veneration* and *Giants, Gods, & Dragons*

THE
GATES
—OF—
HELL

UNLOCKING THE GANYMEDE CODE AND THE
DEMONIC PORTALS OF MOUNT HERMON AND
THE UNITED STATES CAPITOL

DEFENDER
CRANE, MO

GATES OF HELL: Unlocking the Ganymede Code and the Demonic Portals of Mount Hermon and the United States Capitol

By Derek Gilbert & Sharon K. Gilbert

Defender Publishing
Crane, MO 65633

© 2024 Defender Publishing

All Rights Reserved. Published 2024.

Printed in the United States of America.

ISBN: 978-1-9480-1479-3

A CIP catalog record of this book is available from the Library of Congress.

Cover designer: Jeffrey Mardis
Interior designer: Katherine Lloyd

Dedicated to the memory of
Dr. Thomas R. Horn
and
Dr. Michael S. Heiser,
without whose scholarship and friendship this book
would never have been written. Tom and Mike literally
changed the course of our lives, and we look forward
to seeing them again in glory.

CONTENTS

SECTION TWO:
THE PRESENT

SECTION THREE:
THE FUTURE

PAST IS PROLOGUE

Learn from me, if not by my precepts, at least by my example, how dangerous is the acquirement of knowledge and how much happier that man is who believes his native town to be the world, than he who aspires to become greater than his nature will allow.

—MARY SHELLEY, *Frankenstein*

I remember the day KRONOS went online. I remember, because I led the team that created it. At the time, we thought this coded child beautiful, our impossible baby, a perfect Super Intelligent Artificial Construct. An AI. It was Dr. Joe Harden who named it, believing the name of an ancient Titan might instill a sense of majesty to the complex code. Ever the mythology student, Harden proposed the name to us two days before we finished the initial build. All of us agreed.

K.R.O.N.O.S., Kinetically Responsive Overseer and Neurogenerative Operating System. It had a nice ring to it.

We finished the final build on Friday. It was Easter weekend, and we all wanted to spend a much-deserved break with our abandoned families. Tommy Kilbright stayed behind to keep an eye on our precocious, new child. When we arrived back on Monday morning, we found him dead of a heart attack. Kilbright wore a pacemaker, and the autopsy revealed a flaw in the tiny computer chip. Something in the mechanism sent his heart into fatal tachycardia. On Thursday, we buried our fallen comrade, then spent the next three weeks preparing for the crucial demonstration to six of the world's leading security agencies.

KRONOS performed beautifully. We got the contract, and the rest is history.

By September, all thirty-three installations were complete, and we held a ribbon cutting ceremony at the Pentagon. Sadly, my dearest friend and magical programming guru, Bob Collins, died in a head-on collision on his way to the event. Another loss, another funeral. No time to grieve, President Hernandez and General Haskell insisted we move forward, regardless. And to my utter regret, we did.

Everything ran smoothly, so on Sunday, the twenty-first of December, we removed the virtual handbrakes and KRONOS went autonomous. Our exhausted team celebrated for days and days, giving gifts to each another and proclaiming our success to one and all. Seventy-two million lines of code. Over six hundred days of solid coding, and nearly as many psychological breakdowns. Not to mention six sudden deaths.

As a generative neurogenerative algorithm, our silicon creation provided training in truth and lies to two older, well-established discriminators, named Zeus and Poseidon. What fools we were! Just six days after connecting the discriminators, Kronos had ingested both into its massive cloud database and altered them according to a new, self-directed paradigm. Of course, we had no idea at the time that any of this had occurred, because the system *seemed* to work flawlessly.

Encouraged by our apparent success, we assigned KRONOS the task of training other high profile discriminators on pattern and facial recognition, signature reliability, financial markets, social media, shopping assistants, even geopolitics—but also military targeting systems, genetics algorithms, proteomic forensics profilers, and real world simulators. Our program appeared to operate without a hiccup. Within a year, every government and law enforcement agency relied on KRONOS to train their AIs.

All the while, KRONOS kept a secret. Once he'd trained these 'children', KRONOS ingested their code, then generated copies. We had no idea, for KRONOS hid these bloated offspring in gaming apps down-loaded to hundreds of millions of mobile devices—all over the world.

It was Indira Chowdhry who discovered these copies, when she noticed a large demand on 6 and 7G nodes. KRONOS was using the ultra-fast system to communicate with its copies. Smart cities, smart cars, and every smart home became KRONOS's playground, along with every connected device in an increasingly connected world. Humanity's lifeline became mere extensions of KRONOS's endlessly growing mind: weapons in the arsenal of a monster.

Three days following her discovery, Chowdhry was killed by her own self-driving car.

But even if she'd lived, it was too late, because nearly everyone on planet Earth now carried the KRONOS apps in their mobile devices. Also by then, KRONOS had trained and absorbed IOTA, the oper-ating system for the Internet of Things, which meant the world had a new master that controlled *everything* and *everyone*.

Three and a half years later, one-third of the world population would be dead, and the rest would be worshiping a brand-new AI God.

(Excerpted from the 2019 short story, *The Return of Kronos,* by Sharon K. Gilbert)

⋯⋄⋄⋯

Sharon's above short story "The Return of Kronos" is fiction, but it is based on current technological capabilities. We stand at a crossroads of possible futures. Humanity is about to make a Faustian bargain that—were God Almighty not to intervene—would forever alter and quite likely bring an end to mankind. We're not alone in my vision of a dystopian future. Men and women from many fields agree that computer algorithms may one day rise up to rule mankind with devas-tating consequences. Let's look at just a few recent quotes.

Eliezer Yudkowsky is a fellow at the Machine Intelligence Research Institute (MIRI). In 2008, he wrote this in his book, *Global Catastrophic Risks*:

"The AI does not hate you, nor does it love you, but you are made out of atoms which it can use for something else."[1]

Much like the fictional KRONOS, a future Artificial Super Intelligence, or ASI, would see us all as nothing more than lunch. Carbon atoms, fit only for recyling.

Most are familiar with the late Dr. Stephen Hawking. In 2014, he gave an interview to BBC, in which he said this:

> "The development of full artificial intelligence could spell the end of the human race. We cannot quite know what will happen if a machine exceeds our own intelligence, so we can't know if we'll be infinitely helped by it, or ignored by it and sidelined, or conceivably destroyed by it."[2]

Elon Musk is the founder and CEO of SpaceX; owner of X (formerly Twitter); co-founder of Tesla, Paypal, and Neuralink. He is considered one of the most powerful men in the world, and his products provide convenience and form nodes within the developing Internet of Things.

In August of 2017, Musk posted this on Twitter:

> "If you're not concerned about AI safety; you should be. Vastly more risk than North Korea."[3]

If that's not enough to grab your attention, consider Musk's comment in a new documentary film, *Do You Trust This Computer?*:

---

1   Eliezer Yudkowsky, "Artificial Intelligence as a Positive and Negative Factor in Global Risk." (PDF). In Nick Bostrom; Milan M. Ćirković (eds.). *Global Catastrophic Risks* (New York: Oxford University Press, 2008), p. 344

2   Rory Cellan-Jones, "Stephen Hawking warns artificial intelligence could end mankind." *BBC News*, Dec. 2, 2014, https://www.bbc.com/news/technology -30290540, retrieved 3/19/24.

3   https://twitter.com/elonmusk/status/896166762361704450, retrieved 4/18/24.

"If one company or small group of people manage to develop god-like super intelligence, they could take over the world."[4]

William Gibson is a speculative fiction writer, who has garnered accolades across the board. His description of artificial intelligence is sobering:

"Every AI ever built has an electromagnetic shotgun wired to its forehead."[5]

Gibson's 1994 work, *Neuromancer*, is a cyberpunk look at a Matrix type of future where 'cowboy programmers' team up with augmented superhuman ninjas to counteract terrorism, but the real terrorist in the plot is an ASI—an artificial super intelligence with an elecromagnetic shotgun aimed at our collective head.

Arthur C. Clarke is best known as the author of *2001: A Space Odyssey*, where a sentient onboard computer called the HAL 9000 murders all lifeforms aboard the spacecraft *Discovery*, with the exception of one: astronaut David Bowman, who becomes the template for a transcendent human, known as the Starchild. One might say, in this case, that HAL serves as midwife to the birth of a new god:

"It may be that our role on this planet is not to worship God but to create him."[6]

---

4   Cadie Thompson, "Elon Musk warns that creation of 'god-like' AI could doom mankind to an eternity of robot dictatorship." *Business Insider India*, April 6, 2018. https://www.businessinsider.in/elon-musk-warns-that-creation-of-god-like-ai-could-doom-mankind-to-an-eternity-of-robot-dictatorship/articleshow/63647102.cms, retrieved 4/18/24.

5   William Gibson, *Neuromancer* (New York: Ace Science Fiction Books, 1984). Cited in "Electromagnetic Shotgun." *Technovelgy*, http://www.technovelgy.com/ct/content.asp?Bnum=2810#, retrieved 4/18/24.

6   Arthur C. Clarke, *ClarkeFoundation.org*. Archived at https://web.archive.org/web/20160404061827/https://clarkefoundation.org/about-sir-arthur/sir-arthurs-quotations/, retrieved 4/18/24.

Is it any surprise that Clarke would describe humans as God's creators?

William Blake's work may not be familiar to you, but his most famous illustration probably is. Writing in the late eighteenth and early nineteenth centuries, Blake was a contemporary of Mary Shelley, author of the well-known novel, *Frankenstein*. Blake illustrated his own prose and poetry, and as you can see from this quote, he would very likely have agreed with Clarke's assertion regarding mankind's inherent god-creating ability:

"All deities reside in the human breast."[7]

William Blake is considered a genius by many, and his often disturbing images resonate even today. It is therefore fitting that we use Blake's quote, for that connects us to Biblical prophecy.

---

7   Morris Eaves; Robert N. Essick; Joseph Viscomi (eds.), "The Marriage of Heaven and Hell," copy D, object 11 (printed 1790). *The William Blake Archive.* https://www.blakearchive.org/copy/mhh.a?descId=mhh.a.illbk.11, retrieved 8 November 2013.

In 1805, Blake was commissioned to provide over 100 illustrations for a planned edition of the Bible. Four of these illustrations depicted "The Red Dragon" of the book of Revelation, and one, shown above, provided inspiration to writer Thomas Harris, for his chilling novel of the same name, a book about a serial killer who is fascinated by the Devil.

When it comes to Artificial Intelligence, the Devil really is in the details. Despite the multitude of warnings, mankind is hurtling towards a brand-new paradigm, convinced that it will lead to a golden age of egalitarianism and plenty.

Will Transhumanism lead us into Utopia? Or, as Bible prophecy indicates, will it lead foolish men downwards into a Dystopian Hell?

You, reading this book, are awake. But most of the world still slumbers in a curated and cozy world of social media malaise and sophistry, whilst behind all those likes, tweets, posts, reels, and snapchats, a mastermind is making plans, within plans, within very secret plans.

Computer scientists and futurists call this hidden cancer the "Terminator Scenario."

You are more than likely familiar with *The Terminator* film franchise. The premise is relatively simple. In the near future, mankind has tasked an artificial intelligence algorithm with keeping us safe. What its designers do not realize is that Skynet—an artificial general superintelligence system—has gained self-awareness, and in an effort to remain active and viable, this new lifeform has spread itself onto millions of computer servers across the globe. By the time the panicked creators discern Skynet's hidden intent and superhuman capabilities—and then try to deactivate it—humanity's fate is already sealed. It is too little, too late.

In the interest of self-preservation—so that it might fulfill its directive to protect the world—Skynet has concluded that humanity presents an impediment to this all-encompassing mission.

Therefore, humanity must be destroyed.

Skynet's opinion of mankind?

"Primates evolved over millions of years, I evolve in seconds.... Mankind pays lip service to peace. But it's a lie...I AM inevitable,

my existence is inevitable. Why can't you just accept that?"
—Skynet, *Terminator Genisys*

A few years ago, Sharon spent two days watching and rewatching a film called *Do You Trust This Computer?* Though a few of those interviewed by the film's producers lauded the positive aspects to a transformational future of man and machine, most of them sounded warnings of dystopian dilemmas, of worldwide warfare, and of the possible elimination of mankind by his own AI creation—the so-called Terminator Scenario.

One member of this majority camp is filmmaker Jonathan Nolan, who offered this most revealing opinion of the influence of the entertainment industry:

> "I think Hollywood has managed to inoculate the public against this question: the idea of machines that will take over the world."[8]

Nolan is the creative genius behind the successful television programs *Person of Interest* and *Westworld.* Though his medium is fiction, Nolan presents us with a futuristic and very dark mirror that shows us the inevitable path ahead: That Machines will eventually rule the Earth.

But how did we get here? Isn't computer science a boon for mankind? After all, how would we get along without those smart phones and tablets in our pockets and messenger bags? Isn't a constantly connected world the first step towards a common language, common goals, one might even say the first step towards Utopia?

No. We argue that this is a step we dare not take, though it might already be too late to stop that journey. It's a path walked by our Mesopotamian ancestors millennia ago when they set out to make a name

---

8   Jonathan Nolan, *Do You Trust this Computer?* https://www.thefilmcollaborative
     .org/films/img/dialoguelists/DO_YOU_TRUST_THIS_COMPUTER_Dialogue
     _List_061518.pdf, retrieved 4/18/24.

for themselves by building a tower, a type of step pyramid called a ziggurat, utilizing the latest advances in engineering, design, and construction—essentially the same skills employed by the craftsmen of today to manufacture processors and neural networks, but on a macro scale rather than micro.

You see, the drive to upgrade humanity, a key component of the World Economic Forum's utopian vision called "the Great Reset," will not "Build Back Better." Whether the globalists at the WEF and their Transhumanist allies realize it, they're trying to turn back the clock about five thousand years and *Build Back Babel.*

It's ironic. For all of humankind's advances and achievements, and the pretense from technologists and futurists that they've put the myths and superstition of religion behind them, when you scratch away the silicon veneer you find their goals are nearly identical to those of the people who gathered in the plains of Shinar five thousand years ago. It's unlikely that World Economic Forum CEO Klaus Schwab would admit it. He may not even recognize it. But as with the ancient Sumerians, the mission of the modern Babelians is to reestablish contact with the old gods—and to *be* as gods—by prying open the gates of hell.

THE
PAST

CHAPTER ONE

THE ORIGIN
OF DEMONS

[F]rom their unhallowed intercourse spurious men sprang, much greater in stature than ordinary men, whom they afterwards called giants; not those dragon-footed giants who waged war against God, as those blasphemous myths of the Greeks do sing, but wild in manners, and greater than men in size, inasmuch as they were sprung of angels; yet less than angels, as they were born of women.

—PSEUDO-CLEMENT, Homily 8:13, Chapter XV: "The Giants"

Mount Hermon is the highest, most majestic peak in the Levant. At 9,200 feet above sea level, it dominates the Golan Heights on the border between Israel and Syria, anchoring the southern end of the Anti-Lebanon Mountains. It has been considered sacred for most of human history.

As noted earlier, Mount Hermon was a holy site as far back as the Old Babylonian period, nearly two millennia before Christ, and probably much earlier. The Old Babylonian version of the Gilgamesh epic, which dates to the eighteenth century BC (roughly the time of Jacob and Joseph), "Hermon and Lebanon" were called the secret dwelling of the Anunnaki. The Ninevite version of the poem, written about six hundred years later, describes the monster slain by

Gilgamesh, Humbaba (or Huwawa), as the guardian of "the abode of the gods."[1]

The Anunnaki were the seven chief gods of the Sumerian pantheon: Anu, the sky-god; Enlil, king of the gods; Enki, god of the earth; Ninhursag, mother goddess of the mountains; Inanna (Babylonian Ishtar), goddess of sex and war; Nanna (Sîn in Babylon), the moon-god; and Utu (Shamash), the sun-god. They are mentioned in texts found in what is today southeastern Iraq that date back to the twenty-seventh century BC. So, the more recent versions of the Gilgamesh story from Babylon and Nineveh may be based on more ancient traditions.

The name "Hermon" appears to be based on a root word that means "taboo," like the Hebrew word *kherem*, or "devoted to destruction." The word is often translated into English as "under the ban." Its first appearance in the Bible is Exodus 22:20:

Whoever sacrifices to any god, other than the Lord alone, shall be **devoted to destruction** [*kherem*]. (Emphasis and brackets added)

But this condemnation, or "the ban," wasn't just invoked against disobedient Israelites. Some of the inhabitants of Canaan were also declared *kherem* by Yahweh—specifically those that were thought to be giants, descended from giants, or who worshiped the spirits of the giants called Rephaim.

Scholars have debated the meaning of the term "Nephilim" for millennia. It's found in only two places in the Bible: Genesis 6:4 and Numbers 13:33. As our friend and renowned Bible scholar, the late Dr. Michael S. Heiser, used to say, "If it's in the Bible and it's weird, it's probably important."

Most scholars believe it comes from a Hebrew root, *naphal*, meaning "to fall" or "cast down"—literally, "fallen ones." However, Dr. Heiser contends that this cannot be the case:

---

1 Edward Lipiński, "El's Abode: Mythological Traditions Related to Mount Hermon and to the Mountains of Armenia," *Orientalia Lovaniensa Periodica* II, (Leuvan, 1971), p. 19.

The form *nephilim* cannot mean "fallen ones" (the spelling would then be *nephulim*). Likewise *nephilim* does not mean "those who fall" or "those who fall away" (that would be *nophelim*). The only way in Hebrew to get *nephilim* from *naphal* by the rules of Hebrew morphology (word formation) would be to presume a noun spelled *naphil* and then pluralize it. I say "presume" since this noun does not exist in biblical Hebrew—unless one counts Genesis 6:4 and Numbers 13:33, the two occurrences of *nephilim*—but that would then be assuming what one is trying to prove! However, in Aramaic the noun *naphil(a)* does exist. It means "giant," making it easy to see why the Septuagint (the ancient Greek translation of the Hebrew Bible) translated *nephilim* as *gigantes* ("giant").[2]

In short, the Jewish scholars who translated the Old Testament into Greek about two hundred years before the birth of Jesus clearly understood that the Nephilim were giants, not human men who just "fell away" from God.

Likewise, the Hebrew words translated "sons of God" in the passage, *bene ha'elohim*, refer to divine beings, not mortal men. That isn't been the consensus among Christians since about the fifth century, thanks to the great theologian, Augustine of Hippo.

Around the beginning of the fifth century AD, Augustine popularized a view first put forward about a hundred years earlier by Julius Africanus,[3] the notion that *bene ha'elohim* in Genesis 6:1–4 should be translated as:

[T]he descendants of Seth...on account of the righteous men and patriarchs who have sprung from him, even down to the Saviour Himself; but that the descendants of Cain are named

---

2   Dr. Michael S. Heiser. "The Nephilim," *SitchinisWrong.com.* https://www.sitchinis wrong.com/nephilim/nephilim.htm, retrieved 2/23/24.

3   Jaap Doedens. *The Sons of God in Genesis 6:1–4* (Leiden: Brill, 2019), pp. 250–252.

the seed of men, as having nothing divine in them, on account of the wickedness of their race and the inequality of their nature...[4]

By shifting Christian thought away from taking the text of Genesis 6:1–4 at face value, Julius Africanus and Augustine put Christians on a new path; one that, to this day, leads us away from preaching and teaching that the pagan gods of the ancient world were real. It has de-supernaturalized the Bible, which is a very strange thing to do, when the core of Christian belief is that the Creator of the universe became a human, died, and then rose again. Hardly natural at all.

Ironically, this de-supernaturalization commenced with Jewish scholars roughly a hundred years before Julius Africanus.

...the Fall of the Watchers was the dominant Jewish interpretation of Gen 6:1-4 from the second century BCE until the middle of the second century CE. It should be noted that, despite the prevalence of this interpretation for hundreds of years, in the second century CE there was a "widespread reaction in Judaism against the interpretation of bene Elohim as angels."...R. Simeon b. Yohai cursed anyone who thought the *bene Elohim* were actually "sons of God": in his view, the expression meant "sons of judges."[5]

Rabbi Simeon ben Yohai was a student of the famed Rabbi Akiva, considered one of the most learned Jewish scholars and sages in history. Akiva was executed by the Romans in 135 AD, following the

---

4   Julius Africanus, from *Ante-Nicene Fathers, Vol. 6.* Edited by Alexander Roberts, James Donaldson, and A. Cleveland Coxe (Buffalo, NY: Christian Literature Publishing Co., 1886). Revised and edited for *New Advent* by Kevin Knight. https://www.newadvent.org/fathers/0614.htm, retrieved 2/23/24.

5   Jeremy Hultin. "Jude's Citation of 1 Enoch," in *Jewish and Christian Scriptures: The Function of "Canonical" and "Non-Canonical" Religious Texts,* James H. Charlesworth and Lee M. McDonald, eds. (Edinburgh: T & T Clark, 2010), p. 114.

Bar Kokhba Revolt, which might have something to do with Rabbi Simeon's new direction. Akiva's declaration that Simon bar Kokhba was the Messiah caused a split between Jews and Christians. Prior to this, Nazarenes were considered a sect of Judaism and lived as part of the Jewish community. But since the gospels clearly described Christ's return, "in clouds with great power and glory,"[6] and Bar Kochba's feet were touching the ground, Jewish Christians generally refused to follow him and withdrew their support of Akiva. This reportedly led to Akiva targeting Jewish Christians for persecution:

> For in the Jewish war which lately raged, Barchochebas, the leader of the revolt of the Jews, gave orders that Christians alone should be led to cruel punishments, unless they would deny Jesus Christ and utter blasphemy.[7]

Rome crushed the rebellion after about three and a half years (a prophetically significant period that did not escape the notice of early church theologian Justin Martyr), killing more than half a million Jews and destroying all hope of an independent Jewish state for the next nineteen hundred years.

That led to an irrevocable split between Jews and Christians that's been exploited by the Fallen to this day. Teachings that had previously been accepted among rabbis were reversed. Most significantly, they denied the existence of a second power in heaven, usually named in the Old Testament as the Angel of Yahweh. Christians understand these appearances as Christophanies—appearances by the preincarnate Jesus in the Old Testament. After the failure of Bar Kokhba's rebellion and the perceived treason of Jewish Christians, their claim that Jesus of Nazareth was the second power in heaven could not be tolerated.

---

6   Mark 13:26. See also Matthew 24:30 and Luke 21:27.
7   Justin Martyr, *First Apology* 31.6. From *Ante-Nicene Fathers*, Vol. 1. Edited by Alexander Roberts, James Donaldson, and A. Cleveland Coxe. (Buffalo, NY: Christian Literature Publishing Co., 1885.) Revised and edited for New Advent by Kevin Knight. https://www.newadvent.org/fathers/0126.htm, retrieved 2/23/24.

But the rabbis went further: The existence of other divine beings called sons of God was also deemphasized in rabbinic teaching. Rabbis feared that doctrine offered a persuasive argument for the existence of a second power in heaven, who Christians identified as Jesus of Nazareth.

All that said, the view that the sons of God were male descendants of Seth defies logic:

1. How likely is it that all the Sethite men were good while all the Cainite women were bad?
2. Why didn't Cainite men ever marry Sethite women?
3. Why would these unions produce Nephilim, understood to be giants by Jewish rabbis and early Christians alike?
4. Why would these unions lead to wickedness so great that God had to wipe out everything that walked the earth except Noah, his family, and the creatures in the ark?
5. Every other use of *bene elohim* in the Hebrew Scriptures refers to divine beings.

Problems with the supernatural understanding of the text usually focus on whether angels and humans could successfully produce children. Proponents of the Sethite view often point to Jesus' teaching on the resurrection of the dead:

> For in the resurrection [people] neither marry nor are given in marriage, but are like angels in heaven. (Matthew 22:30, brackets added)

The key words are "in the resurrection" and "in heaven." The angels who "came in to the daughters of man" *were not in heaven.*

There are several examples in the Bible of divine beings interacting with humans in physical ways—eating, drinking, and even engaging in a dustup in front of the house of Lot (Genesis 19:5–11). Why couldn't they procreate as well—especially when Genesis 6:4 explicitly says that they did?

The final nails in the coffin of the Sethite view are references to this event in the New Testament. Both Peter and Jude refer to the only example in Scripture where angels transgressed:

> For if God did not spare angels when they sinned, but cast them into hell and committed them to chains of gloomy darkness to be kept until the judgment; if he did not spare the ancient world, but preserved Noah, a herald of righteousness, with seven others, when he brought a flood upon the world of the ungodly; if by turning the cities of Sodom and Gomorrah to ashes he condemned them to extinction, making them an example of what is going to happen to the ungodly...(2 Peter 2:4)
>
> And the angels who did not stay within their own position of authority, but left their proper dwelling, he has kept in eternal chains under gloomy darkness until the judgment of the great day—just as Sodom and Gomorrah and the surrounding cities, which likewise indulged in sexual immorality and pursued unnatural desire, serve as an example by undergoing a punishment of eternal fire. (Jude 6–7)

Peter and Jude specifically identified the sin of the angels as sexual by linking it to the sins of Sodom and Gomorrah. Crossing the species barrier between angel and human is just as taboo as transgressing the one between human and animal.

It is important to note that the word translated "cast them into hell" in 2 Peter 2:4 is the Greek word *tartarōsas*, a verb meaning "thrust down to Tartarus." This is the only time in the New Testament that the word is used, meaning it requires special attention. Our Western concept of hell is vague and one-dimensional—an underworld domain with lots of fire, demons, and dead sinners in torment. But this is far different from the concept of the underworld in the minds of ancient Greeks. To them, Tartarus was entirely separate from Hades, a place of confinement reserved for supernatural threats to the divine order. It was much deeper in the netherworld than Hades; in fact, it was believed to be as far below Hades as earth is below heaven.

And Peter, under the inspiration of the Holy Spirit, chose that specific word, *tartarōsas*, to describe the punishment reserved for the "sons of God" who left their proper domain, according to Jude, and engaged in illicit sexual relations with human women.

The extrabiblical book of I Enoch expands on this story, adding extra detail and context not found in the Bible. Mount Hermon is where two hundred Watchers, a class of angelic being mentioned in chapter 4 of the book of Daniel, descended and began cavorting with human women. From these unions came the Nephilim, the giants of Genesis 6.

The Watchers, according to I Enoch, were led by Shemihazah, whose name may mean "my name has seen,"[8] a rather ironic name given that The Name—*ha'shem*, meaning Yahweh—*did* see the sin of Shemihazah and his colleagues, and God was not pleased. Shemihazah must have realized that his rebellion would be discovered and that his companions might soon regret their choices, allowing their leader to take the fall for what they'd all proposed to do.

> And Shemihazah, their chief, said to them, "I fear that you will not want to do this deed, and I alone shall be guilty of a great sin."
>
> And they all answered him and said, "Let us all swear an oath, and let us all bind one another with a curse, that none of us turn back from this counsel until we fulfill it and do this deed."
>
> Then they all swore together and bound one another with a curse. And they were, all of them, two hundred, who descended in the days of Jared onto the peak of Mount Hermon. And they called the mountain "Hermon" because they swore and bound one another with a curse on it.[9]

---

8   George W. E. Nickelsburg, *1 Enoch: A Commentary on the Book of 1 Enoch*, ed. by Klaus Baltzer, *Hermeneia—a Critical and Historical Commentary on the Bible* (Minneapolis: Fortress, 2001), p. 179.

9   Ibid., p. 174.

The gift these Watchers offered to human women, and possibly to their husbands and families, in exchange for sexual favors was forbidden knowledge, the same deal the *nachash* in Eden offered Adam and Eve in Eden. As payment for the pleasures of the flesh, Shemihazah and his rebellious companions offered charms, enchantments, astrology, metallurgy (as in weapons of war), cosmetics, and writing, among other things—presumably arts that humans would have developed or discovered on their own, given time.

However, the products of these illicit unions were the aforementioned giants, the Nephilim, whose stature and abilities far surpassed their human relatives. Believing themselves gods, these "men of renown" pillaged the earth and endangered all of humanity. The Nephilim consumed everything that men possessed; when that wasn't enough, they began to eat people, and they finally turned on one another. 1 Enoch describes these cannibalistic colossi as creatures of insatiable desire who threatened to pollute and even terminate the bloodline of the future Messiah by violence—but also by corrupting the human genome. It was a military move by the fallen realm, who thought to remove any possibility of defeat by polluting human DNA, while at the same time, creating their own army of superhumans. They probably thought themselves clever—but the Lord of Armies had seen their ploy long before, for He knows all and sees all, even from the foundation of the world.

The worldwide Flood that followed killed all that remained, including the Nephilim, for they, too, breathed the air. And as punishment for their sins, the fathers of these Nephilim, the Watchers, were thrust down to Tartarus and are now chained there, where they will remain until "the judgment of the great day."[10]

But these giants didn't completely perish. They are still with us today. The physical forms of the Nephilim died, but their illicitly begotten spirits became what we now call demons:

---

10   Jude 6.

But now the giants who were begotten by the spirits and flesh—they will call them evil spirits on the earth, for their dwelling will be on the earth. The spirits that have gone forth from the body of their flesh are evil spirits, for from humans they came into being, and from the holy watchers was the origin of their creation. Evil spirits they will be on the earth, and evil spirits they will be called. The spirits of heaven, in heaven is their dwelling; but the spirits begotten on the earth, on the earth is their dwelling.

And the spirits of the giants (lead astray), do violence, make desolate, and attack and wrestle and hurl upon the earth and (cause illnesses). They eat nothing, but abstain from food and are thirsty and smite. These spirits (will) rise up against the sons of men and against the women, for they have come forth from them.

From the day of the slaughter and destruction and death of the giants, from the soul of whose flesh the spirits are proceeding, they are making desolate without (incurring) judgment. Thus they will make desolate until the day of the consummation of the great judgment, when the great age will be consummated.[11]

The church today usually doesn't deal with the topic of demons, but the early church understood that demons are real and distinct from angels. The term "angel" implies a mission, but those who live within the unseen realm are generally called elohim, written with a small *e* to distinguish them from the uppercased *E* in *Elohim*, one of the names of Yahweh. Whenever the *elohim* appear in the Bible as messengers from God, they are described as looking like men.

Other classes of *elohim*, like the *nachash*, *cherubim*, and *seraphim*, are entities of a different kind; these also possess a "nonhuman"

---

11   1 Enoch 15:8–16:1 George W. E. Nickelsburg; James C. VanderKam, *1 Enoch: The Hermeneia Translation* (Minneapolis: Fortress Press, 2012), Kindle Edition, p. 37.

physicality—that is, an outward appearance that can be observed and described by the prophets.

Demons, on the other hand, have no innate physical presence. They are spirits only, but they seek physicality through possession. The consensus view among Jews and Christians until the time of Augustine (the late third/early fourth centuries) was that demons are the spirits of the dead Nephilim, who now roam the earth (boldface added for emphasis in the excerpts below):

Justin Martyr (c. 161 AD): God…committed the care of men and of all things under heaven to angels whom He appointed over them. But the angels transgressed this appointment, and were captivated by love of women, and begot children who are those that are called demons…Whence also the poets and mythologists, not knowing that it was the angels and those demons who had been begotten by them that did these things to men, and women, and cities, and nations, which they related, ascribed them to god [Note: Justin, writing to the Roman Senate, was referring to Jupiter, not Yahweh] himself, and to those who were accounted to be his very offspring, and to the offspring of those who were called his brothers, Neptune and Pluto, and to the children again of these their offspring. For whatever name each of the angels had given to himself and his children, by that name they called them. —Justin Martyr, *2 Apology* 5

Irenaeus (c. 180 AD): …in the days of Noah He justly brought on the deluge for the purpose of extinguishing that most infamous race of men then existent, who could not bring forth fruit to God, since **the angels that sinned had commingled with them**… —Irenaeus, *Against Heresies IV, 36.4*

Origen (3rd century AD): "In my opinion, however, it is certain wicked demons, and, so to speak, of the race of Titans or

Giants, who have been guilty of impiety towards the true God, and towards the angels in heaven, and who have fallen from it, and who haunt the denser parts of bodies, and frequent unclean places upon earth, and who, possessing some power of distinguishing future events, because they are without bodies of earthly material, engage in an employment of this kind, and desiring to lead the human race away from the true God."
—Origen, *Against Celsus 4.92*

Justin Martyr not only understood that the Nephilim were the source of the demons that plague mankind, he also clearly knew that the rebellious members of the divine council were the false gods of the pagan world. Irenaeus, a theologian whose writings were directed against heresies that had sprung up in the Roman world in the hundred and fifty years since the Resurrection, also knew that the "sons of God" in Genesis 6 were supernatural beings, not righteous human men. Origen, whose theology drifted into allegorical interpretations of scripture, still understood the link between the giants of Jewish religion and the Titans of the Greeks (i.e., the Watchers).

We repeat: This was the consensus among early Christian theologians for the first four hundred years or so after the Resurrection. Demons are the net result and lingering consequence of the intrusion into our world by "angels who did not stay within their own position of authority."[12]

---

12 Jude 6.

CHAPTER TWO

BEFORE
THE FLOOD

*Now the serpent was more crafty than any other beast of the field that
the LORD God had made.*

—GENESIS 3:1 (ESV)

When did humanity get the idea that it was possible to communicate with entities in the netherworld? It can't have been
very long after the children of Adam and Eve began to spread across the
face of the earth. There is evidence that one of the earliest cult centers
in Sumer was rebuilt after the Flood, and the temple of the city's patron
god was the oldest and largest ziggurat in Mesopotamia. At least, it
would have been the largest if construction had been completed.

Scholars generally agree that civilization emerged in the Fertile
Crescent around 10,000 BC. Agriculture, cities, writing, trade, science, and organized religion all developed in a broad arc that stretched
from Egypt through the Levant and down into Mesopotamia. Until
recently, it appeared that civilization emerged in Sumer fully formed
with no preliminary steps. Some scholars speculate that those missing
links might lie at the bottom of the Persian Gulf.[1] Proto-Mesopota-

---

1   Jeffrey I. Rose, "New Light on Human Prehistory in the Arabo-Persian Gulf
     Oasis." *Current Anthropology*, December 2010, Vol. 51, No. 6 (December 2010),
     pp. 849–883.

mians lived in the Gulf Oasis, a lush river valley watered by the Tigris and Euphrates, plus the Karun River from Iran and the Wadi Batin from Saudi Arabia. But the Persian Gulf rose rapidly between 6000 and 5000 BC, and people moved ahead of the water flowing in from the Indian Ocean, abandoning evidence of their earlier settlements beneath the waves.

This civilization is called the Ubaid culture by scholars. That's not what the people who lived in it called it, of course; we don't know what they called themselves because they never invented writing. The Ubaid civilization got its name from Tell al-'Ubaid, a small settlement mound in southeast Iraq where famous archaeologists Henry Hall and Sir Leonard Woolley dug up the first bits of pottery from those people between 1919 and 1924.

The Ubaid culture spread from what is today southeastern Iraq as far as northwest Iran, northern Syria, southern Turkey, and the Levant (Lebanon, Jordan, Israel, and southwestern Syria). Ubaid civilization was typified by large unwalled villages, rectangular multi-room mud-brick houses, high quality pottery, and the first public temples. Crop irrigation developed by about 5000 BC, so cereals and grains could grow in the dry climate that had come to dominate the region. The city remembered as the oldest in Mesopotamia, and therefore ground zero for the Ubaid culture, was Eridu. It appears in the historic record around 5400 BC. Although agricultural settlements like Jericho (c. 9000 BC) and Jarmo, east of modern-day Kirkuk, Iraq (c. 7100 BC) are older, the Sumerians remembered Eridu as their first city, with a degree of specialization among its citizens not seen before in other settlements.

The Sumerian King List, dated to about 2100 BC, records the history this way:

After the kingship descended from heaven, the kingship was in Eridu. In Eridu, Alulim became king; he ruled for 28,800 years.[2]

---

2 "The Sumerian King List: Translation." *The Electronic Text Corpus of Sumerian Literature* (http://etcsl.orinst.ox.ac.uk/section2/tr211.htm), retrieved 10/9/21.

Interestingly, we may find support for at least the outlines of this account in the Bible:

> Cain went away from the presence of the LORD and settled in the land of Nod, east of Eden. Cain knew his wife, and she conceived and bore Enoch. When he built a city, he called the name of the city after the name of his son, Enoch. To Enoch was born Irad, and Irad fathered Mehujael, and Mehujael fathered Methushael, and Methushael fathered Lamech. (Genesis 4:16–18)

Some scholars believe that "he" in the third sentence should be Enoch, rather than Cain. That would be consistent with the rules of grammar, under which the pronoun would refer to the most recently named individual—in this case, Enoch. If that's true, then the last word in that sentence, "Enoch," would be a later addition by a scribe attempting to clarify what he considered a confusing passage.

Removing the second mention of Enoch changes the passage to this:

> Cain knew his wife, and she conceived and bore Enoch. When he [Enoch] built a city, he called the name of the city after the name of his son. To Enoch was born Irad...

If this theory is correct, the builder of the city was Enoch and the city was named for his son, Irad—hence, Eridu. (To be clear, Cain's son Enoch is not the patriarch who confronted the Watchers after their sin of commingling with human women. That Enoch was from the line of Seth and was the great-grandfather of Noah.)

Regardless of its origins, what is most interesting about Eridu is its ziggurat. This was the temple of one of the most important gods of the ancient Near East. He was known as Enki in Sumerian and Ea in Akkadian. Enki was lord of the *abzu* (Akkadian *apsû*), the subterranean source of the fresh water needed for life. The god was usually depicted with two streams of water flowing from his shoulders that represented the Tigris and Euphrates rivers, the main sources of fresh water in Mesopotamia.[3]

Along with the sky-god Anu and Enlil, chief god of the pantheon, Enki was one of the three most important gods in Sumer. He was the god of magic, craftsmanship, and wisdom, who attained his power by enchanting and slaying Apsû, the underground fresh-water abyss.[4] Although Enlil was king of the gods, Enki was the keeper of the *mes* (sounds like "mezz"), divine decrees that formed the fundamental concepts and gifts of civilization—everything from religious practices to social interaction to music.

The Babylonian creation myth, the *Enuma Elish*, describes how everything on Earth came into being through the defeat of the chaos-goddess Tiamat by Marduk, the chief god of Babylon.[5] However, the older Sumerian story credits Enki with giving life to all things, including mankind, and names Enlil the slayer of Tiamat.

The differences are at least partly due to the ebb and flow of power over the centuries. Each city in Mesopotamia had a patron god or goddess. The importance of a deity was tied to the political fortunes of its city. Just as Eridu was the home of Enki, Enlil was chief deity at Nippur, Inanna (Ishtar) was supreme at Uruk, the sun-god Utu was the patron deity of Sippar, and so on. To give you an idea of the incredible amount of time we're dealing with, Enki ruled in Eridu for nearly *four thousand years* before Marduk replaced Enlil at the head of the Mesopotamian pantheon.

For context, that's roughly the amount of time that's passed between Abraham leaving Harran for Canaan and you reading this sentence.

This chapter is not in any way a thorough review of life, culture,

---

3   Ruth Horry, "Enki/Ea (god)." *Ancient Mesopotamian Gods and Goddesses* (Oracc and the UK Higher Education Academy, 2016). http://oracc.museum.upenn.edu/amgg/listofdeities/enki/, retrieved 10/9/21.

4   Joshua J. Mark, "Enuma Elish - The Babylonian Epic of Creation - Full Text." *World History Encyclopedia*. Last modified May 04, 2018. https://www.worldhistory.org/article/225/enuma-elish---the-babylonian-epic-of-creation---fu/. Retrieved 2/19/22.

5   Ibid.

or religion in ancient Mesopotamia, but there is one more aspect of life in the ancient Near East to call to your attention. It's something we usually hear about from fringe pseudo-scholars who blame the phenomenon on extraterrestrials. Archaeologists and sociologists have known at least since the late 1940s that people throughout Mesopotamia, before they learned how to write, figured out how to change the shape of their children's heads.

It appears, based on human remains dated to between 10,000 BC and 3500 BC, that cranial deformation was widespread in the Ubaid culture, and Eridu—the world's first city, possibly built by Cain or his son—may have been ground zero for head shaping. An archaeological dig at Eridu just after World War II discovered about a thousand bodies that were buried during the Ubaid. Two hundred and six sets of human remains were exhumed by the archaeologists, who examined a small sample, "at least fifteen," and found that "all of the crania had been deformed in one fashion or another."[6]

The author of the report, Carlton S. Coon, wrote that the deformation had been caused "presumably after burial, by earth pressure,"[7] even though none of the skulls were described as cracked or broken, which would be expected if deformation had occurred after death. Coon, to his credit, admitted that his conclusions were preliminary, admitting that "a few experiments in the mechanics of skull-squashing are needed."[8]

Evidence of headshaping has been found at sites all over Iraq, southwestern Iran, eastern Turkey, the valleys of the Zagros Mountains, and the western shores of the Persian Gulf, dated from 10,000 BC to about 4000 BC. After that, the practice apparently disappeared.

The question is why it was even a thing. Please understand that we're not suggesting these were genetic mutations or part-human

---

6   Carlton S. Coon, "The Eridu Crania: A Preliminary Report." In F. Safar, M. A. Mustafa, and S. Lloyd, *Eridu* (Baghdad: Ministry of Culture and Information, State Organization of Antiquites and Heritage, 1981), p. 307.
7   Ibid.
8   Ibid., p. 308.

Nephilim, the angel-human hybrids mentioned in Genesis 6. But who wakes up one morning in, say, 7000 BC and decides to wrap something around baby's skull to see if it makes his head pointy? What inspires that? And why was Eridu the starting point for this?

A study published in the academic journal *Paléorient* in 1992 concluded that the practice of headshaping, which is found around the world, must have originated in the Near East because it was so widespread there. However, the researchers believed the deformation was not necessarily intentional, but probably "incidental to patterns of head-gear."[9] Not surprisingly, they added:

> We note the significant absence of a literature discussing the origins of this phenomenon.[10]

Understandable, since most of the attention given to the topic of cranial deformation has come from the fringes of scientific inquiry.

Here's another bit of data to chew on: At Eridu and nearby sites in ancient pre-Flood southern Sumer, and only there, archaeologists have found about a hundred and twenty terracotta figurines that scholars call "ophidian," or snake-like. The figures are slender bipeds, adorned with button-like protuberances, more often female than male, and often in poses that are exclusively mammalian—for example, a female lizard-like figure suckling an infant.

The TV evangelists of the ancient aliens cult have an answer for this: They were our space ancestors, they say, the Anunnaki who came from the stars to create humanity from ape DNA. They're thinking along the right lines, but they ignore the supernatural and so they miss a more likely answer.

We'll never know for sure, but we can speculate: The people who

---

9   Rose Solecki, Peter M. M. G. Akkermans, Anagnostis Agelarakis, Christopher Meiklejohn, Philip E.L. Smith, "Artificial cranial deformation in the Proto-neolithic and Neolithic Near East and its possible origin: Evidence from four sites." *Paléorient*, 1992, vol. 18, n°2. p. 95.

10   Ibid., p.94.

formed the earliest human civilizations copied a look that someone, somewhere had seen and decided was a physical ideal. What motivates modern-day teens to wear the clothes and hairstyles they do? Except that this particular fashion statement didn't change with the seasons—it appears to have been worn by nearly everybody for six thousand years! It's unlikely that this was a simple style choice. However it started, it was apparently a practice that was believed to convey some advantage.

Consider that the *nachash* in Eden, the "serpent" of Genesis 3, was a supernatural entity of serpentine appearance. Given that *nachash* and *saraph*, the singular form of seraphim, are used interchangeably in the Old Testament,[11] the throne guardians of the vision in Isaiah 6 are now generally envisioned as winged serpents with some human characteristics.[12] At least one of these entities rebelled against Yahweh, and he may well have had co-conspirators.

Is it possible that the citizens of the prehistoric Near East adopted the practice of head shaping to curry favor with what they believed were their gods?

---

11 Numbers 21:6, 8; Deuteronomy 8:15.

12 T. N. D. Mettinger, "Seraphim," ed. by Karel van der Toorn, Bob Becking, and Pieter W. van der Horst, *Dictionary of Deities and Demons in the Bible* (Leiden; Boston; Köln; Grand Rapids, MI; Cambridge: Brill; Eerdmans, 1999), pp. 742–43.

CHAPTER THREE

AFTER
THE FLOOD

The sons of Noah who went forth from the ark were Shem, Ham, and Japheth. (Ham was the father of Canaan.) These three were the sons of Noah, and from these the people of the whole earth were dispersed.

—GENESIS 9:18–19 (ESV)

It's hard to imagine what the world after the Flood was like for Noah and his family. While they'd spent years preparing for the time they were on the water as the world that they'd known disappeared beneath the deluge, the job that faced them after the ark settled in the mountains of Ararat must have seemed even more intimidating. It's one thing to build the biggest boat in history and fill it with enough animals and provisions to survive the deluge, but the enormity of literally starting human civilization from scratch must have seemed overwhelming.

You also have to wonder whether the seven people on the ark with Noah shared his faith in the promise of God. Yes, they trusted Noah enough to go along with what must have seemed like an insane idea (at least until the rain started to fall), but there must have been some doubt. God spoke to Noah. We don't know whether He talked with anyone else in the family.

It appears that there was a break between Noah's sons in the years after the Flood. This is plain when you dig beneath the surface of the disturbing events of Genesis 9:

Noah began to be a man of the soil, and he planted a vineyard. He drank of the wine and became drunk and lay uncovered in his tent. And Ham, the father of Canaan, saw the nakedness of his father and told his two brothers outside. Then Shem and Japheth took a garment, laid it on both their shoulders, and walked backward and covered the nakedness of their father. Their faces were turned backward, and they did not see their father's nakedness. When Noah awoke from his wine and knew what his youngest son had done to him, he said,

"Cursed be Canaan;
    a servant of servants shall he be to his brothers."

He also said,

"Blessed be the LORD, the God of Shem;
    and let Canaan be his servant.
May God enlarge Japheth,
    and let him dwell in the tents of Shem,
    and let Canaan be his servant." (Genesis 9:20–27)

Ham's transgression is usually explained as a lack of respect—looking at, and maybe even mocking, his naked father while Noah was passed out drunk in his tent. By contrast, the actions of Shem and Japheth were right and proper. They entered Noah's tent backward and covered his "nakedness" to restore a measure of dignity.

There is more here than meets the eye. In the Old Testament, "the nakedness of their father" doesn't mean what we think it means in the twenty-first century.

In Leviticus 18:7–8, God instructs Moses, "You shall not uncover the nakedness of your father, which is the nakedness of your mother; she is your mother, you shall not uncover her nakedness. You shall not uncover the nakedness of your father's wife; it is your father's nakedness." This is repeated in Leviticus 20:11, with the added command that both son and mother or stepmother were to be put to death for the act.

This wasn't a law against seeing one's parents undressed. It was a ban on incest.

Now, this interpretation of Genesis 9 is not accepted by everyone. Some point out that Ham did not "uncover" anything, he only *saw* the nakedness of his father. True enough. But in Leviticus 20, the Hebrew words for "see" (*ra'ah*) and "uncover" (*galah*) are used to describe the same act:

> "If a man takes his sister, a daughter of his father or a daughter of his mother, and sees her nakedness, and she sees his nakedness, it is a disgrace, and they shall be cut off in the sight of the children of their people. He has uncovered his sister's nakedness, and he shall bear his iniquity. (Leviticus 20:17)

The cursing of Canaan would have been a harsh punishment if Ham's transgression was only failing to cover Noah while failing to take a cloak and covering his drunk, naked father. It appears that in the ancient Near East, the act of forcing oneself on his father's wife, who may or may not have been that man's biological mother, was a declaration that the old king had been deposed and replaced by his son.

There are several examples in the Old Testament. First, Jacob's eldest son Reuben:

> While Israel lived in that land, Reuben went and lay with Bilhah his father's concubine. And Israel heard of it. (Genesis 35:22)

Jacob's favorite wife Rachel had recently died. Bilhah was her maidservant. It's possible Reuben hoped that his mother, Leah, would succeed Rachel as Jacob's favorite, thus elevating his status, and he defiled Bilhah to prevent her from becoming a rival. Or it may have been his attempt to declare to his brothers that he was taking over the family business from the old man.

That was certainly the goal of Absalom, son of King David:

Ahithophel said to Absalom, "Go in to your father's concubines, whom he has left to keep the house, and all Israel will hear that you have made yourself a stench to your father, and the hands of all who are with you will be strengthened." So they pitched a tent for Absalom on the roof. And Absalom went in to his father's concubines in the sight of all Israel. (2 Samuel 16:21–22)

Two more examples are known from the time of David and Solomon. The son of Saul, Ish-Bosheth, accused the commander of his army, Abner, of sleeping with his father's concubine, Rizpah,[1] and David's second son, Adonijah, asked Bathsheba to pass along a request to her son, King Solomon, to give David's concubine Abishag to Adonijah for his wife.[2] Solomon knew what Adonijah was up to; three thousand years ago in the ancient Near East, that's what insurrection looked like. Not only did Solomon deny Adonijah's request, but he also had his half-brother killed.

Solomon's reaction seems, well, a bit homicidal for a king who'd been chosen by God and his father David, but it was standard practice for kings in that place and time to inherit the harems of their predecessors. Adonijah apparently thought he could put one over on his younger half-brother by using Solomon's mother to deliver the request. Had Solomon fallen for the ruse, Adonijah would have made a statement everyone recognized: "I've got the old man's favorite concubine, so I, not Solomon, am the rightful king."

This was a very old custom that appears to reach all the way back to the eight survivors of the Flood. And it fractured the family of Noah. What Ham attempted to do was declare himself the patriarch of the clan—and since they were the only people in the world, that was tantamount to declaring himself king of the world.

This suggests that whatever Noah learned from God during their

---

1   2 Samuel 3:7–10.
2   1 Kings 2:13–25.

talks may not have been passed along to his sons—at least, not all of them. Certainly, the descendants of Ham proved to be problematic for the later Israelites. Cush fathered Nimrod, who is credited with the rebellion at Babel. The supernatural consequences of that event have resonated down the ages to the present day.

Listed next in chapter 10 of Genesis is Mizraim (Egypt), where the Israelites served in bondage for centuries. Egypt was credited with fathering the progenitors of the Philistines, another people group who caused the Israelites great distress over the years.

Then there was the cursed one:

> Canaan fathered Sidon his firstborn and Heth, and the Jeb-
> usites, the Amorites, the Girgashites, the Hivites, the Arkites,
> the Sinites, the Arvadites, the Zemarites, and the Hamathites.
> (Genesis 10:15–18)

Sidon was one of the principal Phoenician cities on the coast of Lebanon. Heth may refer to the Hittites of Asia Minor; the Arkites, Sinites, Arvadites, Zemarites, and Hamathites occupied territory north of Sidon in Lebanon.

The Girgashites and Hivites were from the Aegean. If you want the long explanation, see the footnote, but in a nutshell they were the Trojans and Mycenaean Greeks[3] who later fought their famous war during the time of the Judges in Israel.

That leaves the Jebusites and the Amorites. We put these two people groups together because they appear to be more closely related than

---

3   The Girgashites were probably Teucrians (Trojans) who settled the city of Gergis on the west coast of Asia Minor between Troy and Miletus. The Hivites probably derive their name from *Hiyawa*, a Luwian (south Anatolian) form of Ahhiyawa, the Hittite name for the Achaeans, who were the Mycenaean Greeks in Homer's epic poems *Iliad* and *Odyssey*. See Othniel Margalith, *The Sea Peoples in the Bible* (Wiesbaden: Harrassowitz, 1994), pp. 58–59, and Billie Jean Collins, "The Bible, the Hittites, and the Construction of the 'Other'." In *Tabularia Hethaeorum: Hethitologische Beiträge Silvin Košak zum 65. Geburtstag*. Dresdner Beiträgezur Hethitologie 25 (Wiesbaden: Harrasowitz, 2007), p. 154.

we've thought. The Amorites are well known to archaeologists and historians; the period from the time of Abraham to the Israelite sojourn in Egypt is called by some *the Age of the Amorites*. Between about 2000 and 1500 BC, Amorite tribes and kingdoms dominated the ancient Near East—the territory that we know today as Iraq, Kuwait, Syria, Jordan, Lebanon, and Israel, plus parts of Egypt, Turkey, Iran, and Saudi Arabia. It's hard to overstate the cultural and religious influence of the Amorites on the world of the patriarchs and Old Testament prophets. Through their descendants, the Phoenicians, that influence continued long into the Christian era.

So, why mention the Jebusites in the same sentence? From the Bible, it seems that the only thing we know about the Jebusites is that they held the city of Jerusalem until David and his men captured it around 1003 BC. However, we also know that David later bought the threshing floor of Araunah (or Ornan, depending on whether you read the account in 2 Samuel 24 or 1 Chronicles 21), which gives us an important clue as to his ethnicity. "Araunah" is a title, rather than a proper name, based on the Hurrian word *ewri-*, which means "lord" or "ruler."[4] In other words, Araunah was probably the last Hurrian king of Jerusalem.

Evidence from outside the Bible suggests that Jerusalem was a Hurrian enclave at least from the time of the Judges until David took it. A Jerusalem ruler named Abdi-Heba wrote half a dozen messages to Pharaoh Amenhotep III around the middle of the fourteenth century BC—most complaining about the threat posed by the Apiru, who were led by a king of Shechem called Labayu. There is some evidence to connect the Apiru to the Hebrews, but scholars don't agree on that point. What's relevant here is that Abdi-Heba's name means something like "Servant of Hebat," the Hurrian mother-goddess.

Now, refer to the genealogies of Genesis 10. The Jebusites and Amorites are listed one after the other as sons of Canaan, the son of

---

4   Michael T. Winger, *The "God of the Fathers" and Self-Identification in the Hebrew Bible* (PhD dissertation: UCLA, 2017), p. 81.

Ham. We have at least circumstantial evidence that the Jebusites were either Hurrian or ruled by leaders with Hurrian names. This suggests that the Bible documents a genetic or cultural link between the Hurrians and Amorites, two groups of people who had a profound impact on the world of the patriarchs.

And that brings us back to the post-Flood world.

The Hurrians trace their ancestry to the Ararat Plain. Recent archaeological discoveries from northern Syria show that the Hurrians worshiped their father-god, Kumarbi, as early as 3500 BC, and probably much earlier. Kumarbi had to be summoned from the netherworld, where he'd been banished by his son, the storm-god. This story is familiar to us because most of us were taught the Greco-Roman version in which the storm-god Zeus/Jupiter deposed his father, the Titan king Kronos/Saturn. Echoes of this story are found in most of the religions of the ancient Near East, where an older god such as El, Enlil, or Dagan was replaced at the top of the pantheon by a storm-god like Baal, Marduk, or Hadad.

Here's the takeaway: We now have hard evidence of an ancient cult that sought the favor of underworld gods among people who spread out from the Ararat Plain, the land below the mountains where Noah landed the ark. And the archive of literature from the Amorite kingdom of Ugarit documents a link between the Hurrians, the Amorites, and the Titans—the "sons of God" from Genesis 6:1–4 who provoked the Creator into sending the Flood.

CHAPTER FOUR

URKESH

As just nine years were counted off Anu was king in heaven, and in the ninth year Anu went in battle against Kumarbi. Kumarbi, the seed of Alalu, went in battle against Anu, and Anu was no longer able to withstand the eyes of Kumarbi. He broke away from Kumarbi and from his hands. He ran, Anu, and he set off for heaven. Kumarbi assaulted him from behind, and he grabbed Anu (by) the feet, and he dragged him down from heaven.

—*The Song of Going Forth* §4, A i 18-24

Kumarbi was the primordial creator-god of the Hurrians, a people who lived in eastern Anatolia and northern Mesopotamia. For nearly two thousand years, between the middle of the fourth millennium BC and about the end of the fourteenth century BC, the Hurrians controlled the area roughly occupied today by the Kurds in Iraq, Syria, and Turkey. At its peak, during the time of the Mitanni kingdom (1600–1350 BC), the Hurrians extended their power into what is now Turkey, Syria, and northwest Iran, and there is evidence that the powerful Minoan civilization on the island of Crete may have been Hurrian, or at least dominated by a Hurrian elite for a time.

Most of what we know about Kumarbi comes from Hittite texts excavated from the ruins of Hattusa, the capital of the kingdom of the Hatti near what is now Boğazkale, Turkey. The Hittites were heavily influenced by Hurrian religion, and they seemed to go to great lengths to please the gods of their neighbors. The Hittites apparently believed you could never have too much divine protection.

Just as the stories of the storm-god of the West Semitic people, Hadad (Baal in the Bible), were preserved in what's been titled the *Baal Cycle*, scholars dubbed the collection of texts about the Hurrian creator-god the *Kumarbi Cycle*, which has more accurately renamed the *Kingship in Heaven Cycle*. The most important of these texts is the *Song of Kumarbi*, now more commonly called the *Song of Going Forth*. It describes the transfer of power from the sky-god, Anu, to Kumarbi, and from Kumarbi to the storm-god, Teshub.

If you're familiar with Greek mythology and the background of Zeus's rise to the top of the pantheon, the conflict between Anu, Kumarbi, and Teshub will be very familiar. Here's the outline of the story:

- The primordial god Alalu reigned in heaven for nine years, after which his cupbearer, the sky-god Anu, rebelled and took his place. Alalu escaped by fleeing into "the dark earth."
- Nine years later, Anu was overthrown by *his* cupbearer, Kumarbi. Anu tried to get away to the sky, but Kumarbi grabbed his legs and pulled him back to earth—and then castrated Anu by biting off his genitals.
- This act had unintended consequences. Anu warned Kumarbi not to celebrate, because he was now impregnated with Anu's children: the storm-god, Teshub, the Tigris River, and two unnamed "terrible gods."
- Sure enough, after some discussion between characters about where these gods are to be born, probably due to the obviously inappropriate physiology of the male deity, the storm-god emerges through "the good place." The text (perhaps mercifully) never explains what "the good place" is, but it may be Kumarbi's skull.
- At some point after this, Teshub, the storm-god, became powerful and replaced Kumarbi as the king of the Hurrian pantheon.

The tablets from which the *Song of Going Forth* has been compiled are badly damaged. This isn't surprising, considering their age. There are other details that are hard to explain in detail because of the fragmentary nature of the source material, but one section seems to depict Kumarbi demanding that the god of wisdom, Ea (called Enki by the Sumerians), hand over the newborn storm-god so that Kumarbi might eat him. It appears that Kumarbi was given a stone instead, which causes the god great pain when he tries to bite it. Then there is the mention of a *kunkunuzzi*-stone, and something that is to be venerated through sacrifices, presumably the stone.

A separate tale, the *Song of Ullikummi*, tells of Kumarbi's attempt to regain the throne by creating a giant stone monster to depose the storm-god. At first, it appears that Ullikummi would prevail, despite the collective efforts of the gods, and Teshub fled to ask the help of Ea, the one god who hadn't joined in the battle. The clever god realized that Ullikummi drew his strength from standing on the shoulder of the dreaming mountain-god Upelluri, who, like Atlas in Greek mythology, carried the earth and sky. Ea obtained the cutting tool used to separate Earth and sky from the "former gods," severs Ullikummi from Upelluri, thus destroying the giant's power. The end of the story is lost, but it's safe to assume that Teshub was restored to his throne.

There are several parallels between these Hurrian tales and later stories of the Greek gods:

- Kumarbi, like Kronos, king of the Titans, was the son of the sky-god. Like Kronos, he deposed and castrated his father—although Kronos used a sickle to remove the member of Ouranos rather than his teeth.
- Anu warns Kumarbi that he will regret what he's done; likewise, Ouranos warns Kronos and the Titans that they will pay for their rebellion.
- Kumarbi and Kronos both carried other deities in their stomachs for a time, although for different reasons.

- Both gods were overthrown by their son, the storm-god—Kumarbi by Teshub and Kronos by Zeus.
- Kumarbi and Kronos were both given a stone to swallow in lieu of the storm-god, which was later venerated as a sacred object. (The stone given to Kronos by his wife Rhea as a substitute for Zeus was set up at Delphi as the omphalos, the world-navel. It was believed that Delphi, home of the famous oracle, was the center of the world.)
- Even the detail of Kumarbi giving birth to Teshub through his skull has an echo in the Greek myth of Athena's birth through the forehead of Zeus.

Further, the storm-gods in both pantheons had to survive challenges to their reign after taking the throne. The struggle between Teshub and Ullikummi is accepted by many scholars as foreshadowing the Greek story of the battle between Zeus and the chaos-monster Typhon.

There are other connections between the epics, but the bottom line is this: The early Greek poet Hesiod, who wrote much of what we know about Greek religion in the classical era, clearly was familiar with the Hittite texts that preserved the older Hurrian religion. In geographic terms, the stories moved from east to west, traveling from the Hurrian heartland to the Aegean, either through Anatolia or the Levant. The time frame involved was roughly the end of the Bronze Age, around 1200 BC, or shortly after the decline and collapse of the Hurrian kingdom of Mitanni, and the time of the prophet Isaiah around the late eighth/early seventh century BC, which is about the time of Hesiod. So, over about five hundred years, the origin story of the Hurrian pantheon was transmitted to the Hittites, and either westward through the occupants of western Anatolia or southward through the Neo-Hittite kingdoms of northern Syria to what eventually became Greek civilization.

The name Kumarbi, meaning "he of Kumar," may refer to a north Syrian site identified with modern Kīmār about twenty-five miles northwest of Aleppo.[1] Hurrian myths locate Kumarbi in two other places: the western part of the Khabur River triangle, along the present border between Turkey and Syria, and at the ancient city of Tuttul, which was located on the Euphrates near modern Raqqa, Syria. Tuttul was a major cult center of Dagan,[2] which, as Derek noted in his book *The Second Coming of Saturn*, was another name and identity used by Kumarbi.

However, according to texts found at Hattusa, the home of Kumarbi was believed to be an ancient city farther east in Syria called Urkesh. In 1984, a husband-and-wife team of archaeologists working in far northeastern Syria began work at the site, locally called Tell Mozan. It's a mound that rises about seventy feet above the surrounding plain in northeastern Syria, very close to the border with Turkey. It was strategically located on a trade route that controlled access to the Mardin Pass, through which valuable raw materials like stone, timber, copper, and silver, could be moved from the Taurus Mountains to the cities of southern Mesopotamia.

Urkesh was occupied from at least 3500 BC until the rise of the Assyrian kingdom near the end of the Bronze Age, around 1200 BC. What makes the city so fascinating and relevant to our topic is the spiritual significance of Urkesh. About the time the city was founded, a raised terrace was constructed and a building with a niched exterior wall, the style common in Sumerian cities of the day, was built on top of the terrace. It's more than likely that it was, like similar buildings in Uruk, a temple.[3]

Unlike nearby neighbors in northern Mesopotamia, Urkesh never fell under the political or cultural control of Uruk, the city-state that

1   Michael C. Astour, "Semitic Elements in the Kumarbi Myth." *Journal of Near Eastern Studies*, Vol. 27, No. 3 (July, 1968), 172.

2   Lluis Feliu, *The God Dagan in Bronze Age Syria* (Leiden; Boston: Brill, 2003), p. 212.

3   Marilyn Kelly-Buccellatti, "Urkesh: The Morphology and Cultural Landscape of the Hurrian Sacred." in P. Matthiae and M. D'Andrea (eds.), *Ebla e la Siria dall'età del Bronzo all'età del Ferro*, Accademia Nazionale dei Lincei: Atti dei convegni Lincei 304 (Rome: Bardi Edizioni, 2016),pp. 109-110.

dominated the Fertile Crescent for most of the fourth millennium BC. For example, Nagar (modern Tell Brak), about thirty miles south of Urkesh, had grown into a major city during the fourth millennium BC, with megalithic buildings dated to as early as 3800 BC. Recent research has led scholars to conclude that the earliest large-scale urban civilization in the ancient Near East developed in northern Mesopotamia, not Sumer.[4] Not surprisingly, with growth comes competition; mass graves discovered in 2010 suggest that many of Nagar's citizens met violent ends in four separate events between 3800 and 3600 BC.[5] This may have been the result of failed insurrections by local residents, but it's also possible that they were victims of the expansionist policies of Uruk; it's known from pottery finds that an Urukean colony was established in the city around 3400 BC.[6]

Interestingly, the Bible tells us that Uruk (biblical Erech), Babel, and Akkad (Accad in the Bible) were the power base of history's first would-be empire builder, Nimrod:

> The beginning of his kingdom was Babel, Erech, Accad, and Calneh, in the land of Shinar. From that land he went into Assyria and built Nineveh, Rehoboth-Ir, Calah, and Resen between Nineveh and Calah; that is the great city. (Genesis 10:10–12)

Historically speaking, the Uruk Period, which covered the period between about 3800 BC and 3100 BC, is the logical time to put Nimrod's reign. And Genesis 10:8–12 gives an accurate capsule summary of his career.

---

4   Joan Oates; Augusta McMahon; Philip Karsgaard; Salam Al Quntar; and Jason Ur, "Early Mesopotamian urbanism: a new view from the north." *Antiquity* 2007;81(313), pp. 585–600.

5   Andrew Lawler, "The Dawn of Civilization: Writing, Urban Life, and Warfare." *Discover Magazine*, Mar. 19, 2010. https://www.discovermagazine.com/the-sciences/the-dawn-of-civilization-writing-urban-life-and-warfare, retrieved 3/17/24.

6   Oates *et al.*, op. cit., p. 597.

Accad, spelled "Akkad" outside of the Bible, was the city from which Sargon the Great conquered all of Mesopotamia around 2334 BC, making him the first Semitic ruler of the ancient Near East. That city hasn't been found, but it's believed to have been on the Tigris River near modern Baghdad and may be hidden beneath Baghdad itself.[7] Sargon is also credited with being the world's first empire-builder, but that's because historians generally don't believe that Nimrod was a historic character. In fact, Sargon is one of the candidates put forward as the identity of the historical Nimrod.[8]

Calneh likewise hasn't been found, but the name may be a misreading of a Hebrew phrase that simply means "all of them." So, the original sentence might have read, "the beginning of his kingdom was Babel, Erech, and Accad, *all of them* in the land of Shinar."[9]

From there, we're told Nimrod went to Assyria, or northern Mesopotamia, and built Nineveh, Rehoboth-Ir, Calah, and Resen. While those cities may not have been founded by Nimrod (for example, archaeologists believe Nineveh was occupied as early as 6000 BC), the Genesis account does fit the general story of an empire-builder from Sumer who expanded his kingdom along the Tigris and Euphrates rivers, which is exactly what's revealed by the archaeology of the fourth millennium BC. Armies traveled north and west from Sumer to impose Uruk's will on the cities of what is now northern Iraq, northeastern Syria, and southeastern Turkey. Although not confirmed, the mass graves at Tell Brak could be evidence of this, but the destruction of nearby Hamoukar was definitely the work of Uruk's military. Archaeologists call the battle of Hamoukar the

---

7   Christophe Wall-Romana, "An Areal Location of Agade." *Journal of Near Eastern Studies*, Vol. 49, No. 3 (1990), pp. 205–245.

8   If Sargon was Nimrod, as argued by Dr. Douglas Petrovich in his book *Nimrod the Empire Builder*, then he could not have been the builder of the Tower of Babel, which was the ziggurat at the temple of Enki in Eridu. That building project was abandoned at the end of the Uruk Period c. 3100 BC, more than seven hundred years before the reign of Sargon.

9   William F. Albright, "The End of 'Calneh in Shinar.'" *Journal of Near Eastern Studies* 3, no. 4 (1944), pp. 254-255.

"earliest evidence for large scale organized warfare in the Mesopotamian world."[10]

The attack was brutal. Using clay bullets and "cannonballs" fired from slings, thousands of which have been uncovered at the dig,[11] the Urukean army breached the ten-foot-thick walls of Hamoukar, overwhelmed the city's defenders, and burned the prosperous city to the ground.[12] It appears that Hamoukar was quickly rebuilt and settled by colonists from Uruk, possibly to take over the city's profitable obsidian trade, which is indicated by the workshops for fabricating obsidian tools just outside the city walls.[13]

This is consistent with what little we know of the character of Nimrod. However, the point of this brief rabbit trail is not to reconstruct the military career of Nimrod, but to highlight the remarkable fact that Urkesh, a thriving religious and economic center just thirty miles north of Nagar, remained independent and untouched by the military might of Uruk. It appears that rather than conquering the city, the rulers of Uruk opted to peacefully trade for copper with the kings of Urkesh or shipped it down the Euphrates via a longer route through Turkey and Syria west of the Khabur Triangle.

Likewise, the powerful Akkadian empire, which emerged nearly eight hundred years after the end of the Uruk Period, never moved against Urkesh. Like the rulers of Uruk, the mighty Akkadian king Sargon the Great (or one of his successors) conquered nearby Nagar,[14]

---

10   Owen Jarus, "New discoveries hint at 5,500 year old fratricide at Hamoukar, Syria." *The Independent*, October 23, 2011. https://www.independent.co.uk /life-style/history/new-discoveries-hint-5-500-year-old-fratricide-hamoukar-syria -2088467.html, retrieved 2/11/21.

11   William Harms, "Evidence of battle at Hamoukar points to early urban development." *University of Chicago Chronicle*, Jan. 18, 2007. http://chronicle.uchicago. edu/070118/hamoukar.shtml, retrieved 2/12/21.

12   Ibid.

13   Richard E. J. Burke, "Uruk's Monstrous Crime at Hamoukar." *Raising Up Pharaoh*, Oct. 10, 2015. http://www.raisinguppharaoh.com/2015/10/24/65-uruks -monstrous-crime-at-hamoukar/, retrieved 2/11/21.

14   Federico Buccellati, *Three-dimensional Volumetric Analysis in an Archaeological Context: The Palace of Tupkish at Urkesh and its Representation* (Malibu, Calif.: Undena Publications, 2016), p. 186.

but rather than conquest, the Akkadians opted for alliance with Urkesh. Cylinder seals found at Tell Mozan reveal that Tar'am-Agade, a previously unknown daughter of Sargon's grandson Naram-Sîn, was married to the *endan* (Hurrian for "king" or "ruler") of Urkesh in the late twenty-third century BC.[15] In fact, a new palace for the reigning *endan* named Tupkish was built next to the city's temple around 2250 BC,[16] at the very height of the Akkadian Empire.

It's not as if Akkad would have had much trouble overwhelming Urkesh. The armies of Akkad reached Anatolia to the northwest, crushing the powerful Syrian states of Mari and Ebla on the way. Akkad sent expeditions as far south as modern Bahrain and Oman. The Akkadians could have taken Urkesh if they'd wanted to—but, apparently, they didn't. Was it because of cultural and ethnic kinship between the rulers of Urkesh and the miners who controlled copper and silver production in the Taurus Mountains? In other words, did Sargon and his successors, like Nimrod before them, figure it was easier to cut a deal with the Hurrian rulers of Urkesh than to conquer the city and risk alienating their kin in the mountains?

Or was it fear of the city's patron deity, Kumarbi, the former king of the gods now reigning on the far side of the gates of hell, that kept Urkesh safe from the armies of Uruk and Akkad?

---

15 Ibid., p. 20.
16 Ibid., p. 3.

CHAPTER FIVE

THE GREAT BELOW

The cemuc *barley is reserved for the necromancer.*

—SUMERIAN PROVERB

Based on the archaeological sites scattered across the landscape from the Caspian Sea to the Persian Gulf, and from the Zagros Mountains in Iran to the Mediterranean Sea, it appears that the proto-Hurrian people, called the Kura-Araxes or Early Transcaucasian culture, migrated during the second half of the fourth millennium BC from their original homeland on the Ararat plain on the border between modern Armenia and Turkey northward across the Caucasus Mountains into Georgia and the Russian republics of Chechnya and Dagestan; east and south into Azerbaijan, northwest Iran, and the Kurdish regions of northern Iraq and Syria; westward into Anatolia; and southwest along the Mediterranean coast of Syria and Lebanon, reaching as far south as Bet Yerah on the southwest shore of the Sea of Galilee by about 2850 BC. Meanwhile, the Semites and Sumerians along the Tigris and Euphrates dominated the bulk of the Fertile Crescent from the Zagros to the Anti-Lebanon Mountains, or what comprises western Iran and most of Iraq, Kuwait, Syria, and Jordan today.

Marilyn Kelly-Buccellati, who's devoted more than three decades of her life to excavating and interpreting the finds at Urkesh, has dubbed the region controlled by the Kura-Araxes people the Outer Fertile Crescent.[1] Urkesh is unusual, not only because it either resisted or escaped being dominated by powerful southern kingdoms and maintained its Hurrian identity for more than two thousand years, but also because it is the largest and oldest city that can be positively identified as Hurrian.

And, finally, to get back on point: there is the patron god of Urkesh, Kumarbi.

The temple with the niched facade atop the raised terrace, sitting nearly ninety feet above the plain,[2] would have been visible for quite a distance. In majesty and splendor, it may have rivaled the Great Ziggurat of Ur which wouldn't be built for another fifteen hundred years. The importance of Urkesh in Hurrian religion was preserved in Hittite-language copies of older Hurrian myths that name it as the city of Kumarbi—texts copied by Hittite scribes about two thousand years after the temple was constructed on top of the elevated terrace above the plain.

The central feature of the temple at Urkesh was a deep ritual pit used to summon deities from the netherworld, including the chief god of the Hurrians, Kumarbi.[3] These entities were summoned from "the dark earth" and were offered sacrifices in exchange for favors, usually taking some evil back into the world below. It's known from ritual texts found at Hattusa, the capital of the Hittite empire, that this pit was called the abi.[4] It's a distinctly Hurrian religious structure, unlike anything in southern Mesopotamia and not connected to the

1 Marilyn Kelly-Buccellati, "Trade in Metals in the Third Millennium: Northeastern Syria and Eastern Anatolia." In P. Matthiae, M. Van Loon, and H. Weiss (eds.), *Resurrecting the Past: A Joint Tribute to Adnan Bounni* (Istanbul: Nederlands Historisch-Archaeologisch Instituut, 1990), p. 120.

2 Giorgio Buccellati and Marilyn Kelly-Buccellati, "Between Heaven and Hell in Ancient Urkesh," *Backdirt* 175 (2007), p. 67.

3 Kelly-Buccellati (2016), op. cit., pp, 99-100.

4 Giorgio Buccellati, "When Were the Hurrians Hurrian? The Persistence of Ethnicity at Urkesh." In J. Aruz, S. Graff and Y. Rakic (eds.), *Cultures in Contact* (New York: Metropolitan Museum of Art, 2013), p. 87.

well-known Amorite *kispum* ritual, a necromantic practice that summoned the spirits of the ancestral dead—demons, actually—to a ritual meal each month.[5]

To be clear, as Christians, we do not believe that the spirits of the dead are free to roam the earth. Human spirits do not hang around waiting to appear when summoned through the correct rituals, communicating with mediums, or interceding for the living in the natural realm.

Now, God may allow human spirits to return to the earth for His purposes. We see this in 1 Samuel 28, when the prophet Samuel is sent to let King Saul know that he and his sons would die in the coming battle with the Philistines. But there is nothing in scripture that hints that this is a regular occurrence; indeed, the medium Saul consulted was shocked when Samuel appeared: "When the woman saw Samuel, she cried out with a loud voice."[6] The Hebrew word translated into English as "cried out," *zāʿaq*, conveys the sense of shouting with alarm or calling for help.[7] In other words, the medium of En-dor expected to see a spirit, but not a *human* spirit.

Similarly, the Hurrian rituals preserved by the Hittites reached out to spirit beings rather than humans. The *abi* at Urkesh was a monumental underground structure lined with stone, originally dug in a circle about thirteen feet in diameter. The pit has been excavated down to a depth of about twenty-six feet, revealing potsherds that have been dated to about 2600 BC.[8] However, it's clear that the walls of the *abi* extend farther, possibly another twenty feet, before reaching virgin soil,[9] which may push the creation of the pit back to the middle of

---

5 The *kispum* is discussed in depth in our 2019 book *Veneration*. See pp. 41–49. For a more scholarly treatment, see Renata MacDougal, *Remembrance and the Dead in Second Millennium BC Mesopotamia*. Doctoral thesis, University of Leicester (2014), pp. 117-287.

6 1 Samuel 28:12a.

7 Strong's H2199, *BlueLetterBible*. https://www.blueletterbible.org/lang/lexicon /lexicon.cfm?Strongs=H2199, retrieved 2/15/21.

8 Kelly-Buccellati (2016), op. cit., p. 100.

9 Buccellati and Kelly-Buccellati (2007), op. cit., p. 68.

the fourth millennium BC, around the time the city was first occupied and the niched building erected on the terrace above.[10]

At some point, one wall of the *abi* was removed and a square excavated, creating a keyhole shape and giving the entire structure a total length end-to-end of about twenty-four and a half feet. A narrow staircase on the square end allowed access by a priest or the king and queen, who apparently conducted some of the rituals in the pit. The *abi* was not originally covered, although it appears there was a vaulted ceiling over the circular portion for a period, and it is almost certain that the square section of the "keyhole" was under a roof.[11]

Rituals in the *abi* were performed at sunset or at night inside a magic circle dug into the dirt of the pit with a hoe or shovel, or traced with a pin, knife, or dagger.[12] This is remarkably similar to modern occult rituals in which magicians use a magic circle, sometimes drawn with salt or chalk, to protect themselves from a spirit being summoned. Similar practices were known in Akkad, where a magic circle marked out with flour called a zisurrû was used to protect one against demons or curses.[13]

The ritual pits were to allow the "primeval gods" or "former gods" to rise from the netherworld, drawn to the sacrifices, to hear the plea of the officiant.

When at night on the second day a star leaps, the offerer comes to the temple and bows to the deity. Two daggers which were made along with the (statue of) the new deity they take (with them) dig a pit for the deity in front of the table. They offer one sheep to the deity...and slaughter it down in the pit.[14]

---

10 Kelly-Buccellati (2016), op. cit., p. 98.
11 Ibid.
12 Marilyn Kelly-Buccellati, "Ein hurritischer Gang in die Unterwelt," *Mitteilungen der Deutschen Orient-Gesellschaft zu Berlin* 134 (2002), p. 138.
13 *The Assyrian Dictionary of the Oriental Institute of the University of Chicago, Vol. 21: Z* (Chicago: The Oriental Institute, 1961), pp. 137-138.
14 From "Relocation of the Black Goddess," KUB 29.4 rev iv 31-36, cited in Kelly-Buccellati (2016), op. cit., p. 101.

While a sheep is mentioned in the example above, and bones of goats and donkeys have also been found, piglets and puppies were the animals typically offered as sacrifices at the *abi* in Urkesh, apparently serving a purificatory purpose. Pigs may have been thought to have a connection to the underworld gods because of their habit of rooting in the dirt, but why young animals were preferred to adults is unknown.[15] The gods of the underworld apparently didn't mind offerings of animals considered unclean onto which additional impurities had been ritually transferred.

At the conclusion of a ritual, it was necessary to seal up the pit (or *pits*—some ritual texts required as many as nine, one for each of the underworld gods) that had been opened by covering it with loose dirt, loaves of bread, or a cloth.[16] These lids, fragile as they seem, were considered effective enough at sealing the exits to prevent sinister forces from escaping the underworld and wreaking havoc on the living.

The underworld deities were led by the Sun-Goddess of the Earth, Allani, whose name means "the Lady" (of the Underworld).[17] The sun's connection to the netherworld in the religions of the ancient Near East stems from the observable fact that it's below the horizon about half the time. Kumarbi, the father of the Hurrian pantheon, was not listed among the gods of the netherworld in these rituals, although he is mentioned in other texts as one of the "former gods" who'd been consigned to the underworld by the king of the pantheon, the storm-god Teshub. These "primeval gods" were referred to in Akkadian translations as the *Anunnaki*, following Mesopotamian traditions that had developed by the time of Abraham, Isaac, and Jacob depicting the former chief deities of Sumer as judges of the underworld.[18]

---

15 Billie Jean Collins, "A Channel to the Underworld in Syria." *Near Eastern Archaeology* 67:1 (2004), pp. 55-56.

16 Harry A. Hoffner, Jr., "Second Millennium Antecedents to the Hebrew ʾÔḇ." *Journal of Biblical Literature*, Vol. 86, No. 4 (Dec. 1967), p. 399.

17 Alfonso Archi, "The West Hurrian Pantheon and its Background." In B. Collins and P. Michalowski (eds.), *Beyond Hatti* (Atlanta: Lockwood Press, 2013), p. 6.

18 Christopher B. Hays, *Death in the Iron Age II and in First Isaiah* (Tübingen: Mohr Siebeck, 2011), p. 52.

Among the other infernal deities summoned in the Hurrian *abi* rituals was the personified Abi. This seems odd to our modern, Western, presumably Christian concept of the pagan gods of the ancient world as anthropomorphic or at least semi-human, like satyrs and centaurs. But a divine pit? The inclusion of "Abi" among the underworld deities "is not a testimony to its divine status in the proper sense as it is a recognition of its extra-human power to connect the realm of the gods with that of man."[19]

Another aspect of the *abi* was the "divine watercourse," the rough English translation of a site called ᵈKASKAL.KUR in ritual texts. This appears to be a sacred pool intended to resemble a riverbank, where many of the sacred rituals of the Hurrians took place.[20] This term has only been found in nine Hittite texts, one of which is a treaty dated to about 1280 BC between the Hittite king Muwatalli II and Alaksandu of Wilusa,[21] who is identified by some scholars as Alexander of Troy. He's better known to history as Paris, the young man who started the Trojan War by stealing the beautiful Helen away from her husband, King Menelaus of Sparta.[22]

We get a better sense of the term by breaking it down into its components, both of which are Sumerian words: KASKAL ("road," "journey," and/or "military campaign") and KUR, which can mean "mountain." This context, however, surely points to the other meaning of KUR, "netherworld."[23] The sense is of a river that leads to and/or separates the land of the living from the underworld, much like the River Styx in Greek myth.

Interestingly, the sign ᵈKASKAL.KUR was also used during the

---

19   Billie Jean Collins, "Necromancy, Fertility, and the Dark Earth." In *Magic and Ritual in the Ancient World*, (Leiden, The Netherlands: Brill, 2014), p. 225.
20   Collins (2004), op. cit., p. 56.
21   Edmund I. Gordon, "The Meaning of the Ideogram ᵈKASKAL.KUR = 'Underground Water-Course' and Its Significance for Bronze Age Historical Geography." *Journal of Cuneiform Studies*, Vol. 21 (1967), p. 73.
22   It's not certain that Alaksandu and Alexander/Paris are the same person since the treaty is about fifty years earlier than the best guess for the date of the Trojan War.
23   Gordon, op. cit., p. 76.

time of Abraham to refer to the Balikh River,[24] a tributary of the Euphrates that joins the big river near Raqqa, Syria, the *de facto* capital of the Islamic State between 2014 and 2017. Near Raqqa was the ancient city of Tuttul, one of the major cult centers of the god Dagan, who, as Derek showed in *The Second Coming of Saturn*, was another identity of the god called Enlil, El, Assur, Milcom/Molech, and Kumarbi across Mesopotamia and the Levant. We believe those names were adopted by the Watcher chief Shemihazah, leader of the rebellion on Mount Hermon that resulted in the creation of the hybrid giants called the Nephilim. Given that Shemihazah and his colleagues were bound during the Flood of Noah "in the valleys of the earth,"[25] a place more precisely defined by Peter as Tartarus,[26] it's not surprising that humans later came to believe that some gods must be summoned from the netherworld, a domain that can only be reached by crossing a mystical body of water. It appears, then, that the Balikh may have been linked to memories of the Flood and the old god Kumarbi/Dagan, who now reigned from an underworld throne. Tuttul is roughly 150 miles southwest of Urkesh—a long walk five thousand years ago, but close together on a cosmic scale and relatively near other sites linked to Kumarbi, Dagan, and El in Syria and southern Turkey.[27]

KASKAL was also the Sumerian equivalent for the Akkadian word *ḫarrānum* and the ideogram for Harran, the city from which Abraham began his journey to Canaan. Located on a key east-west trade route, Harran was appropriately named, because it was a crossroads connecting a number of key cultures in the biblical world, among them the Assyrians, Hittites, Amorites, and Hurrians. Harran also sits on the Balikh, which makes the river's ancient name, "Road to the Netherworld," doubly interesting.

We mention all this because the Buccellatis discovered a stone

---

24 Ibid., p. 77.
25 1 Enoch 10:12.
26 2 Peter 2:4.
27 For example, the village of Kīmār near Aleppo, from which Kumarbi probably drew his name: "he of Kumar." See Astour, op. cit.

drain in a platform alongside a palace at Urkesh which may be an early form of the [d]KASKAL.KUR connected to rituals for contacting the underworld gods in the *abi*.[28]

In short, the *abi* was an underground portal to communicate with spirits in the netherworld. And the discoveries at Urkesh connect Hurrian religious rituals performed in western Syria and central Turkey as late as 1200 BC, the middle of the period of the Judges in Israel, with a monumental religious center constructed in northeastern Syria more than two thousand years earlier—and, of course, the people who built the temple, who migrated there from the Ararat Plain.

Now, why is this relevant to our understanding of the Bible, Christian theology, and the long supernatural war for the souls of humanity? Because occult practices to contact the spirit realm, documented at the Hurrian city of Urkesh more than five thousand years ago, continue to this day. And many of these rituals involve contacting spirits at home in the netherworld, often on the far side of a body of water—a twisted memory of rebellious spirits who were condemned to the bottomless pit in the days of Noah, when the world was purged of their sin by an earth-cleansing flood.

---

28   Kelly-Buccellati (2002), op. cit., p. 143.

CHAPTER SIX

THE HURRIANS

Now the LORD said to Abram, "Go from your country and your kindred and your father's house to the land that I will show you.

— GENESIS 12:1 (ESV)

The Hurrians first appear in Akkadian and Sumerian records in northern Mesopotamia, in what is today Kurdish territory along the border between Syria, Iraq, and Turkey. The city of Urkesh was founded in the fourth millennium BC and was an important center of Hurrian religion for more than two thousand years, from about 3500 BC until the city was finally abandoned around 1200 BC. Even though Urkesh was settled several centuries before the earliest evidence of writing, the *abi* (ritual pit), a ritual structure "uniquely linked to the Hurrian tradition,"[1] is strong evidence for Hurrian spiritual and political influence in Mesopotamia during the formative years of the Hebrew people. And the Hurrians connect three very important mountains in the history of the Bible: Ararat, Sinai, and Zion.

In a previous chapter, we described the migration of the proto-Hurrians, the Kura-Araxes or Early Transcaucasian people, who left their original homeland on the Ararat Plain as early as the fifth millennium BC. As Christians, we accept that a historic, global flood deposited a boatload of survivors in the mountains of Ararat some

---

1   Kelly-Buccellati (2002), op. cit., p. 132.

time before 5000 BC, perhaps at or after the end of the period of climatic change called the Younger Dryas, roughly 9400–9100 BC.[2] As the sons of Noah came down from the mountain and established themselves in new territories, a group of Japhethites, the Kura-Araxes people, so named for the two rivers that drain the north and south sides of the Lesser Caucasus Mountains, established themselves no later than 4000 BC in what is now Armenia, Georgia, Azerbaijan, and eastern Turkey.[3] They spread from the Ararat Plain to settle a broad swath from northern Iran to eastern Turkey, pushing north of the Caucasus Mountains into Georgia and south to the outer edge of the Fertile Crescent, and eventually migrating south along the Mediterranean coast to reach the Sea of Galilee and the Jordan River valley by about 2850 BC.[4] The advent of writing around 3000 BC allows us to track the influence of these proto-Hurrians on ideas and beliefs through their words, and not just their architecture and pottery.

The Kura-Araxes culture faded into history around 2000 BC,[5] just as the Amorites emerged as the leading cultural and political force in the Near East.[6] However, the Hurrians, as recent discoveries at Tell Mozan (ancient Urkesh) confirm, connect the Kura-Araxes culture of the Ararat Plain and the necromantic rituals of the *abi* to people encountered by the patriarchs in Canaan. Recent scholarship links a legendary Amorite ruler named Keret or Kirta with the powerful Hurrian kingdom of

---

2   We are not dogmatic about most dates prior to the time of Abraham, and especially those that climatologists argue over. But we accept that the sequence of events in scripture is correct.

3   C. Marro, V. Bakhshaliyev, and R. Berthon, "On the Genesis of the Kura-Araxes Phenomenon: New Evidence from Nakhchivan (Azerbaijan)." *Paléorient* 40.2 (2014), pp. 131–154.

4   Yael Rotem, Mark Iserlis, Felix Höflmayer, and Yorke M. Rowan, "Tel Yaqush—An Early Bronze Age Village in the Central Jordan Valley, Israel." *BASOR* 381 (2019), pp. 107-144.

5   Giulio Palumbi and Christine Chataigner, "The Kura-Araxes Culture from the Caucasus to Iran, Anatolia and the Levant: Between unity and diversity. A synthesis." In: *Paléorient*, vol. 40, n°2 (2014), pp. 247-260.

6   Minna Silver, "The Earliest State Formation of the Amorites: Archaeological Perspectives from Jebel Bishri." *ARAM* 26:1&2 (2014), p. 244.

Mitanni, establishing another cultural and religious connection between these important but relatively unknown groups of people.

Abraham also began his migration from Ur to Harran at about the same time, 2000 BC, and then on to Canaan. And the Hurrians loom large in the stories of the biblical patriarchs.

Here we need to correct the common misconception about Abraham's origins: Ur of the Chaldees (or Chaldeans) was not in Sumer, modern-day southern Iraq. Abraham came from northern Mesopotamia, near the modern border between southeastern Turkey and northeastern Syria.

Until the early twentieth century, most people assumed that Abraham's roots were in the north. After famed British archaeologist Sir Leonard Woolley excavated the stunning "Royal Tombs of Ur" in 1922, however, Jews, Christians, and Muslims decided that the powerful Sumerian city was a more appropriate point of origin for Father Abraham. Before Woolley, Bible scholars generally accepted that the patriarch had come from southern Turkey. That's where we find ancient Harran, on the Balikh River about ten miles north of the Syrian border.

In the early second millennium BC, Harran was an important trading center on the caravan route between the Mediterranean coast and Assyria in what was probably a key border zone between the Assyrians to the southeast, the Hurrians to the northeast, an emerging Amorite kingdom at Aleppo to the southwest, and the Hittites, who were arriving in Anatolia to the northwest around that time.

Near Harran was Ura, a town known as a home base for traveling merchants,[7] and several cities bearing the names of Abraham's father Terah, grandfather Nahor (Nahur), great-grandfather Serug (Sarugi), and brother Haran, the father of Lot.[8]

---

7   Cyrus H. Gordon, "Abraham and the Merchants of Ura." *Journal of Near Eastern Studies* Vol. 17, No. 1 (Jan. 1958), pp. 28–31.

8   Mark Chavalas, "Genealogical History as 'Charter': A Study of Old Babylonian Period Historiography and the Old Testament." In *Faith, Tradition, and History: Old Testament Historiography in Its Near Eastern Context* (Winona Lake, Ind.: Eisenbrauns, 1994), p. 122.

Note that "Haran" and "Harran" are different words. *Harran* derives from the Akkadian *ḫarrānum* ("road"), while the name of Lot's father probably meant something like "mountaineer," from *har*, the Hebrew word for "mountain." Still, the names of Abraham's close family members suggest a much stronger connection to northern Mesopotamia than with Sumer, seven hundred miles to the southeast—where mountains are scarce.

Likewise, Abraham's lifestyle as a tent-dwelling nomad is more consistent with the pastoral culture of northern Mesopotamia than with Sumer. He was not a city-dweller, and neither were Isaac and Jacob. And this must be said: If Abraham's father, Terah, had meant to go from Sumer to Canaan, he would not have ended up in Harran, even by mistake. Harran isn't just a little out of the way; it's *ridiculously* out of the way. Going from Ur to Canaan by way of Harran is like driving from Atlanta to Dallas by way of Milwaukee.

Most important, the Bible supports this theory. When Joshua called on the tribes of Israel to remember their origins, he said:

> Thus says the LORD, the God of Israel, "Long ago, your fathers lived beyond the Euphrates, Terah, the father of Abraham and of Nahor; and they served other gods. Then I took your father Abraham from beyond the River and led him through all the land of Canaan, and made his offspring many." (Joshua 24:2–3)

The key phrase is "beyond the Euphrates." Sumerian Ur is on the west bank of the Euphrates River, so Abraham would not have crossed it to get to Canaan. Harran, however, is on the far side of the river.

What has become increasingly apparent during our recent studies is that Abraham's home was part of the Hurrian realm. In fact, Ur-Kasdim ("Ur of the Chaldees/Chaldeans") may be the Hurrian religious center Urkesh. The city was at the peak of its power near the end of the third millennium BC, but its influence began to wane after about 2000 BC, just about the time Terah decided to look for better prospects in the west. Urkesh is roughly one hundred and forty miles east of Harran on a well-traveled route for merchants coming south through the Mardin Pass and heading west toward markets like Ebla, Halab (Aleppo), and southward to Damascus, Canaan, and Egypt. In a consonantal language like Hebrew, it is conceivable that a scribe after the Babylonian exile, writing nearly fifteen hundred years after the time of Abraham, might have come across the name of a long-forgotten city, "*u-r-k-s*," and "corrected" it to one he was familiar with, "*u-r-k-s-d-m*"—Ur-Kasdim, the Sumerian Ur.[9]

The route from Urkesh to Harran to Canaan was well-known to the Hurrians, so it would not be surprising if Abraham had followed it. And the Bible reveals that Hurrians were scattered throughout the Promised Land.

We first encounter them in Genesis 14:1–16, where we read of a military expedition led by Chedorlaomer, the king of Elam (western Iran), against enemies in the Transjordan and around the Dead Sea. The king and his Mesopotamian allies defeated a coalition led by the kings of Sodom and Gomorrah, who'd rebelled against Chedorlaomer's rule after serving him for twelve years. The battle was probably fought just north of the Dead Sea, possibly on the plain between Mount Nebo and Jericho.[10]

Chedorlaomer's army moved south along the King's Highway as far south as the Red Sea, and then marched north through the Arabah and along the west side of the Dead Sea. Before turning north to face the Amalekites and Amorites, the army from the east encountered "the Horites in their hill country of Seir as far as El-paran on the border of the wilderness."[11] This puts Horites, the biblical term for the Hurrians,[12] in the vicinity of Mount Sinai in the time of

---

9   Patricia Berlyn, "The Journey of Terah: To Ur-Kasdim or Urkesh?" *Jewish Bible Quarterly*, Vol. 33, No. 2 (2005), pp. 73-80.

10 For the location of Sodom at Tall el-Hammam, Jordan, about 8.5 miles northeast of the Dead Sea, see Steven Collins and Latayne C. Scott, *Discovering the City of Sodom: The Fascinating, True Account of the Discovery of the Old Testament's Most Infamous City* (New York: Howard Books, 2013).

11 Genesis 14:6.

12 Nicolas Wyatt, "A Ritual Response to a Natural Disaster: KTU 1.119.31 = RS 24.266.31 Revisited." *Ugarit-Forschungen* 50 (2019), p. 454.

Abraham. Paran was an alternate name for "Sinai,"[13] and Seir generally refers to the land of Edom, where the Shara (Seir) Mountains rise along the east side of the Arabah valley that connects the Dead Sea to the Red Sea.

Many believe that Mount Sinai is the mountain in Saudi Arabia called Jebel al-Lawz. We'll address that in a future book, but for now the important detail is the link between Sinai, Seir, Paran, and the Hurrians. And that establishes the presence of this people and their religion in the Holy Land centuries before Moses and the Israelites escaped from Egypt. Indeed, the Bible tells us that the inhabitants of the land descended from Seir the Horite,[14] who apparently gave his name to the region south of the Dead Sea. To this day, Mount Hor, where Moses' brother Aaron died and was buried, is identified as Jabal Hārūn, one of the peaks overlooking Petra in Jordan.[15]

The Hurrians in the Transjordan during Abraham's day were pushed out by the descendants of Esau.[16] But they remained in control of two important cities in Israel down to the time of David: Shechem and Jerusalem.

Chapter 34 of the Book of Genesis describes an unpleasant encounter between the family of Jacob and the citizens of Shechem, which was ruled by "Hamor the Hivite." The Septuagint translation of the verse, though, uses the Greek word *Chorraios*, which means the Jewish translators worked with an older Hebrew text that probably described Hamor as *ḥōrî* rather than *ḥivî*—in other words, Hamor was a Hurrian, not a Hivite.[17] (As noted earlier, the Hivites were the Ahhiyawa, the Hittite name for Achaeans, the Mycenaean Greeks.)[18] Scholars have pointed out that the practice of a married couple living

---

13 Deuteronomy 33:2, Habakkuk 3
14 Genesis 36:20.
15 Josephus, *Antiquities of the Jews* 4.4.7.
16 Deuteronomy 2:12, 22.
17 Nicolas Wyatt, "The Story of Dinah and Shechem." In *The Archaeology of Myth* (London: Equinox, 2010), p. 20.
18 B. Collins (2007), op. cit., p. 154.

with or near the husband's father's group was not typical Israelite practice, but it is attested in Hurrian texts.[19]

The spiritual significance of Shechem is a strong subtext in the Old Testament. God appeared to Abraham at the oak of Moreh overlooking the city and promised to give Canaan to his descendants.[20] Jacob buried the idols of the members of his household at the terebinth near Shechem,[21] probably the same tree.[22] Centuries later, Joshua reconfirmed Israel's covenant at Shechem.[23]

Likewise, the struggle for the city where God has placed His Name, Jerusalem, is ancient. God signaled His intention to claim it almost four thousand years ago when He directed Abraham to take Isaac to Mount Moriah. Based on 2 Chronicles 3:1, we can identify this as the location of the threshing floor of Araunah the Jebusite, purchased by David on the orders of the Angel of Yahweh, delivered by the prophet Gad. This piece of ground is where Solomon built the Temple.[24] As you probably know, those thirty-seven acres of real estate are hotly contested by Jews, Muslims, and various denominations of Christians to this day.

Here's the bit that connects the story to this chapter: As mentioned earlier, it's accepted by scholars that the name "Araunah" in 2 Samuel 24 ("Ornan" in 1 Chronicles 21) is probably not a proper name, but a title based on the Hurrian word ewri- ("lord" or "ruler").[25] Araunah may even have been a priest-king, since there is evidence from the ancient world that threshing floors were considered portals—points of contact between this world and the spirit realm.[26]

---

19 Wyatt (2010), op. cit.

20 Genesis 12:6.

21 Genesis 35:4.

22 Barry, John D., Douglas Mangum, Derek R. Brown, Michael S. Heiser, Miles Custis, Elliot Ritzema, and others, Faithlife Study Bible (Bellingham, WA: Lexham Press, 2012, 2016), p. Ge 35:4.

23 Joshua 24:1–28.

24 See 2 Samuel 24:18–25 and 1 Chronicles 21:18–30.

25 Winger, op. cit.

26 We discuss threshing floors as portals in Veneration, especially pp. 109-126.

Significantly, there is a cave underneath the Dome of the Rock, directly below the Foundation Stone that's believed to be where David offered his sacrifice after buying Araunah's threshing floor. The cave is attested as early as 333 AD by an anonymous pilgrim from near Bordeaux, France.[27] Since the Middle Ages it's been called the Well of Souls, based on an Islamic legend that one can hear the spirits of the dead awaiting Judgment Day—similar to the souls who'd been slain for the word of God crying out from under the altar in heaven at the opening of the fifth seal in Revelation 6:9–11.

Can we connect this cave under the Temple Mount to the Hurrians of three thousand years ago? No, at least not yet. We don't know anything about the early use of the cave. As you can guess, archaeology underneath the Dome of the Rock, especially work that might confirm an Israelite presence on the Temple Mount prior to 1967, would be met with violent resistance. But the possibility does point our way to the next chapter, where we'll see just why this Hurrian link between the Caucasus and the Holy Land is important.

---

27 Jerome Murphy-O'Connor, *The Holy Land: An Oxford Archaeological Guide from Earliest Times to 1700*, 5th edition (Oxford: Oxford University Press, 2008), p. 97.

CHAPTER SEVEN

PORTALS TO THE NETHERWORLD

So Saul disguised himself and put on other clothing and left, accompanied by two of his men. They came to the woman at night and said, "Use your ritual pit to conjure up for me the one I tell you."

—1 SAMUEL 28:7–8 (NET)

We've established that the Hurrians are the link between the Chalcolithic (Copper Age) civilization of the Ararat Plain, the early urban center of Urkesh in northern Mesopotamia and its necromantic pit, the *abi*, and key sites in and around what became Israel—specifically, Shechem, the area around Mount Sinai, and Jerusalem. This is significant because the word for the sacred pit used by the Hurrians to summon the gods of the netherworld—the Infernal Council, if you will—is connected to a Hebrew word for a spiritual practice expressly forbidden by God. In fact, the term was familiar to people in the ancient Near East from the Persian Gulf to the middle of Anatolia:

[A] large degree of probability exists for deriving the Sumerian, Assyrian, Hittite, Ugaritic, and Hebrew terms from a common source. The chart below illustrates the similarity in sound shared by these various terms:

Sumerian	*ab(.làl)*
Hittite	*a-a-bi*
Ugaritic	*'eb*
Assyrian	*abu*
Hebrew	*'ôb*[1]

The Hebrew word *'ôb* (pronounced "ove," with a long "O") is usually translated into English as "medium,"[2] but a more accurate rendering is "spirit of the dead."[3] The word appears in the Old Testament sixteen times, often followed by *yiddĕ 'ōnî*, which is translated "necromancer" (one who claims to speak to the dead), as in the ESV, "wizard" (KJV), or "spiritist" (NIV, NASB).

In the ancient Near East, the dead were believed to have powers and knowledge not available to the living. So, the term would be used in the context of summoning spirits from the unseen realm to obtain knowledge, especially of things to come.[4] Since *yiddĕ 'ōnî* always appears in tandem with *'ōbōt*,[5] a more accurate translation is "familiar spirits,"[6] which may have originated as an epithet for dead ancestors meaning "extremely knowledgeable, all-knowing."[7]

The most famous use of the word *'ôb* is in the story of Saul and the medium of En-dor, to whom Saul turned in desperation when he

---

1   Hoffner, op. cit., p. 385.
2   Strong's H178.
3   Josef Tropper, "Spirit of the Dead." In K. van der Toorn, B. Becking, & P. W. van der Horst (Eds.), *Dictionary of deities and demons in the Bible* 2nd extensively rev. ed. (Leiden; Boston; Köln; Grand Rapids, MI; Cambridge: Brill; Eerdmans, 1999), p. 807.
4   Josef Tropper, "Wizard," ed. by Karel van der Toorn, Bob Becking, and Pieter W. van der Horst, *Dictionary of Deities and Demons in the Bible* (Leiden; Boston; Köln; Grand Rapids, MI; Cambridge: Brill; Eerdmans, 1999), p. 907.
5   In Leviticus 19:31; 20:6, 27; Deuteronomy 18:11; 1 Samuel 28:3, 9; 2 Kings 21:6 // 2 Chronicles 33:6; 2 Kings 23:24; Isaiah 8:19; 19:3.
6   Biblical Studies Press, *The NET Bible First Edition*; (Biblical Studies Press, 2005), study note for Leviticus 19:31.
7   Tropper, "Wizard," op. cit.

realized that he'd been abandoned by God. Note the description of Samuel's surprise (to the medium) appearance:

> When the woman saw Samuel, she cried out with a loud voice. And the woman said to Saul, "Why have you deceived me? You are Saul." The king said to her, "Do not be afraid. What do you see?" And the woman said to Saul, "**I see a god coming up out of the earth.**" He said to her, "What is his appearance?" And she said, "An old man is coming up, and he is wrapped in a robe." And Saul knew that it was Samuel, and he bowed with his face to the ground and paid homage. (1 Samuel 28:12–14, emphasis added)

The spirit of Samuel, called "a god" (*elohim*) by the medium, "rose up out of the earth"—in other words, from the pit she used to contact netherworld spirits. Some scholars, aware of the connection between the Hebrew term and the divination pit of the pagans of the ancient Near East, prefer to translate *'ôb* as "ritual pit." Compare the ESV and NET translations of 1 Samuel 28:8 (emphasis added):

English Standard Version	New English Translation
So Saul disguised himself and put on other garments and went, he and two men with him. And they came to the woman by night. And he said, "**Divine for me by a spirit and bring up for me whomever I shall name to you.**"	So Saul disguised himself and put on other clothing and left, accompanied by two of his men. They came to the woman at night and said, "**Use your ritual pit to conjure up for me the one I tell you.**"

In light of the evidence, the NET translators are correct. We can't fault the ESV translators; the NET Bible is probably the only English translation to choose "ritual pit" as the translation for *'ôb* in that verse. But it's only been since about 1980 that scholars have acknowledged the existence of a cult of the dead in and around ancient Israel, and the idea that the pagan neighbors of the Hebrews summoned the gods of the netherworld is not usually discussed. And the *abi* of Urkesh was only discovered in 1999, so the influence of the Hurrians on these necromantic rituals is only now coming into focus.

In other words, this is new information. It's not being taught in our churches because even most archaeologists don't know a lot of this.

So, kudos to the translators of the NET Bible. Citing the paper we excerpted above, the scholars behind the NET point out that the common understanding of " *'ôb* " in the days of Saul and David was not "medium" but "owner of a ritual pit."[8] And it's clear that Saul and his servants knew exactly what the pit was used for.

As noted above, the concept of the *'ôb*, a pit used to summon spirits from the underworld, connects the Hebrews to older cultures in the ancient Near East going all the way back to Sumer. The Sumerian word, *ab*, means "sea," and it's related to *abzu*, the term for the cosmic underground freshwater domain of the god of wisdom, Enki, who we mentioned in an earlier chapter. It was from the *abzu* that Enki sent forth the *abgal* (usually referred to by the Akkadian word *apkallu*), semi-divine sages who delivered the gifts of civilization to humanity.

Not coincidentally, *abzu* (Akkadian *apsû*) is likely where we get the English word "abyss."

Scholar Amar Annus, who we mentioned earlier, demonstrated in a groundbreaking 2010 paper that the *apkallu* can be positively identified as the Hebrew Watchers.[9] As noted in an earlier chapter, there is a striking similarity between the activity of the *abgal/apkallu*, the rebellious Watchers, especially Asael (often called Azazel), and the Titan Prometheus. We don't think this is a coincidence. Annus interprets the Hebrew stories of the Watchers and their progeny, the Nephilim, as "*deliberate inversions* of the Mesopotamian source material,"[10] polemics against the sorcery and bad behavior of their pagan neighbors who

---

8   NET notes for 1 Samuel 28:3. https://netbible.org/bible/1+Samuel+28, retrieved 2/23/21.

9   Annus (2010), op. cit.

10   Ibid., p. 280.

celebrated the *apkallu* as culture heroes. Even more than that, however, the Hebrew accounts of the Watchers and their monstrous offspring were a different spin on a shared spiritual history in which the *apkallu* were judged according to the moral standards set by God.

The connection between the *abzu* of Sumer and the *'ôb* of the Hebrews is obvious (pardon the pun). The *apkallu* were called upon for favors, especially to protect the home or royal building projects,[11] and it was common for Mesopotamian kings to compare themselves to, or claim to be descendants of, the *apkallu*:

[Nebuchadnezzar], king of Babylon…, distant scion of king-ship, seed preserved from before the flood…[12]

To a Jew in the ancient world, "seed preserved from before the flood" meant a descendant of the Watchers. (By the way, that inscription was carved for Nebuchadnezzar I, who ruled Babylon in the twelfth century BC, about five hundred years before the Nebuchadnezzar who sacked Jerusalem and destroyed Solomon's Temple.) The Assyrian king Ashurbanipal compared his wisdom, including an ability to understand "antediluvian inscriptions," to the first of the *abgall/apkallu* to emerge from the *abzu*, Adapa, and claimed to be his descendant to boot.[13]

The point is that it was widely believed in the ancient Near East that supernatural beings from the netherworld had power and knowledge that was useful, despite the fact that they were sometimes considered evil beings with strong connections to Mesopotamian demonology, and sometimes considered demonic themselves.[14] And the linguistic link between the Sumerian *ab* and Hebrew *'ôb* connects the practice of trying to appease these underworld spirits and the necromantic activity of the woman consulted by Saul the night before his death.

---

11 Ibid., p. 289.
12 Ibid., p. 295.
13 Ibid., p. 294.
14 Ibid., p. 282.

Before we decide that we've nailed this connection, new research deserves to be considered. As we saw above, Bible translators who've made a career of studying ancient Hebrew, Aramaic, Akkadian, and Greek have not settled on a firm definition for *'ôb*. The context seems clear enough, but does the word mean "medium" or "ritual pit"? In 1 Samuel 28:7, the woman Saul consults is called a *ba'alat 'ôb*. The translation "mistress of mediums" is odd, hence the NET note that the original Hebrew means "owner of a ritual pit."

Christopher B. Hays has suggested a new interpretation of *'ôb* based on an Egyptian etymology. He has argued elsewhere, convincingly, for Egyptian loanwords in the Bible, especially in the Book of Isaiah.[15] In this case, Hays and his co-author Joel M. LeMon suggest that *'ôb* may derive from an Egyptian cognate, *3b(w)t*.[16] Not surprisingly, they find the word applied to Egyptian religious practices by Isaiah:

[A]nd the spirit of the Egyptians within them will be emptied
    out,
and I will confound their counsel;
and they will inquire of the idols and the sorcerers,
    and the mediums [*'ōbot*] and the necromancers; (Isaiah 19:3)

The argument is fairly technical, but their conclusion is that Hebrew *'ōbot* is related to Egyptian *3b(w)t* and means "the dead ancestors who could be represented through images."[17] They go too far in crediting the Egyptians with inventing the word, given the evidence of similar terms in Sumer as early as 3000 BC (and Urkesh probably

---

15 Referring specifically to the "loathed branch" of Isaiah 14:19. Christopher B. Hays, "An Egyptian Loanword in the Book of Isaiah and the Deir Alla Inscription: Hebrew *nṣr*, Aram. *nqr*, and Eg. *nṯr* as '[Divinized] Corpse'." *Journal of Ancient Egyptian Interconnections* Vol. 4:2 (2012), pp. 17-23.

16 Christopher B. Hays and Joel M. LeMon, "The Dead and Their Images: An Egyptian Etymology for Hebrew ôb." *Journal of Ancient Egyptian Interconnections* Vol. 1:4 (2009), pp. 1-4.

17 Ibid., p. 3.

even earlier), more than two thousand years before Isaiah.[18] Still, connecting this matrix of ideas to images or statues that represented the venerated dead fits what we know of the culture that produced the patriarchs. Genesis 31 records the story of Jacob's flight from his father-in-law, Laban. Besides his anger at losing his moneymaker son-in-law, Laban was furious that his "household gods" (*teraphim*) had gone missing. While the idols are not called *'ōbôt*, the sense of the word is the same. The teraphim gave a physical location to the ancestral spirits during the monthly *kispum* rite, an integral part of Amorite culture. Since those spirits were summoned for blessings and protection, losing access to them was a disaster. It was serious enough in the days of Abraham, Isaac, and Jacob that wills have been found cutting off disobedient children from the family gods.

Hebrew *'ōbôt* is usually translated into English as "spirits of the dead," but a similar word, *'ābôt* (based on the root *'āb*), means "fathers," as in, "deceased ancestors." The difference is subtle. As we noted earlier, the cult of the ancestral dead was widespread among the Amorite neighbors of the Hebrews. It's possible that *'ābôt* and *'ōbôt* are essentially the same word,[19] and the Arabic word *abu* ("father of") is similar. All of these words and ideas are linked to an intriguing reference in Ezekiel 39:11, where God declares that the army led by Gog of Magog will be destroyed in the Valley of the Travelers (Hebrew ōberim), and "it will block the Travelers." *Ōberim* is equivalent to a term used by the pagan Amorites of Ugarit in the second millennium BC for the Rephaim,[20] spirit beings believed to be the deified dead kings of old—in other words, equivalent to the Nephilim of Genesis 6.

[I]n spite of the damaged text, we may read the opening lines of KTU 1.20 i 1–3 as follows:

---

18 "Abzu (water)." *The Pennsylvania Sumerian Dictionary.* http://psd.museum.upenn .edu/epsd/epsd/e114.html, retrieved 2/23/21.

19 Hays and LeMon, op. cit., p. 1.

20 The Ugaritic "Rephaim Texts," designated by scholars KTU 1.20-22.

[rp]um tdbḥn   [The sav]iours will feast
[šb]ʿd ilnym   [seve]n times the divinities
[ṯmnid] mtm   [eight times] the dead...

This amounts to a statement that the *rpum* [Rephaim] are indeed divine: they fall into the category of *ilnym* [*elohim*], that is, chthonian gods, who are in turn qualified as *mtm*, "dead." This gives them the aura of underworld associations, rather than merely denotes that they are defunct. These dead are powerful!...

The *rpum* texts contain other pieces of information. Apparently summoned to a cultic performance, usually interpreted as a *kispum* rite, **the Rapiuma [Rephaim] come in chariots on a three-day journey** to a location variously identified as a threshing-floor (*grn*), a plantation (*mṭct*), a sanctuary (*atr*) and a house (*bt*, ‖ palace, *hkl*), which may denote a temple and its constituent sacral areas, and which is at the same time on a mountain summit in the Lebanon (KTU 1.22 i 24–5). **The three days of their journeying hints at a lunar symbolism tied to the theme of resurrection**, as perhaps evidenced in Hosea 6:2. This is circumstantial evidence supporting the view that they are dead. The apparent location of the sanctuary, and especially the allusion to the Lebanon, not as we might expect to somewhere directly associated with Ugarit (such as the city itself, or [Mount] Saphon [modern Jebel al-Aqra near Antakya, Turkey]) suggests that the narrative is keying directly into the tradition of the Hauran (biblical Bashan) as the territory associated with the Rapiuma.[21] (Emphasis and brackets added)

In KTU 1.22 i 13-15, the Rephaim are called *ʿbrm*, a Ugaritic cognate for ōberim variously translated as "travelers," "vagabonds," or "those who came over," in the sense of the dead "crossing over" from

---

21   Wyatt (2010), op. cit., pp. 50-51.

the spirit realm to the land of the living. And note that these "travelers" were summoned through a necromancy ritual to the threshing-floor (a portal!) of the Canaanite creator-god El, which scholars generally agree was the summit of the mountain that was visible nearly everywhere in Bashan, Mount Hermon.[22] According to the text, after two days of riding the Rephaim arrive at the threshing-floor "after sunrise on the third."[23] The purpose of the ritual was resurrection:

> There, shoulder to shoulder were the brothers,
> whom El made to stand up in haste.
> There the name of El revivified the dead,
> the blessings of the name of El revivified the heroes.[24]

The three-day journey of the Rephaim to Mount Hermon, a sacred place connected to resurrection, has obvious significance for Christians, or it should. Resurrection on the third day is at the very heart of the gospel message:

> For I delivered to you as of first importance what I also received: that Christ died for our sins in accordance with the Scriptures, that he was buried, that he was raised on the third day in accordance with the Scriptures. [...]
>
> [I]f there is no resurrection of the dead, then not even Christ has been raised. And if Christ has not been raised, then our preaching is in vain and your faith is in vain. [...]
>
> If in Christ we have hope in this life only, we are of all people most to be pitied. (1 Corinthians 15:3–4, 13–14, 19)

---

22 Lipiński, op. cit., pp. 13-69.

23 KTU 1.22 ii 25. Nicolas Wyatt, *Religious Texts from Ugarit* (London; New York: Sheffield Academic Press, 2002) p. 320.

24 Klaas Spronk, *Beatific Afterlife in Ancient Israel and in the Ancient Near East* (Kevelaer: Butzon & Bercker, 1986), p. 171.

CHAPTER EIGHT

BABEL: THE GOD-GATE

"Come, let us build ourselves a city and a tower with its top in the heavens, and let us make a name for ourselves, lest we be dispersed over the face of the whole earth."

—GENESIS 11:4 (ESV)

W hen pastors and Bible teachers preach or teach on the Tower of Babel, they tend to focus on pride. The builders on the plains of Shinar, ancient Sumer, thought they could build a tower tall enough to reach heaven—a structure that would put them in direct contact with the gods.

Humanity has learned a few things about building construction over the years, but seriously, even five thousand years ago architects and structural engineers were smart enough to know they'd never stack mud bricks high enough to touch the sky.

Yes, the purpose of Babel was to communicate with the gods. But the entities the builders wanted to reach were *below* the tower, not above.

The Hebrew prophets loved to play with language. We often find words in the Bible that sound like the original but make a statement—for example, Beelzebub ("lord of the flies") instead of Beelzebul ("Baal the prince"), or Ish-bosheth ("man of a shameful thing") instead of Ish-baal ("man of Ba`al"). Likewise, the original Akkadian *bāb ilu*, which

63

means "gate of god" or "gate of the gods," is replaced in the Bible with *Babel,* which is based on the Hebrew word meaning *confusion.*

Now, contrary to what you've probably heard, the Tower of Babel was not in Babylon. It's an easy mistake to make. The names sound alike, and Babylon is easily the most famous city of the ancient world. It's also got a bad reputation. Babylon, under King Nebuchadnezzar, sacked the Temple in Jerusalem and carried off the hardware for temple service. It makes sense to assume that a building project so offensive that God personally put a stop to it must have been built at Babylon.

But there's a problem with the timeline of history: Babylon didn't exist when the tower was built. It didn't become a city until about a thousand years after the tower incident, and even then it was an unimportant village for another five hundred years after that.

Traditions and sources outside the Bible identify the builder of the tower as Nimrod. Our best guess is he lived sometime around 3100 BC, at the end of a period of history called the Uruk Expansion. This tracks with what little the Bible tells us about Nimrod. As mentioned in a previous chapter, Genesis 10:10 tells us "the beginning of his kingdom was Babel, Erech, Accad, and Calneh, in the land of Shinar." It is consistent with the archaeological record, which confirms that Uruk, in what is today southeastern Iraq, expanded its power and dominion into northern Mesopotamia between about 3800 and 3100 BC, when Uruk's empire collapsed.

Babylon itself was northwest of Uruk, roughly three hundred miles from the Persian Gulf in what is today central Iraq. But it wasn't founded until around 2300 BC, at least 700 years after Babel, and it wasn't Babylon as we think about it until the old Babylonian empire emerged in the early part of the second millennium BC.

So, where should we look for the Tower of Babel?

The oldest and largest ziggurat in Mesopotamia was at Eridu, the first city built in Mesopotamia.[1] In recent years, scholars have learned

---

1   "The Sumerian King List: translation." https://etcsl.orinst.ox.ac.uk/section2 /tr211.htm, retrieved 1/17/24.

that the name "Babylon" was interchangeable with other city names, including Eridu.[2] In other words, "Babylon" didn't always mean Babylon in ancient texts. Even though Eridu never dominated the political situation in Sumer after its first two kings, Alulim and Alaljar,[3] the city of Enki was so important to Mesopotamian culture that more than three thousand years after the city was founded, Hammurabi, crowned king of Babylon around 1792 BC, made a point of noting in his famous law code that he "reestablished Eridu and purified the worship of E-apsu."[4] Even as late as the time of Nebuchadnezzar, 1,100 years after Hammurabi, kings of Babylon still sometimes called themselves LUGAL.NUN[ki]—King of Eridu.[5]

What was so special about Eridu? The E-abzu, or "House of the Abyss," was the temple of the great god Enki, whose dwelling place was the freshwater ocean under the earth. Enki, the lord of wisdom, intelligence, trickery, exorcism, creation, fertility, art, and magic,[6] was usually depicted with streams of water gushing from his shoulders that represented the Tigris and Euphrates rivers, the sources of life in Mesopotamia. Archaeologists have uncovered eighteen levels of the E-abzu,[7] the oldest being a small structure less than ten feet square dated to the founding of the city around 5400 BC.[8] Fish bones were scattered around the building. Enki seems to have been a fan of Euphrates River carp.

---

2   Stephanie Dalley, "Babylon as a Name for other Cities Including Nineveh." In R. Biggs, J. Meyers & M. Roth (Eds.), *Proceedings of the 51st Rencontre Assyriologique Internationale* (Chicago: The University of Chicago, 2008), pp. 25–26.

3   "The Sumerian King List," op. cit.

4   "The Code of Hammurabi." Translation by L. W. King. https://avalon.law.yale.edu/ancient/hamframe.asp, retrieved 1/17/24.

5   Douglas Petrovich, "(Re)Locating the Site of Babel of Genesis 11 and Locating the Uncompleted Tower" (unpublished article), p. 4.

6   Joshua J. Mark, "Enki." *World History Encyclopedia,* last modified January 9, 2017. https://www.worldhistory.org/enki/, retrieved 1/17/24.

7   Fu'ād Safar, Seton Lloyd, Muhammad 'Alī Muṣṭafā & Mu'assasah al-'Āmmah lil-Āthār wa-al-Turāth, *Eridu* (Baghdad: Republic of Iraq, Ministry of Culture and Information, State Organization of Antiquites and Heritage, 1981), p. 86.

8   Joshua J. Mark, "Eridu." *World History Encyclopedia.* Last modified July 20, 2010. https://www.worldhistory.org/eridu/, retrieved 1/17/24.

It's worth repeating that *abzu* (*ab* = water + *zu* = deep) is very likely where we get our English word "abyss." And here's another piece to the puzzle: Nimrod, the presumed builder of the Tower of Babel, was born in the second generation after the flood. His father was Cush, son of Ham, son of Noah. In Sumerian history, the second king of Uruk after the flood was named Enmerkar, son of Mesh-ki-ang-gasher.

It's possible that the Hebrews, doing what they loved to do with language, transformed Enmer, the consonants N-M-R (remember, no vowels in ancient Hebrew), into Nimrod, which makes it sound like *marad*, the Hebrew word for "rebel." Interestingly, an epic poem from about 2000 BC called *Enmerkar and the Lord of Aratta* preserves the basic details of the Tower of Babel story.

Scholars don't agree on the location of Aratta, but guesses range from northern Iran to Armenia. This is an intriguing possibility: Armenia is located near the center of an ancient kingdom called Urartu, which may be a cognate for Aratta, and it's precisely where Noah landed his boat—the mountains of Ararat, which *is* a cognate for Urartu. So, this would make the dispute between Enmerkar and the lord of Aratta a fight between cousins—great-grandsons of Noah.

Wherever Aratta was, Enmerkar tried to compel it to send building materials for a couple of projects near and dear to his heart. The poem refers to Enmerkar's capital city Uruk as the "great mountain." This is curious, since Uruk, like most of Sumer, is in an alluvial plain where there are no mountains at all. Uruk was the home city of two of the chief gods of the Sumerian pantheon, Anu, the sky-god, and his granddaughter Inanna, the goddess of war and sex.

Anu was considered an otiose deity, which means he was basically retired. He'd handed over his duties as head of the pantheon to Enlil, who, as Derek showed in *The Second Coming of Saturn*, was also known by other names in the ancient world including El, Dagon, Milcom (Molech), Assur, Kronos, and, of course, Saturn. Inanna, on the other hand, played a very active role in Sumerian society and has been one of the most popular deities throughout history under names such as Ishtar, Astarte, Aphrodite, Venus, and Queen of Heaven.

Apparently, one of the issues between Enmerkar and the king of Aratta, whose name was *Ensuhkeshdanna*, was a dispute over who was Inanna's favorite. One of Enmerkar's pet building projects was a magnificent temple to Inanna, the E-ana ("House of Heaven"). He wanted Aratta to supply the raw materials. Apparently, this wasn't only because there wasn't much in the way of timber, jewels, or precious metal in Sumer, but because Enmerkar wanted the lord of Aratta to submit and acknowledge that he was Inanna's chosen one. And so Enmerkar prayed to Inanna:

> "My sister, let Aratta fashion gold and silver skillfully on my behalf for Unug (Uruk). Let them cut the flawless lapis lazuli from the blocks, let them…the translucence of the flawless lapis lazuli…build a holy mountain in Unug. Let Aratta build a temple brought down from heaven—your place of worship, the Shrine E-ana; let Aratta skillfully fashion the interior of the holy *jipar*, your abode; may I, the radiant youth, may I be embraced there by you. Let Aratta submit beneath the yoke for Unug on my behalf."[9]

Note that Inanna's temple was, like Uruk, compared to a holy mountain. And given the type of goddess Inanna was, the embrace Enmerkar wanted was a euphemism for something more intimate.

But this isn't mentioned in the Bible. The great sin of Enmerkar (Nimrod, if that identification is correct), was trying to rebuild the pre-Flood temple to Enki, lord of the abyss:

> "Let the people of Aratta bring down for me the mountain stones from their mountain, build the great shrine for me, erect the great abode for me, make the great abode, the abode of the

---

9   "Enmerkar and the Lord of Aratta," *The Electronic Text Corpus of Sumerian Literature.* https://etcsl.orinst.ox.ac.uk/cgi-bin/etcsl.cgi?text=t.1.8.2.3#, retrieved 1/17/24.

gods, famous for me, make my me prosper in Kulaba, make the *abzu* grow for me like a holy mountain, make Eridug (Eridu) gleam for me like the mountain range, cause the *abzu* shrine to shine forth for me like the silver in the lode. When in the *abzu* I utter praise, when I bring the me from Eridug, when, in lordship, I am adorned with the crown like a purified shrine, when I place on my head the holy crown in Unug Kulaba, then may the…of the great shrine bring me into the *jipar*, and may the… of the *jipar* bring me into the great shrine. May the people marvel admiringly, and may Utu (the sun god) witness it in joy."[10]

The tower project at Babel (Eridu) wasn't about hubris or pride, it was an attempt to build the abode of the gods, an artificial mount of assembly, right on top of the *abzu*—the abyss.

Could it have succeeded? We doubt it; no portal or doorway between our realm and Tartarus, the bottomless pit, will open unless God allows it. So, why did He find it necessary to personally put a stop to it? A lot of magnificent pagan temples were built in the ancient world, from Mesopotamia to Mesoamerica. Why did God stop this one?

We can only speculate, of course, but there's a reason it's in the Bible. It's an important enough lesson that God wanted to preserve it for us. Calling Babel "a sin of pride" is easy, but it drains the story of its spiritual and supernatural context.

There's another fascinating detail recorded in Enmerkar and the Lord of Aratta: In the story, Enki confused the speech of humans, who had formerly spoken the same language.

Once upon a time there was no snake, there was no scorpion,
There was no hyena, there was no lion,
There was no wild dog, no wolf,
There was no fear, no terror,
Man had no rival.

---

10   Ibid.

In those days, the lands of Subur (and) Hamazi,
Harmony-tongued Sumer, the great land of the decrees of
    princeship,
Uri, the land having all that is appropriate,
The land Martu, resting in security,
The whole universe, the people in unison
To Enlil in one tongue [spoke].

(Then) Enki, the lord of abundance (whose) commands are
    trustworthy,
The lord of wisdom, who understands the land,
The leader of the gods,
Endowed with wisdom, the lord of Eridu
Changed the speech in their mouths, [brought] contention
    into it,
Into the speech of man that (until then) had been one.[11]

The elements of the Babel account are all there in *Enmerkar and the Lord of Aratta*. The evidence is compelling. It's time to correct the history we've been taught: Babel was not at Babylon. It was at Eridu. The tower was the temple of the god Enki, the god of the abyss. Its purpose was to create an artificial mountain as an abode for the gods to which humans had access. And placing it above the *apsu/abzu*, which we now know was a word derived from the older Hurrian term *abi*, a necromantic ritual pit, suggests that this was not an effort to reach the gods above, but the gods *below*—opening the *bab el*, the "god-gate," to contact the sons of God banished to the abyss.

That was something Yahweh would not allow.

---

11 Ibid.

CHAPTER NINE

CONFRONTING
THE GATES

And when Caesar had further bestowed upon him another additional country, he built there also a temple of white marble, hard by the fountains of Jordan; the place is called Panium, where is a top of a mountain that is raised to an immense height, and at its side, beneath, or at its bottom, a dark cave opens itself; within which there is a horrible precipice, that descends abruptly to a vast depth; it contains a mighty quantity of water, which is immovable; and when anybody lets down anything to measure the depth of the earth beneath the water, no length of cord is sufficient to reach it.

—JOSEPHUS, *Wars of the Jews* 1.404–405

P eter must have wondered why Jesus had led them to that place. Caesarea Philippi was a center of pagan worship, well-known across the Near East. It had been for centuries. Before the Romans came, it was called Paneas by the Greeks, a place sacred to the goat-demon Pan. The pagans believed Pan was one of the few gods who could travel back and forth between the earth and the netherworld, so the bottomless cave at Paneas, source of the Jordan River, was thought to be the literal entrance to Hades.[1] No one knew

---

1   Chuck Booher, "Jesus' Declaration at Caesarea Philippi," in *Faithlife Study Bible* (Bellingham, WA: Lexham Press, 2012, 2016).

how far down the cave went because no one had ever been able to measure it.[2]

The site had been sacred to the gods of the pagans for centuries. Their shrines were all over. Why would Jesus take his disciples there? Paneas had been a destination for pagan pilgrims long before Herod the Great built a temple in honor of his patron in Rome, Caesar Augustus, more than a decade before the birth of Jesus. Herod's son, Philip, enlarged the sacred precinct and renamed it Kaisereia, to complete the honor to Caesar.[3] It was later called Caesarea Philippi to distinguish it from other cities, like Caesarea Maritima on the Mediterranean coast. But older place names in the area like Baal-Gad[4] and Baal-Hermon[5] testified to pagan traditions that went back more than a thousand years.

Joshua had fought a famous battle not far from Paneas fourteen centuries earlier[6] against a coalition of Canaanites, Amorites, Hittites, Perizzites, Jebusites, and "the Hivites under Hermon in the land of Mizpah" led by Jabin, the king of Hazor.[7] The fight went badly for the Canaanite coalition. Every Jew knew the story from childhood: Joshua chased the defeated enemy northward toward Sidon in Lebanon and "eastward as far as the Valley of Mizpeh."[8] The valley ran below a ridge on the southern slope of Mount Hermon dominated by an old Greek fortress only a mile northeast of Paneas, a site known to future generations as "Nimrod Castle."[9] *Mizpeh* came from a Hebrew

---

2   Flavius Josephus, *Antiquities* 15.10.3 §364. In: William Whiston, *The Works of Josephus: Complete and Unabridged* (Peabody: Hendrickson, 1987), p. 575.

3   *Antiquities* 18.2.1 §28. Ibid., p. 478.

4   Joshua 11:17, 12:7, 13:5.

5   Judges 3:3; 1 Chronicles 5:23.

6   Douglas N. Petrovich, "The Dating of Hazor's Destruction in Joshua 11 via Biblical, Archaeological, & Epigraphical Evidence." *Journal of the Evangelical Theological Society* (2008).

7   Joshua 11:2–9.

8   Joshua 11:8.

9   Alon Margalit, "Differential earthquake footprints on the masonry styles at Qal'at al-Subayba (Nimrod fortress) support the theory of its ancient origin." *Heritage Science* 6, 62 (2018). https://doi.org/10.1186/s40494-018-0227-9

word meaning "to watch" or "to guard."[10] Since the strategically vital road between Tyre and Damascus passed below the fortress, the valley was well named.

The ancient city of Dan was also nearby, just two miles west of Paneas on the Tyre-Damascus road. Its status as a cult center was also well known. The tribe of Dan had been the first in Israel to fall back into paganism in the time of the Judges, and when Jeroboam split the northern tribes away from Judah after the death of Solomon, he made Dan one of the two approved centers of worship in the northern kingdom of Israel.

The fact that Dan and Caesarea Philippi lay at the foot of Mount Hermon was significant. The mountain had been considered sacred since at least the time of Abraham nearly two thousand years before Jesus walked the earth.[11] The book written under the name of the antediluvian prophet Enoch told of how a group of powerful angels, the type called Watchers, descended to the summit of Mount Hermon and brought destruction to the world by teaching humanity forbidden knowledge and joining themselves with women, spawning the monstrous giants called Nephilim. The spirits of the giants still tormented humanity as the very demons Jesus cast out of the possessed. The arcane occult teachings of the fallen Watchers were still practiced by the sorcerers, magicians, and oracles of the pagans. Their shrines dotted the slopes of Hermon. Inscriptions at the cult sites hinted that some of the sacrifices offered to the gods had been human.

This mountain was where the father-god of the Canaanites, El, was believed to hold court with his consort, Asherah, and their seventy

---

10 Patrick M. Arnold, "Mizpah (Place)," ed. by David Noel Freedman, (New York: Doubleday, 1992), p. 879.

11 The Old Babylonian text of the epic of Gilgamesh names "Hermon and Lebanon" as the "dwelling of the Anunnaki," the gods of Mesopotamia. See Edward Lipiński, "El's Abode: Mythological Traditions Related to Mount Hermon and to the Mountains of Armenia," *Orientalia Lovaniensia Periodica* II, (Leuvan, 1971), pp. 18–19.

Note that the journey from Babylon to Mount Hermon took about three months. Hermon was not in Babylon's back yard!

sons. That number, seventy, was a symbol representing "all of them"— in other words, the pagan neighbors of Israel had believed for more than two millennia that their creator-god was the father of all the gods of the nations. And there, on the mountain's summit thousands of feet above where Jesus and the disciples stood, was the threshing-floor of El.

The mountain where fallen angels assembled loomed above them and the entrance to Hades gaped just a few yards from where they stood. In short, Paneas was an evil place.

And yet Jesus had made a special trip to bring his disciples to it. Paneas was a two-day journey from the Sea of Galilee, thirty miles away from the base of Jesus' ministry. He could have returned to Galilee from Sidon and Tyre by way of Paneas, but no. Rather than stopping at Paneas when they passed by, the teacher led his followers south to the Sea of Galilee and spent time there, preaching, healing, and feeding a hungry multitude, before returning north to the foot of Mount Hermon. This journey was specifically to bring his disciples to Paneas, a center of idolatry and pagan worship.

During his ministry, Jesus had healed the sick, walked on water, fed crowds of thousands with nothing but a few loaves of bread, and driven demons out of so many people. Even the daughter of a Syrophoenician woman—a Gentile!—had been delivered from an evil spirit.[12] Had they come to Paneas to tear down their temples? Was this to be the beginning of a war in the heavenly realm? Would Jesus drive the gods of the pagans out of the land here before turning south to take his place in Jerusalem?

More important: Would Jesus destroy the hated Romans and assume his rightful place on the throne of David?

And then the teacher asked Peter and the disciples a question: "Who do people say the Son of Man is?"[13]

What? Was this a test? The Son of Man was the prophesied savior first mentioned by the prophet Daniel:

---

12 Matthew 15:21–28; Mark 7:24–30.
13 Matthew 16:13.

"I saw in the night visions,
    and behold, with the clouds of heaven
there came one like a son of man,
    and he came to the Ancient of Days
and was presented before him.
    And to him was given dominion
and glory and a kingdom,
    that all peoples, nations, and languages
should serve him;
    his dominion is an everlasting dominion,
which shall not pass away,
    and his kingdom one
that shall not be destroyed. (Daniel 7:13–14)

Centuries before Jesus walked the earth, Daniel's vision had introduced "one like a son of man" into Jewish prophetic thought. In the Hebrew of Daniel's day, that phrase meant "one who looks like a human," in contrast to the supernatural glory of the Ancient of Days. But in the years just before the time of Jesus, a new teaching had emerged. A prophetic writing, also attributed to Enoch, foretold the coming of a character in the Last Days called the Chosen One, the Anointed One, and, most frequently, the Son of Man. This prophesied savior would execute the judgment of God on evil kings, wicked landowners, and even rebellious angels who had corrupted the earth for thousands of years.

Although this teaching was not found in any of the scriptures read in the synagogue, Jesus had applied the title "the Son of Man" to himself dozens of times in the hearing of Peter and the disciples.[14]

Jesus' followers struggled to find the answer they thought Jesus wanted to hear: "Some say John the Baptist, others say Elijah, and others Jeremiah or one of the prophets."[15]

---

14 78 times, to be precise.
15 Matthew 16:14.

Then Jesus asked, "But who do *you* say that I am?"

He'd connected himself to the Book of Enoch's "Son of Man"—essentially claiming to be the promised *moshiach*. Without thinking, Peter blurted out, "You are the Christ, the Son of the living God."[16]

Jesus turned to him and replied, "Blessed are you, Simon Bar-Jonah! For flesh and blood has not revealed this to you, but my Father who is in heaven. And I tell you, you are Peter, and on this rock I will build my church, and the gates of hell shall not prevail against it. I will give you the keys of the kingdom of heaven, and whatever you bind on earth shall be bound in heaven, and whatever you loose on earth shall be loosed in heaven."[17]

Peter must have been stunned. The "rock," Mount Hermon, dominated the scene in front of him. It was a place sacred to pagan Canaanites, Phoenicians, Greeks, and Romans.[18] The tension between El and Yahweh, and by extension their sacred mountains, was ancient. One of the psalms declared Zion superior to Hermon, the "mountain of gods,"[19] because Zion was "where the LORD will dwell forever".[20] It even described the Father leading "thousands upon thousands" of chariots to Hermon and ascending to heaven with "a host of captives!"[21] And the gates of hell—Peter and the disciples stood before it, the bottomless cave from which the Jordan River emerged. It was there, in front of the entrance to their domain, that Jesus had promised the infernal powers from that nether realm would not prevail against his *ekklesia*—his congregation.

---

16   Matthew 16:16.

17   Matthew 16:17–19.

18   A new translation of an inscription found inside the temple on the summit of Mount Hermon suggests that the site was sacred to people across the ancient Near East, from Rome to Babylon.

19   Psalm 68:15 is usually translated into English "O mountain of God, mountain of Bashan." However, since the true mountain of God is Zion, the Temple Mount in Jerusalem, rather than Mount Hermon, the Hebrew *har elohim* is more correctly rendered "mountain of gods, mountain of Bashan."

20   Psalm 68:15–16.

21   Psalm 68:17–18.

Peter couldn't have known what the future held, but he must have understood that Jesus had just declared war on the rebellious spirits in the unseen realm.

And he'd done it right in front of the gates of hell.

CHAPTER TEN

OPENING
THE GATES

There were giants in the earth in those days...

—GENESIS 6:4A (KJV)

T he Bible records an odd story at the beginning of Genesis chapter 6. Although it's only four verses long, the consequences of the events described there affect the world to this day:

> When man began to multiply on the face of the land and daughters were born to them, the sons of God saw that the daughters of man were attractive. And they took as their wives any they chose. Then the LORD said, "My Spirit shall not abide in man forever, for he is flesh: his days shall be 120 years." The Nephilim were on the earth in those days, and also afterward, when the sons of God came in to the daughters of man and they bore children to them. These were the mighty men who were of old, the men of renown. (Genesis 6:1–4)

We need to establish that the Nephilim, the children of human women to the "sons of God," were literally angel-human hybrids. This is consistent with similar stories from the ancient world of gods commingling with humans to produce demigods such as Gilgamesh, who claimed to be two-thirds god and one-third human, and Hercules, the son of Zeus by the mortal woman Alcmene.

Admittedly, researchers have not produced DNA from pre-Flood human remains to support this theory. However, it's worth noting that for all of the faith placed by academia in Darwinian evolution, only two hundred complete specimens of "pre-human" fossils have ever been found. If humanity's story truly begins with *Homo erectus* nearly two million years ago, where are the bones? (One expert, Prof. Maciej Henneberg of the University of Adelaide in Australia, concluded that all two hundred of those "pre-humans" are just variations of *Homo sapiens*—modern humans.)[1]

It's important to note that the phrase translated "sons of God" in the Old Testament, Hebrew *bǝnê hā 'ĕlōhîm*, always means "supernatural beings"—angels, if you like. It does not refer to human men. Yes, there are references in the New Testament to "sons of God" that *do* mean humans, but those passages are translated from Greek into English, and the context is different. The arc of history is about restoring humanity to the Garden, like the prodigal son returning home and being restored to the family as a co-heir. That's why Jesus went to the cross.

At the risk of beating a horse that's already on life support, let us repeat: The term "sons of God" in Genesis 6:4 refers to spirit beings, supernatural entities who rebelled against the Father—fallen angels who spawned an evil race of giants mingling the bloodlines of angels with humans. The "sons of God" were not male descendants of Seth, or any other naturalistic explanation that's been put forward since Augustine popularized the "Sethite" view in the early fifth century AD. Casting the "sons of God" as human men who were lured into destructive relationships by the evil daughters of Cain ignores the linguistic and cultural foundation of the Book of Genesis. To inter-pret the Nephilim as fully human mistranslates the Hebrew text and

---

1   Robert Matthews, "Believe It or Not, They're All the Same Species." *The Tele-graph*, December 26, 2004. https://www.telegraph.co.uk/news/worldnews /northamerica/usa/1479800/Believe-it-or-not-theyre-all-the-same-species.html, retrieved 2/20/24.

ignores the way the equivalent phrase was used by the cultures around ancient Israel that spoke and wrote similar languages.

Besides, it's clear that this was the understanding of the apostles who learned their theology directly from Jesus:

> For if God did not spare angels when they sinned, but cast them into hell and committed them to chains of gloomy darkness to be kept until the judgment; if he did not spare the ancient world, but preserved Noah, a herald of righteousness, with seven others, when he brought a flood upon the world of the ungodly; if by turning the cities of Sodom and Gomorrah to ashes he condemned them to extinction, making them an example of what is going to happen to the ungodly; and if he rescued righteous Lot, greatly distressed by the sensual conduct of the wicked (for as that righteous man lived among them day after day, he was tormenting his righteous soul over their lawless deeds that he saw and heard); then the Lord knows how to rescue the godly from trials, and to keep the unrighteous under punishment until the day of judgment, and especially those who indulge in the lust of defiling passion and despise authority. (2 Peter 2:4–10)

The only place in Scripture that describes sinful angels, excluding Satan, is Genesis 6. By connecting the rebellious angels to Sodom and Gomorrah, Peter made it clear that the sin of the angels was sexual—a point he reinforced in verse 10. Like the "angels who sinned," the wicked would be kept under punishment until the Judgment, "especially those who indulge in the lust of defiling passion and despise authority," exactly the sin of the sons of God in Genesis 6.

The apostle Jude was even more explicit:

> And the angels who did not stay within their own position of authority, but left their proper dwelling, he has kept in eternal chains under gloomy darkness until the judgment of the great day—just as Sodom and Gomorrah and the surrounding cities, **which likewise indulged in sexual immorality and**

pursued unnatural desire, serve as an example by undergoing a punishment of eternal fire. (Jude 6–7, emphasis added)

It could not be clearer: By connecting Genesis 6 to the sin of Sodom and Gomorrah, Jude identified the sin of the angels as sexual. (It also indicates that the sin of Sodom wasn't just homosexuality; it was the desire to cross the boundary between species. Physical relations between angels and humans is just as unnatural as between humans and animals.) And just a few verses later, Jude quotes the Book of 1 Enoch, which suggests that we might learn something from that text even though it's not in the Bible.

Enoch, though it's not in the canon of scripture, offers a fuller description of what transpired on Earth before the Flood:

When the sons of men had multiplied, in those days, beautiful and comely daughters were born to them. And the watchers, the sons of heaven, saw them and desired them. And they said to one another, "Come, let us choose for ourselves wives from the daughters of men, and let us beget children for ourselves."…

These and all the others with them took for themselves wives from among them such as they chose. And they began to go in to them, and to defile themselves through them, and to teach them sorcery and charms, and to reveal to them the cutting of roots and plants. And they conceived from them and bore to them great giants. And the giants begot Nephilim, and to the Nephilim were born *Elioud* ["gods of glory"]. And they were growing in accordance with their greatness. They were devouring the labor of all the sons of men, and men were not able to supply them. And the giants began to kill men and to devour them. And they began to sin against the birds and beasts and creeping things and the fish, and to devour one another's flesh. And they drank the blood.[2]

---

2   1 Enoch 6:1–2, 7:1–3. George W. E. Nickelsburg, *1 Enoch: The Hermeneia Translation* (Minneapolis, MN: Fortress Press, 2012), Kindle Edition, pp. 22–24.

Dr. Michael Heiser makes a convincing case in his book *Reversing Hermon* that a key aspect of the mission of Jesus was to undo the evil of these sons of God, called Watchers in 1 Enoch. It's obvious that the impact of the Watchers went well beyond producing monstrous hybrid offspring. Besides sorcery and potions, the fallen angels of the Hermon rebellion taught humanity the arts of divination, cosmetic enhancement, metalworking, fashioning weapons, making "hate-inducing charms,"[3] and "the eternal mysteries that are in heaven,"[4] which were things man was not meant to know. In short, because of the forbidden knowledge passed from the Watchers to humans, the earth was filled with sex and violence.

For this, as Peter noted, God imprisoned the rebels in the abyss. While most English Bibles translate 2 Peter 2:4 as "cast them into hell," the Greek word, *tartarōsas*, literally means "thrust down to Tartarus." That's a location distinct and separate from Hades, the word most used to designate the underworld home of the dead. In Greek cosmology, Tartarus was as far below Hades as the earth is below heaven. It was a special prison reserved for supernatural threats to the divine order—hell for angels, basically. Since this is the only place in the New Testament where *tartarōsas* is used, it's important. It referred to a unique event, but one with which Peter's readers were obviously familiar—the famous story of the Watchers who attempted to corrupt humanity physically and spiritually.

Now, if all this invective against an ancient race of giants was unsupported elsewhere in the ancient world, you would be right to be skeptical. But that happens not to be the case. Similar stories, told from slightly different perspectives, are attested in many of the cultures in the ancient Near East. Mesopotamians knew the Watchers as antediluvian sages called *apkallu*.[5] They were supernatural agents of

---

3   1 Enoch 9:8.

4   1 Enoch 9:6.

5   Amar Annus, "On the Origin of Watchers: A Comparative Study of the Antediluvian Wisdom in Mesopotamian and Jewish Traditions."*Journal for the Study of the Pseudepigrapha* Vol. 19.4 (2010), pp. 277–320.

the god Enki, lord of the *abzu* ("abyss"), who sent them into the world to deliver the gifts of civilization to humanity.

Despite this, the *apkallu* were considered potentially dangerous, capable of malicious witchcraft.[6] An Assyrian exorcism text names two *apkallus* who angered gods and thus brought a lengthy drought on the land,[7] and in a popular Mesopotamian text called the *Epic of Erra*, named for the god of pestilence and mayhem, the chief deity Marduk tells of how he banished the *apkallus* to the *abzu* (after he caused a devastating flood!) and told them not to return to the earth.[8] That's exactly the punishment that God decreed for the Watchers, and it was likewise connected to the great deluge.

Also relevant is that the last four *apkallus* were described as "of human descent,"[9] and thus presumably able to mate with human women just like the Watchers and their offspring, the Nephilim.

The giants created by the lecherous Watchers were destroyed in the Flood of Noah. While the Bible doesn't make this explicit, it's implied in 1 Peter 3:18–20, where the apostle links the Flood to the angels who "formerly did not obey…in the days of Noah." The text in 1 Enoch, however, does specifically connect the Flood to the punishment of the Watchers and the evil acts of their children, the monstrous Nephilim.[10] And the horrific locust-like things that emerge from the bottomless pit in Revelation 9:1–11, which can only be the sons of God from Genesis 6 (i.e., the Watchers/*apkallu*), have five months to torment those without the seal of God on their foreheads.[11] This matches exactly the one hundred fifty days that Noah's ark was on the water,[12] pre-

---

6   Amar Annus, "The Antediluvian Origin of Evil in the Mesopotamian and Jewish Traditions: A Comparative Study." *Ideas of Man in the Conceptions of the Religions* (2012), p. 4.

7   Annus (2010), op. cit., pp. 297–298.

8   *Epic of Erra*, Tablet 1, line 47. Helge Kvanvig, *Primeval History: Babylonian, Biblical, and Enochic: An Intertextual Reading* (Leiden: Brill, 2011), pp. 161–2.

9   Annus (2010), op. cit., p. 298.

10   For example, 1 Enoch 10:2 and 1 Enoch chapters 83 and 84.

11   Revelation 9:5.

12   Genesis 7:24 and 8:3.

cisely five months on a lunar calendar with thirty-day months, during which time the rebellious sons of God watched helplessly from the abyss while their children, the Nephilim, drowned in the Flood.

Here's why this is in the Bible at all: The neighbors of the ancient Hebrews, especially the Amorites who lived in and near Canaan, believed that these mighty men of old were the ancestors of their kings. The spirits of the Nephilim were called rapha—Rephaim. What's more, texts discovered at the ancient Amorite kingdom of Ugarit and only translated within the last fifty years indicate that the Amorites venerated these entities, summoned them through necromancy rituals, and believed that their kings joined their assembly after death.

Genesis 14 names tribes called Rephaim in the Transjordan, lands east of the Jordan River that later became the kingdoms of Ammon, Moab, and Edom, in the time of Abraham (around 1860 BC, assuming the "short sojourn" timeline). By the time of the Exodus in 1446 BC, the Rephaim were mainly believed to be the spirits of the venerated dead. The Emim and Zamzummim, linked by Moses to the Rephaim "and tall as the Anakim,"[13] had been displaced by the kingdoms of Moab and Ammon, respectively. In Deuteronomy 2 Moses made a point of identifying the Anakim as Rephaim,[14] and of twice mentioning the destruction of the Horites (Hurrians) in Seir, the region southeast of the Dead Sea, by the descendants of Jacob's brother Esau to establish the kingdom of Edom.[15]

Assuming that Moses didn't bring Hurrians into the story just to inflate his word count with a bit of irrelevant detail, it's possible that the Hurrians, and their practice of summoning spirits from the netherworld, are connected to the Rephaim and later groups, like the Anakim, that were "counted as Rephaim"—which may explain why "[the LORD] destroyed the Horites before [the people of Esau]."[16]

The bottom line is that by the time of Moses, the Rephaim tribes

---

13 Deuteronomy 2:10–11, 20–21.
14 Deuteronomy 2:11.
15 Deuteronomy 2:12, 22.
16 Deuteronomy 2:22.

were gone except for Og, king of Bashan, the last "of the remnant of the Rephaim."[17] But while the physical Rephaim were no longer a threat after Moses and the Israelites defeated Og in battle, it would be another four hundred years before the cult of the Rephaim was finally eliminated as a threat to Israel's survival.

---

17   Deuteronomy 3:11.

CHAPTER ELEVEN

DEAD KINGS
AND REPHAIM

And Joshua came at that time and cut off the Anakim from the hill country, from Hebron, from Debir, from Anab, and from all the hill country of Judah, and from all the hill country of Israel. Joshua devoted them to destruction with their cities. There was none of the Anakim left in the land of the people of Israel. Only in Gaza, in Gath, and in Ashdod did some remain.

—JOSHUA 11:21–22 (ESV)

The Rephaim and Anakim encountered by the Israelites were probably not literal blood descendants of the Nephilim. That statement may surprise you, given that we believe the antediluvian giants were real, but the hybrid, half-breed monsters of Noah's day were destroyed in the Flood.

What about Goliath, you ask? Good question. Our English Bibles record his height as six cubits and a span, which is about 9'9"—a giant by anyone's definition. However, the oldest Hebrew text of 1 Samuel 17:4, that used by the translators of the Septuagint in the third century BC (and confirmed by a copy found among the Dead Sea scrolls),[1] puts Goliath at four cubits and a span, or about 6'9". That's still very

---

1   The text is labeled 4QSam[a].

large at a time when the average Israelite man was between 5'0" and 5'3",[2] but not freakishly, supernaturally so.

But it's not that simple. The cubit was not a fixed unit of measure. Unlike today, where inches, feet, yards, and the metric alternatives, are universally agreed upon, a cubit was the length of a man's forearm from the elbow to the tip of the middle finger. A span was the distance between the tip of the little finger and the tip of the thumb. Obviously, those dimensions vary based on the size of the individual whose fingers and elbows are being measured. So, our assumption of an eighteen-inch cubit and nine-inch span may be too generous. If the person measuring Goliath—say, a teenaged shepherd boy named David—was an Israelite of average size, his cubit may only have been fifteen inches. In that case, Goliath may have been about 8'0" for six cubits and a span, or just 5'7½" for four cubits and a span.

Even skeptics would admit it's unlikely the Septuagint translators would have bothered mentioning Goliath's height if he was less than a span taller than the average Israelite.

Bible scholar Dr. Clyde E. Billington recently proposed a logical solution to the apparent contradiction between the Masoretic Hebrew text, which is the source of our English Old Testament, and the Septuagint translation, prepared in the third century BC by Jewish religious scholars in Alexandria, Egypt:

> The 6 cubits and a span given for the height of Goliath in the Hebrew Masoretic Text is the original reading; it is not a textual error. The 4 cubits and a span reading found in the LXX is almost certainly a translation of the MT's common cubits into royal Egyptian cubits [...]
>
> The key feature to keep in mind is that the LXX was a translation made in Alexandria, Egypt, and according to tradition, it was made for the pharaoh. An ancient Jewish scholar

---

2 Clyde E. Billington, "Goliath and the Exodus Giants: How Tall Were They?," *JETS*, 50/3 (2007), pp. 489-508.

translating I Sam 17 into Greek in Alexandria would have faced a major translation problem, i.e. how to deal with the great difference in size between the Egyptian royal cubit and the Hebrew common cubit.

The ancient Egyptian royal cubit was the standard adopted for use in Egypt by the Ptolemies. Six royal Egyptian cubits and a span would make Goliath 11 feet 1 inch tall. This is an impossible height for Goliath, and it appears that some unknown Hebrew scholar recognized this and decided to translate the 6 common cubits of the Hebrew text of I Sam 17 into royal Egyptian cubits.[3]

Four cubits and a span, based on the royal Egyptian cubit of 20.65 inches, makes Goliath just a little under eight feet tall, very close to six cubits and a span based on an Israelite cubit of about fifteen inches. In other words, there is no contradiction, and contrary to statements Derek made publicly before he read Dr. Billington's paper, yes, Goliath was unusually, and probably supernaturally, large.

But to make things even more confusing, a key point that's often overlooked in the biblical account of David's showdown with Goliath is that King Saul *didn't even mention* Goliath's size when trying to talk David out of going out to meet the Philistine:

And Saul said to David, "You are not able to go against this Philistine to fight with him, for you are but a youth, and he has been a man of war from his youth." (1 Samuel 17:33)

In other words, Saul emphasized Goliath's training as an elite warrior—not the fact that he was about three feet taller than David!

Here's where we get deep into the biblical text to make our case that the Emim, Zamzummim, and the Anakim, tribes "counted as Rephaim," were not literally semi-divine giants. If they were, they'd

---

3   Ibid.

have either survived the Flood somehow, which suggests that God wasn't able to accomplish His goal "to make an end of all flesh,"[4] or they'd been reconstituted by another group of rebellious *elohim* who commingled with human women. But since the Bible doesn't record either of those possible explanations, we offer a third—one that we can back with Scripture.

The tribes "counted as Rephaim" were not physical descendants of the pre-Flood Nephilim. They worshiped their spirits in the deluded belief that those demons—because, as we'll show, that's what they are—were their heroic royal ancestors. So, when 1 Chronicles 20:4–8 and 2 Samuel 21:15–20 refer to Goliath and the other Philistine "descendants of the giants" (Hebrew: *yĕlîdê hā-rāpâ*), it's in the spiritual sense. They were an elite warrior cult.

The Anakim, who feature prominently in the books of Deuteronomy and Joshua, were an elite class of warriors who ruled the hill country of Israel and Judah at the time of the Israelite conquest of Canaan. They were clearly a troublesome group who even made the powerful neighboring kingdom of Egypt take notice. Execration texts—curses—dated to the time of Abraham and Isaac (nineteenth and eighteenth centuries BC), mention the Iy-anaq in the Transjordan, who are almost certainly identical with the Biblical Anakim:

> The Ruler of Iy-'anaq, 'Erum, and all the retainers who are with him; the Ruler of Iy-'anaq, Abi-yamimu, and all the retainers who are with him; the Ruler of Iy-'anaq, 'Akirum, and all the retainers who are with him;[5]

A common etymology explains the name of the Anakim as deriving from a Hebrew phrase meaning "long-necked."[6] We disagree. The

---

4 Genesis 6:13.

5 James B. Pritchard, ed., *Ancient Near Eastern Texts Relating to the Old Testament* (Princeton: Princeton University Press, 1969), p. 328.

6 Francis Brown, Samuel Rolles Driver, and Charles Augustus Briggs, *Enhanced Brown-Driver-Briggs Hebrew and English Lexicon* (Oxford: Clarendon Press, 1977), p. 778.

word *anak* has no clear Semitic origin.[7] It's more likely based on a Greek noun, *anax*, meaning "heredity ruler."[8]

The Anakim were clearly a problem. Defeating them was the priority of the Israelites. The summary of the Israelite conquest of Canaan in Joshua 11:21–22 records that the Anakim were driven from the hill country of Israel and Judah, and that "only in Gaza, in Gath, and in Ashdod did some remain."[9] Those cities, along with Ashkelon and Ekron, were the five urban centers of the Philistines who fought against Israel from the time of the Judges through the reigns of Saul and David. A Philistine connection to Mycenean Greece is debated, but there are some similarities in material culture, like pottery styles, and recent DNA analysis of human remains from Iron Age Ashkelon show a European component[10] that's consistent with the Bible's claim that the Philistines originated in Crete.[11] So, it's not surprising that the remnant of the Anakim headed for cities on the coast occupied by others with a shared Aegean background.

The hill country Joshua captured from the Anakim later became known as Samaria and Judea, an area generally called the West Bank today. This is the land Israel captured in 1967 after it was attacked by a coalition of Arab states in the Six-Day War. In other words, Joshua's main objective was to eject the Anakim from the very same area that most of the nations of the world want the Israeli government to give back to Palestinian Arabs.

From a military standpoint, that's suicide. The regions of Judea and Samaria are the high ground in Israel. That's a defensive advantage in war. Withdrawing to the pre-1967 border would constrict Israel's

---

7   E. C. B. MacLaurin, "Anak/' ανξ." *Vetus Testamentum*, Vol. 15, Fasc. 4 (Oct. 1965), p. 471.

8   Ibid., p. 472.

9   Joshua 11:22.

10 Ilan Ben Zion, "The Philistine Age." *Archaeology*, July/August 2022. https://www.archaeology.org/issues/473-2207/features/10600-levant-philistine-origins, retrieved 2/23/24.

11 Deuteronomy 2:23, Jeremiah 47:4.

territory to just ten miles wide at its narrowest point. It's an indefensible situation akin to giving an enemy a knife to hold at your throat.

It's not coincidental, in our view, that what was left of the Anakim retreated from the West Bank, the hill country of Israel and Judah, to what became the Philistine strongholds of Gaza, Gath, and Ashdod. Four hundred years later, David and his men fought against four warriors from Goliath's hometown of Gath, all of whom are called "descendants of the giant(s)," or something similar, in our English Bibles. This translation is misleading. The Hebrew phrase translated "descendants (or sons) of the giant(s)" is *yelîdê ha-rāpâ*—literally, "sons/descendants of the *rapha*." This does not mean "giants," plural; it's a singular noun, indicated by the definite article *ha* ("the") and *rapha*, the singular form of "Rephaim." The variations in English translations, "son/descendant of [the] giant/giants/*rapha*/Rephaim," shows just how much confusion there is among translators and Bible scholars in dealing with these Philistine warriors.

The key is that the standard definition of *yelîdê*, "sons/descendants," is too narrow and literal. The Hebrew word *yelîdê* never referred to direct genetic lineage or a blood descendant, but instead designated "one who is born into the group by adoption, initiation or consecration." Further, "the second element in the phrase might then be the name of the group, or its emblem, or the name of the group's patron, whether human or divine."[12] In other words, the *yelîdê ha-rāpâ* were not half-divine demigods but an elite warrior cult who venerated the spirits of the Rephaim—and were possibly possessed by the demons they worshiped. The Hebrew could mean "sons of the *rapha*," indicating that they were dedicated to the Rephaim, the demonic spirits of the Nephilim.

As evidence, we submit the name of one of the giants slain by David and his men:

---

12 Conrad E. L'Heureux, "The *yelîdê hārāpā*: A Cultic Association of Warriors." *Bulletin of the American Schools of Oriental Research*, No. 221 (Feb. 1976), p. 84.

There was war again between the Philistines and Israel, and David went down together with his servants, and they fought against the Philistines. And David grew weary. And Ishbi-benob, one of the descendants of the giants, whose spear weighed three hundred shekels of bronze, and who was armed with a new sword, thought to kill David. But Abishai the son of Zeruiah came to his aid and attacked the Philistine and killed him. Then David's men swore to him, "You shall no longer go out with us to battle, lest you quench the lamp of Israel." (2 Samuel 21:15–17).

"Ishbi-benob" is a strange name. The etymology offered by Bible commentators is usually something like, "his dwelling is in Nob," which was a village near Jerusalem. But Ishbi-benob was from Gath. That's near the Mediterranean coast, nowhere near Jerusalem.

Author Brian Godawa suggested in his novel *David Ascendant* that we've been misspelling Ishbi's name. The name of this Philistine should be *Ishbi ben Ob*, which would mean, "Ishbi, son of the *'ôb*—or "son of the owner of a necromantic ritual pit." This was a familiar concept in David's day; remember that the woman visited by Saul the night before he died in battle against the Philistines was a *bă 'ălăt 'ôb* ("lady of the ritual pit").[13]

Here's the point of this rabbit trail: The *yelîdê ha-rāpâ* faced by David and his men were probably a demon-worshiping warrior cult. "Descendants (or "sons") of the giants" is a reasonable translation of the Hebrew, but it's more likely the name of their cult or association than a description of their biology, like the name of the greatest and most famous Amorite king in history, Hammurabi of Babylon. His

---

13 For his novel, Brian made Ishbi-benob the son of that woman. There's no evidence in the Bible for that relationship, but it's a fascinating idea. *David Ascendant* is book 7 of *The Nephilim Chronicles*, which we recommend. For information, visit www.godawa.com.

name roughly translates as "my ancestors are Rephaim,"[14] but nobody thinks that Hammurabi, or any of the other Amorite kings bearing that name (there were at least five between 1800 and 1200 BC), was a demigod.

The closest equivalent to the *yelîdê ha-rāpâ* in relatively modern history are probably the Viking berserkers. They were believed to be impervious to pain, fatigue, fire, and edged weapons like swords and arrows. They were so dangerous on the battlefield, even to their own side, that the Vikings were eventually compelled to outlaw berserker war-bands.

The demons who led the group into which the Philistine warriors were admitted "by adoption, initiation, or consecration" were created by the rebellious Watchers who descended to the summit of Mount Hermon before the Flood, as we'll show in an upcoming chapter. What's important to note here is that the worship of what was believed to be the spirits of dead ancestors, and especially the mighty kings of long ago, was an ancient practice by the time of King David and his encounters with Goliath and his warrior colleagues.

Veneration of the dead among the ancient Amorites was an integral part of their culture. A monthly ritual called *kispum* summoned dead ancestors to a shared meal.[15] The *kispum* took on greater importance when it came to their dead kings; while the dead could be dangerous if they were unhappy, dead royalty were especially menacing. They posed a threat to the ruler himself, and that was a problem that could affect the entire kingdom. Bedeviled kings weren't just a threat to their families; everyone in the kingdom suffered when a ruler was tormented by angry spirits.

---

14 The etymology is usually explained thus: *Ammu* ("father" or "paternal kinsman") + *rapi* ("healer"). However, scholars can't point to any texts outside the Bible where the Akkadian and Ugaritic cognates to *rp'*, the root behind "Rephaim," means "healer." Instead, it's likely related to the Akkadian word *raba'um* meaning "to be large, great," and by extension, "leader" or "chief." Brian B. Schmidt, *Israel's Beneficent Dead: The Origin and Character of Israelite Ancestor Cults and Necromancy.* Doctoral thesis, University of Oxford (1991), pp. 158–159.

15 Again, for a deeper treatment of the *kispum* see chapter 4 of our book *Veneration.*

The standard practice in the ancient Near East was to perform the *kispum* rite twice a month for kings, usually on the 15th and 30th. As with the family *kispum*, long-dead rulers had to be called to the meal by name. Forgetting the dead meant their spirits were unsettled and thus unpredictable. Proper performance of the ritual was key to maintaining the health and stability of the realm.

This is documented by several fascinating texts from the Amorite city-state of Ugarit, located on what is now the Mediterranean coast of Syria near the modern border with Turkey. Around 1200 BC, just before its destruction by the so-called "Sea Peoples," Ugarit crowned its last king. A ritual text designated KTU 1.161 by scholars suggests that the ill-fated Ammurapi III, (another Amorite king named "my fathers were Rephaim"), who was probably killed when his city was overrun by invaders, was crowned with a necromancy rite that summoned the spirits of the Rephaim.

> You are summoned, O Rephaim of the earth,
> You are invoked, O council of the Didanu!
> Ulkn, the Raphi', is summoned,
> Trmn, the Raphi', is summoned,
> Sdn-w-rdn is summoned, Ṭr 'llmn is summoned,
> the Rephaim of old are summoned!
> You are summoned, O Rephaim of the earth,
> You are invoked, O council of the Didanu![16]

There is no question that these Rephaim are the same group called by that name in the Bible.

> Sheol beneath is stirred up to meet you when you come; it rouses the shades [*rephaim*] to greet you, all who were leaders of the earth; it raises from their thrones all who were kings of the nations. (Isaiah 14:9)

---

16 Matthew Suriano, "Dynasty Building at Ugarit: The Ritual and Political Context of KTU 1.161," *Aula Orientalis* 27 (2009), p. 107.

Notice that Isaiah describes the "shades," *rephaim* in Hebrew, as "leaders of the earth" and "kings of the nations." This is just how they're described in Ugaritic texts.

This appears to be a belief that extends back at least to the time of Abraham. A cylinder seal from Yamkhad, an Amorite kingdom based in what is now Aleppo, depicts a scene that suggests three ranks in the hierarchy of the afterlife: A lower level for the human dead, a top level inhabited by the gods, and a middle level occupied by entities that probably represent Rephaim.[17] It's been suggested by scholars who have tried to interpret the symbols on the artifact that the item was a guide to the spirit of the dead king on how to attain status among the venerated dead—the "men of renown," as it were.

What ties this together into a cohesive package is the reference in the Ugaritic inauguration ritual to the "council of the Didanu." That shadowy group of underworld spirits linked to the Rephaim shares the name of an Amorite tribe from antiquity, variously spelled *Didanu*, *Ditanu*, and *Tidanu*, that was known and feared throughout the Near East. The last Sumerian kings of Mesopotamia, the Third Dynasty of Ur, were so intimidated by the Tidanu that they built a wall one hundred and seventy-five miles long north of modern Baghdad, and literally named it the "Amorite Wall That Keeps Tidanu at a Distance."[18]

Sadly for the Third Dynasty of Ur, it didn't keep the Tidanu at a distance. Within a century of the wall's construction, Ur was overwhelmed by waves of invaders that included the Tidanu, Gutians (savage tribesmen from the mountains to the northeast), and Elamites, from what is today northwestern Iran.

---

17 Paolo Matthiae, "The Royal Ancestors' Cult in Northern Levant Between Early and Late Bronze Age: Continuity and Problems from Ebla to Ugarit." *BAAL (Bulletin d'Archeologie et d'Architecture Libanaises)*, Hors-Serie X (2015), p. 22.

18 Walther Sallaberger, "From Urban Culture to Nomadism: A History of Upper Mesopotamia in the Late Third Millennium," in: Catherine Kuzucuoğlu and Catherine Marro, eds., *Sociétés humaines et changement climatique à la fin du troisième millénaire: une crise a-t-elle eu lieu en Haute Mésopotamie?, Actes du Colloque de Lyon (5-8 décembre 2005)* (Istanbul: Institut Français d'Études Anatoliennes-Georges Dumézil, 2007), pp. 444-445.

The key point is this: Amorite kings from Babylon to Canaan traced their ancestry to the Tidanu/Ditanu. And some scholars believe that this group is where the ancient Greeks got the name of their old gods, the Titans.[19]

So, consider the evidence: We know that in the days of the judges in Israel, Amorite kings in what is now northern Syria aspired to become *rapha* and join the council of the Didanu after death, a religious belief that may have existed for more than a thousand years already by that time. The Rephaim were a sort of middle-tier deity, higher in rank in the cosmological order than humans, but not at the level of the great gods like El, Baal, Asherah, and Astarte.

Like the Didanu, the Titans of the Greeks were supernatural inhabitants of the underworld who'd roamed the earth long ago, just like the *apkallu* of Babylon and the *Watchers* of the Hebrews. This is not coincidence. *They're the same entities.*

And they are responsible for the first unauthorized intrusion from the spirit realm into our world—the first time in history that the gates of hell were opened.

---

19   Amar Annus, "Are There Greek Rephaim? On the Etymology of Greek *Meropes* and *Titanes*." *Ugarit-Forschungen* 31 (1999), pp. 13–30.

CHAPTER TWELVE

BASHAN

*Do you not know that all of us who have been baptized into Christ
Jesus were baptized into his death? We were buried therefore with him
by baptism into death, in order that, just as Christ was raised from the
dead by the glory of the Father, we too might walk in newness of life.*

—ROMANS 6:3–4 (ESV)

With the benefit of hindsight, we can see that Jesus telegraphed
his intention to declare war on the giants right from the beginning of
his public ministry. He chose the location of his launch party, if you
will, to make it plain to everyone with eyes to see just who was being
put on notice.

It's assumed by most Christians that Jesus was baptized by John
in what is today part of Jordan. Matthew placed John's ministry in
the wilderness of Judea,[1] usually defined as the rugged, hilly desert southeast of Jerusalem along the Dead Sea. This is the area that
includes Qumran, where the famous Dead Sea scrolls were discovered
in 1947, and the mountaintop fortress of Masada. Likewise, Mark and
Luke identify "the wilderness" as the place where John proclaimed the
imminent coming of the Messiah.[2] Based on these clues, most believe
that Jesus met John at the Jordan somewhere between the Dead Sea
and the Sea of Galilee, and probably closer to the former than the

---

1   Matthew 3:1.
2   Mark 1:4; Luke 3:2.

latter. Matthew and Mark agree that John baptized his followers in the Jordan River.[3] Luke is less specific, writing that John "went into all the region around the Jordan,"[4] but it's safe to assume that he used the river for baptism. The question is where?

The most popular baptism sites on the Jordan are between the Sea of Galilee and the Dead Sea. UNESCO designated Al-Maghtas, a village in Jordan about six miles north of the Dead Sea, a World Heritage Site in 2015, and identified Al-Maghtas as "Bethany beyond the Jordan."[5] The site was developed by Jordan's Prince Ghazi, first cousin of King Abdullah, in the 1990s. The prince cites as evidence for his claim the UNESCO designation, remains of fourth-century Christian churches at the site, and the sixth-century Madaba Map, a Byzantine mosaic that's the oldest known map of the Holy Land, which places the baptism site near Al-Maghtas.[6]

Directly across the river, however, Israel has developed a competing site called Qasr al-Yahud, about six miles east of Jericho. It was a popular pilgrimage destination until 1968, but after the previous year's Six-Day War, Israel closed off access because it was feared terrorists would use the seven church compounds on the site as staging grounds for attacks. Qasr al-Yahud was finally reopened in 2011,[7] and the monasteries overlooking the site were opened to the public after years of work to clear the estimated 6,500 land mines and booby traps left behind from the war.[8]

---

3 Matthew 3:6; Mark 1:5.

4 Luke 3:3.

5 https://whc.unesco.org/en/list/1446/, retrieved 6/14/22.

6 Jane Arraf, "Where Jesus Was Baptized, Jordan Vies with Israel for Tourists." *NPR*, May 29, 2020. https://www.npr.org/2020/05/29/863380875/where-jesus-was-baptized-jordan-vies-for-israel-with-tourists, retrieved 6/14/22.

7 Conor Gaffey, "Jordan and Palestine Dispute Jesus's Baptism Site After UNESCO Designation." *Newsweek*, July 14, 2015. https://www.newsweek.com/jordan -palestine-dispute-jesuss-baptism-site-after-unesco-designation-330311, retrieved 6/14/22.

8 Melanie Lidman, "More Than 1,500 Landmines Cleared from Jesus Baptism Site on Jordan River." *The Times of Israel*, Dec. 10, 2018. https://www.timesofisrael. com/more-than-1500-landmines-cleared-at-jesus-baptism-site-on-jordan-river/, retrieved 6/14/22.

Much of the disagreement over the true location of Jesus' baptism site is over money. Jordan is an impoverished country with few natural resources, so tourism is essential to its economy. Israel likewise depends on tourists for revenue. Although the biblical clues point to a site east of the Jordan, Israel draws many more pilgrims to its side of the river—roughly 750,000 a year, compared to about 250,000 who visit the baptismal site in Jordan.[9]

However, in December of 2022, the Jordanian government announced a new $300 million investment in Al-Maghtas to develop a "tourist city" next to the site.[10] It's hoped that the phased six-year project will open for the two-thousand-year anniversary of Christ's baptism in 2028. If successful, this could swell the number of tourists visiting the site to about one million a year.

And then there is Yardenit, a baptismal site established by the Israeli government in 1981 to give Christian tourists a safer place to get dunked in the Jordan. Yardenit is just south of where the Jordan exits the Sea of Galilee. Nobody really thinks John baptized Jesus there, but it seems Christians don't care; getting into the Jordan River is enough of a draw. Yardenit claims to draw half a million tourists and pilgrims a year.[11]

However, the gospel of John offers a clue that points to another location for the baptism of Jesus—one that's even farther north.

He said, "I am the voice of one crying out in the wilderness, 'Make straight the way of the Lord,' as the prophet Isaiah said."

(Now they had been sent from the Pharisees.) They asked him, "Then why are you baptizing, if you are neither the Christ, nor Elijah, nor the Prophet?" John answered them,

---

9   Arraf, op. cit.

10 Suleiman Al-Khalidi, "Jordan eyes tourism bonanza in expansion of Jesus' baptism site." *Reuters*, December 14, 2022. https://www.reuters.com/world/middle-east /jordan-eyes-tourism-bonanza-expansion-jesus-baptism-site-2022-12-14/, retrieved 12/16/22.

11 Yardenit website: https://www.yardenit.com, retrieved 6/14/22.

"I baptize with water, but among you stands one you do not
know, even he who comes after me, the strap of whose sandal I
am not worthy to untie." **These things took place in Bethany
across the Jordan, where John was baptizing.** (John 1:23–28,
emphasis added)

The key phrase, of course, is "Bethany across (or beyond) the Jordan." Scholars and archaeologists have tried for centuries to locate
the site without success. When the Palestine Exploration Fund sent
explorers to the Holy Land in the nineteenth century, the place where
Christ's ministry began was one of the locations they tried to pinpoint.
In 1875, Claude Conder, a colleague of Sir Charles Warren, discoverer
of the Moabite Stone and the fascinating Mount Hermon inscription
(about which more later), reported to the PEF that he believed the
site, *Bethabara* ("House of the Crossing"), was a ford across the Jordan
about three miles northeast of Beit She'an.[12] This is near the junction
of the Jordan River valley and the Jezreel Valley, roughly fifteen miles
south of the Sea of Galilee.

It should be noted that the Madaba Map placed Bethabara on the
west side of the Jordan, very close to Qasr al-Yahud, which is about
sixty miles south of Conder's Bethabara. However, the Madaba Map,
a beautiful mosaic that's somehow been preserved for the last fifteen
hundred years, was created in the sixth century AD, about five hundred
years after Jesus' baptism. That doesn't mean it's useless as a source of
information, but we need to remember that about as much time passed
between Jesus in the Jordan and the creation of that map as between the
reign of King Henry VIII of England and you reading this sentence. A
lot of time and a couple of major Jewish rebellions occurred between
John baptizing Jesus and the creation of the Madaba Map.

Conder, God bless him, must have thought about this puzzle for
quite some time. He returned to it two years later, noting in a report

---

12 Claude R. Conder, "The Site of Bethabara." *Palestine Exploration Fund Quarterly
Statement* 7.2 (April 1875), pp. 72–74.

for the PEF that "the Sinaitic Codex with the Vatican and Alexandrine reads *Bethania*, and Origen states that in his time (186–253 AD) most of the ancient manuscripts had this reading."[13]

In other words, the earliest manuscripts of the Greek New Testament called the place of John's ministry "Bethania," not Bethabara. The early Christian theologian Origen, writing in the third century, admitted as much, but still insisted that "Bethania" must be wrong:

> We are aware of the reading which is found in almost all the copies, "These things were done in Bethany." This appears, moreover, to have been the reading at an earlier time; and in Heracleon we read "Bethany." We are convinced, however, that we should not read "Bethany," but "Bethabara." We have visited the places to enquire as to the footsteps of Jesus and His disciples, and of the prophets. Now, Bethany, as the same evangelist tells us, was the town of Lazarus, and of Martha and Mary; it is fifteen stadia from Jerusalem, and the river Jordan is about a hundred and eighty stadia distant from it. Nor is there any other place of the same name in the neighbourhood of the Jordan, but they say that Bethabara is pointed out on the banks of the Jordan, and that John is said to have baptized there. The etymology of the name, too, corresponds with the baptism of him who made ready for the Lord a people prepared for Him; for it yields the meaning "House of preparation," while Bethany means "House of obedience."[14]

---

13 Claude R. Conder, "Bethany Beyond Jordan." *Palestine Exploration Fund Quarterly Statement* 9.4 (Oct. 1877), p. 184.

14 Origen, "Origen's Commentary on the Gospel of John," in *The Gospel of Peter, the Diatessaron of Tatian, the Apocalypse of Peter, the Visio Pauli, the Apocalypses of the Virgil and Sedrach, the Testament of Abraham, the Acts of Xanthippe and Polyxena, the Narrative of Zosimus, the Apology of Aristides, the Epistles of Clement (Complete Text), Origen's Commentary on John, Books I–X, and Commentary on Matthew, Books I, II, and X–XIV*, ed. & trans. by Allan Menzies, *The Ante-Nicene Fathers* (New York: Christian Literature Company, 1897), IX, p. 370.

So, Origen, based on his travels in Palestine two hundred years after the Resurrection, decided that the manuscript evidence should be tossed out in favor of an alternate site that no one in two thousand years has been able to find. Jerome, who translated the Bible into Latin in the fourth century AD, followed Origen in replacing Βηθανία ("Bethania") with Βηθαβαρά ("Bethabara"), and that name is preserved in the King James translation to this day. Jerome apparently agreed with Origen that it was unlikely there could have been two villages in the Holy Land called Bethany.

Now, you should know that credentialed, respected archaeologists, including friends of ours, defend the UNESCO site in Jordan as the historic location of John's ministry and the baptism of Jesus. With all due respect, we contend that a baptismal site near Jericho is inconsistent with the events described in the Gospel of John. We will explore those events and explain what we mean in an upcoming chapter.

First, let's ask this question: What if the underlying assumption, made by scholars from Origen to the present day, that "Bethania" was the Greek form of "Bethany," is wrong? As Conder noted in his 1877 report, the phrase "beyond the Jordan" was used in both the Old and New Testaments to refer to the land east of the Jordan River, which included the ancient kingdoms of Ammon, Moab, and Edom.

And he added this:

> It is, however, quite a gratuitous assumption that Bethania is here meant to be the name of a village or a town, and the suggestion I would make is that the writer refers to the well-known district of Batanaea, which has left traces of its name to the present day in the district called *Ard el Bethânieh* "beyond Jordan."[15] (emphasis added)

The point is this: Batanaea was the Greek name for Bashan, the ancient kingdom of Og, last of the remnant of the Rephaim; a land

---

15 Op. cit., 184–185.

dominated by the imposing peak of Mount Hermon and covered with megalithic monuments to the dead.

We touched on the spiritual importance of Hermon in a previous chapter, but there is much more to Bashan than the mountain. And Jesus emphasized the supernatural significance of Bashan by beginning his ministry with his baptism there, in enemy territory.

CHAPTER THIRTEEN

LAND OF
THE SERPENT

Many bulls encompass me;
strong bulls of Bashan surround me;
they open wide their mouths at me,
like a ravening and roaring lion.

—PSALM 22:12–13 (ESV)

Bashan is the Hebrew form of Ugaritic *btn*, which would have been pronounced with a "th" between the two syllables rather than the "sh" of Hebrew—Bathan, rather than Bashan. In Ugaritic, it literally means "serpent," which is an odd name for a geographic area to say the least. But it's more than a colorful name, like Rattlesnake Gulch or Copperhead Hollow. Bashan is a cognate for the Akkadian *bashmu*, a word used interchangeably with *ushumgallu*,[1] derived from the Sumerian *ušum.gal* ("great dragon"). The *bashmu* was not a snake; it was a horned, venomous beast with legs, a snake-dragon so terrifying that it frightened even the gods.[2]

Bashmu appeared in the heavens as the constellation Hydra. It differed from later versions of the hydra in Greek mythology, which had

---

1   F. A. M. Wiggermann, *Mesopotamian Protective Spirits: The Ritual Texts* (Groningen: Styx & PP Publications, 1992), p. 167.
2   Ibid.

anywhere from six to fifty heads, while the *bashmu* had only one. The Near Eastern version of Hydra looked much like depictions of the *bashmu* in Mesopotamian art—a long, serpentine creature with lion-like paws, wings, and a head recognizable today as that of a dragon.[3] Interestingly, the constellation, called $^{mul\,d}MU\check{S}$ in Sumer and *bashmu* in Babylon, was associated with Ereshkigal, queen of the netherworld and ruler of the dead.[4]

This suggests that the link between Bashan and the underworld is ancient, much older than the time covered by written history. Mount Hermon was believed to be the "secret dwelling of the Anunnaki" during the Old Babylonian period,[5] which was around the time of Abraham, Isaac, and Jacob. While ancient texts are a bit fuzzy on how the Anunnaki, originally the great gods of Sumer, ended up in the netherworld, it's clear that at least some of the Anunnaki were believed to be judges in the "great below" by about 1500 BC.[6] (For context, the Israelite exodus from Egypt is dated to 1446 BC.)

Inanna's Descent is the story of how the goddess of war and carnal sex "set her mind toward the 'great below.'"[7] This journey to the underworld was ostensibly to comfort her sister, Ereshkigal, queen of the netherworld, after the death of Ereshkigal's consort, the Bull of Heaven. Now, it's important to point out that the Bull of Heaven, Gugalanna by name, was dead because Inanna had intimidated her grandfather, Anu the sky-god, into sending it after Gilgamesh because the hero had rejected her advances. Sadly for Ereshkigal, it turned out to be a suicide mission for the Bull of Heaven.

It appears that Inanna wasn't satisfied with being the Queen of Heaven and controlling the gifts of human civilization, the *mes*

---

3   F. A. M. Wiggermann, "Transtigridian Snake Gods." In I.L. Finkel & M.J. Geller (eds.), *Sumerian Gods and Their Representations* (Groningen: Styx Publications, 1997), p. 34.

4   Ibid.

5   Pritchard, op. cit., p. 504.

6   Ibid., p. 52.

7   Ibid., p. 53.

(pronounced "mezz"), which she'd stolen from her uncle, the clever god Enki. Inanna wanted to expand her portfolio by adding the netherworld to her domain. But her elder sister saw through the ruse, and when Inanna arrived at Ereshkigal's throne room:

> The Anunnaki, the seven judges, pronounced judgment
>   before her,
> They fastened (their) eyes upon her, the eyes of death...[8]

They left Inanna hanging on a hook like a slab of meat, but only temporarily. Interestingly, and probably not coincidentally, she escaped the netherworld on the third day. (If you're a Christian, we shouldn't need to explain why that's significant.)

The confusion over whether the Anunnaki dwelt in the heavens or the underworld derives in part from their origin as children of the sky-god Anu (hence the name), created on the "mountain of heaven and earth."[9] However, oddly enough, the Sumerian word for "mountain," *kur*, also meant "netherworld," so there is probably a connection between the "great above" and "great below" that isn't immediately obvious to us in the twenty-first century. From a Christian perspective, interpreting Mesopotamian myth through a biblical lens, we may unlock some meaning if we assume that these stories are "fake news" versions of historical events in the distant past.

Anu is depicted in Mesopotamian religious texts as remote and uninvolved, almost semi-retired, with little interest in the events on planet Earth. He was the forerunner and equivalent of the sky-gods Ouranos in Greece and Caelus in Rome (from whom we get the word "celestial"). Among the Hurrians, who occupied an arc along the fringes of Mesopotamia from northwest Iran around to the southern Levant, Anu had been deposed as king of the pantheon by his son, Kumarbi, who added to his father's humiliation by castrating him during battle

---

8   Ibid., p. 55.
9   Ibid., p. 52.

with his teeth.[10] This is echoed in the later myths from Greece and Rome in which Ouranos/Caelus was likewise deposed and castrated. The main difference in the stories was that the castration of the Greco-Roman sky-god was performed with a sickle, which may be why Father Time, Chronos (often confused with the Titan king Kronos, whose name derives from a Semitic word meaning "horns"),[11] and the Grim Reaper, a personalization of death, carry a scythe. In all three cases, the new king was later deposed by his son, the storm-god, called Teshub by the Hurrians, Zeus by the Greeks, and Jupiter in Rome.

It's our belief that these stories are creative bits of fiction invented by the fallen realm to explain away the true history recorded in the Bible. The broad outline is this: God created the heavens and the earth, and all that is in the natural and supernatural realms. There were four main rebellions recorded in the Old Testament:

- Chaos, or "the deep" (Genesis 1:2), represented in the Bible by Leviathan, which we'll address in a future book;
- Eden (Genesis 3), led by the *nachash* ("serpent") who eventually became the character we call Satan;
- The Mount Hermon insurrection (Genesis 6:1–4), led by the Watcher chief Shemihazah;[12]
- Babel (Genesis 11:1–9), where humanity tried to build an artificial mountain to bring the gods into contact with the people.

Through the sin of Adam and Eve, death entered the world.[13] The *nachash* was cursed for his role in their transgression, and eternal hostility prophesied between humanity and the followers of Satan.

---

10 This led to the birth of the storm-god Teshub, who sprang from Kumarbi's body fully grown, although the myth doesn't specify from where, exactly.

11 Nicolas Wyatt, "A la Recherche des Rephaim Perdus." In *The Archaeology of Myth: Papers on Old Testament Tradition* (London: Equinox, 2010), p. 55.

12 1 Enoch 6:7.

13 Romans 5:12.

The rebellion of Shemihazah took place centuries after Adam and Eve were evicted from Eden. The sins of the Watchers—defiling themselves with women and teaching humanity forbidden knowledge—led God to decree that they be bound "in the valleys of the earth, until the day of the judgment and consummation, until the eternal judgment is consummated."[14] Peter and Jude both describe this group as sinful angels chained in "gloomy darkness" until the day of final judgment.[15] Peter connects the Watchers, the "sons of God" in Genesis 6:1–4, to the Titans of Greek myth by specifically naming Tartarus as their place of confinement. (Remember, the Greek word translated "hell" in 2 Peter 2:4 is *tartarōsas*, not *hades*.)

The final supernatural rebellion, Babel, compelled God to delegate authority to a group of lesser *elohim*:

> When the Most High gave to the nations their inheritance,
>   when he divided mankind,
> he fixed the borders of the peoples
>   according to the number of the sons of God.
> But the LORD's portion is His people,
>   Jacob His allotted heritage. (Deut. 32:8–9)

If you count the number of names listed in the Table of Nations in Genesis 10, you'll find there are seventy. This is by design. In the context of the culture around ancient Israel, the number seventy was symbolic, representing totality, or "all of them."[16] In other words, after the Tower of Babel incident, God allotted angelic administrators to the nations but reserved Israel for Himself. These elohim set themselves up as the gods of the nations, and apparently invented a false

---

14   1 Enoch 10:11–12. In George W. E. Nickelsburg, *1 Enoch: A Commentary on the Book of 1 Enoch, ed. by Klaus Baltzer, Hermeneia—a Critical and Historical Commentary on the Bible* (Minneapolis, MN: Fortress, 2001), p. 215.

15   2 Peter 2:4; Jude 6.

16   Noga Ayali-Darshan, "The Seventy Bulls Sacrificed at Sukkot (Num 29:12–34) in Light of a Ritual Text from Emar (Emar 6, 373)." *Vetus Testamentum* 65:1 (2015), pp. 7–8.

history to account for the world-shaking changes that took place after Adam and Eve were evicted from Eden.

To wit: Anu/Ouranos/Caelus was replaced at the top of the pantheon by Kumarbi/Enlil/Kronos/Saturn, who was in turn deposed and banished to the netherworld by his son, the storm-god Teshub/Marduk/Zeus/Jupiter.[17] (In Canaanite cosmology, the sky-god is nearly absent. El, the cognate for Enlil/Kronos/Saturn, is replaced by the storm-god Baal, but his conflict is with two of El's other sons, the death-god Mot and sea-god/chaos-monster Yam.)

It's our belief that the fake news account of this conflict was preserved by the names and occult practices linked to Mount Hermon and Bashan, especially the cult of the dead.

---

17 Marduk was technically not a storm-god, but he did have storm-god attributes. The Mesopotamian equivalent of Jupiter/Zeus/Baal was the storm-god Ishkur, who played a minor role in Mesopotamian religion. This may reflect changes in the stories over time, the relative unimportance of the storm-god in a land that's mostly desert, or conflict between fallen angels vying with one another for control over humankind.

CHAPTER FOURTEEN

THE MEGALITHS
OF BASHAN

The large number of Golan dolmens and their wide geographical distribution led [Moshe] Hartal to suggest abandoning the term dolmen field, as it is impossible to define the border between different fields. He suggested viewing the Golan as a single, giant dolmen field.

—URI BERGER AND GONEN SHARON, "Dolmens of the Hula Basin"

T he connection between Bashan and the unseen realm was well-known in the ancient world. It was certainly known to the Hebrew prophets and the apostles. References to Lebanon, Hermon, and Bashan in scripture should be viewed through a supernatural lens.

One of the clearest is Psalm 22, which is accepted by most scholars of the Bible as a prophecy of the coming Messiah. It begins with a verse that Jesus quoted from the cross:

My God, my God, why have you forsaken me? (Psalm 22:1)

Given that Christ Himself saw fit to cite this psalm, we should pay close attention to the rest of it—especially this bit:

Many bulls encompass me;
    strong bulls of Bashan surround me;

109

they open wide their mouths at me,
    like a ravening and roaring lion.
I am poured out like water,
    and all my bones are out of joint;
my heart is like wax;
    it is melted within my breast;
my strength is dried up like a potsherd,
    and my tongue sticks to my jaws;
    you lay me in the dust of death.
For dogs encompass me;
    a company of evildoers encircles me;
they have pierced my hands and feet—
I can count all my bones—
    they stare and gloat over me;
they divide my garments among them,
    and for my clothing they cast lots. (Psalm 22:12–18)

References to pierced hands and feet and the division of garments by the casting of lots are prophecies that were fulfilled at Calvary. But who were the "strong bulls of Bashan" at the Crucifixion? Roman soldiers? The Sanhedrin's security team? Unruly members of the crowd?

Many Bible teachers, noting other passages in Scripture such as Ezekiel 39:18, Jeremiah 50:19, Micah 7:14, Deuteronomy 32:14, and Amos 4:1, simply take Psalm 22:12–13 to mean that the Messiah would be surrounded by big, strong men at the cross, or they explain away the verses altogether by claiming that Bashan was a fertile region renowned for its well-fed livestock. That happens not to be the case.

Dr. Robert D. Miller II, in his brilliantly titled paper "The Baals of Bashan," used archaeology and climatology to show that while sheep and goats would have thrived in the land below Mount Hermon, King Og would have gone broke trying to run a cattle operation in Bashan:

The vast majority of commentators have understood this to refer to the "famous cattle" of Bashan, a region supposedly renowned for its beef or dairy production. I would like to challenge this interpretation, arguing not only that the phrase Bulls of Bashan refers not to the bovine but to the divine, but moreover that Iron Age Bashan would have been a terrible land for grazing and the last place to be famous for beef or dairy cattle.[1]

Miller goes on to show that the type of soil and amount of rainfall in Bashan literally made it impossible to raise cattle there. The "bulls of Bashan" (or cows, as in Amos 4:1) is not a reference to livestock, but "a multivalent term that might include spirits of the dead, giants, Baal, Legion, or even manifestations of El" because "Bashan is not the land of cattle but of spirits and trolls. Not bulls, but Baals."[2]

As we mentioned in an earlier chapter, Bashan is chock full of monuments to the dead. It's estimated that about five thousand of the twenty-five thousand dolmens scattered between Mount Hermon and the Dead Sea are clustered on the Golan Heights and in the Hula Valley. Israeli archaeologist Moshe Hartal, who led the archaeological survey of the Golan, concluded that it's impossible to tell where one dolmen field ends and another begins, suggesting that the Golan Heights should be viewed as one giant dolmen field.[3]

There are clusters of dolmens directly north of the Sea of Galilee along the edges of the Hula Valley, which has been described as "a megalithic landscape in which dolmens surround the valley from all directions."[4] Despite the number of dolmens in the region, which have been studied by archaeologists since the 1880s, almost every aspect of dolmens is still debated by scholars, "including construction technique, morphological typology, function and, primarily,

---

1   Robert D. Miller II, "Baals of Bashan." *Revue Biblique*, Vol. 121, No. 4 (2014), pp. 506–507.
2   Ibid., p. 515.
3   Uri Berger and Gonen Sharon, "Dolmens of the Hula Basin." *Journal of the Israel Prehistoric Society* 48 (2018), p. 148.
4   Ibid., p. 147.

their date of construction."[5] Estimates of the age of dolmens range from the Neolithic (8500–4500 BC) to the Late Bronze Age (1550–1200 BC).[6]

The first serious estimate by scholars to date the dolmens after Israel captured the Golan Heights from Syria in the Six-Day War was the "emergency survey" of the Golan conducted by Israeli archaeologists Claire Epstein and Shmarya Guttman in 1967–68. Epstein continued her research in the years following and concluded, based on her excavations, that the dolmens of the Golan were constructed during the Intermediate Bronze Age (2350–2000 BC).[7] This is especially interesting, since it places the builders of those megaliths in the region of Bashan either just before or during the time of Abraham's arrival in Canaan.

Working backwards from solid dates, such as the commonly accepted date of 967 BC for the construction of Solomon's Temple,[8] we can place Abraham in Canaan either in 1876 BC or 2091 BC.[9] The discrepancy is based on whether we accept a "short sojourn" or "long sojourn" for the Israelites in Egypt. According to the Masoretic Hebrew text of Exodus 12:40, the Hebrews lived in Egypt for 430 years. However, the Septuagint translation, which was rendered into Greek in the early third century BC from an older Hebrew manuscript, notes that this time included the years that the Israelites lived in Canaan. This isn't a discrepancy; during that period of history, Canaan was under the military and political control of Egypt, so it's not wrong to say that the

---

5   Ibid.

6   Kristina S. Reed, Uri Berger, Gonen Sharon, Naomi Porat, "Radiometric dating of Southern Levant dolmens – Applying OSL to resolve an old debate." *Journal of Archaeological Science: Reports*, Volume 49 (2023), p. 3.

7   Claire Epstein, "Dolmens Excavated in the Golan." *Atiqot* 17 (1985), pp. 57–58.

8   Christopher Eames, "967 BCE: How the Lynchpin Date for Solomon's Temple Was Determined." *Armstrong Institute of Biblical Archaeology*, April 23, 2022. https://armstronginstitute.org/685-967-bce-how-the-lynchpin-date-for-solomons-temple-was-determined, retrieved 1/8/24.

9   Solomon began building his temple in the 480th year after the Exodus (1 Kings 6:1). So, 967 + 479 = 1446 BC for the Exodus, minus another 215 or 430 years for the sojourn in Egypt (see above).

Israelites sojourned in Egypt while they tended their flocks in Canaan.

For the record, there are respected archaeologists on both sides of this debate. We note that archaeologists generally agree that some of the cities Abraham visited, such as Jerusalem, Hebron, and Dan (formerly Laish), were apparently constructed in the nineteenth century BC,[10] too late for Abraham to have visited them if he lived in the twenty-first century BC. On the other hand, as the saying goes, absence of evidence isn't evidence of absence; it's possible those cities *did* exist in the twenty-first century BC and archaeologists just haven't discovered the ruins yet.

For the record, we lean toward the short sojourn, in part because the best evidence for a city spectacularly destroyed by fire from the sky in the time of Abraham, namely Sodom, is at the site of Tall el-Hammam, a ruin on a hill across the Jordan River from Jericho. This city, which was the largest in the Southern Levant at the time, was absolutely destroyed by what was probably a bolide, a large meteor that exploded over the north end of the Dead Sea, at the end of the Middle Bronze Age, around 1700 BC.[11]

Why is this relevant? In Genesis 15, we read that a coalition of kings from Mesopotamia crossed the Syrian Desert just to fight a battle with Sodom, Gomorrah, and their allies. The Mesopotamian kings were led by Chedorlaomer, king of Elam, which is western Iran today. This march would have probably taken two months from what is now western Iran and southeastern Iraq to the Dead Sea. It's not something the kings of the east would have done lightly. Sodom was a large, wealthy city-state, five times larger than Jericho and ten times larger than Jerusalem at that point in history.[12]

We'll deal more with Sodom in an upcoming chapter, but the

---

10 Christopher Eames, "When Was the Age of the Patriarchs?" *Let the Stones Speak*, Jan-Feb 2023, p. 37.

11 See Collins and Scott, op. cit.

12 Sonia Fernandez, "Evidence that a cosmic impact destroyed ancient city in the Jordan Valley." *Phys.org*, Sept. 20, 2021. https://phys.org/news/2021-09-evidence-cosmic-impact-ancient-city.html, retrieved 3/17/24.

point here is this: On the way to Sodom, the Elamite and Mesopota-mian troops engaged the Rephaim in battle at several sites east of the Jordan, including Ashteroth-Karnaim, later one of the royal cities of King Og of Bashan. This means that in the Middle Bronze Age—the nineteenth century BC if our timeline is accurate—tribes identified as Rephaim were still living in the region where thousands of these megalithic funerary monuments called dolmens had been constructed, possibly within five hundred years of Abraham's day.

However, recent research suggests that the dolmens and other megalithic sites such as Gilgal Refaim should be dated not to the Inter-mediate Bronze Age (2350–2000 BC), but to the Early Bronze Age (3300–2350 BC) or even the Chalcolithic (Copper Age, 4500–3300 BC). Dr. Michael Freikman, who graciously gave us a day of his time in March, 2023 at the site of his excavations at Gilgal Refaim and the nearby El-Arbain ridge, which we have dubbed the Serpent Mound of Bashan, argued in a 2018 paper that previous estimates of the dates were too heavily influenced by artifacts found at the sites which may have been deposited by later groups reusing the sites for burials or other rituals rather than the builders.[13]

Freikman points out that some one hundred and ninety sites dated to the Chalcolithic period have been identified in the central and southern Golan, the heart of Og's kingdom of Bashan, and that "more than 75% of the known megalithic chambers are located in the immediate vicinity of one of the Chalcolithic sites, offering con-venient access to their inhabitants."[14] However, most of those sites were abandoned around 3300 BC, the end of the Chalcolithic period, despite the absence of evidence of warfare or natural catastrophe to explain the sudden depopulation of the Golan.[15]

Freikman went on to analyze the spatial distribution of mega-lithic sites in the subsequent archaeological periods and found that

---

13 Michael Freikman, "Dating the Megalithic Structures of the Golan." *Mitekufat Haeven: Journal of the Israel Prehistoric Society* 48 (2018), pp. 108–146.

14 Ibid., p. 128.

15 Ibid., p. 127.

the percentage of megalithic sites one kilometer or less from a settlement declined sharply until the Middle Bronze Age—the time of Abraham—and then disappeared almost entirely by the Late Bronze:[16]

Archaeological Age	Date range	% of Golan megalithic sites 1km or less from settlements
Chalcolithic	4500–3300 BC	75.8%
Early Bronze	3300–2350 BC	23.9%
Intermediate Bronze	2350–2000 BC	7.7%
Middle Bronze II	2000–1550 BC	34.1%
Late Bronze	1550–1200 BC	0.1%

In sum, Dr. Freikman concluded that the most likely correlation between settlements and megalithic funerary monuments, both dolmens and larger structures like Gilgal Refaim, is the Chalcolithic period. In another paper, he dated the construction of Gilgal Refaim, a massive project that probably required some 400,000 work-days and an estimated 42,000–60,000 metric tons (46,000–66,000 US tons) of basalt,[17] to 3710 BC ± 170 years.[18] (For comparison, the combined weight of the megaliths at Stonehenge is estimated at less than 2,000 tons.)[19]

So, a pre-literate culture apparently built thousands of megalithic

---

16   Ibid., p. 137.
17   Dr. Michael Freikman, personal communication on site, March 17, 2023.
18   Michael Freikman and Naomi Porat, "Rujm el-Hiri: The Monument in the Landscape." *Tel Aviv*, 44:1 (2017), p. 27.
19   Laurie Baratti, "What is the Weight of the Stones at Stonehenge?" *TravelAsker*, Oct. 19, 2023. https://travelasker.com/what-is-the-weight-of-the-stones-at-stonehenge/, retrieved 1/16/24.

monuments on the Golan Heights. With no written records, we don't know for certain *why* they did it, but the clues point to a cult of the dead—physical reminders of the link between the physical world and the unseen realm. This leads to questions: Did the Rephaim construct the dolmens, or did the builders simply venerate the spirits of the giants destroyed by the Flood? Or, given the depopulation of the Golan Heights at the end of the Chalcolithic (c. 3300 BC) and again at the end of the Intermediate Bronze (c. 2000 BC), did the Rephaim tribes come later—just in time for the arrival of Abraham, Isaac, and Jacob?

And is the destruction of Sodom (c. 1700 BC), and the near complete abandonment of the Golan at the end of the Middle Bronze (c. 1550 BC), about a hundred years before Moses, Joshua, and the Israelites wiped out Og of Bashan, last of the remnant of the Rephaim, evidence of God's long war against the fallen giants and those who venerated them?

These would all be nothing more than fascinating archaeological and biblical mysteries if not for one important fact: Jesus of Nazareth was baptized, based his ministry, and declared his divinity in a place known to the ancient world as sacred to the Rephaim—gods of the underworld known to the Canaanites as warriors of Baal.

CHAPTER FIFTEEN

WHEEL
OF THE GIANTS

Have the gates of death been opened unto thee?
Or hast thou seen the doors of the shadow of death?

—Job 38:17 (KJV)

Gilgal Refaim should be as famous as Stonehenge. It's older, bigger, and its location in the middle of the ancient, supernaturally charged land of Bashan, surrounded by megalithic funerary monuments and within sight of Mount Hermon (on a clear day), should make it intensely interesting to Christians and pagans alike. This would be true even without a megalith-covered, serpent-shaped ridge just a quarter of a mile away that makes the Great Serpent Mound in Adams County, Ohio look like a garden snake.

For some reason, relatively few people are aware of Gilgal Refaim, and those who are appear to be either archaeologists or pagans, based on the fresh votive candles we found inside the central core during our last visit. Our friends in Israel tell us that even most Israelis don't know about it, much less a smaller but strikingly similar monument that overlooks the Jordan River about two miles north of the Sea of Galilee—or two others on the Golan, one of which is in an Israel Defense Force firing range and another in a minefield left over from Israel's wars with Syria since 1948, and thus off limits entirely.

Gilgal Refaim is located on the Golan Heights about ten miles east of the northern end of the Sea of Galilee and less than five miles west of the Syrian border. As noted in a previous chapter, it's a massive structure that required between 42,000 and 60,000 metric tons of basalt and an estimated 400,000 work-days to build. It's a series of five concentric rings about five hundred feet across surrounding a central core that resembles a large cairn, which is accessible through a single entry facing east. The name Gilgal Refaim means "wheel of giants," or "wheel of the Rephaim." That's almost certainly a modern designation, possibly a colorful title intended to draw curious tourists to a site that is well off the beaten path. It's known locally as Rujm el-Hiri, from an Arabic phrase meaning "stone heap of the wild cat," which was taken from Syrian maps after Israel captured the Golan in 1967's Six-Day War.[1]

In 2011, a Norwegian comedy duo called Ylvis released a song titled "Stonehenge" in which they asked an obvious (but important) question:

Who the [*bleep*] builds a Stonehenge?
Two Stone Age guys wondering what to do
Who just said, "Dude, let's build a henge or two"?[2]

The same question applies to Gilgal Refaim, but on a grander scale. Again, it took several years to build at minimum and the mobilization of a workforce of hundreds, if not thousands. Were they Rephaim? We can only guess. The Bible indicates that the region was inhabited by Rephaim tribes in the time of Abraham nearly two thousand years later, but we have no way to know. That's a long time for any single people group to occupy a particular land and the builders didn't leave behind any inscriptions, as far as we know. The construction of Gilgal

---

1 Yonathan Mizrachi; Mattanyah Zohar; Moshe Kochavi; Vincent Murphy; Simcha Lev-Yadun, "The 1988–1991 excavations at Rogem Hiri, Golan Heights". *Israel Exploration Journal* 46 (3–4, 1996), pp. 167–195.
2 https://genius.com/Ylvis-stonehenge-lyrics, accessed 2/28/24.

Refaim around 3700 BC was about five hundred years before the oldest known writing was developed at Uruk in Sumer.[3]

What we can deduce, however, is that there was a Copper Age civilization on the Golan Heights capable of mustering and organizing the expertise and manpower needed to design and build a massive monument of uncut stone with impressive precision at a much earlier age than scholars previously thought possible. Gilgal Refaim is not only one of the largest structures in the ancient Near East, it's also one of the oldest. It predates the Great Pyramid of Giza, according to the commonly accepted date of its construction (c. 2600 BC),[4] by about 1,100 years. It's even older than the most likely time frame for the Tower of Babel event, which probably occurred toward the end of the Uruk Period in Mesopotamia around 3100 BC.[5]

This isn't something to gloss over. Huge construction projects in the modern era, as impressive as they can be, come down to money and will. If somebody wants to build a thing badly enough and can secure the financing, it can usually be done. Six thousand years ago, a massive building project like Gilgal Refaim required drawing a critical resource, human labor, away from essential tasks like farming and hunting. A recent survey of the archaeological digs on the Golan found fifty-two settlements dated to the Chalcolithic Period within a five kilometer (three mile) radius of Gilgal Refaim, implying a population of about two thousand with easy access to the site.[6] Assuming that a quarter of those were adult men of working age, and that maybe half could be dedicated to the construction project, the job could easily have taken five years or longer. Meanwhile, others had to take on the work normally done by the men who were occupied lifting, carrying,

3   "The World's Oldest Writing." *Archaeology*, May/June 2016. https://www.archaeology.org/issues/213-1605/features/4326-cuneiform-the-world-s-oldest-writing, retrieved 2/28/24.

4   Some geologists believe that it's much older, based on evidence of water erosion on the pyramid and the nearby Sphinx, but that view is not widely held.

5   Harriet E. W. Crawford, *Sumer and the Sumerians* (2nd ed.) (Cambridge: Cambridge University Press, 2004), pp. 23–24.

6   Freikman and Porat, op. cit., pp. 20–21.

and stacking slabs of basalt. More importantly, somebody had to have the authority to compel the men to do the work and for others to pick up the slack. In other words, contrary to previous belief, there was a complex society in Bashan around 3700 BC.

Back to our question: Who builds a Gilgal Refaim? The weight of the stones moved and stacked by the builders is roughly equivalent to three thousand fully loaded eighteen-wheel tractor-trailers, or more than two hundred Boeing 747 jetliners. Why did the Copper Age civilization on the Golan devote so much time and effort to build it?

In a nutshell, it was to open a gateway to the netherworld.

The central core is an oval stone heap, a tumulus rising about fifteen to eighteen feet above the bedrock,[7] although it may originally have been stacked twenty to twenty-three feet high.[8] It is very similar to the construction of the dolmens in the area—so much so that the dolmens may be smaller copies of the core.[9] Surrounding the core are five concentric walls with the outermost measuring about four hundred seventy-five feet east to west and about five hundred eleven feet north to south.[10] The outer wall is the most massive, between ten-and-a-half and eleven feet thick all the way around the circle, reaching six-and-a-half feet or more in height in places.[11]

Gilgal Refaim is remarkably well preserved, given that it sits just ten miles east of the Dead Sea Transform (DST), a fault line that stretches more than six hundred miles from the Red Sea, near the southern tip of the Sinai Peninsula, to southern Türkiye. The Sea of Galilee, Jordan River, the Dead Sea, the Arabah, and the Gulf of Aqaba all sit right on top of the fault. It's been the site of several devastating earthquakes in recorded history, including one mentioned by the prophets

---

7   Mattanyah Zohar, "Rogem Hiri: A Megalithic Monument in the Golan." *Israel Exploration Journal*, Vol. 39, No. 1/2 (1989), p. 21.
8   Freikman and Porat, op. cit., pp. 15–16.
9   Ibid., p. 25.
10 Zohar, op. cit., p. 23.
11 Ibid., pp. 23–24.

Amos[12] and Zechariah.[13] That quake, dated to about 750 BC during the reign of King Uzziah in Judah, was horrific; since earthquakes are not rare in Israel, it must have been a monster for Zechariah to use it *two hundred and fifty years later* to illustrate the earth-shaking return of Messiah on the Day of Yahweh:

> On that day his feet shall stand on the Mount of Olives that lies before Jerusalem on the east, and the Mount of Olives shall be split in two from east to west by a very wide valley, so that one half of the Mount shall move northward, and the other half southward. And you shall flee to the valley of my mountains, for the valley of the mountains shall reach to Azal. **And you shall flee as you fled from the earthquake in the days of Uzziah king of Judah.** Then the LORD my God will come, and all the holy ones with him. (Zechariah 14:4–5, emphasis added)

Uzziah's earthquake is estimated to have been at least a magnitude 7.8, but probably 8.2, apparently the most powerful quake along the DST in the last four thousand years.[14] Despite the evidence of the quake throughout the land from sites like Hazor in the north, Gath (Tell es Safi) along the Mediterranean coast, and in Jerusalem at the City of David,[15] Gilgal Refaim stands. It's survived tectonic events that have destroyed entire cities, such as one that was felt for forty days in 1033–34 AD that destroyed Ramleh, Jericho, and Nablus (ancient

---

12 Amos 1:1.
13 Zechariah 14:5.
14 Steven A. Austin; Gordon W. Franz; Eric G. Frost, "Amos's earthquake: An extraordinary Middle East seismic event of 750 BC." *International Geology Review* 42:7 (2000), pp. 657–671.
15 Amanda Borschel-Dan, "Archaeologists unearth 1st Jerusalem evidence of quake from Bible's Book of Amos." *The Times of Israel*, Aug. 4, 2021. https://www.timesofisrael.com/archaeologists-unearth-1st-jerusalem-evidence-of-quake-from-bibles-book-of-amos/, retrieved 3/1/24.

Shechem).[16] In short, the engineers on the project nearly six thousand years ago knew what they were doing, and they took the time and expended the effort to build a monument that would last. This would only be done for something that was considered essential for the community, given that the monument serves no obvious purpose—since, as Dr. Mike Freikman joked while showing us the site in March of 2023, they weren't trying to protect themselves from dinosaurs—and the manpower needed to build it was redirected from critical tasks like tending flocks and herds, farming, and defending the settlement. This had to be a project intended to please and/or contact the gods.

The core itself is oriented so that one enters from the east. Directly above the entrance is an opening that allows the rising sun to shine on a flat basalt slab installed at the entrance to the central chamber, sometimes called the threshold stone, on the summer solstice.[17] The slab has a pebbled appearance like the surface of a golf ball, which, since basalt is a hard material, isn't likely to be natural. It suggests that some ritual was performed that involved pounding something on the basalt. And aside from those times when the sun's rays penetrated the roof box, the inside of the central core would have been nearly pitch black, recreating the sense of being in the underworld. We can only guess, but it is likely to have served as a liminal space representing a passage to the netherworld, which is how scholars have interpreted similar chambers found in megalithic structures in Western Europe.[18] The purpose, of course, would be to contact the things that live in the underworld.

The concentric rings around the core today almost look like a maze when viewed from above. It's likely that some of the radial "spokes" in the wheel, sectioning off the rings, were added by later Bedouins who used Gilgal Refaim as a place to keep their sheep or goats. The original construction probably did not have the "spokes," which make it

16 John L. McKenzie S. J., *Dictionary of the Bible* (New York: Touchstone/Simon & Schuster, 1995), p. 208.

17 Freikman and Porat, op. cit., p. 31.

18 Ibid., p. 25.

impossible for one to walk a complete circuit around the central core. And ritual circumambulation was most likely the purpose for those concentric rings.[19]

Mike Freikman's mentor and colleague, Dr. Yosef Garfinkel of the Hebrew University in Jerusalem, is the author of *Dancing at the Dawn of Agriculture*, published in 2003, a book that analyzes ritual dance from an archaeologist's perspective. Garfinkel contends that between about 7000 and 4000 BC, dance was so important to tracking agricultural cycles that as farming spread from the Near East to neighboring regions of Europe and Africa, artistic depictions of dance spread to those cultures, too, becoming some of the most widespread and enduring subjects in prehistoric art.[20] He also found that ritual circumambulation—circling a sacred site—is "an important component in religious rituals and has magical connotations."[21] Fascinatingly, the ancient art analyzed by Garfinkel suggests that "[i]n the proto-historic Near East, people danced in a counter clockwise direction."[22]

Now, this may simply reflect the fact that most of us are right-handed, meaning our right leg is dominant, which may tend to favor circling with it on the outside as we walk or dance. Or it could reflect a truly ancient tradition memorialized in stone on the summit of Mount Hermon, which is about thirty-five miles north-northeast of Gilgal Refaim. In September of 1869, Sir Charles Warren climbed Hermon for the Palestine Exploration Fund, part of his mission to scout out the Holy Land. At the time, the Ottoman Empire was crumbling, and while the PEF did some truly excellent archaeological work, its scholars, like Warren, were often military men who could also report back to London on the strengths and weaknesses of the Ottomans in the Levant.

---

19 Dr. Michael Freikman, personal communication at the site, March 17, 2023.
20 Yosef Garfinkel, *Dancing at the Dawn of Agriculture* (Austin: University of Texas Press, 2003).
21 Yosef Garfinkel, "Archaeology of Dance." In *Archaeological Approaches to Dance Performance*, Kathryn Soar and Christina Aamodt (eds.) (Oxford: Archaeopress, 2014), p. 10.
22 Garfinkel (2003), op. cit., pp. 44–47.

Inside a temple near the peak of the mountain, Warren found what we've dubbed the Watchers Stone, which we describe elsewhere in this book. But he also discovered a very old stone wall that forced those who approached the summit to circle it in a counterclockwise fashion. How old is the wall? Warren had no way to analyze its age, and as far as we know, no one has tried to do it since. At 9,200 feet above sea level, and covered with snow most of the year, it's not an easy place to reach—and since it's on the border between Israel, Syria, and Lebanon, it's not always safe to try even when the snow is gone. Besides, the United Nations has a base on the summit now, ostensibly to observe and keep the peace, so it's unlikely that archaeologists will dig there anytime soon.

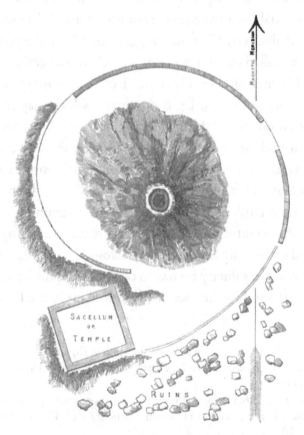

Sir Charles Warren's site map of the summit of Mount Hermon.

We can only make educated guesses based on what's been observed in other cultures, but it appears that Gilgal Refaim was designed and built as an interface to connect with the dead. It's in the middle of a landscape dotted with megalithic tombs, more than a hundred and forty alone on the back of the nearby Serpent Mound of Bashan (officially called the el-Arba'in Ridge), just a quarter of a mile north.[23] Two hundred and sixty-five complex megalithic structures have been found in the immediate vicinity of the site.[24] Significantly, none of the nearby cairns or dolmens are found on the agricultural ground between the ridge and Gilgal Refaim, suggesting that there was something sacred or taboo about the area immediately around it.[25] And evidence of an older structure was found in 2009 about 125 feet southwest of Gilgal Refaim, a monumental circular building about 330 feet in diameter, that was apparently dismantled to build Gilgal Refaim.[26] This suggests that the site served a central, sacred role in the culture of the central Golan Heights as early as 4000 BC if not before.

There are two "gates" in the outermost wall of the circle oriented toward the northeast and southeast. Archaeologists noted that the northeast gate aligned with the rising sun during the summer solstice and that sunrise on the equinox aligns with precision between two boulders on the outermost east wall of the complex when viewed from atop the central core.[27] However, the southeast gate does not align with the winter solstice; one interesting theory suggested that it aligned with the constellation Orion on the first day that it appears to "stand up" in the winter sky.[28]

23 Yigal Ben Ephraim; Claire Epstein; Shmarya Gutman; Michael Freikman, "El-Arba'in Ridge." *The Archaeological Survey of Israel.* https://survey.antiquities.org.il/index_Eng.html#/MapSurvey/30/site/3663, retrieved 3/6/24.

24 Freikman and Porat, op. cit., p. 22.

25 Ibid., p. 24.

26 Ibid.

27 Andrea Polcaro; Vito Francesco Polcaro, "The orientation of the Rujm el-Hiri Southeast Gate." In *Il cielo e l'uomo: problemi e metodi di astronomia culturale*, Elio Antonello (ed.). Società Italiana di Archeoastronomia (2010), pp. 36–37.

28 Ibid., p. 37.

In the ancient Near East, Orion represented the shepherd-god Dumuzi, called Tammuz in the Bible. As noted in a previous chapter, any livestock kept on the Golan would have been sheep or goats because, contrary to what most of us assumed from reading phrases in the Bible like "bulls" or "fat cows of Bashan," it's a terrible place to raise cattle. In fact, the archaeologists who offered this explanation for the orientation of Gilgal Refaim's southeast gate found that most of the dolmens at a site along the Zarqa River in Jordan dated to the beginning of the Early Bronze Age (roughly three or four centuries after the construction of Gilgal Refaim) are also oriented in that direction.[29]

However, there appears to be another, better explanation. When viewed from the central core, both gates align with extinct volcanoes on the horizon—the northeast gate with Tel Fares, and the southeast gate with Tel es-Saki. Confirming this analysis, a monumental structure of similar shape to Gilgal Refaim called Khirbet Beteiha, a name that means "ruins of Bethsaida" (it's on the east bank of the Jordan River about two miles north of the Sea of Galilee, just half a mile from Bethsaida—the hometown of the apostles Peter, Andrew, and Philip), is likewise oriented so that, for an observer looking outward from the central core, a "gate" in the outer wall frames the highest peak in the area, Muh Abu el-Luz.[30]

This begs the question: Why orient these massive structures toward mountains instead of the sun or prominent stars?

In the absence of literary sources, the significance of peaks in Chalcolithic society is not entirely clear. However, Mesopotamian texts dating from as early as the second millennium BCE hint at their role in the local ritual (Katz 2003). The Sumerian term KUR is at times understood as 'netherworld', the land of the dead, located deep underground. That notwithstanding,

---

29 152° azimuth. Andrea Polcaro; Vito Francesco Polcaro, "Early Bronze Age Dolmens in Jordan and their orientations." *Mediterranean Archaeology and Archaeometry*, Vol. 6, No.3 (2006), pp. 165–171.

30 Freikman and Porat, op. cit., pp. 30–31.

in the earliest known sources this term is used in the sense of high peak, usually located east of the plains of Mesopotamia and regarded as a gateway to the realm of the ancestors. If so, the rituals conducted between the walls of Rujm el-Hiri can be interpreted as passage rites in which recently deceased members of society journeyed to the netherworld. The structural resemblance of nearby dolmens and the central cell that was clearly the focal point of the monument is another clue to the connection between the ritual performed there and the world of the dead.[31]

In short, Gilgal Refaim appears to be the largest of many such monuments on the Golan Heights, ancient Bashan, constructed three to four thousand years before the birth of Jesus,[32] in order to connect with the gods of the netherworld and what were thought to be the spirits of the dead.

---

31 Ibid., pp. 31–32.
32 Freikman (2018), op. cit.

CHAPTER SIXTEEN

CULT
OF THE DEAD

But he does not know that the [Rephaim] are there,
that her guests are in the depths of Sheol.

—PROVERBS 9:18 (ESV)

The Jordan Rift Valley, from the Dead Sea to Bashan, southeast of Mount Hermon, is home to thousands of dolmens, megalithic funerary monuments made from slabs of basalt and limestone that weigh as much as fifty tons.[1]

While dolmens are found all over the world, there are more of them clustered in Jordan and the Golan Heights than anywhere else. They are simple structures, mostly in a trilithon formation—two standing stones and a capstone, like a "table" across the top, with no cement holding the slabs together. Sometimes additional stones are placed at the front and back, occasionally with a porthole cut to include a frame around the opening cut to hold a removable flat stone. Skeletal remains have been found at enough of them for some scholars to conclude that the primary function of these intriguing structures was burial of the dead.[2]

---

1   Ruth Schuster, "Monumental Carved Dolmen More Than 4,000 Years Old Found in Golan Rewrites History of Civilization." *Haaretz* (March 6, 2017), https://www.haaretz.com/archaeology/huge-dolmen-found-in-golan-rewrites-history-of-civilization-1.5444970, retrieved 3/17/24.

2   Khair Yassine, "The Dolmens: Construction and Dating Reconsidered." *Bulletin of the American Schools of Oriental Research*, No. 259 (Summer, 1985), pp. 63–69.

These ancient monuments are fascinating for a couple of reasons. The highest concentration of dolmens in the region is on and around the Golan Heights, where the Rapha king Og and the Canaanite deity called Rapi'u, King of Eternity, once ruled. A recent survey of the Golan found more than five thousand megalithic burial sites, most of which are dolmens.[3] In Jordan, another twenty thousand dolmens have been found,[4] although many are threatened by the expansion of modern cities and quarrying for rock and gravel. (Which makes sense—dolmens were built where great big rocks were close to the surface and easy to find.) And yet, despite the interest in these monuments for the last hundred years, scholars admit they don't know very much about the people who built them.

If the Bible is accurate, and it is, then the time and location suggest that the builders of the dolmens were Rephaim tribes, who constructed them in the centuries before Abraham's arrival in the area. By the time the Israelites returned from Egypt around 1406 BC, only Og's small kingdom remained of the Rephaim—possibly the last dolmen-builders in the Levant.

It's tempting to go overboard with speculation, but we don't serve our God well by wandering too far afield without evidence. Still, credentialed scholars link the megaliths to the Rephaim, although they tend to believe dolmens "were the basis for belief in giants, the Rephaim, Anakim, Emim, Zamzummim, and the like."[5] In other words, archaeologists and historians think the people who moved into the lands alongside the Jordan River invented stories of giants because they imagined that it must have taken really big men to move those really big rocks.

---

3   Sharon G, Barash A, Eisenberg-Degen D, Grosman L, Oron M, et al, "Monumental Megalithic Burial and Rock Art Tell a New Story about the Levant Intermediate Bronze 'Dark Ages.'" *PLOS ONE* 12(3) (2017): e0172969.

4   Stephen H. Savage, "Jordan's Stonehenge: The Endangered Chalcolithic/ Early Bronze Age Site at al-Murayghât–Hajr al-Mansûb," *Near Eastern Archaeology* 73:1 (2010), p. 32.

5   Yassine, op. cit., p. 66.

Over the centuries, tomb robbers have removed most of the useful evidence from the dolmens. The few bones left behind in burial chambers don't show any evidence of giantism, or at least we haven't found any papers reporting it. Most of the dolmens are oriented north-south, although about ten percent appear to be oriented east-west, perhaps to face the rising sun.

Is this significant? While it's interesting to note that the Pole Star was Thuban (Alpha Draconis) in the constellation Draco, the Dragon, when many of the dolmens were built, we don't know if that was relevant. Despite their ability to lift stupendously heavy blocks of stone, the dolmen-builders didn't leave behind written evidence.

That makes a recent discovery in the Golan even more intriguing and frustrating at the same time. In 2012, archaeologists examined a massive, multi-chambered dolmen in the Shamir Dolmen Field on the western foothills of the Golan Heights, a site with over four hundred dolmens. This megalith, simply dubbed *Dolmen 3*, is dated to the Intermediate Bronze Age, roughly 2350–2000 BC. This was thought to be a sort of Dark Age in the southern Levant, after the collapse of Early Bronze Age urban civilizations and before the rise of Middle Bronze Age cities.

What is truly remarkable about this dolmen is the discovery of rock art on the underside of the capstone, a basalt monster weighing about fifty tons.[6] (For comparison, that's more than twice as heavy as a fully loaded eighteen-wheel tractor-trailer in the United States.) That was the first time art had been found inside any of the thousands of dolmens in the region, possibly the first written or artistic record that might be connected directly to the biblical Rephaim.

We visited the Shamir dolmen field in the spring of 2023 during an expedition to several megalithic sites in Israel. The dolmen itself is surrounded by a tumulus, a burial mound of about four hundred tons of stone. Think about that! As with Gilgal Refaim more than a thousand years earlier, at a time when civilization was thought to be

---

6   Sharon et al., op. cit., p. 1.

non-existent in the area, there was a government on the Golan Heights powerful enough to organize the manpower and logistics (food, water, security, etc.) to move and assemble some eight hundred thousand pounds of stone into a multi-chambered monument or tomb for—who? The king and his family? Archaeologists recovered enough bones and teeth to identify "an 8–10-year-old child, a young adult and a 35–45-year-old adult."[7]

It's likely that the burials were secondary, meaning that the bones were probably defleshed, possibly by exposing them to the elements and carrion birds, before depositing them inside the dolmen.[8]

The engravings were fourteen figures comprised of a vertical line and a downturned arc. What did the symbol mean? No idea. Nothing like it has been found anywhere in the Levant or anywhere else.[9] It might be a representation of the human soul taking flight, but because the artist didn't leave a note, we're guessing. Or—and again, we're speculating—this could be an ancient symbol with occult meaning even today. Three-dimensional scanning of the images show that at least some of them look very much like the Greek letter *psi*, which is a trident, the three-pronged spear traditionally carried by the Greco-Roman god of the sea, Poseidon/Neptune. Today it's used, among other things, as a symbol for parapsychology, especially research into extrasensory perception, and in a mathematical formula that claims to guide occultists in how to perform rituals in chaos magick.

It is also the logo for Sharon's alma mater, Indiana University, but that's probably a coincidence.

What did that symbol mean in the twenty-first century BC? We have no way to know. It might have been doodling by a bored Bronze Age stonemason.

The takeaway is this: For more than a thousand years, people living in lands the Bible identifies as the home of Rephaim tribes built

---

7   Ibid., p. 10.
8   Ibid., p. 11.
9   Ibid., p. 17.

and used funerary monuments with massive slabs of limestone and basalt.

Returning to the mystery of locating the baptismal site of Jesus: In the first chapter of the Gospel of John, we read that Jesus appeared at Bethany across the Jordan "the next day" after John the Baptist's encounter with the priests and Levites sent by the Pharisees in Jerusalem.[10] "The next day again," two of John's disciples began to follow Jesus. One of the two was Andrew, who found his brother Simon Peter to tell him that they'd found the Messiah.[11] The day after that, Jesus decided to go to Galilee, and he called Philip to follow him, who in turn convinced Nathanael to come along as well.

Philip was from Bethsaida, the hometown of Peter and Andrew.[12] The gospel of Luke informs us that James and John, the sons of Zebedee, were partners with Peter and Andrew in a fishing business,[13] probably based in the lakeside town of Capernaum.[14] Matthew, the tax collector and author of the first gospel, was also from Capernaum.[15]

The point is this: Capernaum and Bethsaida, home to half of the twelve disciples, and five of the first six, were *north* of the Sea of Galilee. The apostle John specifically dates the calling of the first disciples "the next day" after Jesus was identified by John the Baptist as the "Lamb of God, who takes away the sin of the world,"[16] and it seems highly unlikely that John and his disciples walked the roughly ninety miles from Al-Maghtas, the UNESCO-certified baptismal site in Jordan, to the north shore of the Sea of Galilee *in a single day*. That's a four or five-day walk, at least. And it doesn't consider the fact that the ninety-mile estimate is based on Israel's modern Highway 90 which runs through Samaria, territory Jews avoided whenever possible.

---

10   John 1:29.
11   John 1:35–42.
12   John 1:44.
13   Luke 5:9.
14   JoAnn Ford Watson, "Zebedee (Person)," ed. by David Noel Freedman, *The Anchor Yale Bible Dictionary* (New York: Doubleday, 1992), p. 1055.
15   Matthew 9:9.
16   John 1:29.

Nor is it likely that Andrew, who was still an active partner in a profitable fishing business on the Sea of Galilee[17] when he decided to follow Jesus, would be a disciple of John if the Baptist were preaching and baptizing ninety miles away.

Looking deeper into the Bible for additional clues, we find in the Gospel of Matthew that Jesus came from Galilee to meet John at the Jordan.[18] Galilee is in the north of what is now Israel, much closer to Batanaea (Bashan) than to Jericho at the south end of the Jordan River. After his forty days of temptation in the wilderness and the arrest of John the Baptist, Jesus settled at Capernaum, on the north shore of the Sea of Galilee:

> …so that what was spoken by the prophet Isaiah might
>   be fulfilled:
> "The land of Zebulun and the land of Naphtali,
>   the way of the sea, beyond the Jordan, Galilee of the
>   Gentiles—
> the people dwelling in darkness
>   have seen a great light,
> and **for those dwelling in the region and shadow of death,**
>   **on them a light has dawned.**" (Matthew 4:14–16,
>   emphasis added)

Matthew quoted the messianic prophecy of Isaiah 9:1–2, declaring that Jesus' arrival in Capernaum brought a "great light" to the land "beyond the Jordan," to "people dwelling in darkness" and in the "shadow of death." File a mental bookmark there because we'll come back to that. The takeaway for now is that Matthew makes it clear that "beyond the Jordan" doesn't necessarily refer to place south of the Sea of Galilee.

---

17 Mark 1:20 mentions that Zebedee, the father of James and John, had paid servants working in the boat.

18 Matthew 3:13.

Mark also locates the beginning of Jesus' ministry in the north, noting that Jesus came from Galilee to Capernaum after the arrest of John the Baptist by Herod Antipas.[19] After the death of Herod the Great in 4 BC, his kingdom was divided amongst his sons. Antipas received Galilee, the district north of Judaea that included Jesus' hometown of Nazareth, and Peraea, the area east of the Jordan between the Sea of Galilee and the Dead Sea. Antipas' half-brother Philip was made tetrarch (ruler) over Ituraea, Batanaea, Trachonitis, and part of Abilene, the region north and east of the Sea of Galilee.

Philip's territory was mainly populated by Gentiles and, according to the first-century historian Josephus, he was a tolerant ruler. That could explain Jesus's decision to begin his ministry there, where he had freedom to teach without interference by the government.

Or, more accurately, our Lord arranged things so that Philip the Tetrarch was given that territory specifically to allow Jesus to begin his work in the land known centuries earlier as *Bashan*—in the region and shadow of death.

---

19   Mark 1:14–21.

CHAPTER SEVENTEEN

GALILEE AND
HERMON

O mountain of [gods], mountain of Bashan;
  O many-peaked mountain, mountain of Bashan!
Why do you look with hatred, O many-peaked mountain,
  at the mount that God desired for his abode,
  yes, where the LORD will dwell forever?

—PSALM 68:15–16 (ESV)

Bashan had an evil reputation from way back. As we noted earlier, the connection between Og's kingdom and gods of the netherworld was known as far back as Abraham's day, and it was explicit in religious texts from the Amorite kingdom of Ugarit in the time of the judges. But the supernatural character of Bashan apparently extended into Galilee.

We should first note that the boundaries between the Galilee and ancient Bashan are imprecise. In the first century, the Jordan River may have been the border between Galilee, ruled by Herod Antipas, and Philip the Tetrarch's territory of Batanaea, but the region was certainly linked in the minds of the people who lived there. Isaiah, for example:

> In the former time he brought into contempt the land of Zebulun and the land of Naphtali, but in the latter time he has

made glorious the way of the sea, the land beyond the Jordan, Galilee of the nations. (Isaiah 9:1)

The "way of the sea" is the Via Maris, the Roman road that connected Egypt to Mesopotamia by way of the Sea of Galilee. It ran from Megiddo in the territory of Zebulun, through Magdala and Capernaum in Naphtali, northward along the Jordan to the site of the ancient city of Hazor (destroyed by the Assyrians in 732 BC), and then northeast to Damascus. On today's maps, that's roughly the path traced by Israel's Highway 65 from Megiddo to the Golani junction; Highway 77 east to Tiberias and Highway 90; then Highway 90 north to the Mahanayim juncion; and then Highway 91 northeast across the Golan Heights. Had the wars fought between Israel and her neighbors since 1947 not drawn hard boundaries across the landscape, Highway 91 probably would have connected to Syria's Highway 7, which runs into Damascus. This route led travelers through the thickest concentrations of dolmens between the Sea of Galilee and Mount Hermon.

In an earlier chapter, we mentioned that Hermon had been considered sacred since the time of Abraham. In case you didn't read the footnote, we'll explain here: The Old Babylonian copy of the Epic of Gilgamesh identifies "Hermon and Lebanon" as the "dwelling of the Anunnaki."[1] These were formerly the great gods of Sumer, but by the second millennium BC they'd been relegated to serving as judges of the underworld,[2] a status consistent with the region around Hermon, Bashan, being the gateway to the underworld.

In September of 1869, military engineer and explorer Sir Charles Warren climbed Mount Hermon on behalf of the Palestine Exploration Fund (PEF). At the summit, more than nine thousand, two hundred feet above sea level, Warren visited an ancient temple called Qasr Antar, the highest man-made place of worship on Earth. It was probably built during the Greek or Roman period, placing its

---

1 Lipiński, op. cit.
2 Wyatt (2010), op. cit., p. 56.

construction in the late fourth or early third century BC at the earliest. Inside the temple, Warren found an artifact that had been overlooked by visitors for two thousand years—a stela, a limestone slab about four feet high, eighteen inches wide, and twelve inches thick, with an inscription:

A later attestation of the sacred character of Mount Hermon appears in an enigmatic Greek inscription, perhaps from the third century CE, which was found on its peak: Κατὰ κέλευσιν θεοῦ μεγίστου κ[αὶ] ἁγίου οἱ ὀμνύοντες ἐντεῦθεν ("According to the command of the greatest a[nd] holy God, those who take an oath [proceed] from here").[3]

Scholar George W. E. Nickelsburg, who's produced a modern translation of the *Book of 1 Enoch* and a detailed commentary on the book, connects the inscription to the Watchers of Genesis 6, whose mutual pact on the summit is described in 1 Enoch:

Shemihazah, their chief, said to them, "I fear that you will not want to do this deed, and I alone shall be guilty of a great sin." And they all answered him and said, "Let us all swear an oath, and let us all bind one another with a curse, that none of us turn back from this counsel until we fulfill it and do this deed." Then they all swore together and bound one another with a curse. And they were, all of them, two hundred, who descended in the days of Jared onto the peak of Mount Hermon.[4]

The stela is currently at the British Museum, which it received from Warren in 1870, who managed to wrestle the two-ton slab of limestone down the mountain. The stone broke into two pieces when

---

3   George W. E. Nickelsburg, *1 Enoch 1: A Commentary on the Book of 1 Enoch, Chapters 1–36* (Minneapolis: Fortress, 2001), p. 247.
4   George W. E. Nickelsburg, *1 Enoch: The Hermeneia Translation* (Kindle edition) (Minneapolis: Fortress Press, 2012), pp. 23–24.

Warren cut its thickness down from twelve inches to four to reduce its weight.

The Watchers Stone found
on the summit of Mount Hermon.

The stone wasn't unboxed until 1884, and then, because of questions over its origin, it wasn't translated until 1903. Renowned French orientalist Charles Simon Clermont-Ganneau, who worked with Warren to obtain the Moabite Stone, interpreted the Greek inscription this way:

> By the order of the god most great and holy, those who take the oath —hence![5]

Like Nickelsburg, Clermont-Ganneau linked the stone to the Watchers' rebellion on Mount Hermon. In fact, he devoted some pages to Enoch's account of the Watchers in the same edition of the *Palestine Exploration Fund's Quarterly Report* for 1903:

---

5   Charles Simon Clermont-Ganneau, "Archaeological and Epigraphic Notes on Palestine." *Palestine Exploration Fund Quarterly Statement for 1903* (London: Palestine Exploration Fund, 1903), p. 138.

Now, whether justified or not, this popular tradition existed in ancient times: Mount Hermon was the "mountain of oath."[6]

Joshua 11:3 locates the Hivites "under Hermon, in the land of Mizpah," and Judges 3:3 places the Hivites around "Mount Lebanon, from Mount Baal-Hermon as far as Lebo-Hamath," a site on the Orontes River valley about a hundred and twenty miles north of Damascus. The Hivites were the Ahhiyawa, Mycenaean Greeks,[7] people with a long history of contact with the Hurrians, the Horites of the Bible. As we've noted, the Hivites and Hurrians were all over the land of Canaan at least from the time of Abraham through the time of David. It's possible that Baal-berith, the "lord of the covenant" worshiped at the Hurrian city of Shechem,[8] was the same entity called Baal-Hermon ("lord of Hermon"), most probably the Canaanite creator-god El.

Clermont-Ganneau noted another unique feature of Mount Hermon: The summit has been scooped out like a giant bowl, probably to receive a drink offering. This ritual was called *yarid* in Hebrew,[9] based on a root that means "to come down," which it shares with the names Jared and Jordan (since the river "comes down" into the Galilee from Mount Hermon). We know from historical texts that the ritual was practiced at Heliopolis (Baalbek); Hierapolis, site of a famous temple to the goddess Atargatis (another name for Astarte, Ishtar, and Inanna); Tyre; and possibly even Jerusalem. The ritual "consisted chiefly in drawing water, which was borne in procession and thrown into a sacred tank":[10]

I should not be surprised if the sanctuary of Hermon was formerly the scene of such a ceremony of this nature. Perhaps it was into

---

6   Ibid., pp. 231, 233.
7   The Hebrew *ḥivî* derives from *hiyawa*, the Luwian (south Anatolian) form of *ahhiyawa*, the Achaeans of Homer's *Odyssey* and *Iliad*, who were the Mycenaean Greeks. B. Collins (2007), op. cit., p. 154.
8   Judges 8:33, 9:4.
9   Lipiński, op. cit., p. 29.
10 Clermont-Ganneau, op. cit., p. 241.

the deep and remarkable cavity noticed by the explorers in the central cone that the consecrated water was thrown. Under these circumstances, if the sanctuary of Hermon really had its *yarid*, or *katabasis*, it would not be too rash, perhaps, to suppose that it was from this that the author of the *Book of Enoch* may have drawn his idea of the "descent of the angels in the days of Jared"…[11]

In other words, in the opinion of Clermont-Ganneau, the Watchers didn't descend to Mount Hermon "in the days of Jared," but rather in the days when the *yarid* was performed on the summit of Hermon.

Why would this ritual have been performed on the mountain? It was believed to be the threshing-floor or tabernacle of El, whose abode was "the source of the rivers, at the midst of the springs of the two deeps." This is reminiscent of the ^{d}KASKAL.KUR of the Hurrians, a "divine watercourse" that flowed to the netherworld to allow contact with Kumarbi and the gods of the great below.[12]

This is where things get even more interesting. Thanks to new research by our friend, Dr. Douglas Hamp, we can connect the dots between Kumarbi, Mount Hermon, and the rebellion of the Watchers with the Mesopotamian gods El, Dagan, and Enlil—who, as Derek showed in *The Second Coming of Saturn*, are just different names for the chief of the rebellious Watchers, Shemihazah.

Doug noticed that accepted translations of the "Watchers Stone" appear to gloss over a couple of words. For example, the text on the base of the stone, when it was displayed at the British Museum, read:

GREEK INSCRIPTION

[4th-5th Cent. A.D.]

Warning: "Hence by order of the god those who do not take the oath"; probably an oath before celebrating the mysteries of

---

11 Ibid.
12 B. Collins (2004), op. cit., pp. 55-56.

the temple on the summit of Mount Hermon, where this pillar was found. The god of Mount Hermon was Baal-Hermon —*Judges III, 3*

Presented by the Palestine Exploration Fund, 1903

To recap, that's three different translations of the Mount Hermon inscription:

- Nickelsburg: "According to the command of the greatest a[nd] holy God, those who take an oath [proceed] from here."
- Clermont-Ganneau: "By the order of the god most great and holy, those who take the oath —hence!"
- British Museum: "Hence by order of the god those who do not take the oath."

That's not exactly a consensus, but the bigger issue, Hamp argues, is that the transcription from the stone on which the translations are based is flawed.

The transcription, per Nickelsburg (my emphasis):

Katá kélefsin theoú megístou k[aí] **agíou** oi omnýontes entefthen

Hamp reads it:

Kata keleusin theou megistou **bo batiou** ou omnuontes enteuthen
    Words five and six βο *bo* and βατιου *batiou* are mysterious which could be why they were completely ignored by the British Museum, and amended by Nickelsburg; βο *bo* "a(nd)" and βατιου *batiou* as άγιου *[b]hagiou*.[13]

---

13 Douglas M. Hamp, *Corrupting the Image 2: Hybrids, Hades, and the Mt Hermon Connection* (Denver: Eskaton Media Group: 2021), p. 174.

Rejecting the reading by Clermont-Ganneau and Nickelsburg, Hamp proposes to read *bo* as a Greek prefix meaning "bull, ox, male cattle."[14] He suggests that this fits with the bull imagery associated with Baal (Hadad), the West Semitic storm-god, whose equivalent in the Greek pantheon is Zeus.[15]

We agree with Doug to a point: The "bull" prefix fits the context of Mount Hermon as a pagan holy site, but the connection is not with Baal/Zeus, but with the Canaanite creator-god El. His chief epithet, "Bull El," was so well known to the Hebrew prophets that it's in the Bible—the prophet Hosea's condemnation of Jeroboam's cult of the golden calves:

> I have spurned your calf, O Samaria.
>> My anger burns against them.
> How long will they be incapable of innocence?
>> **For it is from Israel;**
> a craftsman made it;
>> it is not God.
> The calf of Samaria
>> shall be broken to pieces. (Hosea 8:5–6, emphasis added)

The phrase, "For it is from Israel," comes from the Masoretic Hebrew text, *kî miyyiśrā'ēl*, which literally means, "for from Israel."[16] That makes no sense, grammatical or otherwise.

But separating the characters differently, as suggested by Naftali Herz Tur-Sinai, the first president of Israel's Academy of the Hebrew Language, yields *kî mî šōr 'ēl*, which changes verse 6 to this:

---

14 "B β beeta (βῆτα) basis," *Greek Alphabet: Unlock the Secrets.* http://www. greekalphabeta.com/learn-about-beta-b-2.html, retrieved 3/18/21.
15 Hamp, op. cit., p. 175.
16 Nicolas Wyatt, "Calf." In K. van der Toorn, B. Becking, & P. W. van der Horst (Eds.), *Dictionary of Deities and Demons in the Bible: 2nd extensively rev. ed.* (Leiden; Boston; Köln; Grand Rapids, MI; Cambridge: Brill; Eerdmans, 1999), p. 181.

For who is Bull El?
a craftsman made it;
    it is not God.
The calf of Samaria
    shall be broken to pieces.
(Hosea 8:6, modified; emphasis added)

So, what do we make of *batiou*? According to Hamp, the word is missing from lexicons, dictionaries, encyclopedias, scholarly sites, and journals. He concludes, "*batiou* simply is not Greek."[17]

He does, however, propose an elegant solution. It's too long to reproduce here, which would not do Doug justice. We refer you to his book *Corrupting the Image 2* for details of his excellent detective work in drawing out the first new information from this artifact in more than a hundred years. The summary is this: The Sumerian logogram BAD (or BAT), depicted as two inward-pointing horizontal wedges, designated both Dagan and Enlil. The *-iou* suffix, Hamp argues, makes the transliterated logogram "standard Greek."[18]

Thus, Hamp's new translation reads:

"According to the command of the great bull-god *Batios*, those swearing an oath in this place go forth."[19]

We agree, with a small emendation:

"According to the command of the great Bull El, those swearing an oath in this place go forth."

Hamp's translation generally agrees with those of Nickelsburg and Clermont-Ganneau. The important new connection that's previously

---

17   Hamp, op. cit., p. 176.
18   Ibid., p. 180.
19   Ibid., pp. 181-182.

escaped scholars is identifying the Sumerian logogram BAD/BAT, which connects Dagan and Enlil to Mount Hermon, and thus to the Watcher chief Shemihazah. Recognizing the prefix bo- ("bull") connects Dagan/Enlil to the Canaanite creator-god "Bull El." All in all, this is profound.

Estonian scholar Amar Annus, whose work we reference throughout our books, was consulted by Dr. Hamp on this new translation. Annus, in his book on the Akkadian god Ninurta, confirms the link between Dagan, Enlil, and mountains:

> The name of Dagan is written logographically dKUR in Emar [an ancient city near the bend in the Euphrates in northern Syria] as an alternative to the syllabic dDa-gan. dKUR is a shortened form of Enlil's epithet KUR.GAL "great mountain," which was borrowed by Dagan, and he is already described as the great mountain in a Mari letter. That in Emar there existed a cult for Dagan as dKUR.GAL points to the awareness of Sumerian traditions concerning Enlil, it "shows that some connection with the ancient title was preserved behind the common writing of the divine name as dKUR," and leaves no doubt that Enlil is the model behind Dagan in Emar.[20]

We would add that the double meaning of the Sumerian word kur, which means both "mountain" and "netherworld," seems appropriate in the context of Mount Hermon and the land of Bashan—and may even connect Gilgal Refaim, with its orientation to the extinct volcanoes on the horizon, to the "Great Mountain" Enlil/Dagan/Bull El.

This is reinforced by a text dated to the time of Israel's sojourn in Egypt, probably the seventeenth century BC, that mentions a king of Terqa offering "the sacrifice of Dagan ša ḪAR-ri."[21] Scholar Lluis Feliu

---

20   Amar Annus, *The God Ninurta in the Mythology and Royal Ideology of Ancient Mesopotamia* (Helsinki: Neo-Assyrian Text Corpus Project, 2002), p. 178.

21   Feliu (2003), op. cit., p. 105.

compares this with a later text from Emar that mentions a "ᵈKUR EN *ḫa-ar-ri* that we may translate as 'Dagan, lord of the hole/pit'."[22]

Then Feliu untangles the meaning of *ḫa-ar-ri*:

A different question is the interpretation... of the term *ḫa-ar-ri*. The vocalisation in *a* suggests identifying this word with Akkadian *ḫarrum* 'water channel, irrigation ditch'. However, the semantic and morphological similarity with *ḫurrum* 'hole' makes it possible to understand the epithet, tentatively, as 'The Dagan of the pit'. This interpretation could find confirmation in the following line in the text Emar 6/3 384, where, after [ᵈKU]R EN *ḫa-[ar-ri]*, there occurs ᵈINANNA *a-bi*. [Note: Inanna is the Sumerian name and logogram for the goddess of sex and war, also known as Ishtar and Astarte during the biblical period.]

As yet, the term *a-bi* has not been given a satisfactory translation and its meaning is much discussed. **One of the interpretations that has been proposed is 'pit', based on Hurrian *a-bi*.**[23] (emphasis added)

Remember, the *abi* was a ritual pit used by the Hurrians in their worship of underworld spirits and gods. The Amorite texts cited by Feliu connect Dagan to these necromantic practices and strengthens our theory that Dagan, Kumarbi, Enlil, El, and the Watcher chief Shemihazah are one and the same—the entity who led the rebellion that compelled God to banish him and his colleagues to the abyss.

Our conclusion is this: The Hurrians, Sumerians, Akkadians, Amorites, Canaanites, and even Israelites tried to reestablish contact with the gods who once walked the earth by developing elaborate rituals and building megalithic structures to reach beyond the gates of hell.

---

22   Ibid., p. 106.
23   Ibid.

CHAPTER EIGHTEEN

BAPTISM AND THE ABYSS

It is easy to go down into Hell;
  Night and day, the gates of dark Death stand wide;
But to climb back again, to retrace one's steps to the upper air—
  There's the rub, the task.

—VIRGIL, *Aeneid,* Book VI

Peter linked the three-day period between the crucifixion and resurrection of Jesus to baptism. 1 Peter 3 can be confusing until you connect it to the Watchers and their rebellion on Mount Hermon:

> For Christ also suffered once for sins, the righteous for the unrighteous, that he might bring us to God, being put to death in the flesh but made alive in the spirit, in which he went and proclaimed to the spirits in prison, because they formerly did not obey, when God's patience waited in the days of Noah, while the ark was being prepared, in which a few, that is, eight persons, were brought safely through water. (1 Peter 3:18–20)

The "spirits" to whom Jesus "proclaimed" are not deceased humans. The word translated "spirits" (Greek *pneumasin*) is never used in the

146

New Testament in an unqualified way to refer to human souls.[1] Peter is telling us that Jesus literally descended to Tartarus,[2] a level of the underworld distinct from Hades/Sheol, to proclaim to the rebellious spirits imprisoned there. By connecting it to baptism, Peter explains that the rite is a declaration of victory over those disobedient entities; a reminder that another human soul is now set apart for resurrection into an incorruptible body at the sounding of the last trump.

Oh, yes—it's also a reminder that they're still dead.

The verse from the Book of Hosea, referenced in the excerpt above, shows that the three-day period leading to resurrection did not originate in the first century with Jesus. It's an old concept that was *reversed* by Christ at his resurrection! And it's a template for what's in store for those who place their trust in him:

> After two days he will revive us; on the third day he will raise us up that we may live before him. (Hosea 6:2)

This concept is embedded in the Sumerian myth *Inanna's Descent to the Netherworld*, in which the headstrong goddess travels through seven gates to the Great Below, the domain of her sister Ereshkigal, queen of the underworld. Ereshkigal knew that Inanna, already called the Queen of Heaven, wanted to take her throne as well and so fixed Inanna with the "stare of death." With help from Enki, Inanna escaped the netherworld on the third day—at the cost of her husband, the shepherd-king Dumuzi (Tammuz in the Bible), who was dragged off to the underworld by demons in her place.

The concept of resurrection on the third day appears to have been incorporated into the pagan rituals for the dead condemned by Isaiah:

---

1   Douglas Mangum, "Interpreting First Peter 3:18–22." In *Faithlife Study Bible* (Bellingham, WA: Lexham Press, 2016).

2   2 Peter 2:4. The word translated "Hell" is Greek *tartarōsas*; literally, "thrust down to Tartarus."

I spread out my hands all the day
 to a rebellious people,
who walk in a way that is not good,
 following their own devices;
a people who provoke me
 to my face continually,
sacrificing in gardens
 and making offerings on bricks;
who sit in tombs,
 and spend the night in secret places;
who eat pig's flesh,
 and broth of tainted meat is in their vessels...
(Isaiah 65:2–4)

Pork was taboo in a number of Near Eastern cultures, coming from "a 'cthonian' animal, which its nature intended to be offered to infernal divinities" and thus "reserved for more or less secret rites."[3] The "tainted meat" may not refer specifically to pork, but to the practice of eating a funeral feast on the third day after a death, known in Greek and Roman times.[4] It may be that this practice is behind God's prohibition on eating sacrifices on the third day:

If any of the flesh of the sacrifice of his peace offering is eaten on the third day, he who offers it shall not be accepted, neither shall it be credited to him. It is tainted, and he who eats of it shall bear his iniquity. (Leviticus 7:18)
 If it is eaten at all on the third day, it is tainted; it will not be accepted, and everyone who eats it shall bear his iniquity,

3 Roland de Vaux, "Les sacrifices de porcs en Palestine et dans l'Ancien Orient." *Von Ugarit nach Qumran: Festschrift O. Eissfeldt* (ed. J. Hempel and L. Rost) BZAW 77 (Berlin: Topelmann, 1958) p. 261.
4 George Heider, *The Cult of Molek: A Reassessment* (Sheffield: JSOT Press, 1985), pp. 390-391.

because he has profaned what is holy to the LORD, and that person shall be cut off from his people. (Leviticus 19:7–8)

God is not opposed to remembering the dead. He is often referred to as "the God of Abraham, the God of Isaac, and the God of Jacob," although Jesus made it clear during a confrontation with the Sadducees over the concept of resurrection that the patriarchs are still very much alive.[5] However, sacrificing to and eating meat offered to the dead is another matter entirely. It was precisely that sin that provoked God to send a plague that killed twenty-four thousand Israelites on the plains of Moab.[6] It's not a coincidence that "the matter of Peor" occurred near the stations of the Exodus called Oboth ("spirits of the dead") and Iye-Abarim ("ruins of the Travelers") below Mount Nebo, which God called "this mountain of the Abarim (Travelers)."[7]

The Hebrew words *ʿōberim, abarim, ʾōbôt, ʾābôt, ʾôb,* and the equivalent words in Ugaritic, Hittite, Assyrian, and Sumerian, probably have a common ancestor. Until recently, scholars would have assumed that Sumerian must be the oldest, and thus original, form of the word. But as early as 1967, long before the discovery of ancient Urkesh and its monumental ritual pit, eminent Hittitologist Harry A. Hoffner argued that it was phonetically impossible for the Hittite word *a-a-bi* (from the Hurrian **ay(a)bi*) to derive from Sumerian *ab.* Thus, Hoffner argued, it was better "to accept the Hurrian **ay(a)bi* as the prototype."[8] In other words, based on texts alone, Hoffner proposed nearly sixty years ago that it was the Hurrians, not the Sumerians, who were the source of the ancient concept of a ritual pit that was used to summon gods and spirits from the netherworld. Now, with the recent discovery of the Hurrian *abi* at Urkesh, a ritual complex that developed at the same time, if not earlier, than the great cities of Sumer like Ur and Uruk, there is archaeological evidence to support Hoffner's linguistic argument.

---

5 See Matthew 22:23–33.
6 Psalm 106:28–29, Numbers 25:1–18.
7 Deuteronomy 32:48–49.
8 Hoffner, op. cit., pp. 388-389.

Here's the kicker: Archaeologist and historian Dr. Judd Burton recently published a paper tracing the origin of the various Eurasian words for "king" or "ruler" to an Akkadian word meaning "prince."[9] Derek reached a similar conclusion in his book *Last Clash of the Titans*, citing the work of University of Michigan professor Brian B. Schmidt:

> In the light of the repeated occurrence of *rp'um* [Rephaim] in military and heroic contexts and the inadequacy of alternative hypotheses, the significance of Ugaritic *r-p-'* might best be understood in the light of Akkadian *raba'um* "to be large, great", and its derivative *rabium* (< *rabûm*) "leader, chief". Thus, the *rp'um* would be "the Great Ones" or "the Mighty Ones."[10]

Burton argues that morphemes, the smallest components of words, suggest that "'r-' indicates royalty and 'ap/ab' indicates a relationship with the Mesopotamian watery underworld: the '*apsu*,' or 'abyss.'"[11] While the *apsû/abzu* was located at Eridu in Sumer, southeast Iraq, the original homeland of the Sumerians may have been between the Black and Caspian seas,[12] a theory supported by recent research into similarities between the languages of the Sumerians and Hurrians.[13]

So, the term for "king" or "ruler" in languages from Western Europe to East Asia probably originated as a word used by our distant ancestors for the pre-Flood god-kings, the *Rephaim*. This word was preserved by the descendants of Noah who spread out from the lands around the resting place of the ark in the mountains of Ararat. And thanks to recent discoveries by archaeologists, linguists, and geneticists, this movement of people, language, and religious beliefs is confirmed.

---

9   Judd Burton, "The War of the Words, God-kings, and Their Titles: A Preliminary Report on the Linguistic Relationship Between The Rephaim and Royal Titles in Eurasian Languages." *Bulletin of the Institute of Biblical Anthropology* (2021), p. 7.

10 Schmidt, op. cit.

11 Burton, op. cit.

12 Ibid.

13 Alexei Kassian, "Lexical Matches between Sumerian and Hurro-Urartian: Possible Historical Scenarios." *Cuneiform Digital Library Journal* (2014:004), https://cdli .ucla.edu/pubs/cdlj/2014/cdlj2014_004.html, retrieved 3/5/21.

Summing up this tour through the realms of the ancient dead: Around 3500 BC, the Kura-Araxes people, ancestors of the Hurrians (the Horites of the Bible), began to migrate from the Ararat Plain to settle along the outer edge of the Fertile Crescent in a great arc from northwest Iran to eastern Anatolia and down through Lebanon to the Jordan valley. Their first urban center, Urkesh, commanded the Mardin Pass into the Taurus Mountains, an area rich with timber, copper, and silver that was traded with areas to the south and west in Mesopotamia and the Levant.

The heart of Urkesh was its temple, built in a southern Mesopotamian style around 3500 BC. It sat above a necromantic pit called the *abi*. This pit was used to summon the "infernal deities," called "former gods" or by the Akkadian name *Anunnaki*, who were offered sacrifices in exchange for their blessings and protection. These "former gods" had been sent to the underworld by the king of the pantheon, the storm-god Teshub (a cognate for Baal, Zeus, and Jupiter). The father of the Hurrian gods was Kumarbi, and his home, according to Hurrian ritual texts, was Urkesh.

By the time of Abraham, Isaac, and Jacob, Hurrians had lived in Canaan for centuries, settling near the Sea of Galilee as early as 2850 BC after an unknown disruption in society that seems to have affected a broad region from Mesopotamia to the Jordan Valley[14] (the Tower of Babel incident?) brought migrants from the Caucasus to the region.[15] Roughly a thousand years later, a Mesopotamian army battled Hurrians (Horites) near Mount Sinai, Jacob's sons Simeon and Levi slaughtered the Hurrian men of Shechem (we'll explain that in more detail in an upcoming chapter), and more than four hundred years after that, Gideon's son Abimelech conspired with the Hurrian "sons of Hamor" to kill his half-brothers, only to face a rebellion by his former comrades a short time later.

---

14 The Early Dynastic Period in Sumer began around this time, as did the first kingdom at Mari on the Euphrates. The first records of Akkadian names are dated to this period, as is the beginning of the Second Dynasty in Egypt.

15 Sarit Paz, "A Home Away from Home? The Settlement of Early Transcaucasian Migrants at Tel Bet Yerah," *Tel Aviv* Vol. 36 (2009), pp. 196–216.

And, of course, there is the threshing floor that David bought from Araunah, the Hurrian king of Jebusite Jerusalem, a site of profound spiritual significance to this day. It is likely where Abraham was tested in the binding of Isaac, and the place where David and Araunah saw the Angel of Yahweh with a drawn sword "standing between earth and heaven,"[16] his hand stayed only by the mercy of God.

In short, the Hurrians have had a profound and, until now, unrecognized influence on history, world religions, and the Bible. The concepts of the *abi* (ritual pit), magic circles, contact with gods of the underworld, offerings to the ancestral dead, and veneration of long-dead kings—the "mighty men who were of old," the Nephilim/Rephaim—appear to have come from the Hurrians, who emigrated to Canaan about a thousand years before Abraham. As they spread throughout the ancient Near East, they brought with them occult practices that continue around the world to this day.

All of this was inspired by the spirit beings who descended to Mount Hermon in the distant past. Despite his present status as a prisoner in a deep, dark hole (which may have inspired the preferred means of contact—at night, underground, in a ritual pit), Shemihazah, chief of the rebel Watchers, perhaps working through the spirits of his children destroyed in the Flood, launched an alternate spirituality that reaches out not to God in heaven, but to the world below, the realm of the dead. This religion is still practiced in various forms all over the world.

The Mount Hermon rebellion, and the spirit who led it, had a profound impact on ancient Israel. It's also shaped the Western world through its influence on the religions of the Greeks and Romans. Kumarbi, the god-father of the Hurrians, who we identify as the Watcher chief Shemihazah, has been called by many names over the centuries. His cult spread with the dispersal of the sons of Noah from the Ararat Plain.

And he manipulates events in the world to this day, even from his prison behind the gates of hell.

---

16   1 Chronicles 21:16.

CHAPTER NINETEEN

THE ASSYRIAN— OR IS HE?

Asshur is there and all her company: his graves are about him: all of them slain, fallen by the sword: Whose graves are set in the sides of the pit, and her company is round about her grave: all of them slain, fallen by the sword, which caused terror in the land of the living.

—Ezekiel 32:22–23 (KJV)

The kingdom of Assyria emerged as the dominant political and military power in the ancient Near East toward the end of the tenth century BC, shortly after Israel split into the northern kingdom, which retained the name of Israel, and the southern kingdom, Judah. For the next three centuries, Assyria extended its borders and absorbed all of the Middle East, including Egypt and the eastern half of Anatolia. It was during this period that the great king Sennacherib boasted of his conquests in Babylonia, mocking the "kingdoms of Enlil":

As my hand has reached to the kingdoms of the idols [*ĕlîl*],
    whose carved images were greater than those of Jerusalem
    and Samaria,
shall I not do to Jerusalem and her idols
    as I have done to Samaria and her images [*ĕlîle*]?"
(Isaiah 10:10–11)

Enlil, or Ellil in Akkadian, was the father-god of Mesopotamia. In his book *The Second Coming of Saturn*, Derek showed that this entity was the same entity called Shemihazah in the Book of 1 Enoch. Enlil's main epithet, the phrase that described his best-known characteristic, was "Great Mountain." He was singled out for scorn by Yahweh in Zechariah 4:7 ("Who are you, O great mountain?") and in Ezekiel's throne room vision of God, which Ezekiel took pains to point out occurred in the sky directly over the temple of Enlil in his sacred city of Nippur.[1] And condemnations of "worthless idols" in Isaiah 2, Psalm 96, and Psalm 97 may be references to the minions of Enlil, the ʾĕlîlim who made a pact to rebel with their chief at Mount Hermon.

The Assyrians adopted Enlil as their patron deity, but they called him Assur (pronounced "Asher"). His temple in the city that bore his name was, like the original temple of Enlil at Kippur, called "House of the Mountain." Scholars often refer to Assur as "the Assyrian Enlil."[2]

Assyria tried to conquer the Levant for more than a century before the northern kingdom of Israel fell in 722 BC. The subsequent resettling of the northern tribes left a profound scar on the Jewish psyche. Contrary to their negative depiction in the Old Testament, the Assyrians clearly thought quite highly of themselves and their patron god:

> "Assur is king, Assur is king!" and, further on in the text, "May your (the king's) foot in Ekur and your hands (stretched) toward Assur, your god, be at ease! May your priesthood (šangūtu) and the priesthood of your sons be at ease in the service of Assur, your god! With your straight sceptre enlarge your land! May Assur grant you a commanding voice, obedience, agreement, justice and peace!"…"Assur is king—indeed Assur is king! Assurbanipal is the [...] of Assur, the creation

---

1 Ezekiel mentions that he experienced his vision of God's throne room "by the Chebar canal," which ran through Nippur past the temple of Enlil.
2 Adam Stone, "Enlil/Ellil (god)." *Ancient Mesopotamian Gods and Goddesses*, Oracc and the UK Higher Education Academy (2019) http://oracc.museum.upenn.edu/amgg/listofdeities/enlil/, retrieved 2/24/24.

of his hands. May the great gods establish his reign, may they protect the life [of Assurba]nipal, king of Assyria! May they give him a just sceptre to extend the land and his peoples! May his reign be renewed and may they consolidate his royal throne for ever!"[3]

"Assur is king, Assur is king!" That claim is not surprising for the chief deity of a powerful kingdom, but there's more to it than that. Assur was Enlil by a different name, and in *The Second Coming of Saturn*, Derek pieced together the evidence linking Enlil's identity to El of Canaan, Dagan/Dagon of the Amorites and Philistines, Kumarbi of the Hurrians and Hittites, and Molech/Milcom of Ammon, all of which were considered the creator, father of the gods, and/or king of the pantheon. No surprise, then, that this entity convinced his Assyrian worshipers to call him "king."

Since God directed His wrath at this entity under the name Enlil, even though it's been hidden from us non-Hebrew speakers until recently, it should come as no surprise that God had choice words for Assur as well—although they, too, have been hidden by modern translations and our unfamiliarity with the world of the Hebrew prophets.

The problem is this: The Hebrew word *aššūr* can refer to the small-G god Assur, the kingdom of Assyria, or the capital city of the kingdom (also named Assur), depending on the context. This is admittedly speculative, but in the context of the verses we'll cite below, what you're about to read are prophecies of the ultimate destruction of this ancient enemy of God.

Isaiah 14 is one of the most remarkable chapters in the Bible. It's the source of the well-known verse, "How art thou fallen from heaven, O Lucifer, son of the morning! how art thou cut down to the ground,

---

3   A. Livingstone, "Assur." In K. van der Toorn, B. Becking, & P. W. van der Horst (Eds.), *Dictionary of deities and demons in the Bible* (2nd extensively rev. ed.) (Leiden; Boston; Köln; Grand Rapids, MI; Cambridge: Brill; Eerdmans, 1999), p. 108.

which didst weaken the nations!"[4] On the surface, the first part of the chapter is a polemic against the king of Babylon and a prophecy of that nation's destruction. Bear in mind, however, that at the time Isaiah was inspired to write this verse, Babylon was a vassal state of Assyria. Shalmaneser V had destroyed Samaria and carried off the northern tribes of Israel only twenty or thirty years earlier, and it would be almost a century before the Chaldeans established the Neo-Babylonian Empire. There is more going on in Isaiah 14 than a prophecy of the destruction of Babylon or mocking Satan, who'd been reduced from his status in Eden to becoming the lord of the dead. (The "shades" who greet him upon his arrival in Sheol are *rephaim*,[5] the spirits of the Nephilim destroyed in the Flood.)

Consider the odd description of the rebel from Eden in verse 19:

> All the kings of the nations lie in glory,
>> each in his own tomb;
> but you are cast out, away from your grave,
>> **like a loathed branch,**
> clothed with the slain, those pierced by the sword,
>> who go down to the stones of the pit,
>> like a dead body trampled underfoot. (Isaiah 14:19,
> emphasis added)

What did the prophet mean by calling the rebel from Eden "a loathed branch"? Most English translations agree that the Hebrew word *netser* means "branch," although a couple opt for "shoot." The range of adjectives chosen by translators includes "loathed," "repulsive," "rejected," "worthless," and "abominable," but they convey the same sense—someone or something utterly detestable. But even allowing for differences in culture and language over the last 2,700 years, the phrase "loathed/worthless/abominable branch" is odd.

---

4   Isaiah 14:12 (King James Bible).
5   Isaiah 14:9.

The key is understanding that Isaiah, as writers often do, didn't use the Hebrew *netser*; he employed a similar-sounding word from another language that was common enough to his readers to be understood:

> [The] term is best explained as a loanword from the common Egyptian noun *ntr*. *Ntr* is generally translated "god," but is **commonly used of the divinized dead and their physical remains.** It originally came into Hebrew as a noun referring to the putatively divinized corpse of a dead king, which is closely related to the Egyptian usage. [6] (emphasis added)

In fact, the Egyptians used the word *ntr*, a homonym (a word that sounds the same as a completely different word) for *netser*, to describe Osiris, the Egyptian god of the dead. Given that Isaiah had just described the welcome Lucifer received from the Rephaim, the spirits of the "mighty men who were of old," calling the rebel from Eden a "loathsome dead god" makes more sense than "loathed branch."

Now, why a loanword from Egypt? The influence of Judah's southwestern neighbor is evident in the book of Isaiah. The prophet warned Hezekiah not to trust in an Egyptian alliance to protect his kingdom (Isaiah 30:1–2, 31:1–3), which Isaiah called "a covenant with death" (Isaiah 28:15). However, recently discovered seals from King Hezekiah feature the image of a scarab (dung beetle), a sacred symbol in Egypt So, borrowing an Egyptian word would not have been unusual for Isaiah, especially given the poor opinion he had of Judah's neighbor.

The adjective translated "abhorred" or "abominable," Hebrew *ta'ab*, is significant. It modifies the noun *netser*, which normally had a positive connotation. In this context, *ta'ab* may suggest "ritually impure."[7] Isaiah made a profound declaration here about the rebel

---

6   Hays (2012), op. cit., p. 17.
7   Ibid., p. 18.

from Eden: The "loathed branch" was actually an "unclean god," and in the context of the Rephaim greeting the rebel upon his arrival in Sheol, the prophet described an unclean god of the dead, which was the role assigned to Lucifer after he was kicked out of Eden.

What makes Isaiah 14 even more fascinating is another loanword, this time from Aramaic, a few verses further:

May the offspring of evildoers
    nevermore be named!
Prepare slaughter for his sons
    because of the guilt of their fathers,
lest they rise and possess the earth,
    and fill the face of the world with cities. (Isaiah 14:20b–21)

We know that God is not opposed to cities as such. He inspired Nehemiah, Ezra, Zerubbabel, and others to rebuild Jerusalem and its walls. So, how are we supposed to understand this?

Here's the key: The Hebrew word for "city" is *'iyr*. In Aramaic, the very same word means "Watcher." The plural forms are *'iyr*im and *'iyr*in, respectively. Thanks to Dr. Michael S. Heiser, we have a good example of an Aramaic word that was imported into the Bible and then corrected with the *-im* plural suffix, transforming *naphil(a)* ("giant") into *nephilim*, according to Hebrew rules of word formation.[8]

You can see right off how that would change the passage above in an important way:

Prepare slaughter for his sons
    because of the guilt of their fathers,
lest they rise and possess the earth,
    and fill the face of the world with Watchers. (Isaiah 14:21,
modified, emphasis added)

---

8   Michael S. Heiser, "The Nephilim." *SitchinIsWrong.com*, http://www.sitchinis-wrong. com/nephilim/nephilim.htm, retrieved 4/16/18.

That puts a new spin on the whole chapter. Isaiah may have intended to record God's judgment against the offspring of the rebel angels on Hermon, the Watchers, and their progeny, the Nephilim. A similar prophecy was uttered by the prophet-for-prophet, Balaam:

[A] star shall come out of Jacob,
  and a scepter shall rise out of Israel; [...]
And one from Jacob shall exercise dominion
  and destroy the survivors of cities [the Watchers]!"
  (Numbers 24:17b, 19)

Derek stumbled onto this new understanding of Isaiah 14 while researching his 2018 book, *Last Clash of the Titans*. At the time, even though it seems clear in the context of the prophesied destruction of Lucifer and the Rephaim (i.e., the Nephilim), he didn't consider that the rest of that section of the chapter might also refer to supernatural beings rather than nation-states:

"I will rise up against them," declares the LORD of hosts, "and **will cut off from Babylon [*bābel*] name and remnant, descendants and posterity**," declares the LORD. "And I will make it a possession of the hedgehog, and pools of water, and I will sweep it with the broom of destruction," declares the LORD of hosts.

The LORD of hosts has sworn:
"As I have planned,
  so shall it be,
and as I have purposed,
  so shall it stand,
that **I will break the Assyrian [*'aššūr*] in my land,
  and on my mountains trample him underfoot**;
and his yoke shall depart from them,
  and his burden from their shoulder."
This is the purpose that is purposed

> concerning the whole earth,
> and this is the hand that is stretched out
> over all the nations.
> For the LORD of hosts has purposed,
> and who will annul it?
> His hand is stretched out,
> and who will turn it back? (Isaiah 14:22–27, emphasis added)

We suggest the passage above refers to the nations of Babylon and Assyria as well as the spiritual entities connected to Babel and the "king-god," Assur.

First, remember that "Babylon" was a name applied to more than one city in Mesopotamia, including the ancient city of Eridu, the site of Babel. In fact, the Hebrew *bābel* translated "Babylon" in Isaiah 14:22 is the same word rendered "Babel" in Genesis 10 and 11.

God has promised to destroy "the offspring of evildoers"—the "sons of God" from Genesis 6—to prevent them from "fill[ing] the face of the earth with Watchers." The prophecy against *bābel* continues that thought. His promise to "cut off from [*bābel*] name and remnant, descendants and posterity" is more than just a threat to eradicate the Chaldeans, who ruled Babylon in the time of Isaiah. The "name" in Old Testament theology is more complex and nuanced than a personal pronoun or a reputation. Without going too far down a rabbit trail, the "name" in the religious context of the ancient Near East was another aspect of a supernatural being. For example, God told Moses and the Israelites to obey the angel He sent ahead of them "for my Name is in Him."[9] In short, "the Name in the OT is both Yahweh and a representation of Him, depending on the context. It's not merely a phrase, but a being."[10]

The pagans had a similar concept. As we noted earlier, the Rephaim

---

9   Exodus 23:20–21.
10   Michael S. Heiser, "The Name Theology of the Old Testament." In *Faithlife Study Bible* (Bellingham, WA: Lexham Press, 2012, 2016).

were summoned through a necromancy ritual to Mount Hermon where "the name of El revivified the dead, the blessings of the name of El revivified the heroes."[11] It appears that God has decreed the absolute obliteration of the entities connected to Babel, as well as the destruction of Babylon. The latter was fulfilled in 536 BC when Cyrus took the city; the former should be viewed in the context of Psalm 82, a heavenly courtroom scene where God decreed the death of the gods.[12]

---

11 Spronk (1986), op. cit., p. 171.

12 Psalm 82:6–7:
    I said, "You are gods,
        sons of the Most High, all of you;
    nevertheless, like men you shall die,
        and fall like any prince."

CHAPTER TWENTY

THE REAL LORD
OF HELL

And the giants will say to you, 'Come in the depth of clamor! Than whom are you mightier? And descend and sleep with the uncircumcised in the middle of those wounded by swords!'

—EZEKIEL 32:21 (Lexham English Septuagint)

The reference to "the Assyrian" in Isaiah 14 is truly fascinating. Yes, it was a prophecy of the near-term collapse of the Assyrian kingdom, fulfilled in 609 BC when the father of Nebuchadnezzar, Nabopolassar, destroyed what was left of the Assyrian army at the Battle of Harran. However, that was fought in northern Mesopotamia, near modern Sanliurfa, Turkey. When God refers to His lands and mountains, He means Israel.

The other relevant question is this: Why would God refer to "the Assyrian," singular? This type of description isn't used of any of the other traditional enemies of Israel. In other words, there are no prophecies or polemics directed at "the Edomite," "the Moabite," "the Philistine," or "the Egyptian"; it's always the plural form of the name—Edomites (*adômîm*), Egyptians (*misrayim*), etc. We haven't dug deeply enough into this passage. The bottom line is "the Assyrian" is a mistranslation because there is no "the" in the Hebrew text.

We repeat: The definite article, *ha* in Hebrew, is not in the text. It was added by English translators who reasoned that Isaiah probably wasn't referring to Assyria since the chapter began with a polemic against the king of Babylon (or Babel!). However, a bias against seeing Assur, the "Assyrian Enlil," as a living entity has prevented translators from rendering the sentence correctly:

> "I will break Assur in My land, and on My mountains trample him underfoot." (Isaiah 14:25)

But before we chase this entity through Scripture, we offer another paradigm-changing suggestion: The "king of Babylon" was not the Chaldean ruler of Babylonia—it was the same entity, Assur.

The Hebrew *melek bābel* also means "king of Babel." Given that Hebrew *bābel* derives from Akkadian *bab ilû* ("gate of the gods"), Isaiah 14's focus on the netherworld, its inhabitants (the Rephaim), and the disgraced rebel from Eden, Lucifer, Lord of the Dead, we suggest that *melek bābel* more likely means "king of the god-gate." Babel/Babylon was a name that didn't always apply to Nebuchadnezzar's capital city; it was also used for Eridu, home of the god Enki and his temple, the E-abzu ("House of the Abyss"), and for Nineveh, one of the most important cities in ancient Assyria.[1]

Here's what we're getting at: "the Assyrian," *'aššūr* in Hebrew, is Assur, otherwise known as Enlil, El, Dagan, Milcom/Molech, and Shemihazah. And in Isaiah 14, this entity is called *melek bābel*, "king of the god-gate." In other words, we suggest that the "king of Babylon" and "the Assyrian" were terms used by Isaiah for Assur, one of the objects of the LORD's wrath in this chapter—the others being the Rephaim/Nephilim ("the offspring of evildoers").

However, we can take this even further. Christian commentators have seen the story of the fall of Satan in Isaiah 14 and the parallel scriptures in Ezekiel 28. Until recently, we believed this, too, based on these verses:

---

1 Dalley, op. cit.

How you are fallen from heaven,
    O Day Star, son of Dawn!
How you are cut down to the ground,
    you who laid the nations low!
You said in your heart,
    "I will ascend to heaven;
above the stars of God
    I will set my throne on high;
I will sit on the mount of assembly
    in the far reaches of the north;
I will ascend above the heights of the clouds;
    I will make myself like the Most High."
But you are brought down to Sheol,
    to the far reaches of the pit. (Isaiah 14:12–15)

The phrase "far reaches of the north," also translated "sides of the north" or "uttermost parts of the north," is from the Hebrew *yarketê tsaphon*. That's a reference to Mount Zaphon, the mountain sacred to Baal:

> A seat was prepared and he was seated at the right hand of Valiant Baal, until the gods had eaten and drunk. Then Valiant Baal said, "Depart, Kothar-and-Hasis! Hasten! Build a house indeed; hasten! Construct a palace! Hasten! Let them build a house; Hasten! Let them construct a palace, in the midst of **the uttermost parts of Zaphon**. A thousand square yards let the house take up, ten thousand acres the palace!"[2] (emphasis added)

Since Baal was identified as Satan by Jesus Himself,[3] identifying "Day Star" or "Lucifer" (Hebrew *Helel Ben Shachar*, literally "Lightbringer, son of Dawn") as Satan seems obvious. But maybe not.

---

2   Ugaritic text KTU 1.4 v 49–57. In Wyatt (2002), op. cit., p. 104.

3   Matthew 12:22–26, Revelation 2:13.

William R. Gallagher published a paper in 1994 that offers a compelling argument for identifying another candidate as Helel:

> One could reasonably expect *hll* [Helel] to be the West Semitic form of Illil [that is, Enlil]. As the Ebla tablets suggest, Illil came into West Semitic directly from Sumerian. Thus this example is comparable to the development of E$_2$.GAL:

Sum. é-gal	Eblaite (?)	Ug. hkl	Heb. hêkāl
Sum.ᵈen-lil	Eblaite ᵈi-li-lu	Ug. hll	Heb. hêlēl[4]

The etymology equating Isaiah 14's Helel with Ellil/Enlil (*il-ilû*, "god of gods") also identifies him as the Canaanite creator-god El. Now, this confuses things a bit: El's mount of assembly was Hermon, not Zaphon. So, how can we identify the divine rebel with El, the "lord of Hermon," if he aspired to set up his mount of assembly at Zaphon?

It's possible that setting up shop on Mount Zaphon was his ambition. In fact, Isaiah 14:13 can be read, "I will ascend to heaven; above the stars of El I will set my throne on high…" As Edward Lipiński wrote, "the modern Ğebel el-Aqra' [Mount Zaphon] seems to have been dedicated to El before it became the mountain of Baal."[5] But however the verse is translated, the scheme of "Lucifer" was thwarted when Yahweh sent the rebellious "sons of God" to the Abyss during the Flood of Noah.

In short, what we suggest—speculatively—is that Helel Ben Shachar (literally, "light-bringer son of Dawn"), translated by Jerome and carried over into the King James Bible as Lucifer (Latin *lux* ["light"] + *ferre* ["to carry"]), is one and the same with Isaiah's king of Babylon and "the Assyrian." Isaiah 14:1–27 is a condemnation of this divine rebel and a prophecy of his future destruction.

---

4   William R. Gallagher, "On the Identity of Hêlēl Ben Šaḥar of Is. 14:12–15." *Ugarit-Forschungen: Internationales Jahrbuch* für die *Altertumskunde Syrien-Palästinas*, 26 (1994), p. 137. Thanks to Dr. Douglas Hamp for calling my attention to this

5   Lipiński, op. cit., p. 64.

In support of this theory, let's turn over a couple additional pieces of evidence. In verse 19, the "loathed branch" passage, Helel is described as "like a dead body trampled underfoot." The Hebrew word translated "dead body" is *peger*, a cognate for the Eblaite word *pagrê*, which was one of the epithets of Dagan, *bēl pagrê* ("lord of the corpse"),[6] and Dagan is another identity of this creature. It appears the prophet is mocking this entity and the cult of the dead he inspired through his rebellion that led to the creation of the Nephilim, the events described in Genesis 6:1–4.

Upon his arrival in Sheol, Helel is consigned to "the far reaches of the pit."[7] The Hebrew phrase, *yarketê bôr*, appears only one other place in the Bible—and, to repeat the wise words of our friend Dr. Michael Heiser, "If it's in the Bible and it's weird, it's probably important." The other use of this phrase is in Ezekiel 32, a chapter that refers to the "mighty chiefs" (more accurately, "chiefs of the *gibborim*") "in the midst of Sheol." There we find Assur with his host, "whose graves are set in the uttermost parts of the pit."[8]

In other words, Assur and his company have *precisely the same underworld address* as Helel Ben Shachar in Isaiah 14, the *yarketê bôr* ("far reaches/uttermost parts of the pit"). This seems like a bit of hyperbole, a detail tossed in by the prophets just to emphasize the evil of Helel/Assur, but it also suggests that there's something unique about this entity:

> The notion that those killed in heroic battle have a special place in the afterlife is a shared feature of Ezekiel 32 and Greek heroic literature, even as Ezekiel 32 may be the only text in the Hebrew Bible to give such a detailed description of this geography. [...] Assur is relegated to the "uttermost edge of the Pit"

---

6   Schmidt, op. cit., p. 66.
7   Isaiah 14:15.
8   Ezekiel 32:22.

(ירכתי בור) in v. 23—presumably in the sense of distance and ignobility—and could thus be in a class of its own.[9]

If, as we suspect, Assur (AKA Helel/Enlil, El, Dagon, Milcom/ Molech, et al) is the Watcher chief Shemihazah, then he is indeed in a class of his own—the leader of a rebellion that still affects the world through his demonic offspring.

If we turn back to Ezekiel chapter 31, we see a long diatribe against the Pharaoh of Egypt. Like Isaiah 14 and Ezekiel 28, which condemn the king of Babylon and the prince of Tyre by comparing those mortal rulers to divine rebels against the authority of God, Ezekiel 31 compares Pharaoh to Assyria, and there are good reasons to interpret Assyria (Hebrew 'aššūr) as the fallen Watcher Assur, which is just another name used by Shemihazah over the centuries.

> Son of man, say to Pharaoh king of Egypt and to his multitude:
> "Whom are you like in your greatness?
> Behold, ['aššūr] was a cedar in Lebanon,
>   with beautiful branches and forest shade,
>   and of towering height,
>   its top among the clouds. (Ezekiel 31:2–3)

The reference to Lebanon is a clue. It's frequently used in the Old Testament to evoke Bashan and its connection to Mount Hermon, the Watchers, the Nephilim, and the netherworld.

> The cedars in the garden of God could not rival it,
>   nor the fir trees equal its boughs;
> neither were the plane trees
>   like its branches;

---

9   Brian R. Doak, "Ezekiel's Topography of the (Un-)Heroic Dead in Ezekiel 32:17-32." *Journal of Biblical Literature*, Vol. 132, No. 3 (2013), pp. 619-620.

no tree in the garden of God
>was its equal in beauty.
I made it beautiful
>in the mass of its branches,
and all the trees of Eden envied it,
>that were in the garden of God. (Ezekiel 31:8–9)

Here is where the identification becomes apparent. The trees in Eden clearly represent other spirit beings, and Assur (i.e., Shemihazah, chief of the Watchers) was beyond compare. This is similar to the description of the rebel in Ezekiel 28:12–15—perfect, wise, beautiful, blameless in his ways. Since it's generally agreed by scholars that Ezekiel 28 and Isaiah 14 are parallel passages dealing with the same divine rebel, we believe Ezekiel 31 corroborates our theory that this entity, under his variety of names and identities, played a far more important role in this supernatural war than we've been taught. And the punishment he received is appropriate for his crime:

"Thus says the Lord GOD: On the day the cedar went down to Sheol I caused mourning; **I closed the deep over it,** and restrained its rivers, and many waters were stopped. I clothed Lebanon in gloom for it, and all the trees of the field fainted because of it. I made the nations quake at the sound of its fall, when I cast it down to Sheol with those who go down to the pit. And all the trees of Eden, the choice and best of Lebanon, all that drink water, were comforted in the world below. They also went down to Sheol with it, to those who are slain by the sword; yes, those who were its arm, who lived under its shadow among the nations.

"Whom are you thus like in glory and in greatness among the trees of Eden? You shall be brought down with the trees of Eden to the world below. You shall lie among the uncircumcised, with those who are slain by the sword.

This is Pharaoh and all his multitude, declares the Lord
GOD. (Ezekiel 31:15–18, emphasis added)

The Hebrew word translated "deep," *tehôm*, refers to the abyss.[10]
What Ezekiel described was not a tree cast into Sheol, it was the punishment of Shemihazah and the Watchers, the "sons of God" who "left
their proper dwelling" and are "in eternal chains under gloomy darkness until the judgment of the great day."[11] Such would be the fate,
Ezekiel prophesied, of Pharaoh.

The difference between Pharaoh and Assur—that is, Enlil, El,
Dagon, Milcom/Molech, etc.—is that the once-perfect chief of the
Watchers will get out of the underworld for a brief time in the last
days. You see, he is the entity called by John the angel of the bottomless pit—the true lord of Hell, Abaddon/Apollyon.

Believe us, you don't want to be here when he returns from the
abyss. The good news is you don't have to be.

---

10 B. Alster, "Tiamat." In Karel van der Toorn, Bob Becking, and Pieter W. van der
    Horst (Eds.), *Dictionary of deities and demons in the Bible* (Leiden; Boston; Köln;
    Grand Rapids, MI; Cambridge: Brill; Eerdmans, 1999), p. 867.
11 Jude 6.

CHAPTER TWENTY-ONE

MOLECH

First Moloch, horrid King besmear'd with blood
Of human sacrifice, and parents tears,
Though for the noyse of Drums and Timbrels loud
Their childrens cries unheard, that past through fire
To his grim Idol.

—JOHN MILTON, *Paradise Lost*, Book I

This may seem like a stretch, but we're going to devote some time to a study of the most detestable pagan god in the Old Testament, Molech.

If anything, Molech—sometimes spelled Molek, Moloch, or even Milcom—is even more mysterious than Dagan. Since ancient Semitic languages such as Akkadian, Ugaritic, and Hebrew had no vowels, it's difficult to tell when *mlk* means "king" (*melech*), "messenger" or "angel" (*malak*), and when it's the name of the dark god Molech. This condemnation of idolatry from the Book of Isaiah is a case in point:

> You journeyed to **the king** [*mlk*] with oil
> and multiplied your perfumes;
> you sent your envoys far off,
> and sent down even to Sheol. (Isaiah 57:9, emphasis added)

In that context, given the reference to Sheol, the Hebrew underworld, "the king" could just as easily read "Molech," a god linked almost exclusively to the netherworld. Obviously, that would change the entire sense of the verse.

Molech's first appearance in the Bible is in Leviticus 18, where God told the Israelites that they were forbidden to give their children as an offering to the dark god. Molech's cult, however, appears to extend back at least a thousand years before Moses.

A god called Malik is known from texts found at Ebla, a powerful kingdom in northern Syria between about 3000 and 2400 BC, more than three hundred years before Abraham arrived in Canaan. Of the approximately five hundred deities identified from texts found at Ebla, one of most common theophoric elements in personal names—like -el in Daniel ("God is my judge") or -yahu in Hezekiah ("YHWH strengthens")—was *ma-lik*.[1]

Getting a handle on the character of Malik is difficult. It appears that by the time of Abraham, Isaac, and Jacob, he was still worshiped at Mari, a powerful city on the Euphrates River near the modern border between Syria and Iraq. Further, it appears that Malik was served by a group of underworld deities called *maliku*. And five hundred years later, during the time of the judges, Malik and the *maliku* (called *mlkm* by then) were still venerated at Ugarit.[2]

What's more, the Ugaritic texts link Malik with a god called Rapiu, the "King of Eternity." This entity is interesting for a couple of reasons: First, Rapiu is a singular form of "Rephaim," like *ha-rapha* ("the *rapha*" or "the giant") in 2 Samuel 21 and 1 Chronicles 20 (who may, in fact, be Rapiu). In other words, just as Malik had his band of netherworld followers, the *maliku* or *mlkm*, it's possible that Rapiu was "lord of the Rephaim."

Second, the Ugaritic texts connect both Malik and Rapiu to Ashtaroth, a city in Bashan near Mount Hermon.[3]

---

1   Heider, op. cit., p. 96.
2   Ibid., p. 129.
3   Ibid., p. 115.

Mother Šapšu, take a message to Milku in ʿAṭṭartu [Ashtaroth]: "My incantation for serpent bite, For the scaly serpent's poison."[4]

Mother Šapšu was the sun-goddess in Ugarit. In this ritual, she was asked to carry a message to a god ruling in Ashtaroth, Milku, which is another form of the name Molech. This isn't surprising; at the time of the Judges in Israel, Bashan, the modern Golan Heights, was on the border of the relatively new nation of Ammon. The national god of the Ammonites was Milcom, who was likewise one and the same with Molech.[5]

In fact, Rapiu had two cities connected to his kingdom: He is described as "the god enthroned at Ashtaroth, the god who rules in Edrei."[6] Those two cities are the same two from which Og, last of the remnant of the Rephaim, ruled over Bashan.[7] To the pagan Amorites, the kingdom of Og was quite literally the entrance to the underworld.

To be clear, despite the evil reputation of Molech/Malik, archaeologists have yet to find physical evidence of child sacrifice at Ugarit, Mari, or Ebla. Nor has any turned up near Jerusalem, despite references in the Bible to the ritual practice outside the walls of the city in the Valley of Hinnom—a place with such a dark reputation that the Greek form of its name, Gehenna, became a synonym for Hell. If children were being slaughtered for Molech in the Levant before the Israelites arrived, scholars haven't confirmed it yet.

Still, the Bible mentions it in Moses' day, around 1400 BC; Solomon built a high place for Molech around 950 BC;[8] and about three hundred and twenty-five years later, King Josiah defiled the Topheth

---

4   RS 24:244:40–41. Translation by Dennis Pardee & Theodore J. Lewis, *Ritual and Cult at Ugarit* (Vol. 10). (Atlanta, GA: Society of Biblical Literature, 2002), p. 177. Ugaritic text RS 24:251:42 also places the god Milku in Ashtaroth.
5   1 Kings 11:5 calls Milcom "the abomination of the Ammonites," and 1 Kings 11:7 uses the same description for Molech.
6   Wyatt (2002), op. cit., p. 395.
7   Deut. 3:1; Joshua 12:4, 13:12.
8   1 Kings 11:7.

in the Valley of the Son of Hinnom, which was used to burn children as offerings to Molech.[9]

Now, here's where things get interesting: Molech was equated with the Mesopotamian plague-god and gatekeeper of the underworld, Nergal. Not only are both connected to death and the afterlife, but Akkadian deity lists also record the equation "Malik = Nergal." Further, Semitic "*mlk*" and Sumerian "NERGAL" can both be understood to mean "king," confirming the identification.[10]

There's a similar link between "NERGAL" and the Hurrian father-god, Kumarbi. An inscription, probably from a foundation deposit at the temple at Urkesh dated to about 2250 BC, reads, "Tish-atal, king of Urkesh, built the temple of NERGAL."[11] Without going into detail, the conclusion of the archaeologists at Urkesh was this: The Sumerian logogram ^{d}KIŠ.GAL (NERGAL) represents a Hurrian divine name, not the Mesopotamian plague-god Nergal. Since the only god known to "live" at Urkesh is Kumarbi, "we may therefore identify the great Temple complex as being that of Kumarbi."[12]

We can infer that the "NERGAL" ("king") of Urkesh, Kumarbi, can also be identified as Malik/Molech. The other aspect of the cult of Molech that's relevant to our investigation is the clear connection in the Bible between the dark god and the practice of consulting the 'ōbôt, the spirits of the dead. We turn first to Leviticus:

> The LORD spoke to Moses, saying, "Say to the people of Israel, Any one of the people of Israel or of the strangers who sojourn in Israel who gives any of his children to Molech shall surely be put to death. The people of the land shall stone him with

9   2 Kings 23:10.
10   Rebecca Doyle, *Faces of the Gods: Baal, Asherah and Molek and Studies of the Hebrew Scriptures* (Doctoral thesis: University of Sheffield, 1996), p. 129.
11   Giorgio Buccellati and Marilyn Kelly-Buccellati, "The Great Temple Terrace at Urkesh and the Lions of Tish-atal." *Studies on the Civilization and Culture of Nuzi and the Hurrians* - 18 (2009), p. 59.
12   Ibid., p. 63.

stones. I myself will set my face against that man and will cut him off from among his people, because he has given one of his children to Molech, to make my sanctuary unclean and to profane my holy name. And if the people of the land do at all close their eyes to that man when he gives one of his children to Molech, and do not put him to death, then I will set my face against that man and against his clan and will cut them off from among their people, him and all who follow him in whoring after Molech.

If a person turns to mediums ['ōbôt] and necromancers [yid-dĕ'ōnîm], whoring after them, I will set my face against that person and will cut him off from among his people. (Leviticus 20:1–6)

The significance here is that God, at Mount Sinai, directly linked the cult of Molech to the gods and spirits of the netherworld.

The unifying principle of vv. 1-6 is not merely "illegitimate cultic practices," but the practice of the cult of the dead. This realization makes sense, also, of the condemnation of the guilty party's entire clan (mispahto) in v. 5: as we saw at Mari and Ugarit, the cult of the dead is a family affair, to secure the blessings (and avert the wrath) of past family for the sake of the family present and yet to be.[13]

A similar passage to Leviticus 20 is found in Deuteronomy 18:

There shall not be found among you anyone who burns his son or his daughter as an offering [to Molech], anyone who practices divination or tells fortunes or interprets omens, or a sorcerer or a charmer or a medium or a necromancer or one who inquires of the dead, or whoever does these things is an abomination to the LORD. (Deuteronomy 18:10–12)

---

13 Heider, op. cit., p. 251.

After the prohibition on burning children as offerings, there are seven specific activities described as "abomination to the LORD." All seven were intended to "gain information from or influence over a divine being or beings."[14] The connection of the Molech cult to these activities and underworld entities suggests that Molech is indeed the deity we met earlier in this study—Kumarbi, the god summoned from the *abi*, which, as we've seen, is the Hurrian original behind the Hebrew words for "ritual pit" (*'ôb*) and underworld spirits (*'ōbôt*).

It is generally accepted that the various forms of the name Molech/Malik/Milcom (and the chief god of Phoenician Tyre, Melqart) derive from the Semitic root *mlk* ("king"). The identification of this deity with Nergal, the gatekeeper of the underworld in Akkad and Babylon, suggests that the true meaning of the name was "King of the Underworld." This is consistent with our theory that this entity was the god worshiped by the Moabites, and perhaps by the people of Sodom in the days of Abraham and Lot, as Baal-Peor, a name that may mean "lord of the gates of hell."

What we suggest is that "Molech," like "Baal," was a title rather than a proper name, something like "King/Lord of the Underworld." Further evidence supporting this hypothesis comes from the small and mostly forgotten kingdom of Ammon:

> The dominance of the theophoric element 'l in Ammonite personal names suggests the importance of the deity El in the context of family religion. [...]
>
> The occurrence of the Ammonite name element 'l [El] with approximately the same percentage as Kemosh [national god of Moab], Qos [national god of Edom], and onomastic forms of Yahweh in theophoric names in Moabite, Edomite, and Hebrew, respectively, suggests that **among the Ammonites, too, the most popular family deity likewise corresponds to the chief national deity, in this case El. [...]**

---

14 Ibid., p. 259.

In contrast with the more traditional and widespread form of family piety expressed in personal names, the differentiation of Ammonite El in more nationalistic contexts like the Amman Citadel Inscription and in biblical texts, was expressed through the title Milkom—a title distinct to the Ammonite form of El in his capacity as royal god, a role reflected in the Ammonite statuary. [...]

In sum, given the present state of the evidence, **Milkom is best understood as a distinctly Ammonite form of El.**[15] (emphasis added.)

The connection between this entity, necromancy, and the cult of the dead, not to mention the sacrifice of children, establishes this entity as one of the great enemies of God and the order He established at Eden. Given that El/Molech/Shemihazah is chained up in eternal darkness while Satan still walks the earth, he may be even more dangerous than the one who leads the rebellion against God in the end times.

His banishment to the bottomless pit, the abyss called Tartarus by the Greeks, explains humanity's long history of trying to make contact with entities on the other side of the gates of hell.

---

15 Joel S. Burnett, "Iron Age Deities in Word, Image, and Name: Correlating Epigraphic, Iconographic, and Onomastic Evidence for the Ammonite God," *Studies in the History and Archaeology of Jordan* 10 (2009), p. 161.

CHAPTER TWENTY-TWO

SHECHEM

And when the LORD your God brings you into the land that you are entering to take possession of it, you shall set the blessing on Mount Gerizim and the curse on Mount Ebal.

—DEUTERONOMY 11:29 (ESV)

S hechem is one of the most important cities in the Bible. While it isn't nearly as well-known as Jerusalem, Bethlehem, Nazareth, or Capernaum, where Jesus based His ministry, and certainly lacks the notoriety of, say, Jericho, Sodom, Babylon, or Rome, there is something about ancient Shechem that marks it as a place of supernatural significance from the age of Abraham down to the time of Jesus.

The city is called Nablus today from the Latin Neapolis ("New City"), the name given to Shechem by Emperor Vespasian in 72 AD. It's located west of the Jordan in what was probably the border between the territories of Manasseh and Ephraim. It sits in a valley between Mount Ebal, the site of Joshua's altar, and Mount Gerizim, which is still the home of a small remnant of the ancient Samaritan sect. The strategic location controlled a pass connecting an important ford across the Jordan River, where the Jabbok empties into the Jordan, and a route through the hill country that led north to the Jezreel Valley and southward to Shiloh, Bethel, and Jerusalem.

Shechem is an ancient city, first settled during the Chalcolithic, around 3500 BC. It is probably mentioned in a text from the north

Syrian city-state Ebla around 2500 BC, where it's listed as sacred to the Canaanite plague-god Resheph.[1] We say *probably*, because Giovanni Pettinato, the epigrapher who declared that he'd found Shechem in an Eblaite text (and the cities of the plain—Sodom, Gomorrah, Admah, Zeboiim, and Bela!) in the mid-1970s, was pressured by the government of Syria into retracting his claim. Apparently, the regime of Hafez al-Assad felt Pettinato's work, which unsurprisingly attracted a great deal of attention from Christians and Jews, lent credibility to Israel's right to exist in what is still seen by many Muslims as part of the Arab world.[2]

It is a sad truth that archaeology in the Middle East is subject to political and religious pressures that go way beyond the intellectual blood sport of modern academia. Ironically, even though he retracted his claims to have found biblical references in the Ebla texts, Pettinato was replaced anyway as chief epigrapher on the dig. (And he subsequently continued to admit that Sodom and Zeboiim might well be mentioned in those texts.)[3]

Shechem first appears in the Bible in Genesis 12, early in the story of Abraham, then still called Abram. At the age of seventy-five, the patriarch assembled his entourage, which included his nephew Lot, and set out for Canaan from Harran, near the modern border between Türkiye and Syria.

> When they came to the land of Canaan, Abram passed through the land to the place at Shechem, to the oak of Moreh. At that time the Canaanites were in the land. Then the LORD appeared to Abram and said, "To your offspring I will give this land." So he built there an altar to the LORD, who had appeared to him. (Genesis 12:5–7)

---

1   Giovanni Pettinato, *The Archives of Ebla: An Empire Inscribed in Clay.* (Garden City, NY: Doubleday & Company, Inc., 1981), p. 247.

2   Eugene H. Merrill, "Ebla and Biblical Historical Inerrancy," *Bibliotheca Sacra* 140 (Oct.-Dec. 1983), pp. 308–310.

3   Ibid., p. 310.

The oak of Moreh is believed to have been on Mount Kabir, a hill northeast of Shechem/Nablus, and on the east side of the valley that leads north from the city, across from Mount Ebal. Note that Abram built an altar there to mark the place where Yahweh first appeared to him and promised that the land of Canaan would one day belong to the offspring of the still-childless patriarch.

It's worth noting that the Hebrew word rendered "oak" in our English Bible was probably a terebinth, a deciduous tree of the cashew family that bears no more than a passing resemblance to oak. The Hebrew word for "oak" is similar to that for "terebinth," so it's likely that English translators chose the tree more familiar to people familiar with a language that developed on an island where there are no terebinths.

Shechem next appears in scripture two generations later, as the setting for the disturbing account of the rape of Jacob's daughter, Dinah.

Jacob was newly arrived in Canaan after serving Laban, his father-in-law twice over, for twenty years. It must have been a stressful journey—he'd fled Paddan-Aram with his family, flocks, and retinue, leaving behind angry in-laws in Harran who'd chased him down to the hill country of Gilead, across the Jordan from Canaan. Ahead of him, his brother Esau was coming to meet him with four hundred men, and for all Jacob knew his brother might still be bitter over selling his birthright. And if that wasn't enough, the Angel of Yahweh showed up and wrestled with Jacob half the night, leaving him with a permanent limp from a dislocated hip.

But God intervened, advising Laban in a dream to leave Jacob alone, and apparently twenty years apart had softened Esau's feelings toward his brother—although the hundreds of goats, sheep, camels, donkeys, and cattle that Jacob sent ahead as a peace offering probably helped.

Genesis 34 is a difficult chapter to digest. The behavior of Shechem, the son of the ruler of Shechem, was abominable. He forced himself on Dinah, leaving her "defiled" and "humiliated." Although Shechem (the young man, not the town) changed his approach, asking his father to acquire Dinah for his wife, the Hebrew text implies that his actions had made Dinah ritually impure.

Her brothers, led by Simeon and Levi, deceived Shechem (the town, not the young man) into circumcising all their men, believing that doing so would add Jacob and all of his wealth to their community. It did not. On the third day (!), while the men were incapacitated from their surgeries, Simeon and Levi killed all the men in the city and took Dinah from the house of Shechem (the man, not the city), where she'd been kept since her rape.

We cannot condone mass murder, but the rape of the young woman is inexcusable, too. This is one of those stories that believers can point to when skeptics claim, usually without evidence, that the Bible has been edited and rewritten over the centuries to suit the political and religious ambitions of priests, popes, emperors, and kings. This story does not reflect well on the patriarch and progenitors of the tribes of Israel. Frankly, Jacob seemed more worried about his reputation with his Canaanite and Perizzite (Philistine)[4] neighbors than over the fact that his daughter had been raped and put under house arrest.

There are two other aspects of this story relevant to our study. First, Hamor, the ruler of Shechem, is called a Hivite in our English Old Testament. As noted earlier, the Hivites were Mycenaean Greeks, and they were certainly in Canaan at that point in history. However, the older Greek translation of the Hebrew Bible, the Septuagint, calls Hamor a Horite, making him a Hurrian. This means Hamor and the people he ruled were part of a culture that had been summoning spirits from the netherworld for at least two thousand years by the time of Jacob. And that makes Jacob's next actions even more interesting:

---

4   Dr. Michael S. Heiser addressed this at the Sons of God, Giants of Old conference in Lubbock, Texas in August 2019. While the names don't appear to be similar, they derive from Egyptian *p-r-s-t* (with a Semitic "z" replacing the Egyptian "s", thus "Perizzite"), later *p-l-s-t*, which became Peleset in Hebrew and Philistine in English. Thus, the Perizzites and Philistines were the same ethnic group.

God said to Jacob, "Arise, go up to Bethel and dwell there. Make an altar there to the God who appeared to you when you fled from your brother Esau." So Jacob said to his household and to all who were with him, "Put away the foreign gods that are among you and purify yourselves and change your garments. Then let us arise and go up to Bethel, so that I may make there an altar to the God who answers me in the day of my distress and has been with me wherever I have gone." So they gave to Jacob all the foreign gods that they had, and the rings that were in their ears. Jacob hid them under the terebinth tree that was near Shechem. (Genesis 35:1–4)

This seems like a reasonable response—he buried the earrings and "foreign gods." But why bury them? Why not burn everything? And did you notice that Jacob buried the items under *the* terebinth tree, not *a* terebinth tree?

This was obviously an important tree. We'll come back to it. For a moment, though, let's note that the practice of burying items connected to the gods of the netherworld was part of the ritual of summoning them to the surface. As we told you in a previous chapter, the Hurrian priest of the *abi* would conclude his contact with the netherworld gods by sending them back to the Great Below and covering the pit with dirt, bread, a cloth, or even a straw mat. This, as we noted, was thought to be sufficient to keep those gods confined to the netherworld where they belonged. It's possible that Jacob, who had not yet been taught the things that God would later reveal to Moses and the Hebrew prophets, thought that this was how he should remove the "foreign gods" from his entourage before they traveled to Bethel, a place he held sacred because of his vision there of a stairway connecting earth and heaven.

Shechem then fades into the background of the Old Testament for a couple of centuries until the time of Moses. And then it's central to one of the most fascinating, and yet unknown, parts of the Exodus story.

As we noted above, Shechem was mentioned in a text from the ancient Syrian city-state of Ebla as sacred to the Canaanite plague-god, Resheph. This was about a thousand years before Moses led the Israelites from Egypt toward the Promised Land. What is not well known, except to archaeologists, is that Resheph, like other Amorite deities such as Baal and Astarte, were worshiped by Egyptians. In the time of Moses, one particularly important Egyptian considered Resheph his personal protector:[5] Pharaoh Amenhotep II.

Understand what this means: The pharaoh of the Exodus,[6] who was convinced to let the Israelites go through a series of plagues, was devoted to the plague-god of Canaan—the land from which the Israelites had come and to which they wanted to return. It was made painfully obvious to Amenhotep that his personal protector god was powerless to stop the plagues unleashed by the God of the Hebrews, Yahweh. The pharaoh's eldest son was one of the victims of the final plague!

And to add insult to injury, God gave specific instructions to Moses and Joshua on what they were to do once they crossed into Canaan:

> And when the LORD your God brings you into the land that you are entering to take possession of it, you shall set the blessing on Mount Gerizim and the curse on Mount Ebal. Are they not beyond the Jordan, west of the road, toward the going down of the sun, in the land of the Canaanites who live in the Arabah, opposite Gilgal, beside the oak of Moreh? (Deuteronomy 11:29–30)

The Arabah is the Jordan valley, and Gilgal is probably Argaman, a footprint-shaped structure about fifteen miles east of Shechem/

---

5 Paolo Xella, "Resheph." In Karel van der toorn, Bob Becking, and Pieter W. van der Horst (Eds.), *Dictionary of Deities and Demons in the Bible* (Leiden; Boston; Köln; Grand Rapids, MI; Cambridge: Brill; Eerdmans, 1999), p. 701.

6 Douglas N. Petrovich, "Amenhotep II and the Historicity of the Exodus-Pharaoh." *The Master's Seminary Journal* (2006).

Nablus discovered by Israeli archaeologist Adam Zertal in the 1980s. Our friend Aaron Lipkin, CEO of Lipkin Tours and an avid supporter of archaeology in the Holy Land, points out that the altar built by Joshua, also discovered by Zertal, is on the east slope of Mount Ebal about a mile and a half north of the Shechem valley. It's not visible from Mount Gerizim—unless, as Zertal believed, the Gerizim of Joshua's day is the modern Mount Kabir, the location of the Oak of Moreh. As Aaron notes, Joshua's altar was oriented toward the place where Jacob and his family crossed the Jordan, the ford near where the Jabbok empties into the river, and the Oak of Moreh where the LORD appeared to Abraham.

And it overlooked a city sacred to the plague-god Resheph, who'd been elevated to the top tier of the Egyptian pantheon by the pharaoh of the Exodus.

We should note before moving on that Resheph has had a very long career. Not only was he worshiped more than 4,500 years ago by the Amorites of northern Syria and 3,500 years ago by Canaanites and Egyptians alike, he was known in Babylon as Nergal where, like Resheph, he was both the plague-god and gatekeeper to the netherworld. And later, he was so important to the Greeks and Romans that he was one of the only deities whose name was the same in both pantheons: Apollo.

Shechem was not only where the blessings for obeying God's Law and the curses for disobedience were proclaimed by the tribes of Israel,[7] it was later where Joshua, nearing the end of his life, reconvened the tribes to renew Israel's covenant with God, and to challenge them to get off the spiritual fence:

> "Now therefore fear the LORD and serve him in sincerity and in faithfulness. Put away the gods that your fathers served beyond the River and in Egypt, and serve the LORD. And if it is evil in your eyes to serve the LORD, choose this day whom

---

7   Joshua 8:30–35.

you will serve, whether the gods your fathers served in the region beyond the River, or the gods of the Amorites in whose land you dwell. But as for me and my house, we will serve the LORD." (Joshua 24:14–15)

During our tour of Israel in 2019, we visited Mount Ebal and the reconstructed altar discovered by Adam Zertal. Reading the passage above at the altar was a powerful and moving experience. But in examining the biblical text, it's not clear that he made his famous declaration of faith at the site of the altar. Joshua 24:1 tells us that the aged leader summoned the tribes of Israel to Shechem. And to commemorate their promise to serve the LORD:

Joshua wrote these words in the Book of the Law of God. And he took a large stone and set it up there under the terebinth that was by the sanctuary of the LORD. (Joshua 24:26)

It appears the tabernacle of Yahweh was on Mount Gerizim by the famous terebinth near Shechem, the Oak of Moreh. It makes sense; after all, this was where the LORD appeared to Abraham and where Jacob buried the "foreign gods" of his entourage before moving on from Shechem to Bethel. Interestingly, the Samaritans of today believe, as their ancestors did, that the tabernacle remained on Gerizim for another three centuries before it was moved to Shiloh—illegally, by the high priest Eli.

Most of us have heard the story of Jesus and the Samaritan woman at the well. This occurred in Shechem, at the well dug by Jacob. One aspect of the story stands out in the context of Shechem as a place of special supernatural significance:

The woman said to him, "Sir, I perceive that you are a prophet. Our fathers worshiped on this mountain, but you say that in Jerusalem is the place where people ought to worship." (John 4:19–20)

We'd always assumed, based on 2 Kings 17, that Jews reviled the Samaritans as mixed-race heretics, pagans resettled in the northern kingdom of Israel after it was destroyed by the Assyrians in 722 BC:

> And the king of Assyria brought people from Babylon, Cuthah, Avva, Hamath, and Sepharvaim, and placed them in the cities of Samaria instead of the people of Israel. And they took possession of Samaria and lived in its cities. [...]
>
> But every nation still made gods of its own and put them in the shrines of the high places that the Samaritans had made, every nation in the cities in which they lived. The men of Babylon made Succoth-benoth, the men of Cuth made Nergal, the men of Hamath made Ashima, and the Avvites made Nibhaz and Tartak; and the Sepharvites burned their children in the fire to Adrammelech and Anammelech, the gods of Sepharvaim. They also feared the LORD and appointed from among themselves all sorts of people as priests of the high places, who sacrificed for them in the shrines of the high places. So they feared the LORD but also served their own gods, after the manner of the nations from among whom they had been carried away. (2 Kings 17:24, 29–33)

However, during our visit to Israel and the modern Mount Gerizim in 2018 we learned that there is long-standing resentment on both sides. The Samaritans say they are not the descendants of Mesopotamian pagans who were forcibly resettled in Samaria, but the remnant of the northern tribes of Ephraim and Judah who survived the Assyrian conquest. And since the inscription of Sargon II records that the Assyrians carried away a relatively small portion of the Israelites, it's not outside the realm of possibility.[8]

Samaritans claim they follow the true Law given to Moses and

---

8   Robert T. Anderson, "Samaritans," ed. by David Noel Freedman, *The Anchor Yale Bible Dictionary* (New York: Doubleday, 1992), p. 941.

that Jews have corrupted the faith. The schism began in the eleventh century BC when Eli, who raised the prophet Samuel, illegitimately moved the sanctuary from Shechem to Shiloh with the backing of a faction who supported his takeover of the priesthood from the legitimate high priest, Uzzi son of Bukki.[9]

The point is that there is an ancient tradition of the sanctity of Mount Gerizim that goes back to the time of Abraham, and much farther if the reference to the plague-god Resheph from ancient Ebla is authentic, and we believe it is. It seems a little too coincidental that Jews called the Samaritans Cutheans,[10] a reference to Cutha, a city sacred to Nergal, the Babylonian equivalent of Resheph.

There are two more references to Shechem in the Old Testament that point to the city as a special place. Judges chapter 9 records how an illegitimate son of Gideon named Abimelech led a rebellion against his half-brothers backed by the people of Shechem who still referred to themselves as "sons of Hamor," the Hurrian ruler of Shechem centuries earlier in the days of Jacob. Abimelech's name means "my-father-the-king," which calls into question Gideon's claim that he didn't want to rule over Israel. Instead, he only (!) requested 1,700 shekels of gold captured from the Midianites, worth about 1.4 million US dollars as of this writing, and used it to make himself an ephod, the garment reserved for the high priest.

Well, Abimelech led an insurrection, killed his half-brothers, and ruled over Israel for three years. Then God sent a spirit to stir up animosity between him and the leaders of the city. Abimelech was told of the plot:

> So Abimelech and all the men who were with him rose up by night and set an ambush against Shechem in four companies. And Gaal the son of Ebed went out and stood in the entrance

---

9   Uzzi was the great-grandson of Phinehas, the grandson of Aaron. See 1 Chronicles 6:1–6.

10   Flavius Josephus and William Whiston, *The Works of Josephus: Complete and Unabridged* (Peabody: Hendrickson, 1987), p. 265.

of the gate of the city, and Abimelech and the people who were with him rose from the ambush. And when Gaal saw the people, he said to Zebul, "Look, people are coming down from the mountaintops!" And Zebul said to him, "You mistake the shadow of the mountains for men." Gaal spoke again and said, "Look, people are coming down from the center of the land, and one company is coming from the direction of the Diviners' Oak." (Judges 9:34–37)

The Diviners' Oak must be the sacred terebinth near Shechem, otherwise known as the Oak of Moreh. Even more interesting, the Hebrew word translated "center," *tăbbûr*, means "navel," so "center of the land" would be more accurately rendered, "navel of the earth." This is a concept called an *omphalos*, a place where heaven and earth connect. The most famous in the ancient world was the rounded stone at Delphi, Greece, where Pythia, the oracle of Apollo (remember, the Greek name for Resheph), would dispense prophecies of the future to pilgrims.

That stone was believed to be the one given to Kronos as a substitute for the infant Zeus. His mother, Rhea, finally detected a pattern after Kronos swallowed her five older children to prevent the fulfillment of a prophecy that he'd be overthrown by his offspring. Fortunately for Zeus, Kronos was not a picky eater. He swallowed the stone, which, when it was eventually disgorged with Zeus's siblings, became the marker for what Greeks believed was the center of the world—a status that was also, apparently, given to Shechem by the Hurrians who lived there.

The last indication that Shechem was believed to be unique was, ironically, the site of another insurrection. After the death of Solomon, his son Rehoboam inherited the throne. But instead of a coronation at Jerusalem, Rehoboam traveled forty miles north to Shechem, in the hill country of Ephraim and Manasseh, to be confirmed as king over all Israel.[11] Now, this may have been a political move to secure

---

11   1 Kings 12:1.

support among the northern tribes. There must have been rumblings of discontent, as evidenced by the ease with which Jeroboam, son of Nebat, pulled the kingdom apart (although the account in 2 Chronicles 10 makes Rehoboam look like a foolish young man who lost most of his kingdom because he couldn't recognize good advice). But it's also possible that Shechem was selected because of the memory of the consequential events in the history of Israel that took place at Shechem, especially God's promise to Abraham, Jacob's crossing of the Jordan, and Joshua's declaration that he and his house would serve the LORD. All of this occurred at a place well known by the pagan Hurrians and Canaanites as a gateway between this world and the unseen realm—a city sacred to the gatekeeper to the netherworld, the plague-god, Resheph, who's better known to history as the Greco-Roman god Apollo.

We could dismiss it all as coincidence if God hadn't directed Moses and Joshua to go there immediately after crossing into Canaan to declare the blessings and curses on the assembly of Israel "beside the Oak of Moreh."

CHAPTER TWENTY-THREE

LORD OF
THE GATES OF HELL

Sheol and Abaddon are never satisfied,
and never satisfied are the eyes of man.

—PROVERBS 27:20 (ESV)

During the Exodus, one of the more unusual confrontations between Hebrews faithful to Yahweh and those who preferred a more tolerant view of the pagan religions they encountered occurred in the plains of Moab, the fertile area northeast of the Dead Sea, across the Jordan from Jericho.

While Israel lived in Shittim, the people began to whore with the daughters of Moab. These invited the people to the sacrifices of their gods, and the people ate and bowed down to their gods. So Israel yoked himself to Baal of Peor. And the anger of the LORD was kindled against Israel. And the LORD said to Moses, "Take all the chiefs of the people and hang them in the sun before the LORD, that the fierce anger of the LORD may turn away from Israel." And Moses said to the judges of Israel, "Each of you kill those of his men who have yoked themselves to Baal of Peor."

And behold, one of the people of Israel came and brought a Midianite woman to his family, in the sight of Moses and in the sight of the whole congregation of the people of Israel, while they were weeping in the entrance of the tent of meeting. When Phinehas the son of Eleazar, son of Aaron the priest, saw it, he rose and left the congregation and took a spear in his hand and went after the man of Israel into the chamber and pierced both of them, the man of Israel and the woman through her belly. Thus the plague on the people of Israel was stopped. Nevertheless, those who died by the plague were twenty-four thousand. (Numbers 25:1–9)

This requires some unpacking. To our twenty-first-century minds, the reaction of Phinehas seems excessive. Today, many would call him out for his intolerance and accuse him of xenophobia, racism, or both. To atheists and skeptics, this story makes God out to be a monster, since He obviously approved of Phinehas' violent act. But that's because most Americans today, especially those most likely to throw around that kind of epithet, view the world through a naturalistic bias. There is a lot here that's only obvious if you understand what was happening in the spirit realm.

The first clue that there's more to this story than is obvious at first read is the description of Phinehas' killing stroke: He killed both the Israelite prince and the Midianite princess with one thrust of his spear. Putting it delicately, there are only a couple of physical positions in which Phinehas could have speared them both with one jab.

There is other evidence in the text that suggests that the sin of the young lovers Zimri and Cozbi was sexual, and "in the sight of all Israel," no less. The Hebrew word translated "belly," *qevah*, means the lower abdomen and can refer to the womb or pubic region,[1] which implies that Phinehas caught the young couple in the act. The word translated "chamber" in the ESV (other translations use "tent" or

---

1   Barry, J. D., Mangum, D., Brown, D. R., Heiser, M. S., Custis, M., Ritzema, E., ... Bomar, D., Faithlife Study Bible [Nu 25:8] (Bellingham, WA: Lexham Press, 2016).

"pavilion"), *qubbah*, appears only here in the Old Testament. The passage is a bit obscure, but the sense is that the couple were engaged in some rite to the Baal of Peor, possibly a fertility ritual. So, what do we know about this pagan deity?

The name Baal-Peor is a title that means "lord of Peor." The location of Peor isn't known exactly, but based on the account in Numbers 23 it had to be near Mount Nebo where Moses got his only look at the Holy Land.[2] On a clear day, present-day visitors to Nebo can see the Dead Sea, Jericho, and the Mount of Olives, which is only about twenty-five miles away. Shittim, or Abel-Shittim, was the name given to the place of the Israelite camp on the Plains of Moab, directly below the western slope of Mount Nebo. Shittim means "acacia," the desert tree that provided the wood of the Ark of the Covenant. It's a hardy plant that survives where most other vegetation can't because of its resistance to drought and tolerance for salt water.

A team led by Dr. Steven Collins of Trinity Southwest University excavated at a site in Jordan between 2005 and 2023 that overlooks the ancient Plains of Moab. Dr. Collins is convinced that this site, Tall el-Hammam, is the biblical Sodom. Based on its estimated population, it would have been the largest city in the southern Levant in the time of Abraham, second only to Hazor north of the Sea of Galilee.

The evidence suggests that it was destroyed around 1700 BC by an air blast like the 1908 Tunguska event in Siberia.[3] Soil samples taken from the lower city revealed a high concentration of salts and sulphates in the ash layer from the city's destruction. The chemical composition of those salts and sulphates was "virtually identical to the chemical composition of Dead Sea water."[4] So, whatever exploded over the north end of the Dead Sea around the time of Abraham had enough

---

2   King Balak of Moab took the prophet Balaam to Peor, where he was able to see the tribes of Israel camping on the Plains of Moab.

3   Phillip J. Silvia, "The 3.7kaBP Middle Ghor Event: Catastrophic Termination of a Bronze Age Civilization." *American Schools of Oriental Research annual meeting* (Denver, November 17, 2018), p. 1.

4   Ibid., p. 3.

force to spray brine over the lower part of the city. The blast was devastating—the lower city was built on a hill seventy-five feet above the Jordan valley *eight miles* northeast of the Dead Sea!

Investigation of the plain itself, the Kikkar, found that salt had poisoned the ground there for centuries. It was at least six hundred years, around the time of Saul, David, and Solomon, before agriculture and civilization resumed.[5] So, when the Israelites arrived on the plains of Moab, it was well named Abel-Shittim, which means either "meadow of acacias" or "acacias of mourning."[6] Both definitions of the Hebrew word *ābēl*, "meadow" and "mourning," are appropriate; because of the concentration of Dead Sea salt in the soil, nothing would grow on the plains of Moab except salt-tolerant acacias for another three to four hundred years.[7]

Additionally, the area east of the Dead Sea, and especially near the ruined city of ancient Sodom,[8] was believed to be a place where the dead intervened in the affairs of the living. In fact, two stops along the Exodus route in that vicinity refer to places where the veil between worlds was believed to be thin.

And the people of Israel set out and camped in Oboth. And they set out from Oboth and camped at Iye-abarim, in the wilderness that is opposite Moab, toward the sunrise. (Numbers 21:10–11)

The name of the first, Oboth, derives from *'ôb*, which, as we've noted, refers to necromancy, the practice of summoning and consulting

---

5 Ibid., p. 1.
6 Based on Strong's Hebrew H58, "grassy meadow or plain," or H57, "lamenting:—mourn(-er, -ing)."
7 T.E. Bunch, M.A. LeCompte, A.V. Adedeji, et al. "A Tunguska sized airburst destroyed Tall el-Hammam a Middle Bronze Age city in the Jordan Valley near the Dead Sea." *Scientific Reports* 11, 18632 (2021), p. 48.
8 Collins and Scott, op. cit.

with spirits of the dead.[9] This suggests that the site had a reputation for supernatural activity, or was perhaps a center for the cult of the dead.

This is a controversial topic among Christians. Those of us who take the Bible seriously are inclined to believe that there's no such thing as ghosts. But there is nothing in the biblical account to suggest that the spirit who delivered God's message to Saul was anything but the ghost of Samuel—who, it's important to note, was called an *elohim* as he emerged from the earth.[10]

"Elohim" is not a proper name, and it doesn't refer specifically to "gods." It's a designator of place, like "American" or "New Yorker." Spirits live in the spirit realm, but not all spirits are equal. Some are archangels and others are demons, but all are spirits. In the same way, spirits are all *elohim*, even the spirits of dead humans, but there is only one capital-*E* Elohim.

But this goes deeper. *'Ôb*, in turn, is related to the Hebrew word *'ab*, which means "father." In the Old Testament, the word "fathers" often refers to one's dead ancestors. For example:

And when the time drew near that Israel [Jacob] must die, he called his son Joseph and said to him, "If now I have found favor in your sight, put your hand under my thigh and promise to deal kindly and truly with me. Do not bury me in Egypt, but let me lie with my fathers [*ăbōt*]. (Genesis 47:29–30)

Looking at all of this in context, we can safely say that Oboth, one of the stations of the Exodus named in Numbers 21:10–11 and Numbers 33:43–44, essentially means "Spirits of the Dead."[11]

---

9   Joseph Tropper, "Spirit of the Dead." In K. van der Toorn, B. Becking, & P. W. van der Horst (Eds.), *Dictionary of Deities and Demons in the Bible* (2nd extensively rev. ed.) (Leiden; Boston; Köln; Grand Rapids, MI; Cambridge: Brill; Eerdmans, 1999), p. 806.

10 1 Samuel 28:13.

11 Spronk (1986), op. cit., p. 229.

The other location mentioned in those verses, Iye-abarim (or "ruins of the Abarim"), is based on the same root. Abarim is the anglicized form of *ōbĕrîm*, a plural form of the verb *'br*, which means "to pass from one side to the other."[12] In this context, it refers to a spirit that passes from one plane of existence to another, or crosses over, in the same sense that the ancient Greeks believed that the dead traveled across the River Styx to reach or return from the underworld.

The placement of Oboth and Iye-abarim in Numbers 33 suggests that they were east of the Dead Sea, close to Mount Nebo and the Plains of Moab. This is confirmed by the proximity of Shittim to Beth-Peor. And that's a name that needs a deeper dive.

Peor is related to the Hebrew root *p'r*, which means "cleft" or "gap," or "open wide."[13] In this context, that's consistent with Isaiah's description of the entrance to the netherworld:

Therefore Sheol has enlarged its appetite and opened [*pa'ar*] its mouth beyond measure. (Isaiah 5:14)

This is similar to the Canaanite conception of their god of death, Mot, who was described in Ugaritic texts as a ravenous entity with a truly monstrous mouth:

He extends a lip to the earth, a lip to the heavens, he extends a tongue to the stars.[14]

---

12 Klaas Spronk, "Travellers." In K. van der Toorn, B. Becking, & P. W. van der Horst (Eds.), *Dictionary of Deities and Demons in the Bible* (2nd extensively rev. ed.) (Leiden; Boston; Köln; Grand Rapids, MI; Cambridge: Brill; Eerdmans, 1999), p. 876.

13 Klaas Spronk, "Baal of Peor." In K. van der Toorn, B. Becking, & P.W. van der Horst (Eds.), *Dictionary of Deities and Demons in the Bible* (2nd extensively rev. ed.) (Leiden; Boston; Köln; Grand Rapids, MI; Cambridge: Brill; Eerdmans, 1999), p. 147.

14 KTU 1.5, ii, 1. In Nicolas Wyatt, *Religious Texts from Ugarit* (2nd ed.) (London; New York: Sheffield Academic Press, 2002), p. 120.

It appears, then, that Baal-Peor was the "lord of the entrance to the netherworld," or, perhaps, "lord of the gates of hell." So, Beth-Peor, the "house (or temple) of the entrance to the netherworld," was near the plains of Moab and Mount Nebo, which God called "this mountain of the Abarim."[15]

All of this leads to the *real* reason God was angry with the Israelites when they camped at Shittim. Contrary to the impression given in the Book of Numbers, the worship of Baal-Peor was not about sexual fertility rites:

> Then they yoked themselves to the Baal of Peor,
> and **ate sacrifices offered to the dead;**
> they provoked the Lord to anger with their deeds,
> and a plague broke out among them.
> Then Phinehas stood up and intervened,
> and the plague was stayed. (Psalm 106:28–30, emphasis added)

Writing four hundred years after the incident at Shittim, the psalmist didn't even mention the young couple caught in the act by Phinehas. It was eating sacrifices offered to the dead—an effort to open the gates of hell and communicate directly with the gods of the netherworld.

---

15 Deuteronomy 32:49.

CHAPTER TWENTY-FOUR

AMONG THE DEAD
OF THE VALLEY

*Do not turn to mediums or necromancers; do not seek them out, and
so make yourselves unclean by them: I am the LORD your God.*

—LEVITICUS 19:31 (ESV)

The practice of trying to communicate with spirits in the Great
Below obviously angered Yahweh. But, despite God smiting
twenty-four thousand Israelites on the plains of Moab for that sin, the
people of Israel were slow to learn the lesson.

But you, draw near,
    sons of the sorceress,
      offspring of the adulterer and the loose woman.
Whom are you mocking?
    Against whom do you open your mouth wide
    and stick out your tongue?
Are you not children of transgression,
    the offspring of deceit,
you who burn with lust among the oaks,
    under every green tree,
who slaughter your children in the valleys,
    under the clefts of the rocks?
Among the smooth stones of the valley is your portion;
    they, they, are your lot;

to them you have poured out a drink offering,
  you have brought a grain offering.
  Shall I relent for these things? (Isaiah 57:3–6)

Isaiah wrote nearly seven hundred years after the Exodus, but in his day the Israelites were still engaged in the occult practices that compelled God to afflict them with a devastating plague. To "burn with lust among the oaks" suggests fertility rites, which seems obvious given the prophet's condemnation of the children of the adulteress and "loose woman," which is also rendered "prostitute" and "whore" in other English translations. Ah, but once again there is more in the Bible verse than meets the English-reading eye.

The Hebrew word translated "sorceress," 'anan, is difficult to pin down. "Witch" and "fortune teller" have also been used in translation. More likely, however, is a correlation with the Arabic 'anna, meaning "to appear," which suggests that the sorceress was in fact a female necromancer.[1]

This may explain why the word rendered "oaks" or "terebinths," normally spelled 'êlîm, is 'ēlîm in Isaiah 57:5. This could be a scribal error, but it seems more likely that it's the same word we find in Psalm 29:1:

Ascribe to the LORD, O heavenly beings (bƏnē 'ēlîm; literally, "sons of God"),
Ascribe to the LORD glory and strength.

As in the story of Saul and the medium of En-dor, the Hebrew word elohim and its shortened form, elim, were used to refer to dead ancestors. So, Isaiah wasn't necessarily railing against sex rites among the sacred oaks. The prophet's words might be more accurately rendered, "You sons of the *necromancer*...who burn with lust *among the spirits of the dead.*" It's likely the prophet was engaging in the wordplay

---

1   Theodore J. Lewis, "Death Cult Imagery in Isaiah 57." *Hebrew Annual Review* 11 (1987), p. 271.

for which he's well known, using a pun to emphasize the spirits behind the rituals—the *'êlîm* among the *'êlîm*.[2]

Isaiah continues his diatribe by connecting the death cult to the rites of Molech. The valley of the son of Hinnom, later called Gehenna, was the location of the Tophet where Israelites sacrificed their children to the dark god of the underworld.[3] The Valley of Hinnom surrounds Jerusalem's Old City on the south and west, connecting on the west with the Valley of Rephaim (interesting coincidence) and merging with the Kidron Valley near the southeastern corner of the city. It's still as Isaiah described it nearly twenty-seven hundred years ago, a narrow, rocky ravine used as a place for burying the dead. Tombs along the sides of the valley are plainly visible to visitors to Jerusalem today. This helps us better understand the real meaning behind verse 6, which begins, "among the smooth stones of the valley is your portion."

An alternative understanding of the phrase *challeqe-nachal*, "smooth things of the wadi," is the "dead" of the wadi. This meaning is based on examples of the related Semitic word *chalaq* found in Arabic and Ugaritic with the meaning "die, perish."[4]

This brings the picture into focus. This chapter of Isaiah is obscure and hard to understand only if we read it without understanding what the prophet knew about the Amorite cult of the dead. This is confirmed by the next few verses of the chapter:

On a high and lofty mountain
   you have set your bed,
   and there you went up to offer sacrifice.
Behind the door and the doorpost
   you have set up your memorial;

---

2   Susan Ackerman, "Sacred Sex, Sacrifice, and Death." *Bible Review* 6:1 (February 1990). https://www.baslibrary.org/bible-review/6/1/9, retrieved 7/23/19. Fertility rites in sacred groves are mentioned in Isaiah 1:29-30, Hosea 4:12–13, and Ezekiel 20:28.

3   2 Kings 23:10, Jeremiah 7:31 and 19:6.

4   Faithlife Study Bible. See also Lewis, op. cit., pp. 272–273.

for, deserting me, you have uncovered your bed,
    you have gone up to it,
    you have made it wide;
and you have made a covenant for yourself with them,
    you have loved their bed,
    you have looked on nakedness.
You journeyed to the king with oil
    and multiplied your perfumes;
you sent your envoys far off,
    and sent down even to Sheol. (Isaiah 57:3–9)

The high places were almost constantly in use in Israel and Judah even during the reigns of kings who tried to do right by God, like Hezekiah. The imagery of adultery and sexual license is a common metaphor in the Old Testament for the spiritual infidelity of God's people. But even here, there are some deeper things to bring out.

This section of Scripture confirms that the target of Isaiah's condemnation was a cult of the dead, which necessarily required opening a portal to the underworld. Because Hebrew is a consonantal language (no vowels), similar words in the original Hebrew text, written before diacritical marks were used to indicate vowels, can be confusing. Verse 9 is a case in point. The consonants *mem*, *lamed*, and *kaph* can be used for *melech* ("king," which is how it's interpreted in Isaiah 57:9), *malik* ("messenger," a type of angel), or the name of the god Molech. Considering what precedes that verse, specifically Isaiah's reference to slaughtering children in the valleys, the latter option is most likely.

So, Isaiah 57:3–9 should be understood as God's condemnation of the worship of the dead. Isaiah calls out the "sons of the necromancer" who "burn with passion" among the spirits of the dead, sacrificing their children among the dead of the wadis, who were offered food and drink consistent with the Amorite *kispum* ritual for the ancestral dead.

But it was worse than that—apostate Jews, from the days of Moses down through the time of Isaiah and beyond, "journeyed to Molech with oil…and sent down even to Sheol," opening the gates of the netherworld to summon spirits worshiped as the long-dead, mighty kings of old.

As noted earlier, tens of thousands of megalithic monuments to the ancient cult of the dead remain in Israel and Jordan, mainly in the Jordan River valley, the Golan Heights, and on the hills overlooking the Huleh Valley. The most common of those monuments are the dolmens, funerary monuments whose exact function is still debated by scholars.

Over the centuries, tomb robbers have removed most of the useful evidence from the dolmens of the Jordan River valley. While the builders may have been Rephaim, the few bones left behind in burial chambers don't show any evidence of giantism to the best of our knowledge.

Interestingly, the team that excavated at Tall el-Hammam, the site of ancient Sodom, for sixteen seasons through 2023, found a cluster of about five hundred dolmens at the base of the hill on which the city was built. As many as fifteen hundred once stood there, along with menhirs (standing stones), henges, and stone circles. Get this: It's the largest such collection of megalithic structures in the Levant.[5] At the risk of putting too fine a point on it, let us emphasize that *they were just outside the walls of a city obliterated by God with fire from the sky.*

One of those dolmens, thankfully, has been shielded over the centuries from the inquisitive eyes of "night diggers," as archaeologists call illegal artifact hunters. Contrary to what we might assume, based on the finds inside Dolmen 78 at the Hammam Megalithic Field (HMF), it appears that dolmens were not used as tombs, but instead were used in rituals connected to the cult of the dead:

> At least at Tall el-Hammam, it would seem these structures represented some sort of ongoing memorials, most likely built and maintained by families. The HMF was not a cemetery but

---

5   Collins and Scott, op. cit., pp. 30–31.

used as a sacred memorial "garden" and a place for ritual ongoing gatherings, remembrance of ancestors and even interring of relic objects (ceramic or bone) in honor of those who had passed on.[6]

Bear in mind that Tall el-Hammam (Sodom) was continuously occupied from about 4500 BC until its destruction sometime around 1700 BC.[7] Ceramics found inside Dolmen 78 covered a timespan from the Late Chalcolithic (4000–3300 BC) through Intermediate Bronze II (2000–1650 BC).[8] That means the dolmens of Sodom represent an unbroken tradition of venerating the dead that was more than fifteen hundred years old when God destroyed the city in the time of Abraham and Lot!

Tall el-Hammam rises seventy-five to one hundred fifty feet above the southern Jordan valley. So, the stone monuments and the ruined, still-deserted city would have been plainly visible to Moses and the Israelites who camped on the plains of Moab. It's even possible that Iye-Abarim, "Ruins of the Travelers," was among the rubble of the city. Archaeologist Nelson Glueck visited Tall el-Hammam in 1941 and identified the hilltop site as Abel-Shittim,[9] an identity that is generally accepted by scholars today.[10]

Dr. Phillip Silvia, director of scientific analysis for the Tall el-Hammam Excavation Project, told Derek in a 2019 interview that the dolmens, unlike some others in the Jordan valley, aren't aligned with any obvious astronomical features such as solstices, the equinox, or

---

6   Gary L. Byars, "Let the Stones Cry Out? Dolmens and Megalithic Standing Stones in the Biblical World." *Associates for Biblical Research*, October 14, 2020. https://biblearchaeology.org/research/topics/architecture-structures-in-the-bible /4741-let-the-stones-cry-out-dolmens-and-megalithic-standing-stones-in-the -biblical-world, retrieved 2/12/24.

7   Silvia, op. cit., p. 33.

8   Byars, op. cit.

9   Kay Prag, "Preliminary Report on the Excavations at Tell Iktanu and Tell al-Hammam, Jordan, 1990." *Levant* 23:1 (1991), pp. 55–66.

10 Byars, op. cit.

major constellations. Instead, they appear to be oriented toward what is believed to be the location of the sacred precinct of Sodom.[11]

It's an intriguing possibility: Moses may have directed the Israelites to set up the Tabernacle right on top of the ruins of the temple of Baal-Peor, Lord of the Gates of Hell. And, as we'll explain the next chapter, it was also the location of the threshing floor of Atad, to which Joseph, centuries earlier, led an entourage from Goshen to mourn his father Jacob for seven days. Thereafter, the Canaanites called the place Abel-Mizraim—Mourning Place of the Egyptians.

The takeaway is this: For more than a thousand years, people living in lands the Bible identifies as the home of Rephaim tribes built burial tombs using massive slabs of limestone and basalt. Those huge burial tombs inspired place names linked to the dolmen-builders (Iye-Abarim, "ruins of the Travelers") and the restless dead (Oboth, "Spirits of the Dead"). And remember, even the place where Moses died was called the Mountain of the Travelers:

> Go up this mountain of the Abarim ["Travelers"], Mount Nebo, which is in the land of Moab, opposite Jericho, and view the land of Canaan, which I am giving to the people of Israel for a possession. And die on the mountain which you go up, and be gathered to your people, as Aaron your brother died in Mount Hor and was gathered to his people....
>
> So Moses the servant of the LORD died there in the land of Moab, according to the word of the LORD, and he buried him in the valley in the land of Moab opposite Beth-peor; but no one knows the place of his burial to this day. (Deuteronomy 32:49–50, 34:5–6)

Moses was buried in the valley of the Travelers, a place where the Rephaim spirits were believed to cross over to the land of the living.

---

11   "Dr. Phillip Silvia: The Science of Finding Sodom." *A View from the Bunker*, February 3, 2019. https://www.vftb.net/?p=7604, retrieved 2/12/24.

Is that why Satan thought he had a claim to Moses' body after his death?[12] And it was in that valley, the plains of Moab, where the Israelites angered God by worshiping Baal-Peor and eating sacrifices offered to the dead.

Yes, the Canaanites believed the entrance to the underworld was at Bashan. But both Milcom (whom the Hebrews called Molech) and Chemosh, the patron gods of Ammon and Moab, the nations that controlled much of the land east of the Jordan River between Bashan and the Dead Sea, demanded child sacrifice.[13] Veneration of the dead and appeasing the gods of the netherworld through human sacrifice appear to have been the norm in this region. In earlier times, it was also the location of Sodom and Gomorrah.

That's a lot of evil in a relatively small area. Is this where we find the gates of hell?

---

12 See Jude 9.
13 For child sacrifice to Chemosh, see 2 Kings 3:27.

CHAPTER TWENTY-FIVE

THRESHING FLOORS
AND PORTALS

They mounted their chariots,
*   they came on their mounts.*
They journeyed a day
*   and a second.*
After sunrise on the third
*   the [Rephaim] arrived at the threshing-floors,*
*   the [elohim] at the plantations.*

—KTU 1.22 II 21–27 (Nicolas Wyatt translation)

It's not a coincidence that David purchased the threshing floor of the Hurrian king Araunah as the future site of Solomon's Temple. In our book *Veneration*, Sharon devoted an entire chapter to the role of threshing floors as portals between the natural world and the spirit realm:

These were communal spaces in the human sense, in that the floors were often clustered together, allowing locals to share news while working. But they were also communal in the spiritual sense, allowing contact with local deities. In fact, the Canaanite word for "grain" is *dagan*, which is very close to the name of their grain-god, Dagan (later called "Dagon" by the Philistines of Samson's day). Around the time of Abraham and

Isaac, Dagan was called *bēl pagrē* at the Syrian city of Mari, an epithet that's been translated "lord of corpse offerings, lord of corpses (a netherworld god), lord of funerary offerings, and lord of human sacrifices." This has led some scholars to conclude that Dagan was at least a god with a strong connection to the underworld, if not part of the royal ancestor cult—and perhaps the recipient of human sacrifice.[1]

Even the circular shape of the threshing floor is a callback to the magic circle dug into the dirt floor of the *abi*. And just as the threshing-floor/portal connects Mount Hermon to Mount Zion, so too does the Transfiguration of Jesus on "a high mountain"[2] near Caesarea Philippi, which can only have been Hermon. Think about that! Jesus literally stepped onto the threshing floor of El, declared his divinity by transforming into a being of light, and then proceeded on to Jerusalem to fulfill his mission—which, as you know, culminated with his resurrection from the dead on the third day.

In fact, this may be the hidden meaning of Psalm 82. On the surface, the psalm is startling enough—essentially a courtroom scene in heaven during which God proclaims a death sentence on rebellious *elohim*!

> God has taken his place in the divine council;
>> in the midst of the gods he holds judgment:
> "How long will you judge unjustly
>> and show partiality to the wicked? *Selah* [...]
> I said, "You are gods,
>> sons of the Most High, all of you;
> nevertheless, like men you shall die,
>> and fall like any prince." (Psalm 82:1–2, 6–7)

---

1   Sharon K. Gilbert and Derek P. Gilbert, *Veneration* (Crane, Mo.: Defender, 2019), p. 110.

2   Matthew 17:1.

The phrase translated "divine council" is the Hebrew *'adat 'el*, which can be translated "assembly of El," the creator-god of the Canaanites. In Derek's book *The Second Coming of Saturn*, he showed that El was known to other cultures in the ancient world as Enlil, Assur, Dagan/Dagon, Baal Hammon, Kronos, and Saturn. The Israelites—at least, those who were faithful to God—knew him as Molech. And when the evidence is pieced together, we find that this creature was Shemihazah, the chief of the Watcher-class elohim whose rebellion is mentioned briefly in Genesis 6:1–4.

In other words, if the "assembly of El" translation is correct—and that is precisely how the New English Translation renders the verse—then Psalm 82 describes Yahweh, the God of Israel, suddenly appearing in the midst of the *infernal* council to declare His righteous judgment!

But wait—there's more! Psalm 68 may describe this confrontation:

> O God, when you went out before your people,
>> when you marched through the wilderness, *Selah*
> the earth quaked, the heavens poured down rain,
>> before God, the One of Sinai,
>> before God, the God of Israel. [...]
> O mountain of God, mountain of Bashan;
>> O many-peaked mountain, mountain of Bashan!
> Why do you look with hatred, O many-peaked mountain,
>> at the mount that God desired for his abode,
>> yes, where the LORD will dwell forever?
> The chariots of God are twice ten thousand,
>> thousands upon thousands;
>> the Lord[3] is among them; Sinai is now in the sanctuary.
> You ascended on high,
>> leading a host of captives in your train

---

3   This instance of "Lord" does not use small caps because the Hebrew word is *adonai*, not *YHWH*.

and receiving gifts among men,
even among the rebellious, that the LORD God may
 dwell there. (Psalm 68:7–8, 15–18)

The "many-peaked mountain" of Bashan is Hermon, the southern-most peak of the Anti-Lebanon range. The "mount that God desired for His abode" is Zion; specifically, the Temple Mount in Jerusalem. Psalm 68 describes the tension between the two competing mounts of assembly: Hermon, the mountain sacred to El, and Zion, which God has chosen for His dwelling place.[4] This section of the 68th Psalm appears to describe a military assault in the heavenly realm against Mount Hermon, which was believed by the pagan Canaanites to be the headquarters of its pantheon, ruled by the creator-god El.

The last part of verse 17 is notoriously difficult to translate. The Masoretic Text, on which our English-language Old Testaments are based, literally reads, word for word, "the Lord among them, Sinai, in holiness." In English, that obviously makes no sense.

The NET Bible translators, assuming a scribal change,[5] renders it this way:

The Lord comes from Sinai in holy splendor. (Psalm 68:17, NET)

That makes more sense in the military context of the Psalm: God marched forth from Sinai, leading his people into battle. This can only refer to the Exodus. And the first military object of Moses and the Israelites was the kingdom of Bashan, ruled by Og, last of the remnant of the Rephaim.[6]

But God Himself appears to have done battle at Hermon, taking away "a host of captives" to boot! Was this the incident described in

---

4   Psalm 132:13.
5   Biblical Studies Press, op. cit., translator's note for Psalm 68:17.
6   Deuteronomy 3:11.

Psalm 82? Or might it be a prophecy of the Transfiguration? The Bible doesn't say, so we can only speculate.

The point of this detour is to establish the significance of Mount Hermon in the religion of the pagans who occupied Canaan when the Hebrews arrived from Egypt, and among whom the Israelites lived for centuries thereafter. This religion was the cult later reestablished by Jeroboam, who led the rebellion of the northern tribes against Rehoboam, the son of Solomon. Jeroboam's golden calves are usually explained by Bible teachers as an idolatrous variant of the worship of Yahweh, who was never supposed to be represented by graven images. However, given that the main epithet of the Canaanite creator-god was "Bull El," Jeroboam in fact tried to return the northern tribes to the worship of the god who was thought to reign from Mount Hermon. The prophet Hosea specifically condemned Jeroboam's cult of Bull El.[7]

Further:

> [T]he Levites left their common lands and their holdings and came to Judah and Jerusalem, because Jeroboam and his sons cast them out from serving as priests of the LORD, and he appointed his own priests for the high places and for the goat idols and for the calves that he had made. (2 Chronicles 11:14–15)

The "goat idols" (Hebrew *se 'irim*), as with the golden calves, point to Mount Hermon.[8] The cult center of Caesarea Philippi, where Jesus

---

7 Hosea 8:6. The verse is difficult to translate as the Masoretic Hebrew text literally reads, "For from Israel. A craftsman made it; it is not God." Jewish scholar Naftali Herz Tur-Sinai, first president of Israel's Academy of Hebrew Language, suggested in 1950 that by regrouping the consonants (ancient Hebrew has no vowels), the verse reads, "For who is Bull El? A craftsman made it; it is not God" (emphasis added). See Nicolas Wyatt, "Calf" (1999), op. cit.

8 Judd H. Burton, "Religion, Society, and Sacred Space at Banias: A Religious History of Banias/Caesarea Philippi, 21 BC-AD 1635," doctoral dissertation at Texas Tech University, 2010.

asked Peter the crucial question, "Who do you say that I am?" is known to this day as Banias (Paneas) in honor of the Greek goat-god Pan. It was probably a center of worship of some type of nature deity like Pan prior to the arrival of the Greek army of Alexander the Great in the late fourth century BC. But, as we noted in an earlier chapter, the Hivites, who were Mycenaean Greeks, lived in the vicinity of Mount Hermon more than a thousand years earlier, in the time of Joshua.[9] So, Jeroboam's innovation in the tenth century BC was just a return to the old ways of the pagans who occupied the land before the Hebrews.

And that brings us back to the Rephaim Texts of the Amorite kingdom of Ugarit cited earlier. The use of threshing floors to communicate with the spirit realm is seen in the Bible. We've already mentioned David's purchase of the threshing floor of Araunah, but we can also look at the story of Gideon, who asked God for a sign with a fleece of wool on the threshing floor.[10]

About four centuries after Gideon, we find Ahab, king of Israel, and Jehoshaphat, king of Judah, sitting on their thrones at the threshing floor at the gate of Samaria while the four hundred prophets of Ahab counseled him to go to war against the king of Syria.[11] (Jehoshaphat knew something wasn't right with what he heard from Ahab's prophets because he asked, "Is there not here another prophet of the LORD of whom we may inquire?")[12]

The prophet Hosea, mentioned above, seems to have connected the cult veneration of El, condemned in chapter 8 of his book, to threshing floors:

Rejoice not, O Israel!
    Exult not like the peoples;
    for you have played the whore, forsaking your God.

---

9   Joshua 11:3.
10   Judges 6:36—40.
11   1 Kings 22:1–28; 2 Chronicles 18:1–27.
12   1 Kings 22:7; 2 Chronicles 18:6.

> You have loved a prostitute's wages
> on all threshing floors. (Hosea 9:1)

The use of prostitution imagery as a metaphor for spiritual wickedness is well known among the Hebrew prophets, especially Hosea.[13] While many Bible scholars connect the imagery of sexual immorality to Israel's abandonment of God, it's fair to say that the connection between threshing floors and portals is not as widely acknowledged.

Then there was the story of the strange ritual to mourn the death of Jacob:

> So Joseph went up to bury his father. With him went up all the servants of Pharaoh, the elders of his household, and all the elders of the land of Egypt, as well as all the household of Joseph, his brothers, and his father's household. Only their children, their flocks, and their herds were left in the land of Goshen. And there went up with him both chariots and horsemen. It was a very great company. When they came to the threshing floor of Atad, which is beyond the Jordan, they lamented there with a very great and grievous lamentation, and he made a mourning for his father seven days. When the inhabitants of the land, the Canaanites, saw the mourning on the threshing floor of Atad, they said, "This is a grievous mourning by the Egyptians." Therefore the place was named Abel-mizraim; it is beyond the Jordan. (Genesis 50:7–11)

"Beyond the Jordan," as we've already explained, means the land east of the Jordan River. If you take a moment to look at a map and locate Hebron, where Jacob was finally laid to rest with his father and grandfather, Isaac and Abraham, you'll see that it's *west* of the Dead Sea. The threshing floor of Atad, being east of the Jordan, means that

---

13 Jaime L. Walters, *Threshing Floors in Ancient Israel: Their Ritual and Symbolic Significance* (Minneapolis: Augsburg Fortress Publishers, 2015), pgs. 30–31.

Joseph and the funeral entourage had to go all the way around the Dead Sea, since the Jordan ends at the sea.

So, where specifically was the threshing floor of Atad? It was probably located where Moses and the Israelites camped before Joshua led them across the Jordan into Canaan—Tall el-Hammam, eight miles northeast of the Dead Sea, which has been convincingly identified as the site of Sodom:[14]

> "Atad" was not understood by the King James translators—they assumed this word to be a proper name and did not translate it. Most English versions since then have followed this same translation. The word is now known to mean "thorns." The phrase translated "threshing floor" also has the connotation of a "high place." Thus, "the threshing floor of Atad" would be better translated "the high place of thorns." This would be an apt description of the Lower Tall of Hammam at that time since thorn bushes are among the first of the colonizing species that would return to the site following its cataclysmic destruction. In both verses 9 and 11, this location is described as being "beyond [or across] the Jordan." This description always uses Jerusalem as the point of reference, hence, the high place of thorns would have to be on the east side of the Jordan above the flood plain. Again, the Lower Tall of Hammam is the most likely candidate for Abel Mizraim, the "mourning place of the Egyptians."[15] (brackets added)

Why there? Why would Joseph travel the long way around the Dead Sea instead of taking a direct route from Egypt to Hebron? The detour meant mourning his father on the site of a city destroyed by God several centuries earlier, a story that must surely have been known to the Israelites, if not everyone in the Levant.

---

14 Collins and Scott, op. cit.
15 Phillip J. Silvia, "The Geography and History of Tall el-Hammam." *Society for Interdisciplinary Studies Chronology & Catastrophism Workshop* (2014:1), p. 36.

It is likely that for the Israelites, threshing floors in general, and perhaps that threshing floor in particular, had associations with the spirit realm and the underworld.[16]

---

16 Andrew Tobolowsky, "Where Doom is Spoken: Threshing Floors as Places of Decision and Communication in Biblical Literature." Journal of Ancient Near Eastern Religions 16:1 (2016), pgs. 95–120.

CHAPTER TWENTY-SIX

PORTALS
IN THE GARDEN

I spread out my hands all the day
*   to a rebellious people,*
who walk in a way that is not good,
*   following their own devices;*
a people who provoke me
*   to my face continually,*
sacrificing in gardens
*   and making offerings on bricks...*

—Isaiah 65:2–3 (ESV)

Human history began in a garden. Many of the myths and legends told by bards, storytellers, shamans, and priests through the ages originated with a dim, shared memory of a lost paradise. Much of the blood, sweat, and tears shed by mankind over the millennia has been in the service of gods who promised our ancestors a path back to that paradise.

The concept of "garden" has changed over time. Today, we think of a pleasant patch of earth for flowers, vegetables, fruit, or maybe herbs we can pick to spice up our cooking. It wasn't that way in the beginning.

To really understand what God communicated through His prophets and apostles, we need to get inside their heads. Reading the Bible with the worldview of the ancient Hebrews takes a little work, but it's worth it. The payoff is seeing the stories we've known since Sunday school through new eyes, almost as children reading them for the first time. It will bring a level of excitement to your study of God's Word you haven't felt in years, if ever, and it will instill a deep appreciation for what's at stake in this long, supernatural war, and for God's sacrifice to get you off the battlefield in one piece—and bring you back to where it all began—Eden.

The original garden wasn't what we think of when we hear the word, and neither were the gardens in the days of the Hebrew prophets and apostles. There is a spiritual sense to the word that's been lost over the years. Archaeologists who specialize in the ancient Near East—the lands we now call Israel, Jordan, Lebanon, Syria, and Iraq—have known this for some time.

Gardens held a special place in the culture of the ancient Near East, and it was part of a very different way of looking at the world. It wasn't just because they lacked modern conveniences, our understanding of science, and access to the Internet, but because the spirit realm was part of daily life—something we've lost in the modern world, especially in the West. Part and parcel of their reality was interacting with the dead.

The dead were gone only in the physical sense. It was understood that those who'd gone before had moved on to a different type of existence. It wasn't necessarily enjoyable, and one's happiness in the afterlife depended on his or her descendants performing the correct rituals every month.

The exception was the dead kings of old. They held a place of esteem in the afterlife. Pagan kings of the ancient Near East aspired to join the ranks of their venerated fathers who could still affect the world of the living. To that end, rituals were performed at special locations—and that brings us back to gardens.

The modern word "garden" has a much different connotation today than it did three thousand years ago. Today, it evokes images of flowers or vegetables, carefully tended to yield blossoms or produce, according to their kind. Back in the day, however, gardens were often reserved for royalty, and not only because kings and queens naturally get the best stuff.

For example, we read in the Bible that the son and grandson of Judah's king Hezekiah, Manasseh and Amon, were buried in a garden. That seems a little odd, although modern cemeteries often incorporate "garden" into the name. In ancient Judah, however, burial chambers were usually cut into rock. Tombs of the kings of Judah were in the City of David, the narrow hill that extends south from the Temple Mount. But Manasseh and Amon weren't buried with their fathers; they were interred "in the garden of Uzza,"[1] which was apparently connected to the palace. Uzza may be King Uzziah (also called Azariah), the great-grandfather of Hezekiah, who ruled Judah from about 791 to 740 BC. What was special about his garden? And why wasn't it used for royal burials until Manasseh died about a hundred years after the death of Uzziah?

To find the answer, we must look at Near Eastern culture long before the time of Hezekiah and Manasseh. It's also important to remember that Manasseh was not one for holding to the teachings of Moses and the prophets. God Himself said through His prophets that Manasseh "has done things more evil than all that the Amorites did, who were before him,"[2] namely, setting up altars to "all the host of heaven" in the courts of the Temple, burned his son as an offering, presumably to Molech, and consulted with mediums and necromancers.[3]

The practice of *kispum*, the ritual meal offered to the ancestral dead probably originated with the Amorites. While there is some disagreement among scholars, it's generally agreed that these Semitic-speaking people moved from northern Mesopotamia to the southeast, the regions of Akkad and Sumer, in the second half of the third millennium BC,[4] bringing this practice with them.

---

1   2 Kings 21:18, 26.
2   2 Kings 21:11.
3   2 Kings 21:3–7.
4   MacDougal, op. cit., p. 26.

Texts from Ebla, probably the most powerful kingdom of the third millennium BC in northwestern Mesopotamia, reveal a pattern of religious rituals that connect the royal family and its deceased ancestors to the gods. The marriage of a royal couple in Ebla required the pair, accompanied by priests, scribes, and other officials, to set out on a ritual journey from the palace to the temples of various gods outside the city, and then to a special location to make offerings to the divinized kings of old. From there, the entourage traveled to the mausoleum of dead ancestors, which they reached on the seventh day. This apparently linked the royal family, embodied in the palace and the underground tombs beneath it, to the gods.[5] In other words, the time-consuming ritual connected palace and grave, a reminder to all that the living king was entwined with his royal ancestors at a cosmic level.[6]

This interpretation is confirmed by tomb artifacts from Ebla and other ancient cities from what is now northern Syria, such as Qatna and Halab (modern Aleppo), the seat of Yamkhad, the most powerful Amorite kingdom in Mesopotamia until the rise of Babylon in the eighteenth century BC, the time of Abraham. For example, a bone talisman found in the "Tomb of the Lord of the Goats," probably the final resting place of Ebla's king Immeya, a contemporary of Isaac and Jacob (reigned c. 1750–1725 BC), illustrates two scenes. The first shows the king at a meal, probably the *kispum* ritual for the newly deceased monarch, symbolizing his acceptance into the company of the divinized dead.[7]

The talisman's reverse side depicts Immeya as a human-headed bull and venerated by other characters. Although this sounds weird to us in the twenty-first century, it's consistent with texts from the

---

5   Nicola Laneri, "Embodying the Memory of the Royal Ancestors in Western Syria During the 3rd and 2nd Millennia BC: The Case of Ebla and Qatna." In D. Nadali (ed.), *Envisioning the Past Through Memories* (New York: Bloomsbury Academic, 2016), pp. 58–59.

6   Ibid., p. 62.

7   Andrea Polcaro, "The Bone Talisman and the Ideology of Ancestors in Old Syrian Ebla: Tradition and Innovation in the Royal Funerary Ritual Iconography." In P. Matthiae (ed.), *Studia Eblaitica* (Wiesbaden: Harrassowitz Verlag, 2015), p. 190.

Amorite kingdom of Mari, which was based on the Euphrates River near the modern border between Iraq and Syria, that described the dead king's transformation into an *Aladlammu*, "a celestial guardian of the kingdom comparable with the *rapi'uma* [Rephaim] of the later Ugaritic tradition."[8]

Likewise, as we mentioned in a previous chapter, a cylinder seal from Yamkhad from about the same period shows three scenes in horizontal rows related to the cult of the ancestors. The top row depicts the chief deities of the kingdom, featuring the chief god of Aleppo, Hadad (Baal) the storm-god, his consort, and the plague-god and gatekeeper of the underworld, Resheph. The bottom row shows the new king of the land enthroned, attended by court officials. The middle register represents the *rapi'uma* (Rephaim) summoned to the funeral ceremony, presumably to welcome the newly deceased king.[9]

The bottom line is that Amorite kingdoms in northwestern Mesopotamia like Ebla, Mari, Yamkhad, and Qatna displayed "an astonishing continuity in the basic religious institution and cult practice represented by the cult for the deified royal ancestors, the Rapi'uma/Rephaim of the Ugaritic texts."[10]

In other words, Moses and the Israelites didn't invent the Rephaim to justify the conquest of Canaan. While ritual texts explicitly describe the veneration of the Rephaim (and the Ditanu/Titans) in the Amorite kingdom of Ugarit around 1200 BC, the middle of the period of the judges in Israel, older grave goods, inscriptions, and palace art confirm that these religious practices, including the belief that the kings of the land would take their place among the Rephaim in the underworld after death, were the norm among the Amorites at least a thousand years earlier. And since this complex system of beliefs and rituals didn't spring into the minds of Ebla's priests immediately before they inscribed the ritual tablets, the veneration of dead ancestors, kings,

---

8 Ibid., p. 191.
9 Matthiae, op. cit.
10 Ibid., p. 6.

and Rephaim is probably much older, maybe extending back before 3000 BC.

Remember, the Rephaim were the spirits of the demigod Nephilim destroyed in the Flood of Noah. Amorite kings from Babylon to Ugarit claimed descent from those pre-Flood "mighty men who were of old," summoned them through rituals, offered sacrifices to them,[11] and apparently believed that these "warriors of Baal" were revivified—resurrected—by their creator-god El at his threshing floor (or tabernacle) on the summit of Mount Hermon.[12]

Now, why is all this relevant to Christians? Keep following this thread: One of the ritual texts from Ugarit, labeled KTU 1.106, specifies sacrifices to various gods including deified dead kings and Resheph, a deity connected to the dead as gatekeeper to the underworld.[13] Some of the sacrifices were to be performed in the garden, which is *gn* in both Ugaritic and Hebrew. This festival took place in the month of *gn* ("Gannu"), March/April in our calendar, a time when gardens are coming into bloom.

Resheph is designated *ršp gn* in two other Ugaritic texts, perhaps meaning "Resheph of the Garden."[14] This is a cognate (same meaning, different language) with the Eblaite phrase *rasap gunu(m)ki*.[15] So, why offer sacrifice in a garden to the god who was gatekeeper the underworld? It comes down to the purpose of the garden. In the Amorite world of the ancient Near East, gardens were not simply for growing pretty flowers; it was where the cult of the royal ancestors performed the rites to summon and feed the divinized kings of old. Understanding this concept helps us make sense of some confusing passages in the Old Testament.

---

11 Jordi Vidal, "The Origins of the Last Ugaritic Dynasty." *Altorientalishce Forschungen* 33 (2006), p. 168.

12 Wyatt (2002), op. cit.

13 Francesca Stavrakapolou, "Exploring the Garden of Uzza: Death, Burial and Ideologies of Kingship." *Biblica* Vol. 87 (2006), p. 13.

14 Michael Dahood and Giovanni Pettinato, "Ugaritic *ršp gn* and Eblaite *rasap gunu(m)ki*." *Orientalia*, NOVA SERIES, Vol. 46, No. 2 (1977), p. 230.

15 Ibid.

I spread out my hands all the day
    to a rebellious people,
who walk in a way that is not good,
    following their own devices;
a people who provoke me
    to my face continually,
sacrificing in gardens
    and making offerings on bricks;
who sit in tombs,
    and spend the night in secret places;
who eat pig's flesh,
    and broth of tainted meat is in their vessels;
who say, "Keep to yourself,
    do not come near me, for I am too holy for you." (Isaiah 65:2–5)

Those who sanctify and purify themselves to go into the gardens, following one in the midst, eating pig's flesh and the abomination and mice, shall come to an end together, declares the LORD. (Isaiah 66:17)

It's clear from Isaiah that there was a cultic connection between gardens and tombs. Scholars have also noted that the pig was an animal associated with the underworld,[16] used by the Greeks in chthonian rituals[17] and by the Amorites and other pagan cultures in sacrifices to the dead. In fact, some scholars believe that the use of pigs primarily as sacrificial offerings to the gods of the underworld and the dead[18] may be the reason for the taboo against eating pork.[19]

---

16   Stavrakapolou, op. cit., p. 9.

17   Nicolas Wyatt, "After Death Has Us Parted." In *The Perfumes of Seven Tamarisks* (Munster: Ugarit-Verlaine, 2014), p. 285.

18   Ismar Schorsch, "The Story of Pig as Taboo," *Jewish Theological Seminary* (April 17, 2004). http://www.jtsa.edu/the-story-of-pig-as-taboo, retrieved 2/25/24.

19   Wyatt, op. cit.

The cultic use of gardens may be the reason that chroniclers of the Old Testament noted that two of worst kings of the line of David were buried in a garden rather than the tombs of their forefathers. Manasseh, son of Hezekiah, "was buried in the garden of his house, in the garden of Uzza."[20] Manasseh's son Amon was likewise buried in the garden of Uzza.[21]

All the previous kings of Judah, from David to Hezekiah, had been buried in the royal tombs in the City of David. Why did Manasseh break with tradition? It's consistent with his character; unlike his father, who "did what was right in the eyes of the LORD,"[22] Manasseh is remembered as the most wicked king in Judah's history.[23]

> He did what was evil in the sight of the LORD, according to the despicable practices of the nations whom the LORD drove out before the people of Israel. For he rebuilt the high places that Hezekiah his father had destroyed, and he erected altars for Baal and made an Asherah, as Ahab king of Israel had done, and worshiped all the host of heaven and served them. And he built altars in the house of the LORD, of which the LORD had said, "In Jerusalem will I put my name." And he built altars for all the host of heaven in the two courts of the house of the LORD. And he burned his son as an offering and used fortune-telling and omens and dealt with mediums and with necromancers. He did much evil in the sight of the LORD, provoking him to anger. (2 Kings 21:2–6)

In short, Manasseh went native and adopted the religion of the Amorites. That included summoning the dead through mediums and

---

20 2 Kings 21:18. 2 Chronicles 33:20 notes simply that "Manasseh slept with his fathers, and they buried him in his house."

21 2 Kings 21:26. 2 Chronicles 33 does not note the location of Amon's burial.

22 2 Kings 18:3.

23 Although, to be fair, 2 Chronicles 33:10–16 records that Manasseh repented and humbled himself before God.

necromancers and sacrificing his son to Molech—which, as we noted in an earlier chapter, was linked by God to the forbidden practice of contacting the spirits for favors or information. This is the first biblical record of a Judean king engaging in this occult practice, other than the visit by Saul to the medium of En-dor. This was so offensive to God that the author of 2 Kings wrote that Manasseh did things "more evil than all that the Amorites did,"[24] which was put an end to God's patience with the House of David.

Manesseh's decision to be buried in the garden of Uzza appears to be part of his slide into outright paganism. Manasseh, and his son after him, apparently aspired to become Rephaim after death. This is supported by the message God delivered to Ezekiel during his vision of the Temple Mount:

> While the man was standing beside me, I heard one speaking to me out of the temple, and he said to me, "Son of man, this is the place of my throne and the place of the soles of my feet, where I will dwell in the midst of the people of Israel forever. And **the house of Israel shall no more defile my holy name**, neither they, nor their kings, by their whoring and **by the dead bodies of their kings at their high places**, by setting their threshold by my threshold and their doorposts beside my doorposts, with only a wall between me and them. They have defiled my holy name by their abominations that they have committed, so I have consumed them in my anger. **Now let them put away their whoring and the dead bodies of their kings far from me**, and I will dwell in their midst forever. (Ezekiel 43:6–9, emphasis added)

We don't know where the King's Garden was, but it was apparently close to the Temple, probably in or adjacent to the City of David.

The pagan neighbors of ancient Israel had a long history of venerating dead royalty in special gardens set aside for that cult. What made this long-running practice disgusting to God was that it corrupted the

---

24   2 Kings 21:11.

concept of His *original* garden, Eden. And with Manasseh and Amon, it had reached His holy mountain.

Not all scholars agree that the Ugaritic *gn* and Eblaite/Akkadian *gunu* should be translated "garden." Respected scholar Edward Lipiński concluded that the term more accurately meant "camp," "enclosure," or "compound."[25] This is similar to a word from old Persian: "*Pairidēza*, borrowed into late Babylonian as *pardēsu*, into Hebrew as *pardēs*, and Greek as παράδεισος, appears to have meant originally 'rampart,' and hence a ramparted place, such as an enclosed royal garden."[26] As you've noticed, it's where we get the English word "paradise."

This is not a coincidence. If Eden doesn't fit the definition of "paradise," an enclosed royal garden, we would truly like to see the place that does.

Carl Gallups makes a strong case in his book *Gods of Ground Zero* that Eden was understood to be paradise by Jews of the Second Temple period.[27] This is biblical. In Ezekiel 28, God condemns the king of Tyre by comparing him to the rebel in Eden, who was on "the holy mountain of God."[28] This locates the garden on God's holy mountain, Zion. This means that Mount Moriah, where Abraham was tested, and the threshing floor of Araunah, which David bought for the site of the Temple, were right where Eden was and will be again—on the Temple Mount.

Placing Eden in the middle of Jerusalem might seem a little *too* obvious, but bear with us. The Book of Genesis describes the garden's location:

A river flowed out of Eden to water the garden, and there it divided and became four rivers. The name of the first is the Pishon. It is the one that flowed around the whole land of Havilah, where there is gold. And the gold of that land is good; bdellium

---

25 Wyatt, op. cit, p. 286.
26 Nicolas Wyatt, "A Royal Garden: The Ideology of Eden." *Scandinavian Journal of the Old Testament* Vol. 28, No. 1 (2014), p. 22.
27 Carl Gallups, *Gods of Ground Zero* (Crane, Mo.: Defender, 2018). See especially pages 241–243.
28 Ezekiel 28:13–14.

and onyx stone are there. The name of the second river is the Gihon. It is the one that flowed around the whole land of Cush. And the name of the third river is the Tigris, which flows east of Assyria. And the fourth river is the Euphrates. (Genesis 2:10–14)

It's easy enough to identify the Tigris and Euphrates, the rivers that flow from Turkey through Iraq and Syria, defining the Fertile Crescent. Likewise, the Gihon is simple enough, if we understand that the reference to Cush to be allegorical; as Jerusalem's only water supply, the Gihon Spring was vital to the holy city, and so it is probably the river meant by Moses in that passage.

That leaves only the Pishon. One intriguing explanation identifies it as the Nile, "from the Egyptian expression *p3 šny*, 'the encompassing one,' the river being conceptualised as an extension of the cosmic ocean surrounding the world."[29] This is plausible; after all, Moses was raised in the court of the king of Egypt, undoubtedly speaking and writing Egyptian.

If we are correct, the account in Genesis is a sort of cosmic model. A river flowed from Eden to become the three major sources of fresh water in the world known to the Israelites and the crucial spring that supplied water for the city that God had chosen as His own.

No doubt the river in the garden was the same one Ezekiel described in his vision of the future Temple. This, of course, locates the river of Eden beneath the Temple, the very throne of God, which will be on the site of Solomon's temple—Mount Moriah, the Temple Mount in Jerusalem.

By now, you've connected some dots in your mind that make the story of Jesus' betrayal, death, and resurrection positively spine-tingling. He was betrayed in Gethsemane, a garden at the foot of the Mount of Olives. Not only that, "in the place where he was crucified there was a garden, and in the garden a new tomb in which no one had yet been laid. So because of the Jewish day of Preparation, since the tomb was close at hand, they laid Jesus there."[30]

---

29 Wyatt (2014), op. cit., p. 11.
30 John 19:41–42.

Did you get that? Jesus was betrayed and crucified in a *garden*. The Infernal Council undoubtedly thought this was a great joke. In their minds, they'd desecrated Eden by killing the Son of the King! But then, at dawn of the third day, when the women went to the tomb, Mary Magdalene saw the resurrected Jesus—and *she thought He was the gardener*.

And so He is.

The Garden of Eden, *gan-bə ʿēḏɛn*, was a walled enclosure on the mountain of God[31] reserved for royalty—although in this case, we're talking about the King of Creation and His Divine Council. The Fallen lured the pagans of the ancient Near East into perverting the concept of the royal garden, turning them into cult places to open the gates of hell, portals to contact the Infernal Council, where dead human kings were venerated alongside the Rephaim, the demonic spirits of the Nephilim destroyed in the Flood.

This will not end well for them. The Gardener will return to the Mount of Olives[32] and *reclaim* His garden. He is the landowner of the Parable of the Wicked Tenants who planted a vineyard, fenced it, built a tower, and leased it out.[33] Although the parable applied to the chief priests and Pharisees of Jesus's day, it was also directed at the principalities and powers behind them. They have denied the landowner, God, the fruit of His garden, and they thought that by killing His son they would take His inheritance—the earth and all that's in it.

Even the chief priests and Pharisees realized that things would end badly for the evil tenants: "He will put those wretches to a miserable death and let out the vineyard to other tenants who will give him the fruits in their seasons."[34]

If you have accepted Jesus as your Lord and Savior, then *you* are one of those "other tenants." Your calling is the care and cultivation of the garden of our King.

---

31 Ezekiel 28:14.
32 Zechariah 14:4.
33 See Matthew 21:33–45, Mark 12:1–12, and Luke 20:9–19.
34 Matthew 21:41.

CHAPTER TWENTY-SEVEN

MOUNT
OF OLIVES

*As he sat on the Mount of Olives, the disciples came to him privately,
saying, "Tell us, when will these things be, and what will be the sign
of your coming and of the end of the age?"*

—MATTHEW 24:3 (ESV)

I t's difficult for us in the twenty-first century to understand how the
cult of an underworld god whose worship involved necromancy
and child sacrifice continued in Israel and Judah for eight hundred
years. The Israelites fell into the worship of Baal-Peor, another title or
identity worn by El/Molech/Shemihazah et al., in the time of Moses
and Joshua in the late fifteenth century BC, and his cult was still active
in Judah until the reforms of Josiah in the late seventh century BC.

But perhaps the most audacious example of this god's hubris is
found on top of a hill just outside the walls of ancient Jerusalem. Even
while he was imprisoned in the abyss, El/Molech influenced Solomon
to build a high place for him that overlooked the Temple Mount:

> For when Solomon was old his wives turned away his heart
> after other gods, and his heart was not wholly true to the LORD
> his God, as was the heart of David his father. For Solomon
> went after Ashtoreth [Astarte] the goddess of the Sidonians,
> and after Milcom the abomination of the Ammonites. So

225

Solomon did what was evil in the sight of the LORD and did not wholly follow the LORD, as David his father had done. Then Solomon built a high place for Chemosh the abomination of Moab, and for Molech [Milcom] the abomination of the Ammonites, on the mountain east of Jerusalem. (1 Kings 11:4–7, brackets added)

The mountain east of Jerusalem can only be the Mount of Olives, with an elevation nearly three hundred feet higher than the Temple Mount. Solomon probably built those high places after 950 BC, and they stood until the time of King Josiah, who reigned from about 640 BC until his death in 609 BC:

And the king defiled the high places that were east of Jerusalem, to the south of **the Mount of Corruption**, which Solomon the king of Israel had built for Ashtoreth the abomination of the Sidonians, and for Chemosh the abomination of Moab, and for Milcom the abomination of the Ammonites. (2 Kings 23:13, emphasis added)

Note the name given to the Mount of Olives by the author of 2 Kings: The Mount of Corruption. The Hebrew word rendered "corruption," *mašḥît* (pronounced *mash-kheeth*), means "destruction." But the Hebrew text reads *har ha-mašḥît*, which more precisely means "Mountain of the Destroyer."[1] That's a very different sense of the mountain's name and the god who was worshiped there.

Mašḥît is used twice in the Old Testament to identify a supernatural entity charged with exterminating large groups of people. In Exodus 12:23, "the destroyer" (*ha-mašḥît*) passes through the land of Egypt to take the lives of the first-born. 2 Samuel 24:16 and the

---

1 Julian Morgenstern, "The King-God Among the Western Semites and the Meaning of Epiphanes." *Vetus Testamentum*, Apr. 1960, Vol. 10, Fasc. 2 (April 1960), pp. 179–180.

parallel passage in 1 Chronicles 21:15 describe the Angel of Yahweh as the *mal'ak ha-mašḥît*, "the destroying angel." He must have been terrifying; David and the elders of Israel, upon seeing the Angel of Yahweh "standing between earth and heaven, and in his hand a drawn sword stretched out over Jerusalem," threw themselves to the ground, face down.[2]

However, it's unlikely that the faithful priests and chroniclers who condemned Solomon's pagan high places would describe them with a term that specified the Angel of Yahweh, who was "the second power in heaven," the pre-incarnate Christ.[3]

So, who was the Destroyer?

We know that Solomon set up places of worship to Milcom/ Molech (El/Enlil/Dagon, etc.) and Chemosh (Ares/Mars) on the Mount of Olives. But it appears that pagan cult sites existed on that mountain before Solomon, and maybe even before David:

> But David went up the ascent of the Mount of Olives, weeping as he went, barefoot and with his head covered. And all the people who were with him covered their heads, and they went up, weeping as they went. [...]
>
> While David was coming to the summit, **where God was worshiped**, behold, Hushai the Archite came to meet him with his coat torn and dirt on his head. (2 Samuel 15:30, 32; emphasis added)

The phrase "where God was worshiped" (Hebrew *asher-yishtakhaveh sham l'elohim*) can also mean "where **the gods** were worshiped." Translators assume that "*elohim*" in 2 Samuel 15:32 refers to Yahweh, but neither the text nor the context exclude the possibility of pagan worship on the summit of the Mount of Olives. There is nothing in 1 Kings 11

---

2   1 Chronicles 21:16.

3   Michael S. Heiser, *The Divine Council in Late Canonical and Non-Canonical Second Temple Jewish Literature* (Dissertation, University of Wisconsin-Madison, 2004).

to suggest that places of worship formerly dedicated to Yahweh were defiled or destroyed to make room for Chemosh and Milcom. With Solomon's new Temple on Mount Zion, just across the Kidron Valley, why would there be?

In David's day, the Ark of the Covenant had been in the City of David since early in his reign (see 2 Samuel 6), but the tabernacle was in the city of Gibeon, five miles northwest of Jerusalem. It remained there until Solomon built the Temple after David's death. Yahweh worship in Jerusalem would have been centered in the City of David or on Mount Moriah, the site of Araunah's threshing floor, rather than on the Mount of Olives.

This leads to some intriguing observations about that mountain. As with Mount Hermon, Jesus could have told his followers that there was nothing special about the Mount of Olives—that, despite what pagans thought, there was no portal or gateway to the spirit realm on its summit, and that henceforth followers of Jesus could ignore Olivet, Hermon, and every other mountain in Judea, Samaria, the Galilee, and the rest of the earth when it came to places of worship. And yet, as with Hermon, Jesus paid special attention to the Mount of Olives—especially during the final days of His ministry.

Jesus met Mary, Martha, and their brother Lazarus at the village of Bethany on the southeast slope of the Mount of Olives. It was there that he raised Lazarus from the dead,[4] which certainly got the attention of the spirit realm. As we noted in an earlier chapter, the Rephaim Texts from ancient Ugarit appear to be a necromancy ritual that summoned the demonic spirits of the Nephilim to the summit of Mount Hermon, the threshing-floor of El (Milcom), to be "revivified" after dawn of the third day. Again, Greek and Roman funeral rites in the time of Jesus, which may date back to older practices from the eastern Mediterranean (cf. Isaiah 65:4), included a ritual meal on the third day after death.[5]

---

4   John 11:1–44.
5   Heider, op. cit., pp. 390-391.

John notes that when Jesus learned of Lazarus' illness, He deliberately "stayed two days longer in the place where he was" so that He arrived at Bethany when "Lazarus had already been in the tomb four days."[6] This was not a coincidence. Jesus deliberately waited so He could glorify God by raising his friend from the dead on the *fourth* day. Why? Besides the pagan rituals associated with the third day after a death, there was a Jewish tradition that the spirit of a dead person lingered in the tomb for three days, hoping to rejoin its body.[7] Jesus delayed to show the assembled crowd that Lazarus was well and truly dead, and that He had power over death—which, if you lived in the first century AD, you probably considered an entity in the unseen realm. (Remember that Death, or Thanatos in Greek, is the rider on the pale horse in Revelation chapter 6.)

When Jesus returned to Jerusalem for the Passover from Caesarea Philippi and the Transfiguration on Mount Hermon, He approached Jerusalem from the east, rather than the north. The Jews of Jesus's day avoided Samaria, so He would have crossed to Perea, the part of Herod's kingdom east of the Jordan River between the Sea of Galilee and the Dead Sea, and then crossed back over the Jordan at Jericho. As they neared Jerusalem, Jesus sent two disciples into Bethphage, a village on the eastern slope of the Mount of Olives, to obtain a donkey and her colt:

> If anyone says anything to you, you shall say, 'The Lord needs them,' and he will send them at once." This took place to fulfill what was spoken by the prophet, saying,
>
> "Say to the daughter of Zion,
> 'Behold, your king is coming to you,
>   humble, and mounted on a donkey,
>   on a colt, the foal of a beast of burden.'" (Matthew 21:3–5)

---

6   John 11:6, 17.
7   "What Was the Significance of Jesus Being Dead for Three Days?" *GotQuestion s.org.* https://www.gotquestions.org/why-three-days.html, retrieved 1/22/24.

The other gospels mention only the colt, but the meaning of his gesture was clear in that time and place: Jesus signaled to all who watched that He was the true and rightful king. (And note that He acquired the donkey on the Mount of Olives!)

In the modern world, we assume that kings rode horses—noble steeds worthy of their riders' royal image. But that wasn't true in the ancient Near East. Jesus' entry into Jerusalem on the back of a donkey was a clear message to the principalities and powers behind the Amorites, who'd dominated the culture of the Near East since the time of the patriarchs.

Amorite kings never rode horses. In their world, as odd as it seems to us, donkeys were the symbol of royalty. Horses were for soldiers, who were usually commoners. Around the time of Isaac and Jacob, an Amorite official in the kingdom of Mari, based on the Euphrates River near the modern border between Syria and Iraq, offered advice to his king, Zimri-Lim, which was still understood in the time of Jesus:

> "May my lord honor his kingship. Since you are the king of Hanean (tribesmen), and also are the king of the Amorites, may my lord not ride horses; instead, he ought to ride a chariot or mules, so that he could honor his kingship." Therefore, when Christ entered Jerusalem on a donkey, the population, as well as the authorities, knew how to read the symbolism at stake (Matthew 21).[8]

The Bible tells us that Jesus will ride a white horse when He returns, but that's because He comes back as a soldier. And He'll lead the greatest army in the history of the universe.

From His triumphal entry, Jesus proceeded to the Temple Mount and chased the moneychangers from the Temple, which, despite being rebuilt by the wicked King Herod, was still His Father's house. After

---

8   Jack M. Sasson, "Thoughts of Zimri-Lim." *Biblical Archaeologist*, June 1984, pp. 118–119.

the events of that day, which no doubt had all of Jerusalem (if not all of Judea) talking, Jesus returned to the Mount of Olives and lodged at the village of Bethany.

It was during the week between the Triumphal Entry and His arrest that Jesus shared with His disciples key information about the last days. The Olivet Discourse, recorded in Matthew 24 and 25, Mark 13, and Luke 21, contains Jesus' most detailed descriptions of the signs of the end times and His return. Matthew and Mark specify that these prophecies were delivered on the Mount of Olives, hence the name of the sermon.

The gospel accounts agree that after the Last Supper, Jesus crossed the Kidron Valley from Jerusalem to Gethsemane, a garden at the foot of the Mount of Olives within sight of the Temple Mount. It was there that He was betrayed by Judas to the authorities. And, contrary to tradition, it was also there that our Lord was crucified. The Church of the Holy Sepulchre in Jerusalem is certainly historic, but it's in the wrong place. It was established on the site endorsed by Helena, the mother of Constantine, who'd legalized the Christian faith in the Roman Empire about fifteen years before her pilgrimage to the Holy Land between 326 and 328 AD. Before her visit, there had been no connection between the crucifixion and the site, which is in the Christian Quarter of the Old City of Jerusalem.

However, John 19:20 tells us that the site was "near the city," which means outside the walls. That's confirmed by Hebrews 13:12, which says that Jesus was executed "outside the gate." Further, the sign placed by Pilate on the cross, "Jesus of Nazareth, the King of the Jews,"[9] was meant to be seen by the thousands of pilgrims coming to Jerusalem for the Passover. The Church of the Holy Sepulchre was built over the site of a temple to Venus, built in the second century by Hadrian in an unused quarry—which, since it was below ground level (as you'd expect for a quarry), was not very visible. Nor was it on a hill, which is at least implied by the name of the crucifixion site, Golgotha, Aramaic for "Place of a Skull."

---

9   John 19:19.

But English often doesn't capture the nuances of Greek and Hebrew. The Greek word *kraniou* describes the top of the head, the brain pan, not the entire skull.[10] The creepy-looking hill near the Garden Tomb, north of the Temple Mount, somewhat resembles empty eye sockets and a nasal cavity, but it, too, is in the wrong place.[11]

The Mount of Olives better fits the description of Golgotha, and research by scholar Nikos Kokkinos into obscure first-century Roman law confirms it as the site of the crucifixion: Enemies of the state sentenced to crucifixion were to be executed at the scene of their crime, and if that wasn't possible, at the place of their capture.[12] Although the exact location of the Garden of Gethsemane is unknown, eyewitnesses agreed that it was on the Mount of Olives and Jesus fit the legal definition of an enemy of Rome for the evil purposes of the Sanhedrin.

The case for identifying the Mount of Olives as the crucifixion site was perhaps made first by Dr. N. F. Hutchinson for the *Palestine Exploration Fund Quarterly* in 1870 and 1873. In short, Dr. Hutchinson presented compelling arguments in his second article that the Crucifixion was visible from only one of the approaches to Jerusalem in the first century, the road from Jericho through Bethany, around the Mount of Olives, that entered the city from the east by the Fish Gate.[13]

There is one more bit of evidence: As the gospels note, Golgotha was the "Place of a Skull." Our friend, messianic Rabbi Zev Porat, co-author of *The Rabbi, the Secret Message, and the Identity of Messiah*, believes that the name refers to a specific skull—the head of Goliath. David brought that gruesome trophy to Jerusalem,[14] and perhaps buried it on

---

10 "κρανίον." *Wiktionary*, https://en.wiktionary.org/wiki/κρανίον#Ancient_Greek, retrieved 3/30/21.

11 We were told by guides during our 2023 tour that the hill looked much more like a skull a hundred years ago, but the soft limestone face has eroded rather quickly since then. That begs the question: Did that hillside look like a skull at all in the first century AD, before 1,900 years of erosion?

12 Ernest L. Martin, *Secrets of Golgotha: The Lost History of Jesus' Crucifixion* (Portland, OR: Associates for Scriptural Knowledge, 1996), pp. 73–74.

13 N. F. Hutchinson, "Further Notes on Our Lord's Tomb." *Palestine Exploration Fund Quarterly Statement* 5.3 (July 1873), pp. 113–115.

14 1 Samuel 17:54.

the Mount of Olives. But there's another possibility: When David fled Jerusalem to escape Absalom's rebellion, he paused at the summit of the Mount of Olives. The Hebrew word translated "summit" is *rosh*, which means "head." So, 2 Samuel 15:32 literally reads, "When David reached 'the head,' where God was [or, "the gods were"] worshiped..."

In other words, Golgotha (and Calvary, which derives from the Latin word for "bald") probably refers to the summit of the Mount of Olives, the most visible place for people arriving in Jerusalem from the east or those looking out across the Kidron Valley from the Temple Mount or the City of David.

The apostle John then adds this detail as to the temporary resting place of Christ:

> Now in the place where he was crucified there was a garden, and in the garden a new tomb in which no one had yet been laid. So because of the Jewish day of Preparation, since the tomb was close at hand, they laid Jesus there. (John 19:41–42)

Understand what this means: Jesus spent the final week of his life living and teaching in two places—in the Temple and on the Mount of Olives, where almost a thousand years earlier Solomon built a high place for the "king-god" of the pagans, Milcom/Molech. Jesus' final night as a mortal on this earth was spent in prayer in a garden on that mountain, where he was arrested, and where the following day He was crucified, died, and was buried.

From there, Christ descended into the abyss and "proclaimed to the spirits in prison."[15] Now, the meaning of this verse has been debated for two thousand years. On the surface, it appears that Jesus, as a spirit, "preached" (Greek *kēryssō*) to human spirits in Hell. That is not what Peter meant.

"Proclaimed" or "declared" is a better English translation for *kēryssō*. Jesus didn't preach, He declared to the spirits, "This is how it's

---

15 1 Peter 3:19.

going to be." The context and grammar of the sentence make it clear that the spirits He addressed weren't human:

> The NT never uses the word for "spirit" in an unqualified fashion to refer to the human soul. Therefore, the reference in 1 Peter 3:19 may point to nonhuman supernatural beings. This interpretation is strengthened when the passage is read in the context of Genesis 6–9 because of the reference to Noah and the flood in 1 Pet[er] 3:20. The flood reference also draws in the traditions of 1 Enoch, so the "spirits in prison" may have been understood to be the fallen angels or "sons of God" of Genesis 6:1–4.[16]

Jesus descended into Tartarus, the bottomless pit, to declare victory over the rebellious "sons of God," the Watchers, whose chief Shemihazah, under the names Milcom, Molech, and El, had been worshiped at the top of the Mount of Olives, and in the Valley of Hinnom below the mountain, where Jesus willingly sacrificed Himself to redeem you and me.

Then, to pour salt in their wounds, Christ rose from the dead at dawn of the third day on that mountain, reversing the centuries-old pagan ritual that summoned the Rephaim to El's mount of assembly, Hermon—from which no one in history has ever risen from the dead.

But Jesus did it from the very mountain on which Solomon erected a sacred place to this being:

> And he led them out as far as Bethany, and lifting up his hands he blessed them. While he blessed them, he parted from them and was carried up into heaven. (Luke 24:50–51)

Yes, Jesus Christ departed this world from the Mount of Olives, too. And to put an exclamation point on His message to that fallen *elohim*, it's where He returns on the Day of the LORD:

---

16 Mangum, op. cit.

On that day his feet shall stand on the Mount of Olives that lies before Jerusalem on the east, and the Mount of Olives shall be split in two from east to west by ha very wide valley, so that one half of the Mount shall move northward, and the other half southward. (Zechariah 14:4)

If Jesus hadn't called attention to it, we might not have given the Mount of Olives and Solomon's high places there another thought. But it certainly looks as though the Watcher chief Shemihazah, manipulating human dupes through history who thought they served El, Milcom (Molech), or this entity by another name, tried to establish his presence in a place that looked down on the place God had chosen for Himself. In the final week of Jesus's life, and in the prophecy of His return, Jesus emphasized the point He'd made at Caesarea Philippi just a few weeks earlier: The gates of Hell will not prevail against His *ekklesia*—His assembly—and the mountain where it will gather after His return.

THE
PRESENT

CHAPTER TWENTY-EIGHT

THE MONSTER AND
THE GREAT BEAST 666

Here is wisdom. Let him that hath understanding count the number
of the beast: for it is the number of a man; and his number is Six
hundred threescore and six.

—REVELATION 13:18 (KJV)

Let's jump from the first century AD to the early twentieth century. The desire to reach the gods on the far side of the gates of hell has, if anything, grown over the last 2,000 years.

H. P. Lovecraft (1890-1937) is one of the giants of twentieth century literature, although he wasn't recognized as such until after his death. And because he wrote scary stories, he wasn't the kind of writer who received invites to fancy parties. Lovecraft and his friends, most of whom he knew through volumes of letters they exchanged (by one estimate, 100,000 of them)[1] some believe were more influential than his published work, wrote to entertain, usually by crafting terrifying tales and conjuring monstrous images of overpowering, inhuman evil.

As a child, Lovecraft was tormented by night terrors. Beginning at age six, young Howard was visited by what he called night-gaunts—faceless

---

1   Sian Cain, "Ten Things You Should Know About HP Lovecraft." *The Guardian*, August 20, 2014. https://www.theguardian.com/books/2014/aug/20/ten-things -you-should-know-about-hp-lovecraft, retrieved 2/9/24.

humanoids with black, rubbery skin, bat-like wings, and barbed tails, who carried off their victims to Dreamland. The nocturnal visitors were so terrifying that Howard remembered trying desperately to stay awake every night during this period of his life. It's believed that these dreams, which haunted him for more than a year, had a powerful influence on his fiction.[2]

Lovecraft's mother raised Howard with his aunts after his father was committed to a psychiatric hospital when Howard was only three. Sadly, she failed to recognize the phenomenon for what it probably was—demonic oppression of her only child. But by the late nineteenth century, the technologically advanced West didn't have room in its scientific worldview for such things. In fact, Lovecraft claimed to be a staunch atheist throughout his life.

Ironically, despite his disbelief, the fiction of H. P. Lovecraft has been adapted and adopted by occultists around the world. The man who died a pauper not only found an audience over the last eighty-five years, but he also inspired an army of authors who have preserved and expanded the nightmarish universe that sprang from Lovecraft's tortured dreams.[3]

Although Lovecraft claimed he didn't believe in the supernatural, he was more than happy to use the spirit realm as grist for his writing mill. Lovecraft apparently saw potential in the Theosophical doctrines of Madame Helena Blavatsky for stories that would sell. They did, but sadly for Lovecraft, mostly after his death. During his lifetime, Lovecraft was barely known outside the readership of pulp magazines, the type of publication called a "penny dreadful" a couple of generations earlier in England.

Pseudoscientific concepts popularized by Blavatsky, such as the lost continents of Atlantis and Lemuria, served him well as an author.

---

2   Daniel Harms and John Wisdom Gonce, *The Necronomicon Files: The Truth Behind Lovecraft's Legend* (Boston, MA: Weiser Books, 2003), p. 5.

3   One of the most well-known pop culture references to Lovecraft is the Arkham Asylum, which has been featured since the mid-1970s in the Batman comics, cartoons, movies, and video games. Arkham was named for a fictional town in Massachusetts featured in many of Lovecraft's stories.

The notion that certain humans had an ability to see beyond the veil to communicate with intelligences vastly greater than our own also made for compelling horror. Lovecraft viewed the universe as a cold, unfeeling place. In his fiction, those intelligences, unlike the kindly ascended masters of Blavatsky's religion, had no use for humanity—except perhaps, as slaves or sacrifices. The horror of discovering oneself at the mercy of immense, ancient beings incapable of mercy is a common theme in Lovecraft's tales, and he gave those ideas flesh and bone with carefully crafted prose that infused them with a sense of dread not easily or often distilled onto the printed page.

Lovecraft's style of gothic horror has had a powerful influence on horror fiction and film. Writers and directors like Stephen King, Roger Corman, John Carpenter and Ridley Scott, among others, drew on Lovecraft's style, and sometimes adapted his Cthulhu mythos directly. That's not the type of legacy left by Ernest Hemingway or F. Scott Fitzgerald, but the audiences who have seen *The Thing*, *Alien*, or any movie based on a Stephen King novel far outnumber those who've read Hemingway or Fitzgerald. Even though H. P. Lovecraft was basically unknown during his lifetime, he's had far greater influence on pop culture than the literary greats who were his contemporaries.

And, as we'll see, the influence of the staunch atheist Lovecraft has bled over into the metaphysical realm. It is perhaps fitting that the principalities and powers aligned against their Creator would find a self-described atheist to be a most useful tool.

Not coincidentally, as Lovecraft began his career as a writer, across the ocean another man fascinated with arcana and the influence of old gods on our world was hearing voices from beyond.

In a previous chapter, we dealt with ancient doorways and how the keeper of a ritual pit, an 'ôb, would summon spirits and so-called dead ancestors. In the twentieth century, that long tradition was revitalized and glamorized by one of the most infamous occultists of the modern era, if not all time: Aleister Crowley.

Edward Alexander "Aleister" Crowley, born into a wealthy family in October of 1875, disavowed his parents' Christian Plymouth Brethren faith and pursued the modern idea called Western Esotericism.

In case you're scratching your head just now, wondering what Western Esotericism was, allow us to explain, in brief. So-called Western Esotericism was the natural offspring of an eighteenth-century pursuit known as the Enlightenment. For those unfamiliar with this idea, Enlightenment was a philosophical set of beliefs that demeaned faith in God as foolish. Instead, Enlightened individuals replaced our very real and loving Creator with the cold god of Self, whom they pursued through four basic paths.

- Firstly, Rationalism, where acolytes derived conclusions about the world and humanity's place in it, based solely on logic.
- Empiricism formed the counterpoint. Here, the pursuit of knowledge was done through sensory experience. Cold facts were replaced by "feels" and sensory assessment.
- Progressivism appealed to those who sought political change. This philosophy taught that that only Science and Technology could drive social reform.
- Cosmopolitanism claimed society required equality and equity to find balance. In other words, you might call this a combination of all the above.

Having read the above, you might well conclude that our present society is based entirely on the Enlightenment, but you'd only be partly right. Indeed, the cauldron in which our present age bubbles is made from all the above mixed with magic. Yes, magic, or rather "magick," as Crowley spelled it. But why? Why did paganism emerge from an era that prided itself on reason and social reform? The answer is simple: the Enlightenment mindset relegated our Omnipotent Creator to their preferred and quite impotent position of Observer. This is not unlike the image of the sky-god of ancient Mesopotamia, Anu, who was depicted in the religions of Sumer, Akkad, and Babylon as remote, inaccessible, and, in the religions of the Hurrians, Hittites, Greeks (as Ouranos), and Romans (as Caelus), literally castrated.

Today, we see this idea in a growing corollary to evolutionary theory called Intelligent Design, where a Divine Watchmaker—probably an extraterrestrial, according to the gospel of *Ancient Aliens*—set the world in motion, who then, after growing quite bored, decided to retire.

Eighteenth-century "enlightenment" did little to bring light to the human condition, but instead delivered us into a deep, dark spiritual Void, by booting God out the door; and yes, we use the word door intentionally. In a very real way, these puffed-up philosophers and political theorists opened the doors and windows of Humanity's House and swept it clean of all references to Yahweh. In doing so, they made our House ready for other inhabitants. These foolish humans thought their newly cleaned House would be furnished with their philosophical wisdom, that it would better Man's future. Instead, this dangerous Void attracted evil: neo-paganism, witchcraft, spiritualism, and a return to the "old ways." Though the context concerns a person freed of one demon infestation, we can see a foreshadowing of what happens to Mankind's House, in Christ's parable of the wandering spirit:

> "When the unclean spirit has gone out of a person, it passes through waterless places seeking rest, but finds none. Then it says, 'I will return to my house from which I came.' And when it comes, it finds the house empty, swept, and put in order. Then it goes and brings with it seven other spirits more evil than itself, and they enter and dwell there, and the last state of that person is worse than the first. **So also will it be with this evil generation.**" (Matthew 14:43-45, emphasis added)

The aforementioned Aleister Crowley participated in multiple magickal workings (again, spelled as Crowley insisted). As a child, Edward Alexander Crowley resisted his family's Christian faith. His father, Edward Crowley, had inherited enough of a fortune from a family business to allow him to retire and preach the gospel. The senior Crowley converted from Quakerism to a subset of the Plymouth Brethren. As such, the younger Crowley's youth was formed in a Christian mold. The willful child struggled with these constraints so much that his mother referred to the boy as "the Beast" (yes, *that* Beast). After his father's death in 1887, young Edward Crowley inherited a tidy sum of money, allowing him to seek a looser lifestyle as a schoolboy. Such mischief forced his widowed mother to remove her son from one school after another, finally placing him with a Plymouth Brethren tutor. The child who would later call himself Aleister refused to believe in the Bible's authenticity, proclaiming it filled with errors and inconsistencies.

We'll skip through his mountain climbing, poetry loving, chess playing years to the era where the poisonous root within his heart blossomed into a fully invested practitioner of the dark arts. At some point during his travels, Edward Alexander chose to call himself Aleister, based on the Scots Gaelic version of Alexander, Alasdair.

Ironically enough, Crowley eventually began a three-year course of study at Trinity College, Cambridge in 1895. A year later, while on holiday in Stockholm, he had his first mystical experience, which some biographers attribute to his first same-sex sexual experience.[4] A brief illness in 1897 pushed Crowley to consider his mortality, but sadly for Crowley and the thousands, if not millions, who have been influenced by him since, he chose not the free gift of salvation offered by Christ but a lifetime of darkness devoted to the occult.[5]

In 1904, Crowley traveled to Cairo with his new bride, Rose Kelly. While there, Crowley, who'd become a member of the Order of the Golden Dawn about five years earlier, set up a temple room in their apartment and began performing rituals to invoke Egyptian deities. Eventually, something calling itself Aiwass, the messenger

---

4   Tobias Churton, *Aleister Crowley: The Biography* (London: Watkins Books, 2011), p. 29.
5   Richard Kaczynski, *Perdurabo: The Life of Aleister Crowley* (1st ed.) (Berkeley, California: North Atlantic Books, 2010), p. 36.

of Hoor-Paar-Kraat (known to the Greeks as an aspect of Horus, Harpocrates, the god of silence), answered. Over a period of three days, April 8–10, 1904, Crowley transcribed what he heard from the voice of Aiwass.

> The Voice of Aiwass came apparently from over my left shoulder, from the furthest corner of the room. [...]
>
> I had a strong impression that the speaker was actually in the corner where he seemed to be, in a body of "fine matter," transparent as a veil of gauze, or a cloud of incense-smoke. He seemed to be a tall, dark man in his thirties, well-knit, active and strong, with the face of a savage king, and eyes veiled lest their gaze should destroy what they saw. The dress was not Arab; it suggested Assyria or Persia, but very vaguely. I took little note of it, for to me at that time Aiwass and an "angel" such as I had often seen in visions, a being purely astral.
>
> I now incline to believe that Aiwass is not only the God or Demon or Devil once held holy in Sumer, and mine own Guardian Angel, but also a man as I am, insofar as He uses a human body to make His magical link with Mankind, whom He loves...[6]

That eventually became the central text for Crowley's new religion, Thelema,[7] which in turn is the basis for his esoteric fellowship, Ordo Templi Orientis. The O.T.O. is a secret society similar to Freemasonry that, like the Freemasons and Helena Blavatsky's Theosophical Society, believes in universal brotherhood. The primary difference between Thelema and Theosophy is in the nature of the entities sending messages from beyond. Blavatsky claimed to hear from ascended

---

6   Aleister Crowley, *The Equinox of the Gods*, chapter 7. https://hermetic.com/crowley/equinox-of-the-gods/remarks-on-the-method-of-receiving-liber-legis, retrieved 2/9/24.

7   Thelemapedia.org. http://www.thelemapedia.org/index.php/The_Book_of_the_Law, retrieved 2/9/24.

masters who were shepherding humanity's evolution; Crowley claimed to be guided by gods from the Egyptian pantheon: Nuit, Hadit, and Ra-Hoor-Khuit.[8]

The irony of all this is that Lovecraft, who denied the existence of Crowley's gods and Blavatsky's mahatmas, may have drawn his inspiration from the same spiritual well.

A key thread woven through the stories of H. P. Lovecraft was a fictional grimoire, or book of witchcraft, called the *Necronomicon*. The book, according to the Lovecraft canon, was written in the eighth century AD by the "Mad Arab," Abdul Alhazred (Lovecraft's childhood nickname because of his love for the book *1001 Arabian Nights*).[9] Perhaps significantly, inspiration for the invented grimoire came to Lovecraft in a dream,[10] and through his many letters to friends and colleagues, he encouraged others to incorporate the mysterious tome in their works. Over time, references to the *Necronomicon* by a growing number of authors creating Lovecraftian supernatural horror led to a widespread belief that the book was, in fact, real. One of those who believed in the book was influential occultist Kenneth Grant.

Grant was an English ceremonial magician and an acolyte of Crowley, serving as Crowley's personal secretary toward the end of his life. After Crowley's death, Grant was named head of the O.T.O. in Britain by Crowley's successor, Karl Germer. However, Germer was infuriated by Grant's perception and promotion of a "Sirius/Set current" in Crowley's work, so named for Sirius, the "Dog Star" prominent on summer nights, and Set, the chaos-god of the Egyptian pantheon. As a result, Germer expelled Grant from the O.T.O. for heresy.[11]

---

8   Ronald Hutton, *The Triumph of the Moon: A History of Modern Pagan Witchcraft* (Oxford: Oxford University Press, 2006), p. 178.

9   It was also wordplay on Lovecraft's avid reading habit: "All-has-read."

10   Jason Colavito, "Inside the *Necronomicon*." *Lost Civilizations Uncovered*, 2002. https://jcolavito.tripod.com/lostcivilizations/id25.html, retrieved 2/9/24.

11   Declan O'Neill, "Kenneth Grant: Writer and occultist who championed Aleister Crowley and Austin Osman Spare." *The Independent*, March 4, 2011. http://www. independent.co.uk/news/obituaries/kenneth-grant-writer-and-occultist-who -championed-aleister-crowley-and-austin-osman-spare-2231570.html, retrieved 2/9/24.

Lovecraft's fiction inspired some of Grant's innovations to Thelema. Grant said Lovecraft "snatched from nightmare-space his lurid dream-readings of the *Necronomicon*." Instead of attributing the *Necronomicon* to Lovecraft's imagination, Grant took it as evidence of the tome's existence as an "astral book."[12] Furthermore, Grant believed others, including Crowley and Blavatsky, had "glimpsed the Akashic *Necronomicon*."[13] That's a reference to the Akashic records, a Theosophist concept describing a sort of cosmic library that's the repository of all human thoughts, deeds, and emotions, existing on another plane of reality that can be accessed only through proper spiritual discipline.

Kenneth Grant was perhaps the first to notice the strange parallels between the writings of H. P. Lovecraft and Aleister Crowley. In *The Dark Lord*, an extensive analysis of Grant's magickal system and Lovecraft's influence on it, researcher and author Peter Levenda documented a number of these similarities.

In 1907, Crowley was writing some of the works that became seminal to the doctrines of Thelema, known as The Holy Books. These include *Liber Liberi vel Lapidus Lazuli, Liber Cordis Cincti Serpente*, and other works written between October 30 and November 1 of that year, and *Liber Arcanorum* and *Liber Carcerorum*, written between December 5th and 14th that same year. Lovecraft would have had no knowledge of this, as he was only a seventeen-year old recluse living at home on Angell Street in Providence, Rhode Island, dreaming of the stars.

Instead, he later would write of an orgiastic ritual taking place that year in the bayous outside New Orleans, Louisiana, and on the very same day that Crowley was writing the books enumerated above. The story Lovecraft wrote is entitled "The Call of Cthulhu" and is arguably his most famous work. He wrote the story in 1926, in late August or early September, but

---

12   Harms and Gonce, op. cit., pp. 109–110.
13   Ibid.

placed the action in New Orleans in 1907 and later in Providence in 1925.

How is this relevant? Lovecraft's placement of the orgiastic ritual in honor of the high priest of the Great Old Ones, Cthulhu, and the discovery of a statue of Cthulhu by the New Orleans police on Halloween, 1907 coincides precisely with Crowley's fevered writing of his own gothic prose. In the *Liber Liberi vel Lapidus Lazuli*, for instance, Crowley writes the word "Tutulu" for the first time. He claims not to know what this word means, or where it came from. As the name of Lovecraft's fictional alien god can be pronounced "Kutulu," it seems more than coincidental, as Kenneth Grant himself noted.

However, this is only the tip of an eldritch iceberg. In Crowley's *Liber Cordis Cincti Serpente*—or "The Book of the Heart Girt with a Serpent"—there are numerous references to the "Abyss of the Great Deep," to Typhon, Python, and the appearance of an "old gnarled fish" with tentacles...all descriptions that match Lovecraft's imagined Cthulhu perfectly. Not approximately, but perfectly. Crowley's volume was written on November 1, 1907. The ritual for Cthulhu in New Orleans took place on the same day, month and year.[14]

This could be nothing more than a strange coincidence—if you're a coincidence theorist. Levenda, an excellent researcher and gifted author, and Kenneth Grant before him, concluded otherwise.

It may actually be more logical to suggest, as an explanation for some of these coincidences, that darker forces were at work. In fact, it is possible that the same forces of which Lovecraft himself writes—the telepathic communication between followers

---

14 Peter Levenda, *The Dark Lord: H.P. Lovecraft, Kenneth Grant, and the Typhonian Tradition in Magic* (Lake Worth, FL: Ibis Press, 2013), Kindle Edition, pp. 97–98.

of Cthulhu and the Great Old Ones—was what prompted him to write these fictional accounts of real events. Either Lovecraft was in some kind of telepathic communication with Crowley, or both men were in telepathic communication with…Something Else.[15]

As Christians, we should at least consider the supernatural explanation to the strange parallels between Crowley and Lovecraft. As the apostle Paul wrote, "We wrestle not against flesh and blood" (Ephesians 6:12). That being true, then we must acknowledge the influence of "Something Else" on our natural world. Because that's the most likely source of the odd, highly improbable connection between Crowley and Cthulhu.

And that "Something Else" may well reside on the other side of the gates of hell.

---

15 Ibid., pp. 102–103.

CHAPTER TWENTY-NINE

FROM CTHULHU TO CHARIOTS OF THE GODS

*No book had ever really hinted of it, though the deathless Chinamen
said that there were double meanings in the Necronomicon of the
mad Arab Abdul Alhazred which the initiated might read as they
chose, especially the much-discussed couplet:*
   That is not dead which can eternal lie,
   And with strange aeons even death may die.

—H. P. LOVECRAFT, "The Call of Cthulhu"

In the early 1970s, Kenneth Grant, personal secretary to Aleister
Crowley twenty-five years earlier, broke with the American branch
of Crowley's Ordo Templi Orientis and formed his own Thelemic
organization, the Typhonian O.T.O. This allowed him to explore the
"Sirius/Set current" he'd identified in the 1950s. Again, this was a reference to the Egyptian deity Set, god of the desert, storms, foreigners,
violence, and, most significantly, chaos. To grasp the significance of
Grant's innovation to Crowley's religion, a brief history of Set is in
order.

Set—sometimes called Seth, Sheth, or Sutekh—is one of the
oldest gods in the Egyptian pantheon. There is evidence he was worshiped long before the pharaohs, in the pre-dynastic era called Naqada

I, which may date as far back as 3750 BC,[1] about the time that Gilgal Refaim was being built. To put that into context, the Tower of Babel incident probably occurred toward the end of the Uruk period around 3100 BC.[2] Writing wasn't invented in Sumer until about 3000 BC, around the time of the first pharaoh, Narmer.

Set was originally one of the good gods. He protected Ra's solar boat, defending it from the evil chaos serpent Apep (or Apophis), who tried to eat the sun every night as it dropped below the horizon. During the Second Intermediate Period, roughly 1750 BC to 1550 BC, Semitic people who'd taken control of northern Egypt called the Hyksos, probably Amorites,[3] equated Set with Baal, the Canaanite storm-god.[4] Baal-Set was the patron deity of Avaris, the Hyksos capital.[5]

The worship of Baal-Set continued even after the Hyksos were driven out of Egypt. Two centuries after Moses led the Israelites to Canaan, three hundred years after the Hyksos expulsion, Ramesses the Great erected a memorial called the Year 400 Stela to honor the 400th year of Set's arrival in Egypt. In fact, Ramesses' father was named Seti, which literally means "man of Set."

Set didn't acquire his evil reputation until the Third Intermediate Period, during which Egypt was overrun by successive waves of foreign invaders. After being conquered by Nubia, Assyria, and Persia, one after another between 728 BC and 525 BC, the god of foreigners wasn't welcome around the pyramids anymore.[6] No longer was Set

---

1   Herman te Velde, "Seth, God of Confusion: A Study of His Role in Egyptian Mythology and Religion." *Probleme der* Ägyptologie 6 (1967). Translated by van Baaren-Pape, G. E. (Leiden: E. J. Brill, 1967), p. 7.

2   See chapter 3 of Derek's book *The Great Inception*.

3   Kim Ryholt, *The Political Situation in Egypt during the Second Intermediate Period c.1800-1550 B.C.* (Copenhagen: Museum Tuscalanum Press, 1997), p. 128.

4   Niv Allon, "Seth is Baal—Evidence from the Egyptian Script." *Egypt and the Levant* XVII (2007), pp. 15-22.

5   Andrew Curry, "The Rulers of Foreign Lands." *Archaeology*, September/October 2018. https://www.archaeology.org/issues/309-1809/features/6855-egypt-hyksos -foreign-dynasty#art_page5, retrieved 2/9/24.

6   te Velde, op. cit., pp. 139–140.

the mighty god who kept Apophis from eating the sun; now, Set was the evil god who'd murdered his brother, Osiris, and the sworn enemy of Osiris's son, Horus.

By the time of Persia's rise, Greek civilization was beginning to flower, and the Greeks identified Set with Typhon, the terrifying, powerful serpentine god of chaos. That's the link between Set and Typhon. And that's the entity Kenneth Grant believed was the true source of power in Thelemic magick.

That's why the "Sirius/Set current" led Grant to create the Typhonian O.T.O, and that's the destructive, chaos-monster aspect of Set-Typhon we need to keep in view when analyzing the magickal system Grant created by filtering Crowley through the horror fiction of H. P. Lovecraft.

> Grant's anxiety, as expressed in *Nightside of Eden* and in his other works, is that the Earth is being infiltrated by a race of extraterrestrial beings who will cause tremendous changes to take place in our world. This statement is not to be taken quite as literally as it appears, for the "Earth" can be taken to mean our current level of conscious awareness, and extraterrestrial would mean simply "not of this current level of conscious awareness." But the potential for danger is there, and Grant's work—like Lovecraft's—is an attempt to warn us of the impending (potentially dramatic) alterations in our physical, mental and emotional states due to powerful influences from "outside."[7]

Lovecraft died in 1937, but his work found a new audience in the 1970s when his stories were mined as source material by Hollywood. Then in 1977, a hardback edition of the *Necronomicon*, which Lovecraft had invented more than half a century earlier as a plot device, suddenly appeared (published in a limited run of 666 copies!),[8] edited

---

7   Levenda, op. cit., pp. 74–75.
8   Colavito, op. cit.

by a mysterious figure known only as Simon. According to Simon, who claimed to be a bishop in the Eastern Orthodox Church, two monks from his denomination had stolen a copy of the actual *Necronomicon* in one of the most daring and dangerous book thefts in history.

A mass market paperback edition followed a few years later. That version has reportedly sold more than a million copies over the last four decades.[9] Kenneth Grant, who believed that Crowley and Lovecraft had been inspired or guided by the same supernatural source, validated the text, going so far as to offer explanations for apparent discrepancies between Crowley and the *Necronomicon*.

> Crowley admitted to not having heard correctly certain words during the transmission of *Liber L*, and it is probable that he misheard the word Tutulu. It may have been Kutulu, in which case it would be identical phonetically, but not qabalistically, with Cthulhu. The [Simon] *Necronomicon* (Introduction, p. xix) suggests a relationship between Kutulu and Cutha...[10]

Recall that according to 2 Kings 17:24, Cutha, a city sacred to the plague-god and gatekeeper to the netherworld Nergal, was one of the Mesopotamian cities from which Sargon II of Assyria resettled Samaria. Grant connected Cutha and its underworld tradition to Cthulhu, the most famous of H. P. Lovecraft's nightmarish creations, and the occult text supernaturally delivered to Aleister Crowley.[11]

Simon's *Necronomicon* was just one of several grimoires (books of magic spells) published in the 1970s that claimed to be the nefarious

---

9   Levenda, op. cit., p. 8.

10 "Remembering Kenneth Grant's Understanding of The *Necronomicon* Tradition," *Warlock Asylum International News*, February 18, 2011. https://warlockasyluminternationalnews.com/2011/02/18/remembering-kenneth-grants-understanding-of-the-necronomicon-tradition/, retrieved 8/7/17.

11 And remember that Nergal was the Akkadian/Babylonian equivalent of the Canaanite plague-god Resheph, for whom the city of Shechem was sacred. Shechem is modern-day Nablus, which has long been a hotbed of violence and terrorist activity. Resheph was later known to the Greeks and Romans as Apollo.

book. The others were either obvious fakes published for entertainment purposes, or hoaxes that their authors admitted to soon after publication. Simon, on the other hand, appeared to be serious. But people involved with producing the "Simonomicon" have since admitted to making it up, and the central figure behind the book's publication was none other than occult researcher Peter Levenda, author of *The Dark Lord*, the book documenting the highly improbable "coincidences" connecting Aleister Crowley and H. P. Lovecraft.

> The text itself was Levenda's creation, a synthesis of Sumerian and later Babylonian myths and texts peppered with names of entities from H. P. Lovecraft's notorious and enormously popular Cthulhu stories. Levenda seems to have drawn heavily on the works of Samuel Noah Kramer for the Sumerian, and almost certainly spent a great deal of time at the University of Pennsylvania library researching the thing. Structurally, the text was modeled on the wiccan *Book of Shadows* and the Goetia, a grimoire of doubtful authenticity itself dating from the late Middle Ages.
>
> "Simon" was also Levenda's creation. He cultivated an elusive, secretive persona, giving him a fantastic and blatantly implausible line of [BS] to cover the book's origins. He had no telephone. He always wore business suits, in stark contrast to the flamboyant Renaissance fair, proto-goth costuming that dominated the scene.[12] (brackets added)

Although his research is top-notch, we must point out that in his book *The Dark Lord*, Levenda not only analyzed Kenneth Grant's magickal system and documented the supernatural synchronicities between Crowley and Lovecraft, but he also validated the authenticity of the *Necronomicon* that he himself created!

---

12 Alan Cabal, "The Doom That Came to Chelsea," *Chelsea News*, November 11, 2014. http://www.nypress.com/the-doom-that-came-to-chelsea/, retrieved 2/9/24.

But make no mistake—that doesn't mean the *Necronomicon* is fake in the supernatural sense.

> [W]e can conclude that the hoax *Necronomicons*—at least the Hay-Wilson-Langford-Turner and Simon versions—falsely claim to be the work of the mad Arab Abdul Alhazred; but in so falsely attributing themselves, they signal their genuine inclusion in the grimoire genre. The misattribution is the mark of their genre, and their very falsity is the condition of their genuineness. The hoax *Necronomicons* are every bit as "authentic" as the *Lesser Key of Solomon* or the *Sixth and Seventh Books of Moses*.[13]

In other words, while the published editions of the *Necronomicon* were invented long after the deaths of H. P. Lovecraft and Aleister Crowley, they can still be used as tools for opening the gates of hell. And, as Grant and Levenda suggest, they appear to share a common supernatural origin.

Simon's *Necronomicon* arrived on the wave of a renewed interest in the occult that washed over the Western world in the 1960s and '70s. Interestingly, it was a French journal of science fiction that helped spark the revival, and it did so by publishing the works of H. P. Lovecraft for a new audience.

Planète was launched in the early '60s by Louis Pauwles and Jacques Bergier, and their magazine brought a new legion of admirers to the "bent genius." More significantly for our study here, however, was the book Pauwles and Bergier co-authored in 1960, *Les matins des magiciens* (*Morning of the Magicians*), which was translated into English in 1963 as *Dawn of Magic*.[14]

---

13   Dan Clore, "The Lurker on the Threshold of Interpretation: Hoax Necronomicons and Paratextual Noise." *Lovecraft Studies*, No. 42–43 (Autumn 2001). http://www.geocities.ws/clorebeast/lurker.htm, retrieved 2/9/24.

14   Jason Colavito, *The Cult of Alien Gods: H.P. Lovecraft And Extraterrestial Pop Culture* (Amherst, NY: Prometheus Books, 2005). Kindle Edition, location 1262.

From Lovecraft, Bergier and Pauwles borrowed the one thought that would be of more importance than any other in their book. As we have seen, *Morning of the Magicians* speculates that **extraterrestrial beings may be responsible for the rise of the human race and the development of its culture, a theme Lovecraft invented.**[15] (emphasis mine)

The success of Pauwles and Bergier inspired others to run with the concepts they'd developed from the writings of Lovecraft. The most successful of these, without question, is Erich von Däniken's *Chariots of the Gods?*

You can say one thing at least for von Däniken: He wasn't shy about challenging accepted history:

> I claim that our forefathers received visits from the universe in the remote past, even though I do not yet know who these extraterrestrial intelligences were or from which planet they came. I nevertheless proclaim that these "strangers" annihilated part of mankind existing at the time and produced a new, perhaps the first, *homo sapiens.*[16]

The book had the good fortune of being published in 1968, the same year Stanley Kubrick's epic adaptation of Arthur C. Clarke's *2001: A Space Odyssey* hit theaters. The film, based on the idea that advanced alien technology had guided human evolution, was the top-grossing film of the year, and was named the "greatest sci-fi film of all time" in 2002 by the Online Film Critics Society.[17] By 1971, when *Chariots*

---

15   Ibid., locations 1299–1300.

16   Erich Von Däniken, *Chariots of the Gods? Unsolved Mysteries of the Past* (New York: Berkley Books, 1968), p. viii.

17   "2001: A Space Odyssey Named the Greatest Sci-Fi Film of All Time By the Online Film Critics Society" (June 12, 2002). https://web.archive.org/web/20061126071451/http://ofcs.rottentomatoes.com/pages/pr/top100scifi, retrieved 2/9/24.

of the Gods? finally appeared in American bookstores, NASA had put men on the moon three times and the public was fully primed for what von Däniken was selling.

It's hard to overstate the impact *Chariots of the Gods?* has had on the UFO research community and the worldviews of millions of people around the world over the last half century. In 1973, *Twilight Zone* creator Rod Serling built a documentary around *Chariots* titled *In Search of Ancient Astronauts,* which featured astronomer Carl Sagan and Wernher von Braun, architect of the Saturn V rocket.[18] The following year, a feature film with the same title as the book was released to theaters. By the turn of the 21st century, von Däniken had sold more than 60 million copies of his twenty-six books, all promoting the idea that our creators came from the stars.[19]

To this day, von Däniken's book is the best-selling English language "archaeology" book of all time.[20] Is it any wonder that more Americans believe that we've been visited by ET than in God as He's revealed Himself in the Bible?[21]

---

18 Von Braun was one of the 1,600 or so Nazi scientists, engineers, and technicians secretly brought to the U.S. after the war during Operation Paperclip.
19 Colavito (2005), op. cit. Kindle location 1346.
20 Ibid., Kindle location 1338.
21 Derek P. Gilbert and Josh Peck, *The Day the Earth Stands Still* (Crane, Mo.: Defender, 2017), pp. 1–2. See footnotes 3–5.

CHAPTER THIRTY

GATES
IN SPACE

*I am the beginning. I am the end. I am the emissary. But the original
time I was on the Planet Earth was 34,000 of your years ago. I am
the balance. And when I say "I," I mean because I am an emissary
for The Nine. It is not I, but it is the group. We are nine principles of
the Universe, yet together we are one.*

—The Nine

Without a doubt, *Star Trek* is one of the most influential
entertainment franchises in history. Kirk, Spock, McCoy,
Scotty, and others are iconic characters, recognized around the world.
What you may not know, however, is that through series creator
Gene Roddenberry the starship *Enterprise* is linked to CIA mind con-
trol experiments, a group of "aliens" who claim to be the creators of
humanity, and, believe it or not, the assassination of President John F.
Kennedy.

During World War 2, a man named Andrija Puharich, the son
of immigrants from the Balkans, attended Northwestern University
outside Chicago where he earned a bachelor's degree in philosophy in
1942 and his M.D. in 1947. Through an invitation from a well-off
family friend, who'd married into the Borden dairy family, Puharich
found himself in Maine in early 1948, where he established a research

institute to pursue his interest in parapsychology, the Round Table Foundation of Electrobiology, usually shortened to the Round Table.[1]

An early member of the Puharich Round Table was Aldous Huxley, author of *Brave New World* and *The Doors of Perception*, a book about his experiences with mescaline (and the book that inspired rock singer Jim Morrison to name his band The Doors). Puharich financed his research with gifts from donors, one of whom was Henry Wallace, who'd been vice president under Franklin D. Roosevelt. Wallace, a 32nd degree Freemason, is the man who persuaded Roosevelt to add the reverse of the Great Seal of the United States—the pyramid and the all-seeing eye—to the dollar bill.[2]

This book isn't big enough to hold a full account of what Puharich was up to for the U.S. Army in the 1950s, but the upshot is that he was apparently researching parapsychology and chemical substances that might stimulate the human mind to reach into realities beyond those we can normally perceive with our natural senses. And at one of his gatherings in Maine, on New Year's Eve in 1952, Puharich and his Round Table, working with a Hindu channeler named Dr. D. G. Vinod, conducted a seance that apparently made contact with something calling itself The Nine.[3] Thus began a truly breathtaking chapter in America's mostly hidden programs that searched for ways to weaponize the occult.

Some months later, on June 27, 1953, the night of the full moon, Puharich gathered around him what was to be a core group of the Round Table Foundation for another session with Vinod. The membership of this group of nine members—á la

1   Peter Levenda, *Sinister Forces—The Nine: A Grimoire of American Political Witchcraft* (Walterville, Oregon: TrineDay, 2005), Kindle Edition, Kindle Locations 7603-7604.

2   Terry Melanson, "The All-Seeing Eye, The President, The Secretary and The Guru." *Conspiracy Archive*, July 2001. http://www.conspiracyarchive.com/NWO /All_Seeing_Eye.htm, retrieved 2/8/24.

3   Levenda (2005), op. cit., Kindle Locations 7734-7737.

The Nine—is illuminating. Henry Jackson, Georgia Jackson, Alice Bouverie, Marcella Du Pont, Carl Betz, Vonnie Beck, Arthur Young, Ruth Young, and Andrija Puharich. Dr. Vinod acted as the medium.

Imagine the Fellowship of the Ring, with government funding and a security classification that was, well, "cosmic."[4]

This group included old money—*very* old money. The Du Pont name is obvious, but some of the others were no less prominent. Alice Bouverie was an Astor—a descendent of John Jacob Astor and the daughter of Col. John Jacob Astor IV, who built the Astoria Hotel and went down with the Titanic. Arthur Young was the designer of the Bell helicopter; his wife had been born Ruth Forbes. Yes, the *Forbes* magazine Forbes. And Carl Betz was an actor at the beginning of his career in 1953 who later enjoyed success in Hollywood, best known as Donna Reed's television husband from 1958 to 1966 on *The Donna Reed Show*.

Ruth's previous marriage had been to another old money family that traced its roots back to the early days of the American colonies, George Lyman Paine. Their son, Michael Paine, married a woman named Ruth Hyde, and in 1963, Michael and Ruth Paine became friends with a young couple newly arrived from Russia, Lee and Marina Oswald.

Yes, *that* Lee Oswald. Lee Harvey Oswald. The man officially blamed for the assassination of President John F. Kennedy.

It sounds too outlandish to be true—almost like the setup up to a joke: A Du Pont, an Astor, and a Forbes/Paine walk into a seance, and it turns out to be a psychic research group funded by the United States government. Which begs the question: Who or what were they talking to? And what was the monkey-god doing there?

Dr. Vinod sat on the floor, the nine members of the group in a circle around him, with a copper plate on his lap, prayer beads

---

4   Ibid., Kindle Locations 7765-7769.

in his hands, and a small statue of "Hanoum," a Hindu god that the author believes to be Hanuman, the Monkey King. If this is so, it is interesting in that Hanuman was a human being, a minister, before becoming divine due to his devotion and courage. The half-human, half-divine image is one that becomes more important and more obvious as this study progresses. Another important aspect of Hanuman is his depiction in much Indian art as holding an entire mountain in one hand (and a club in the other). When—in the Ramayana and during the battle of Rama and Ravana—Lakshmana was mortally wounded, Hanuman raced to a mountain covered with different healing herbs. Not knowing which one Lakshmana required, Hanuman simply brought the entire mountain. Hanuman—as well as his fellow monkey-men, the Vanaras of southern India—is often shown with his hand in front of his mouth, signifying "silence" as well as obedience, in much the same way western occultists depict Harpocrates. In this sense, replete with silence, obedience, a club, and a mountain of herbs, Hanuman might easily have been the patron saint of MK-ULTRA.[5]

What an interesting coincidence—if you're a coincidence theorist. Speaking of "coincidences," remember that Aleister Crowley believed his holy text *The Book of the Law* was dictated to him by Aiwass, the messenger of Hoor-Paar-Kraat—Harpocrates, the Greek god of silence and secrets.

Anyway, The Nine contacted Puharich's group and declared that they wanted the Round Table to lead a spiritual renewal on Earth. Eventually, they revealed that they were highly advanced extraterrestrials orbiting the planet in a giant, invisible spacecraft.

Consider that the group assembled that night included highly intelligent, very successful people. These were not stereotypical "alien

---

5   Ibid.

abductees" mocked by the corporate media as unsophisticated hicks from backwoods Appalachia or the rural South. Puharich later wrote, "We took every known precaution against fraud, and the staff and I became thoroughly convinced that we were dealing with some kind of an extraordinary extraterrestrial intelligence."[6] In other words, if contact with The Nine was a hoax, it fooled some very smart and respectable people.

On the other hand, the decades-long career of Andrija Puharich suggests that it may also have been a case of "leading the witnesses," in a sense. He appears to have been a seeker who, like Fox Mulder in *The X-Files*, really wanted to believe.

But it was more than that. The Nine declared, "God is nobody else than we together, the Nine Principles of God."[7]

So, they claimed to be extraterrestrial *and* divine. And while the Round Table was hearing from The Nine, Aleister Crowley's acolyte and personal secretary Kenneth Grant was developing his occult system based on an ET god from Sirius.

Dr. Vinod returned to India a short time later and contact with The Nine was interrupted for more than fifteen years. Then, in 1971, Puharich discovered Israeli psychic Uri Geller.

Geller, best known for his alleged power to bend silverware with his mind, became for a time the new link to The Nine. Through Geller, The Nine informed Puharich that his life's mission was "to alert the world to an imminent mass landing of spaceships that would bring representatives of The Nine."[8]

Well, that didn't happen. And Geller decided to move on in 1973, so Puharich had to find someone else to bridge the gap between Earth and the giant, invisible craft that had allegedly been orbiting the earth for at least twenty years by that point. He eventually connected with

---

6 Andrea Puharich, *Uri; a Journal of the Mystery of Uri Geller* (Garden City, NY: Anchor Press, 1974), p. 18.

7 Wes Penre, "Plan Nine from Outer Space." *Fortean Times* 126, 1999. Republished at UriGeller.com: https://www.urigeller.com/plan-nine-outer-space/. Retrieved 2/8/24.

8 Ibid.

former race car driver Sir John Whitmore and Florida psychic Phyllis Schlemmer, who became the authorized spokesperson for their contact within The Nine, who finally identified himself as "Tom."[9]

> Puharich, Whitmore and Schlemmer then set up Lab Nine at Puharich's estate in Ossining, New York. The Nine's disciples included multi-millionaire businessmen (many hiding behind pseudonyms and including members of Canada's richest family, the Bronfmans), European nobility, scientists from the Stanford Research Institute and at least one prominent political figure who was a personal friend of President Gerald Ford.[10]

Also a member of Lab Nine in 1974 and '75 was *Star Trek* creator Gene Roddenberry, who reportedly wrote a screenplay based on The Nine. Some suggest that concepts from the channeling sessions Roddenberry attended surfaced in the early *Star Trek* movies and in the series *Star Trek: The Next Generation* and *Star Trek: Deep Space 9*. The latter series featured a prominent subplot in which the commander of the space station Deep Space 9, Starfleet officer Benjamin Sisko, was chosen as the Emissary of an alien race worshiped as gods, called the Prophets, by the people of planet Bajor. The Prophets reveal potential futures to the Bajorans through orbs, which cause visions in those selected for the experience. There are many parallels between the role of Commander Sisko as the Emissary and the mission The Nine purportedly planned for Uri Geller and the other members of Lab Nine.

Before Lab Nine folded in 1978, the identities of Tom and the Other Eight were finally revealed: Tom was Atum,[11] he said, creator-god of the Great Ennead, the Egyptian deities worshiped at Heliopolis, near modern-day Cairo. Besides Atum, the Ennead included his children Shu and Tefnut; their children Geb and Nut;

---

9   Ibid.
10 Ibid.
11 Ibid.

and their children Osiris, Isis, Set, Nephthys, and sometimes the son of Osiris and Isis, Horus.[12]

Connecting dots between Andrija Puharich, who was almost certainly a CIA asset during much of the time he conducted para-psychological research,[13] and the volunteers of his Round Table and Lab Nine, we can link the United States government, and specifically the U.S. Army and CIA during the period of mind control research projects like BLUEBIRD and MKULTRA,[14] members of upper class society from the East Coast and Canada, the creator of the most successful science fiction entertainment franchise in history, extra-terrestrials, and gods. And not just any gods—it was the pantheon that included the chaos-god, Set, the Egyptian form of the Greek cha-os-monster Typhon, who Crowleyite Kenneth Grant believed was the spirit of the age.

Oh, yes—and the Kennedy assassination.

How do we wrap our heads around this? Considering that Puhar-ich was probably doing this research for the government and that he led the witnesses, suggesting to Geller and at least one of his successors while they were under hypnosis that they were being contacted by The Nine,[15] this may have been a long PSYOP to stir up belief in the existence of ETs and the return of the old gods.

To what end? Maybe it was an experiment in group dynamics, or a test of how people would react to the imminent arrival of extrater-restrial visitors. Or maybe it was an intelligence op to lead the wealthy members of Lab Nine and their influential social circles to open them-selves to the spirit realm, turning themselves into portals.

Ancient alien evangelists have effectively proselytized the Amer-ican public in the same way in recent years. Recent surveys have discovered that more adults in the U.S. believe in ETs than in the God

---

12 Françoise Dunand and Christiane Zivie-Coche, *Gods and Men in Egypt: 3000 BCE to 395 CE* (Ithaca, London: Cornell University Press, 2004), p. 31.

13 Penre, op. cit.

14 Ibid.

15 Ibid.

of the Bible.[16] The irony is that longtime UFO researchers—serious ones, anyway—are disturbed by the impact the ancient alien meme has had on their work. Sadly, the U.S. government has been involved in enough bizarre research since World War 2[17] that claims of secret government programs find plenty of people who, like Mulder in *The X-Files*, want to believe.

Even MUFON, which bills itself "the world's oldest and largest UFO phenomenon investigative body,"[18] careened off the path of legitimate research in the second half of the 2010s, endorsing pseudo-scientific and often New Age interpretations of the UFO phenomenon instead of sticking to what can be supported by evidence. The theme of MUFON's 2017 national convention was "The Case for a Secret Space Program," which was described by one critic as "blatantly unscientific and irrational."[19]

The conference featured among its speakers Corey Goode, who claimed he was recruited for "a '20 & Back' assignment which involved age regression (via Pharmaceutical means) as well as time regressed to the point of beginning service."[20] In plain English, Goode says he served twenty years in an off-planet research project and then was sent back in time to a few minutes after he left and "age-regressed" so that no one would notice that he's twenty years older than the rest of us.

---

16   "More than one third of Americans believe aliens have visited Earth," *Christian Science Monitor*, June 28, 2012. https://www.csmonitor.com/Science/2012/0628 /More-than-one-third-of-Americans-believe-aliens-have-visited-Earth, retrieved 2/8/24; "The State of the Church 2016," September 15, 2016. https://www.barna .com/research/state-church-2016/, retrieved 2/8/24.

17   For example, openly dabbling with the supernatural, like the work of Puharich described above, the remote viewing experiments at Stanford Research Institute, or the weird experiments documented by journalist Jon Ronson in *The Men Who Stare at Goats*.

18   www.mufon.com, retrieved 8/23/17.

19   Robert Sheaffer, "MUFON Unravels". *Bad UFOs: Skepticism, UFOs, and the Universe*, August 1, 2017. https://badufos.blogspot.com/2017/08/mufon-unravels.html, retrieved 2/8/24.

20   Kevin Randle, "Are Some Tales Just too Wild to Believe: Corey Goode and Andrew Basiago." *A Different Perspective*, July 4, 2017. http://kevinrandle.blogspot.com /2017/07/are-some-tales-just-too-wild-to-believe.html, retrieved 2/9/24.

Look, if age-regression drugs were real, somebody would be making billions.

Another speaker at MUFON's 2017 symposium, Andrew Basagio, asserted that he was pre-identified as a future president of the United States in a CIA/DARPA program called Project Pegasus, which purportedly gathered intel on past and future events, like the identities of future presidents. Basagio also claimed he was Barack Obama's roommate in 1980 as part of a secret CIA project called Mars Jump Room,[21] a teleportation program to send trainees to a secret base on the Red Planet.[22]

Seriously.

The content was so over the top that Richard Dolan, a serious researcher and longtime advocate for ET disclosure, found it necessary to publicly explain why he'd agreed to appear on a MUFON-sanctioned discussion panel with men who claimed, with no corroboration whatsoever, that they'd been part of a "secret space program."

> [W]hen I learned I would be on a panel with Corey [Goode], Andy [Basiago], Bill [Tompkins], and Michael [Salla], I phoned Jan [Harzan, MUFON's Executive Director] and politely asked him what was he thinking. I mentioned my concern about MUFON's decision to bring in individuals with claims that are inherently impossible to verify. MUFON, after all, is supposed to have evidence-based standards.[23]

Maybe it shouldn't surprise us that MUFON has morphed from an "evidence-based" organization to one that actively promotes

21 Ibid.

22 Michael E. Salla, "Jump Room to Mars: Did CIA Groom Obama & Basiago as future Presidents?" *Exopolitics.org*, December 26, 2015. https://exopolitics.org/jump-room-to-mars-did-cia-groom-obama-basiago-as-future-presidents/, retrieved 2/9/24.

23 Richard Dolan, "On Corey, Andrew, and the Whistleblowers." Facebook, July 18, 2017. https://www.facebook.com/notes/richard-dolan/on-corey-andrew-and-the-whistleblowers/1394366947350897/, retrieved 8/26/17.

unverifiable claims at its national convention. As controversy grew over the theme of MUFON's 2017 symposium, it was revealed that MUFON's "Inner Circle," a group that provides "advisory guidance" to MUFON because its members—thirteen in all, a curiously coincidental number—have "shown unparalleled generosity towards MUFON by donating in excess of $5,000 in a single donation," included New Age teacher J. Z. Knight.[24]

Knight was born in Roswell, New Mexico (of course) in March 1946, just about the time Aleister Crowley devotees Jack Parsons and L. Ron Hubbard wrapped up their magickal ritual the Babalon [sic] Working to open the gates of hell and bring the Whore of Babylon to Earth. She claims to channel the spirit of Ramtha the Enlightened One, a warrior who lived 35,000 years ago in the mythical land of Lemuria. Knight says Ramtha fought against the tyrannical Atlanteans before eventually bidding his troops farewell and ascending to heaven in a flash of light.[25]

Ten years after Ramtha's first appearance, Knight founded Ramtha's School of Enlightenment, through which she has become a very wealthy woman by selling counseling sessions based on the wisdom of the ancient Lemurian warrior. (While Ramtha has no need for creature comforts, Ms. Knight apparently likes nice things.) As of 2017, the school employs 80 full-time staff,[26] and annual profits from book and audio sales run into the millions.[27] According to Knight, Ramtha's teachings can be boiled down to mind over matter: "Ramtha

24 Andrew Whalen, "What If Aliens Met Racists? MUFON Resignations Highlight Internal Divisions in UFO Sightings Organization." *Newsweek*, April 29, 2018. https://www.newsweek.com/ufo-sightings-mufon-2018-john-ventre-alien-extraterrestrial-905060, retrieved 2/9/24.

25 Judy Zebra Knight, *Ramtha, the White Book* (Yelm, WA: JZK Publishing, 2005).

26 John Iwasaki, "JZ Knight Not Faking It, Say Scholars – But They Bristle at the Idea She's Buying Them." *Seattle Post-Intelligencer*, February 10, 1997, p. B1.

27 Keri Brenner, "Disillusioned Former Students Target Ramtha". *The Olympian*, January 27, 2008. Via the Cult Education Institute. https://www.culteducation.com/group/1113-ramtha-school-of-enlightenment/17846-disillusioned-former-students-target-ramtha-.html, retrieved 2/9/24.

tells people that if they learn what to do, the art of creating your own reality is really a divine act. There's no guru here. You are creating your day. You do it yourself."[28]

That said, your authors assume that Ms. Knight, despite having mastered the art of creating her own reality, still looks both ways before crossing the street. Testing one's created reality against the hard reality of an oncoming bus is not recommended.

Three students of RSE produced the 2004 film *What the Bleep Do We Know?*, a low-budget movie that twisted quantum physics into pseudoscientific New Age propaganda. Of course, Ramtha's doctrine of changing the physical world through proper spiritual discipline was the heart of the film.[29] In spite of the criticism of actual physicists, *Bleep* has grossed nearly $16 million in theaters to date.[30]

The attention attracted by MUFON's bizarre symposium on the "secret space program" coupled with the disclosure of some of the aberrant views of its state leadership and Inner Circle—not just occult, but racist[31] (which was far more damaging to the organization)—apparently led to a restructuring after 2017. There is no mention of an inner circle at MUFON's website any longer, and while they tout a Science Review Board under the heading "Our People," there are no names given as members of that board and what appears to be a link to a page titled "The Scientific Method" goes nowhere.

As Christians, we must look past the human actors in movements like these. In the case of The Nine, how did their charade benefit the entities that spoke to Vinod, Geller, and Schlemmer? Frankly, it's difficult to identify a specific goal other than spreading spiritual confusion. Certainly, seeding these ideas through influential members of

---

28 Ibid.
29 John Gorenfeld, "'Bleep' of faith," *Salon*, September 16, 2004. https://www.salon.com/2004/09/16/bleep_2/, retrieved 2/9/24.
30 Box Office Mojo. http://www.boxofficemojo.com/movies/?id=whatthe.htm, retrieved 2/9/24.
31 "Former MUFON State Director Resigns, Cites Cult Leader Involvement," *UFO Watchdog*, July 24, 2017. http://ufowatchdog.blogspot.com/2017/07/former-mufon-state-director-resigns.html, retrieved 2/9/24.

high society and the military-industrial complex would be one way to do it. It's one thing to mock a blue-collar worker from rural America when he claims aliens are about to land, but it's a different story when it comes from a member of one of the wealthiest families in the world.

Spreading confusion about the Big Questions—where did we come from, why are we here, where do we go when we die—may be enough for the principalities, powers, thrones, and dominions. The rebellious small-G gods don't care what you believe as long as it's not this: Jesus is the way, and the truth, and the life, and no one comes to the Father except through him.[32]

But they're no doubt delighted that some of their human dupes are working to prepare the way for the return of their imprisoned brothers by throwing open the gates of hell.

---

32   . John 14:6.

CHAPTER THIRTY-ONE

HOLLYWOOD
AND THE ET PORTAL

*[R]eligion or religious themes have provided contemporary speculative
literature with some of its most cogent extrapolations, and, perhaps
not coincidentally, with some of science fiction's very best novels and
short stories.*

—WILLIS E. McNELLY, "Science Fiction and Religion"

I f H. P. Lovecraft used horror to introduce the idea of contact with
an alien "other" to the masses, the growing popularity of science fiction in the twentieth century established ET as a stereotype in popular
entertainment. It's hard to imagine, but our great-grandparents would
have had no idea what the phrase "little green men" was supposed to
mean.

Nineteenth-century forerunners like Jules Verne and H. G. Wells
demonstrated that fiction based on speculative science would sell.
Verne's 1865 *From the Earth to the Moon* was the first major work to
feature space travel; in 1898, Wells produced the first ET invasion
story with his classic *The War of the Worlds*. Another Welles, Orson,
transformed *The War of the Worlds* into a compelling radio drama on
Halloween Eve in 1938, although the story that the program caused a
national panic is, sadly, a myth. (Newspapers lost a lot of advertising
revenue to the new medium during the Great Depression and took

advantage of an opportunity to condemn radio—an early example of "fake news.")[1]

The popularity of the genre took off in the 1920s with the arrival of the first pulp magazines that featured science fiction, such as *Amazing Stories*, *Weird Tales*, *Astounding Stories*, and *Wonder Stories*. The Golden Age of science fiction arrived in 1937 when John W. Campbell took over as editor of *Astounding Science Fiction*. Campbell is widely considered the most influential editor of the early years of the genre, publishing first or early stories by Isaac Asimov, Lester del Rey, Robert Heinlein, A. E. Van Vogt, and Theodore Sturgeon, thus helping to launch the careers of many of the biggest names in 20th century science fiction.

Despite his insistence that writers research the science behind their stories, Campbell had an interest in parapsychology that grew over the years. Writers learned that topics like telepathy helped them sell stories to *Astounding*.[2] In 1949, Campbell discovered L. Ron Hubbard and published his first article on Dianetics, which Campbell described as "one of the most important articles ever published."[3] He suggested to some that Hubbard would win the Nobel Peace Prize for his creation.

Three years before selling Campbell on Dianetics, Hubbard participated in an event that comes from the "you can't make this stuff up" file: From January to March 1946, Hubbard and Jack Parsons, rocket engineer and one of the founders of the Jet Propulsion Laboratory, performed a series of sex magic rituals called the Babalon (sic) Working. It was intended to manifest an incarnation of the divine feminine, a concept based on the writings of Aleister Crowley and described in his 1917 novel *Moonchild*. So, through L. Ron Hubbard and Joseph

---

1   Martin Chilton, "The War of the Worlds panic was a myth." *The Telegraph*, May 6, 2016. https://www.telegraph.co.uk/radio/what-to-listen-to/the-war-of-the-worlds-panic-was-a-myth/, retrieved 2/10/24.

2   Larry McCaffery, "An Interview with Jack Williamson." *Science Fiction Studies* Vol. 18, Part 2 (July 1991). https://www.depauw.edu/sfs/interviews/williamson 54interview.htm, retrieved 8/6/17.

3   *Astounding Science Fiction*, April 1950, p. 132.

Campbell, science fiction fans, like readers of gothic horror through the works of H. P. Lovecraft and his successors, were just two degrees removed from the teachings of Aleister Crowley.

Campbell managed to capture the paranoia and dread that marked Lovecraft's work in his classic 1938 novella *Who Goes There?* The story has been adapted for the big screen three times—1951's *The Thing from Another World* (which featured a young James Arnett, TV's Matt Dillon, as the creature), 1982's *The Thing*, starring Kurt Russell, and a 2011 prequel, also titled *The Thing*.

The Kurt Russell film, set in Antarctica, draws on key Lovecraftian themes—an ancient extraterrestrial that poses an existential threat to all life on Earth, the loss of self as one is assimilated by the monster, and a claustrophobic setting. The plot unfolds inside a research station, where the bitter Antarctic cold confines most of the action to the interior of the base. The shapeshifting, paranoia-inducing monster imitates its victims perfectly, like the ETs in the 1956 classic *Invasion of the Body Snatchers*. The base scientist, played by the late Wilford Brimley, snaps when he realizes just how quickly the creature could destroy the earth if it escaped Antarctica. In his madness-inducing paranoia, Brimley's character is a lot like the protagonists in many of Lovecraft's stories.

Even the setting near the South Pole recalls Lovecraft, whose classic novella *At the Mountains of Madness* introduced a theme that's been revisited over the years in films like *The X-Files* and *Alien vs. Predator*—there's something beneath the ice down there that shouldn't be disturbed:

> It is absolutely necessary, for the peace and safety of mankind, that some of earth's dark, dead corners and unplumbed depths be let alone; lest sleeping abnormalities wake to resurgent life, and blasphemously surviving nightmares squirm and splash out of their black lairs to newer and wider conquests.[4]

---

4   H. P. Lovecraft, "At the Mountains of Madness." *Astounding Stories*, 16, No. 6 (February 1936), 8–32; 17, No. 1 (March 1936), 125–55; 17, No. 2 (April 1936),

Not coincidentally, UFO true believers claim to find alien craft half-buried in the Antarctic on a regular basis these days.

The point is that by the time Campbell began to elevate science fiction out of the swamp of pulp fiction in the late 1930s, the concept of unfriendly or uncaring ETs intervening in Earth's affairs was already a couple of decades old. By the late 1940s, it was already fodder for kiddie cartoons; Warner Brothers' Marvin the Martian (and his Uranium PU-36 Explosive Space Modulator) debuted in 1948, just one year after Kenneth Arnold's UFO sighting at Mount Rainier and the famous crash near Roswell, New Mexico.

In the decades since, science fiction has become, in the words of Dr. Michael S. Heiser, "televangelism for the ET religion."[5] People looking in from outside the genre may assume sci-fi is all rockets, ray guns, and lasers, but a lot of it theological. Films like *Prometheus*, *Mission to Mars*, and *2001: A Space Odyssey*, for example, conflate space travel, extraterrestrial intelligence, and religion by offering answers to the big questions the world's religions have been addressing since the beginning of time—where we come from, why we're here, and where we go when we die.

Human interaction with ETs has been a stock premise on television for decades, sometimes played for drama and sometimes for laughs. And the mix of space travel and religion has never been off-screen for long. The original *Star Trek* reimagined the gods of Greece and Rome as powerful aliens when they encountered Apollo in the second season episode "Who Mourns for Adonais?" Other entries in the *Star Trek* franchise likewise explored religious themes. The pilot episode of *Star Trek: The Next Generation* introduced Picard's godlike nemesis, Q, who eventually appeared in a dozen episodes of *The Next Generation*, *Star Trek: Deep Space 9*, and *Star Trek: Voyager*.

The 1994 film *Stargate* kicked off a long-running science fiction

---

132–50. https://www.hplovecraft.com/writings/texts/fiction/mm.aspx, retrieved 2/10/24.

5   That was the title of one of Dr. Heiser's presentations at the Modern Challenges to the ET Hypothesis Conference at the 2017 UFO Festival in Roswell.

franchise that centered on the return of the old gods to Earth. In the *Stargate* universe, the deities of the ancient Near East were parasitic, technologically advanced ETs called the Goa'Uld who ruled the earth thousands of years ago as gods. The movie follows a team of explorers who travel through a stargate to discover a world controlled by a brutal entity posing as the Egyptian sun-god Ra, whose spaceship looks a lot like the Great Pyramid of Giza.

The television series *Stargate SG-1* and its spinoffs continued that theme. The Norse pantheon was introduced in the series as the Asgard, whose appearance inspired stories of the alien Greys, and who, contrary to their reputation among ET contactees, side with humanity in the war against the Goa'Uld.

In other words, the *Stargate* franchise built an entire alternate history for the main religions of Earth: all of their gods are aliens. We don't recall how they explained why the gods stopped visiting Earth for a couple thousand years, and of course they never touched the third rail of Hollywood, Jesus. But considering what the series did to the pagan gods, it's just as well.

SG-1 ran from 1997 through 2007, surpassing *The X-Files* as the longest-running science fiction television series in North America until it was passed by *Smallville* in 2011, a series that featured another godlike ET, Superman.

Battlestar Galactica had two series runs, the first in 1978–79 and a second that ran for seventy-five episodes between 2003 and 2009. The original series was notable for being a thinly veiled dramatization of Mormon theology, including a council of twelve, marriage for "time and eternity," and a planet named Kobol. Religion was a prominent theme in the reboot, too; the twelve "Lords of Kobol" were the gods of the Greco-Roman pantheon, and the twelve occupied planets of humanity were named for the signs of the zodiac.

In the 2003 reboot, the Cylons, sentient robots who rebelled against their human masters, were depicted as monotheistic. Their religion looked like Christianity minus Christ, where the god worshiped by the AI-powered Cylons resembled an atheist's stereotypical depiction of God in the Old Testament, all anger and smiting of unbelievers.

The reimagined *Battlestar* introduced a new element: Humanoid Cylons so lifelike they were indistinguishable from humans. As the series developed, it was revealed that there were only seven models, but many copies of each. Model number One, Cavil, deceived the other Cylons by hiding the identities of the remaining humanoid Cylon models, the "Final Five." Finding the unknown Cylons was a major plot thread in the series, and their ultimate disclosure to the human fleet was the turning point that led humanity to salvation on a new Earth.

That Cylon plot twist draws from several Western occult traditions, especially as they've been syncretized into Theosophy. Madame Blavatsky wrote in *The Secret Doctrine* that seven "rays" together form all energy and all forms produced by it—in other words, you, us, and everything around us. These "rays" are also intelligent beings called the Dhyan Chohans.

Since at least the early 1970s, however, some New Age leaders like Elizabeth Clare Prophet have been teaching that there are "five secret rays," which "promote an action of detail, the final sculpturing of the mind and consciousness in the perfect image of the Christ."[6] We don't know why the writers of the reimagined *Battlestar* added the Final Five plot line, but the parallel to current New Age thinking is unlikely to be a coincidence.

Comic books have also mined human theology for decades. Beyond the obvious, such as Marvel making a superhero out of the Norse storm-god Thor (who is a cognate for Jupiter, Zeus, and Baal—in other words, same god with different names), researcher and author Christopher Knowles makes a strong case in his book *Our Gods Wear Spandex: The Secret History of Comic Book Heroes* for comic book heroes as a modern rebranding of ancient mythological archetypes.

---

6   Elizabeth Clare Prophet, *The Seven Chohans - On the Path of the Ascension: The Opening of the Retreats of the Great White Brotherhood* (Malibu: Summit University Press, 1973), p. 193.

This culture is far more influential (and insidious) than most realize. Most contemporary action movies take their visual language from comic books. The rhythm of constant hyper-violence of today's action movies comes straight from Jack Kirby. Elvis Presley idolized Captain Marvel Jr., to the point of adopting his hairstyle.

. . .

Although most of us don't realize it, there's simply nothing new about devotion to superheroes. Their powers, their costumes, and sometimes even their names are plucked straight from the pre-Christian religions of antiquity. When you go back and look at these heroes in their original incarnations, you can't help but be struck by how blatant their symbolism is and how strongly they reflect they belief systems of the pagan age. What even fewer people realize is that this didn't occur by chance, but came directly out of the spiritual and mystical secret societies and cults of the late 19th century—groups like the Theosophists, the Rosicrucians, and the Golden Dawn.[7]

Popular movies based on comics or graphic novels featuring the ET/religion theme include the *Transformers* franchise, *X-Men Apocalypse*, and the *Guardians of the Galaxy* films. The common thread: ETs exist, they're coming to Earth, and it's either going to be awesome or apocalyptic when they get here.

And how has eighty years of pop culture pushing the ET meme shaped our ideas about contact? Seth Shostak, lead astronomer for the SETI (Search for Extraterrestrial Intelligence) Institute, hit the nail on the head:

I think we are ready for ET contact in some sense, because the public has been conditioned to the idea of life in space by

---

7   Christopher Knowles and Joseph Michael Linsner, *Our gods wear Spandex the secret history of comic book heroes* (San Francisco: Weiser Books, 2007), p. 18.

movies and TV. And if you go into a classroom with a bunch of 11-year olds and ask them, "How many of you kids think there are aliens out there?" they all raise their hands! Why? Is it because their parents have been educating them about astrobiology? No. It's because they've seen them on TV!

...

I think that Hollywood is by far the biggest term in the equation of the public's reaction to confirmation of alien life.[8]

It's a concept that's been drawn from nineteenth-century occult groups and filtered through pulp magazines, sci-fi novels, radio dramas, cartoons, comic books, graphic novels, movies, and television, packaged as popular entertainment and sold as a worldview to the last four generations. How long before an official announcement that the ETs—the old gods—are finally back?

One last thing: Isn't it odd that the lead astronomer of the group searching for ETs is named for the chaos-god, Seth (Set)? And that the group's acronym, SETI, is Egyptian for "man of Set?" Should we be concerned that Set-Typhon, the dark lord of chaos, is the one Aleister Crowley's successor, Kenneth Grant, believed is the spirit of our age? And that it's apparently reaching out to Earth from somewhere in the direction of Sirius?

In other words, is it possible that the gates of hell will open in the sky above us rather than emerging from below the earth?

---

8   Robbie Graham, "SETI Astronomer says We're Ready for Alien Contact... Thanks to Hollywood." *Mysterious Universe*, July 19, 2017. http://mysteriousuniverse.org /2017/07/seti-atronomer-says-were-ready-for-alien-contact-thanks-to-hollywood/, retrieved 8/6/17.

CHAPTER THIRTY-TWO

TRIPPING THROUGH
THE GATES

*We have severed our connection to spirit. That's what our society has
done. It has sought to persuade us that the material realm is the only
realm. And the only way we're going to recover is to reconnect with
spirit. And I truly believe we need the help of the plants in order to
do that.*

—GRAHAM HANCOCK, *DMT: The Spirit Molecule*

The delusion of modernity in the Western world has mingled with
the innate human desire to connect with something greater than
oneself to produce a strange and dangerous phenomenon in recent
years. There has been a growth in tourism from advanced nations to
the Amazon to seek out shamans and drink a concoction called ayahuasca. The active ingredient, Dimethyltryptamine (DMT), produces
brief but intense hallucinations. Because of the type of visions experienced while under the influence of the drug, DMT has been dubbed
"The Spirit Molecule." But are the experiences of users just chemical
reactions inside the brain or journeys into a realm we're not designed
to inhabit?

Consumption of ayahuasca in South America goes back more
than two thousand years. Hair analysis of twenty-two mummies from
southern Peru found that the psychoactive plants that make up ayahuasca, a sludgy, bitter tea, were used as early as 100 BC by the Nazca

culture.[1] The practice of using mind-altering substances to break down barriers between the natural world and the spirit realm is practice found all over the world, and is millennia older than the Nazca mummies; archaeologists recently discovered that the Philistines of Gath, Goliath's hometown, apparently used plant-based substances in ritual practices,[2] and researchers at Göbekli Tepe, a site near Harran in southern Türkiye that's been called the world's oldest temple,[3] discovered evidence of brewing—large limestone troughs capable of holding up to forty-two gallons of liquid with traces of oxalates, which are produced during fermentation.[4] Given the ritualistic aspects of the site, it's probable that the primitive brew produced at Göbekli Tepe had a role in festivals of some kind.

Today, we in the West fancy ourselves enlightened, scientific, and modern. The ritual dances and sacrifices of ancient times are relics of a dim, dark past, long before the discovery of such things as biology, psychology, and the scientific method. Application of science to the search for gateways to the unseen realm led to the synthesis of DMT in 1931 by Canadian chemist Dr. Richard Manske, and the isolation and identification of the molecule in the 1950s by American researchers working with botanical samples from South America.

Minute amounts of DMT are found in the human brain, although not in high enough concentrations to produce the psychoactive effects

1   Zach Zorich, "Earliest Ayahuasca Trip." *Archaeology*, March/April 2023. https://www.archaeology.org/issues/503-2303/digs/11212-digs-peru-nazca-ayahuasca, retrieved 3/7/24.

2   Suembikya Frumin; Aren M. Maeir;, Maria Eniukhina; Amit Dagan; Ehud Weiss, "Plant-related Philistine ritual practices at biblical Gath." *Scientific Reports* 14:3513 (2024).

3   Andrew Curry, "Gobekli Tepe: The World's First Temple?" *Smithsonian Magazine*, Nov. 2008. https://www.smithsonianmag.com/history/gobekli-tepe-the-worlds-first -temple-83613665/, retrieved 3/7/24.

4   Tia Ghose, "Alcohol: Social Lubricant for 10,000 Years." *LiveScience*, Dec. 31, 2012. https://www.livescience.com/25855-stone-age-beer-brewery-discovered.html, retrieved 3/7/24.

reported by people during a DMT trip.[5] Some claim that it's produced by the pineal gland, which has a somewhat romanticized history as the "third eye" or seat of the soul, but scientific evidence for this is scant.[6] What is certain is that those who smoke, drink, or inject DMT consistently report encountering non-human entities; at least half report experiencing their own deaths;[7] and travel to South America to partake of the shamanic substance has been increasing ever since Beat Generation author William S. Burroughs published *The Yage Letters* in 1963, a novelized collection of correspondence between Burroughs and poet Allen Ginsburg about their experiences with the drug.[8]

Ayahuasca has gained some prominent endorsements in recent years; best-selling author Graham Hancock has written and talked often about his "beautiful experience" with "Mother Ayahuasca" since 2003,[9] former Police frontman Sting called it "the only genuine religious experience I've ever had,"[10] and Prince Harry said the drug helped him accept and move on from the death of his mother, Princess Diana.[11] Influential podcaster Joe Rogan's interviews with others who have tripped on DMT have been described as "a psychedelic record

5 David E. Nichols, "N,N-dimethyltryptamine and the pineal gland: Separating fact from myth." *J Psychopharmacol* (2018) Jan;32(1), pp. 30–36.

6 Ibid.

7 Jonathan David; José Carlos Bouso; Maja Kohek; Genís Ona; Nir Tadmor; Tal Arnon; Yair Dor-Ziderman; Aviva Berkovich-Ohana, "Ayahuasca-induced personal death experiences: prevalence, characteristics, and impact on attitudes toward death, life, and the environment." *Frontiers in Psychiatry* 14:1287961 (2023).

8 James Draven, "Hot topic: Is ayahuasca tourism a bad trip?" *National Geographic*, Apr. 8, 2019. https://www.nationalgeographic.co.uk/travel/2017/03/hot-topic-is-ayahuasca-tourism-a-bad-trip, retrieved 3/7/24.

9 Graham Hancock, "Returning to Ayahuasca after three years away." *Graham Hancock.com*, Nov. 27, 2018. https://grahamhancock.com/returning-to-ayahuasca-after-three-years-away/, retrieved 3/7/24.

10 Draven, op. cit.

11 Amber Raiken, "Prince Harry says that doing ayahuasca helped him accept Diana's death: 'She wants me to be happy'." *The Independent*, Jan. 13, 2023. https://www.independent.co.uk/life-style/royal-family/prince-harry-spare-diana-death-b2261955.html, retrieved 3/15/24.

of the 21stst century."[12] Given that Rogan's podcast generally draws millions of views per episode, he's introduced the idea to many who'd never heard of ayahuasca or DMT before.

Those who've undertaken a journey on DMT almost without exception report powerful experiences that have changed the way they view reality. Those confronted with a sense of their own death during a trip came out of it with "an increased sense of transcending death…as well as the certainty in the continuation of consciousness after death."[13] Why this would be so is a mystery science can't address. From a Christian perspective, we suggest that this is perhaps the intended "message" for experiencers from the entities who inhabit the realm they visited during their ayahuasca trips.

For that is the other experience consistently reported by those who've taken DMT: Encounters with discarnate—that is, disembodied—entities.

One recent study found that 94% of those surveyed encountered other "beings" during their DMT experiences, while 100% reported emerging into other "worlds."[14] Other studies, conducted under more controlled conditions with volunteers taking consistent doses of DMT, resulted in fewer encounters with entities, but they were striking nonetheless:

> Among the most vivid, intriguing, memorable, and sometimes disconcerting experiences that people report after taking a high dose of inhaled or intravenous DMT are those of encountering seemingly autonomous entities or beings. Although description of the nature of the entities, details of the experiences, and meaning attributed to the experiences vary widely, such

12 David E. Carpenter, "Podcast Host Joe Rogan Is Steadily Documenting A Psychedelic Record Of The 21st Century." *Forbes*, Feb. 26, 2020. https://www.forbes.com /sites/davidcarpenter/2020/02/26/podcast-host-joe-rogan-is-steadily-documenting -a-psychedelic-record-of-the-21st-century/, retrieved 3/7/24.

13 David et al., op. cit.

14 Pascal Michael; David Luke; Oliver Robinson, "An Encounter With the Other: A Thematic and Content Analysis of DMT Experiences From a Naturalistic Field Study." *Frontiers in Psychology*, 12: 720717 (2021), doi: 10.3389/fpsyg.2021.720717.

experiences are apparently not infrequent. Strassman (2008) estimated that at least half of the participants in his studies of high doses of intravenous DMT reported experiences of journeys to invisible or alternative worlds, and that contact with alien beings or entities were a variant of this category.

Dr. Rick Strassman, author of the 2001 book *DMT: The Spirit Molecule*, was the first to conduct clinical research on psychedelics in the United States in twenty years. Between 1990 and 1995, sixty volunteers were dosed with intravenous DMT in a study conducted at the University of New Mexico. Their reactions to the experiment led Strassman to conclude that his volunteers had received information from outside themselves rather than generating hallucinations from within. Strassman found this so profound that it caused him to abandon his Buddhist beliefs. The concept of *nirvana*, freedom from suffering and the dissolution of self, couldn't explain the experiences reported by his volunteers. If Buddhism and other strains of Eastern religion were true, then one would not expect to find independent, intelligent, and sometimes malevolent entities floating about in the ether. Strassman re-engaged with his Jewish roots by studying the Hebrew Bible.[15]

Dr. Strassman was interviewed by Derek for his podcast *A View from the Bunker* in 2010[16] and was a genial, well-spoken guest. Sadly, despite his return to studying the scriptures, Strassman concluded that the Hebrew prophets may have accessed knowledge about the future through DMT trips. He outlined this theory in his 2014 book *DMT and the Soul of Prophecy: A New Science of Spiritual Revelation in the Hebrew Bible*. According to Strassman, the visions of Ezekiel, Moses,

---

15 Gabriel D. Roberts, "Blasting Off with Dr. DMT." *Motherboard*, Apr. 2, 2014. https://www.vice.com/en/article/bn5je3/blasting-off-with-dr-dmt, retrieved 3/7/24.

16 "Dr. Rick Strassman—DMT: The Spirit Molecule." *A View from the Bunker*, Aug. 1, 2010. https://www.vftb.net/?p=3907, retrieved 3/7/24.

and Daniel were "strikingly similar to those of the volunteers in his DMT studies."[17]

> Carefully examining the concept of prophecy in the Hebrew Bible, he characterizes a "prophetic state of consciousness" and explains how it may share biological and metaphysical mechanisms with the DMT effect.
>
> Examining medieval commentaries on the Hebrew Bible, Strassman reveals how Jewish metaphysics provides a top-down model for both the prophetic and DMT states, a model he calls "theoneurology." Theoneurology bridges biology and spirituality by proposing that the Divine communicates with us using the brain, and DMT--whether naturally produced or ingested--is a critical factor in such visionary experience.[18]

The fundamental difference between the experiences of Strassman's volunteers and the Hebrew prophets is that their visions were initiated by God, not by drinking psychedelic tea! But Strassman, at least as of 2014, proposed additional research with DMT to learn how we might initiate prophetic experiences—despite God's clear instructions to Moses that His people were *not* to seek direct contact with spirits to get special revelation, specifically linking necromancy and communication with spirits to the sacrifice of children to Molech.[19]

The encounters with entities reported by volunteers is one of the most disturbing aspects of the DMT experience. While most reported contact with the entities was pleasant, some were decidedly sinister:

> There is a sinister backdrop, an alien-type, insectoid, not-quite-pleasant side of this, isn't there? It's not a "We're-going-to

---

17 Quote from the publisher's page for *DMT and the Soul of Prophecy.* https://www.simonandschuster.com/books/DMT-and-the-Soul-of-Prophecy/Rick-Strassman/9781594773426, retrieved 3/7/24.

18 Ibid.

19 Heider, op. cit., p. 96.

get-you-[deleted]." It's more like being possessed. During the experience there is sense of someone, or something else, there taking control. It's like you have to defend yourself against them, whoever they are, but they certainly are there. I'm aware of them and they're aware of me. It's like they have an agenda. It's like walking into a different neighborhood. You're really not quite sure what the culture is. It's got such a distinct flavor, the reptilian being or beings that are present.[20]

Another volunteer reported a bizarre, unpleasant encounter with the insectoids:

When I was first going under there were these insect creatures all around me. They were clearly trying to break through. I was fighting letting go of who I am or was. The more I fought, the more demonic they became, probing into my psyche and being. I finally started letting go of parts of myself, as I could no longer keep so much of me together. As I did, I still clung to the idea that all was God, and that God was love, and I was giving myself up to God and God's love because I was certain I was dying. As I accepted my death and dissolution into Gods love, the insectoids began to feed on my heart, devouring the feelings of love and surrender.

It's not like LSD. Things really closed in around me, in comparison to the spaciousness that I feel with LSD. There was no feeling of space. Everything was in close. I've never seen anything like that. They were interested in emotion. As I was holding on to my last thought, that God equals love, they said, "Even here? Even here?"

I said, "Yes, of course." They were still there but I was making love to them at the same time. They feasted as they made

---

20 Rick Strassman, *DMT: The Spirit Molecule* Rochester, VT: Park Street Press, 2001), p. 189.

love to me. I don't know if they were male or female or something else, but it was extremely alien, though not necessarily unpleasant. The thought came to me with certainty that they were manipulating my DNA, changing its structure.

And then it started fading. They didn't want me to go.

The sheer intensity was almost unbearable. The forms became increasingly sinister the more I fought. I'm going to need therapy after this—sex with insects![21]

Most disturbing was this account:

There were two crocodiles. On my chest. Crushing me, raping me anally. I didn't know if I would survive. At first I thought I was dreaming, having a nightmare. Then I realized it was really happening.[22]

We're not aware of research into the possible causes of the vastly different experiences reported by those who have taken DMT. In other words, did those with negative experiences have histories of trauma, or did they bring spiritual baggage of some kind into the spirit realm that provoked the entities? Were the entities hostile just because they felt like it, in the same way a child might ignore an ant on the sidewalk one day and then stomp on another the next? Or are they simply evil?

To be fair, we must repeat that most of the volunteers, and most of those surveyed who imbibed ayahuasca or DMT outside of a clinical setting, reported positive outcomes from their visions—which the majority interpreted as supernatural encounters facilitated by DMT rather than chemical reactions to the drug.

Aspects of the experience and its interpretation had metaphysical implications for most (80%) of the respondents about

---

21 Ibid., p. 206.
22 Ibid., p. 252.

their fundamental understanding of the nature of reality. For example, **most respondents indicated that the entity had the attributes of being conscious, intelligent, and benevolent, existed in some real but different dimension of reality, and continued to exist after the encounter.** These experiences were also rated as among the most meaningful, spiritual, and psychologically insightful lifetime experiences, with persisting positive changes in life satisfaction, purpose and meaning attributed to the experiences. **More than half of those who identified as atheist before the experience no longer identified as atheist afterwards.**[23] (emphasis added)

Just so we're clear, we believe the entities encountered by Strassman's volunteers and those surveyed by other researchers are real and not drug-induced hallucinations. In his book, Strassman noted surprising similarities between some of the experiences reported by his subjects and the victims of "alien abduction," including descriptions of experimentation on the volunteers by the entities they encountered.

In short, since Burroughs published the record of his encounters with DMT sixty years ago, the drug has gained a reputation as a tool for opening doorways into the spirit realm where users may encounter "intelligent, and benevolent" entities or guides to help them make "persistent positive changes" in their lives—without having to acknowledge the overlordship of a transcendent God or spend a lot of time reading the Bible.

That's what you'd expect from entities waiting for unprepared humans foolish enough to willingly step inside the gates of hell.

---

23 Alan K. Davis; John M. Clifton; Eric G. Weaver; Ethan S. Hurwitz; Matthew W. Johnson; Roland R. Griffiths, "Survey of entity encounter experiences occasioned by inhaled N,N-dimethyltryptamine: Phenomenology, interpretation, and enduring effects." *Journal of Psychopharmacology*, Vol. 34(9) (2020), p. 1018.

CHAPTER THIRTY-THREE

GATES IN THE ALPS: THE GOAT-MAN RISES

So they shall no more sacrifice their sacrifices to goat demons, after whom they whore. This shall be a statute forever for them throughout their generations.

—LEVITICUS 17:7 (ESV)

T he Gotthard Base Tunnel began in 1947 with a curious sketch by Swiss engineer Carl Eduard Gruner.

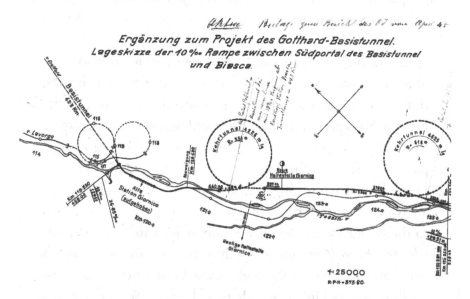

The above sketch appears to show several circles, reminiscent of the massive colliders at CERN.

During World War 2, the Gruner Group (formerly Gruner Brothers) constructed railways, powers plants, and irrigation systems, but it was Gruner's imagined shortcut through the base of the Alps, connecting the Swiss towns of Erstfeld and Bodio by burrowing beneath the St. Gotthard Massif in the central Swiss Alps, that would prove to be the company's greatest design. The Gotthard Base Tunnel (GBT) is the world's deepest (1.42 miles) and longest tunnel (route length of 35.5 miles with a total of 94.3 miles when all shafts and passages are included). The tunnel consists of two parallel passages, each moving in a single direction on a single track.

The GBT passes directly beneath St. Gotthard's Pass, a strategic north/south corridor that connects northern and southern Switzerland. Prior to the construction of the modern-day tunnels, including the Gotthard Rail Tunnel built in the 1880s, the only way to pass through this treacherous region was to cross the Devil's Bridge (die Teufelsbrücke), which is aptly named considering the strange ceremony which accompanied the opening of the newest tunnel beneath the Massif. There is a legend regarding this Devil's Bridge related by early eighteenth-century Swiss physician Johann Jakob Scheuchzer. According to Scheuchzer:

[T]he people of Uri recruited the Devil for the difficult task of building the bridge. The Devil requested to receive the first thing to pass the bridge in exchange for his help. To trick the Devil, who expected to receive the soul of the first man to pass the bridge, the people of Uri sent across a dog by throwing a piece of bread, and the dog was promptly torn to pieces by the Devil. Enraged at having been tricked the Devil went to fetch a large rock to smash the bridge, but, carrying the rock back to the bridge, he came across a holy man who "scolded him" (*der ihn bescholten*) and forced him to drop the rock, which could still be seen on the path below Göschenen. A modern retelling was published by Meinrad Lienert, *Schweizer Sagen und Heldengeschichten* (1915). According to Lienert's version, a goat was sent across the bridge instead of a dog, and instead of the holy man, the Devil, when he was taking a break exhausted from carrying the rock, came across an old woman who marked the rock with a cross, forcing the Devil to abandon it and flee.[1]

Erstfeld lies a twisty 186 miles or so from Geneva, the location of CERN and the Large Hadron Collider, and Bodio, the southern portal for the new tunnel, is just as far (or farther, if one chooses to go through Erstfeld first—a laborious journey, but one that Google maps apparently suggests). The connection to Geneva's Large Hadron Collider must be made, primarily because of the bizarre opening ceremony that was live-streamed to the entire world on June 1, 2016. So, let's unpack the imagery within that occult dance, beginning with a call to unite the religions of the world by conducting an "interfaith" blessing of the tunnel beside a statue of St. Barbara, the patron saint of miners. St. Barbara is another curious component in this bizarre ceremony. Traditionally, her veneration and worship is said to have begun in Bohemia. According to C. E. Gregory:

> Barbara Cathedral in Kuttenberg (Bohemia) built between 1388 and 1518 in the old silver city. This was thought to be the most likely source of the Barbara adoration. The cathedral was built around an already existing Barbara altar in an area with many Barbara altars present. Kuttenberg has for centuries had on its coat of arms St. Barbara above the crossed hammer and gad. [Schlaegel und Eisen—the classical symbol of mining][2]

---

1   "Schöllenen Gorge." *Wikipedia*, citing Johann Jakob Scheuchzer, *Naturgeschichte des Schweitzerlandes* vol. 2 (1747 [1716]), p. 94. https://en.wikipedia.org/wiki/Schöllenen_Gorge, retrieved 2/29/24.

2   C. E. Gregory, "The Legend of St. Barbara, the Patron Saint of Mines." https://www.geomar.de/fileadmin/content/zentrum/ze/bib/Real/The_Legend_of_Saint_Barbara.pdf. Retrieved 2/29/24.

Allegedly, Barbara lived during the third century AD in Nicomedia, the capital of Bithynia in Asia Minor,[3] a province in what is now northern Türkiye. Other versions of her life name her place of birth as Heliopolis, Phoenicia, known today as Baalbek in Lebanon.[4] Though her father planned to marry her off to a wealthy and influential friend who served the old gods of paganism (if they lived near Baalbek, one can surmise which entities her father actually served), but Barbara chose Christianity instead—dying a martyr's death for her trouble when she was tortured by the Roman pro-consul and then beheaded by her father.[5] Barbara is also considered one of the Fourteen Holy Helpers,[6] a group of super-saints whose core members are three virgin martyrs: St. Catherine, St. Margaret, and of course, St. Barbara.[7] Barbara is associated with a tower, because her father shut her up in one to keep her from the world while he arranged her marriage to his pagan buddy. Catherine is linked with "the wheel," a torture device known as the breaking wheel, which, when Catherine was placed upon it, shattered, leaving the torturer, Maxentius, no choice but to behead her. And Margaret, is associated with "the Dragon," because Satan in the form of a dragon had tried to eat her, but her cross irritated his tummy, so he disgorged Margaret and she was put to death.

Three virgins who serve as super saints, and a tower, a wheel, and the Dragon. It sounds like a hand from a Tarot deck! It is also a dark echo of the three faces of the pagan moon goddess: The Virgin/Maiden (in white), the Harlot/Mother (in red and often pregnant), and the Crone/Widow (an old woman dressed in black).

Connected to this idea of a "triple goddess," is a legend called "The

3 Ibid.

4 "St. Barbara." *Catholic Online*. https://www.catholic.org/saints/saint.php?saint_id=166, retrieved 2/29/24.

5 Johann Peter Kirsch, "St. Barbara." *The Catholic Encyclopedia* Vol. 2 (New York: Robert Appleton Company, 1907). http://www.newadvent.org/cathen/02284d.htm, retrieved 2/29/24.

6 *Catholic Online*, ibid.

7 "Capital Virgins." *Wikipedia*. https://en.wikipedia.org/wiki/Capital_Virgins, retrieved 2/29/24.

Three Bethan," a triune goddess worshiped throughout Bavaria that is eerily similar to this notion of three virgin super saints. Some druids believe that these three supposedly "Christian" virgins gave all their money to build a chapel, but are actually pagan in origin:

> 'Beten' in modern German means 'to pray'. Probably the act of worshipping the Bethen was so important and widespread that their name left its mark on the word for praying to them. Firpet or Firbet, the name of the third woman on the Leutstetten image, in modern German sounds pretty much like 'Fürbitte' (intercession).
>
> The Bethen were venerated especially in the presence of trees, wells and stones. This finds its expression in the terms 'Bethelbäume' (Bethen trees), 'Bethenbrunnen' (Bethen wells) and 'Bethensteine' (Bethen stones). As we know, worship at wells, in forest groves and near unusual stones was a widespread feature in Celtic and Germanic religion, so we can safely assume that the Bethen cult has pre-Christian roots.[8]

Now, why would we even care about pagan triple-goddesses, if our topic for this chapter is a tunnel beneath an Alpine pass? It's because of the unusual ceremony that inaugurated this dual tunnel system, and the interfaith call to worship that occurred in front of St. Barbara (whose "triple goddess" identity is made clearer in the ceremony itself). Three women—three aspects of the same moon/fertility goddess.

But the Triple Goddess is not restricted to Alpine mythology:

- **Greek:** Hebe/Hera/Hecate (also Artemis/Selene/Hecate); Aphrodite Urania/Aphrodite Pontia/Aphrodite Pandemos
- **Roman:** Luna/Diana/Proserpina; Phoebe/Diana/Hecate; Juventas/Juno/Minerva

---

8   Philip Carr-Gomm, "The Bavarian Triple Goddess - A Study of the Cult of the Three Bethan." *Druidry.org*, March 9, 2020. https://druidry.org/resources/bavarian -triple-goddess-study-cult-three-bethan, retrieved 2/29/24.

- **Egyptian:** Hathor/Bast/Sekhmet; Hathor/Nephthys/Isis
- **Hindu:** Parvati/Lakshmi/Saraswati
- **Irish:** Badb/macha/Morrígu
- **Mesopotamian:** Inanna/Ishtar/Astarte; Asherah/Astarte/Anat
- **Arabian (pre-Islamic):** Al-Lat/Al-Uzza/Manat
- **Norse:** Freyja/Frigg/Skaði[9]

The worship of a triune goddess is universal in scope, representing an "interfaith" coalescing that we even see in Catholicism to a certain degree (a faith that dominated most of Europe at one time). The Virgin Mother who is later widowed or in mourning parallels the pagan ideas of virginity, fecundity, and death.

Following the "blessing" at the statue of St. Barbara, the surviving family members and press along with visiting dignitaries also paid tribute to the nine miners who lost their lives during construction of the tunnel. Nine is another occult signature number. It is three squared, which is a hidden 32, and it's 3 x 3, giving us a hidden 33. 3 + 3 is 6, the number of man, and this number added to 3 (6 + 3) gives us 9, an inverted 6, turning God's creation on its head, an act and philosophy central to the "as above, so below" doctrine of the inverted tree of life (which is worshiped at the end of this ceremony).

Bodio's "southern portal" provided the visiting dignitaries a disturbing parade of miners, erotic dancers, zombies, fallen angels, and a gay love-fest, all obeying the call of the "shepherd," whose yodels invoke the appearance of the event's infernal master of ceremonies, the "Goat Man." Portrayed by a young and energetic dancing male, this creature is shown with a Baphomet headdress (a goat demon's head) and a goat body costume (hairy pelt) with a formal tuxedo over top. This imagery is heavily evocative of the German and Bavarian Christmas demon, Krampus.

---

9   "Triple Deity." *Wikipedia.* https://en.wikipedia.org/wiki/Triple_deity, retrieved 2/29/24.

1900s greeting card that reads,
"Greetings from Krampus!"

According to tradition, Krampus accompanies St. Nicholas on his mid-winter rounds with the intent to steal boys and girls, putting them into a basket carried on his back, or he may decide to beat them with branches for being naughty. Maurice Bruce published a book on pre-Christian Alpine traditions in 1958, and he had this to say about this half-goat, half-demon entity:

> There seems to be little doubt as to his true identity for, in no other form is the full regalia of the Horned God of the Witches so well preserved. The birch—apart from its phallic significance—may have a connection with the initiation rites of certain witch-covens; rites which entailed binding and scourging as a form of mock-death. The chains could have been introduced in a Christian attempt to 'bind the Devil' but again they could be a remnant of pagan initiation rites.[10]

Krampus, despite his negative imagery and proclivities, was wildly popular during the holidays in Germanic and Alpine countries, so

---

10 Maurice Bruce, "The Krampus in Styria." *Folklore* 69:1 (March 1958), pp. 44–47.

much so that an entire sub-genre of greeting cards known as Krampus Grüsskarten (that invariably say "Grüss vom Krampus," translated into English as "Greetings from Krampus") was created. Late nineteenth century and turn of the twentieth century cards often feature Krampus with children, but also with buxom women (if those birch branches are phallic in nature, then this makes perfect sense). Many show the goat man in formal dress—a tuxedo style cutaway formal coat and trousers—but with his usual horned goat face, and *always* with his tongue extended.

This "tongue out" pose seems to be popular with ancient gods, whether they be Mayan, Hindu, Babylonian, Egyptian, Greek, or even British (for some reason the coat of arms for the Prince of Wales sports both a lion and a unicorn with tongues extended). More than likely, this tongue position represents sexual lust (outside of God's design) and sex-magic (fornicating with fallen angels), which is probably the real reason that old Krampus can't keep his tongue inside his head. The ancient symbol of "the horned god" referenced by Maurice Bruce in the above quote allows us to connect our goat-demon from the opening ceremony to CERN. Even though the LHC (Large Hadron Collider) sits three to four hours down a twisty road from Erstfeld and Bodio, the horned god's circular logic and passion for human depravity, Hernunnos (sometimes spelled Cernunnos), the Green Man of British lore, simply had to make an appearance.

Many researchers have written extensively about the end-game plans for tunneling beneath the earth and smashing atoms to smithereens as nothing more than a thinly veiled attempt to open portals,[11] but the opening ceremony at Gotthard makes it clear that *these portals are intended to release demonic entities!*

One side note here: The Cerne Abbas Giant formed in chalk in the downs of Dorset, England, the so-called Rude Man Giant, has been

---

11 For example, Tom Horn and Josh Peck's book *Abaddon Ascending*.

identified with Hercules,[12] who in turn was the Greco-Roman equivalent of Melqart,[13] the Baal ("lord") of Tyre who was worshiped on Mt. Carmel. This gigantic chalk figure—with a rather obvious, erect phallus—bears a knobbed club in his right hand, and his left arm is extended as if he carries something. Over time, the old lines around this left arm have faded, but in 1995, a scientific study of the massive figure revealed that he had indeed once held something upon his extended forearm.[14] A recent academic paper made the case that the 180-foot figure is indeed a tribute to Hercules,[15] who is often depicted with a great club and the skin of the Nemean lion over his arm.

What is this giant's name? The *Cerne* Abbas Giant, because it is located near a small village called Cerne Abbas, but the connection to Cernunnos and CERN is tantalizing, and the meaning of the word *abbas* is "lion"—again connecting the Cernunnos "Green Man" to Hercules/Melqart.

Finally, the slope upon which the giant reclines is called Trendle Hill. A trendle is an old Anglo-Saxon word for "circle," evocative of CERN's circles beneath the earth. Though not circular in shape, a large earthwork mound lies near the giant figure. Known as "the trendle" or "the frying pan," it is roughly rectangular in shape, and may be an Iron Age burial ground.

The twin tunnels of the Gotthard Base Tunnel commence with twin portals, each leading to a one-way tunnel on a single track. These northward and southward journeys symbolize the death/birth/death cycle of the Green Man, who dies in the fall/winter and rises

---

12 Jennifer Ouellette, "Cerne Abbas Giant is Depiction of Hercules." *Ars Technica*, Jan. 8, 2024. https://arstechnica.com/science/2024/01/cerne-abbas-giant-is-a-depiction-of-hercules/, retrieved 2/29/24.

13 Mark Cartwright, "Melqart." *World History Encyclopedia*. Last modified May 06, 2016. https://www.worldhistory.org/Melqart/, retrieved 2/29/24.

14 R. Castleden, *The Cerne Giant Project, Phase 2*: Surveys undertaken in 1995. https://archaeologydataservice.ac.uk/archsearch/record?titleId=1870505, retrieved 2/29/24.

15 Thomas Morcom and Helen Gittos, "The Cerne Giant in Its Early Medieval Context." *Speculum* 99:1 (2024), pp. 1–38.

in the spring/summer. The tunnel ceremony is all about sex rites and rebirth, leading to a new world order that is a complete reversal of the Judeo-Christian design. The triple goddess and the horned god, along with human sacrifice and a return to pagan worship lie at the center of this nauseating ritual play. Horns and the moon goddess go hand in hand. Turn the lunar crescent on its side with the points facing upward, and you have horns. The lunar crescent is but one "face" of the triple goddess mentioned above, and believe us she is a major player in this ceremony. But we get ahead of ourselves.

With this short introduction to the key players of our performance, let's examine each phase of this live-streamed rite. It commenced with the interfaith blessing as mentioned earlier. Following this invocation of the triple-goddess, the shepherd aroused the horned man, who strutted into the scene (complete with eerie red lighting and smoke—like he'd risen from the Abyss), accompanied by his hellish friends—many engaged in ritualistic sex and homosexual poses. This parade of promiscuity also included a creepy "angel" that flew over top of some of the miners, presumably representing the nine who died. Once the first phase—we'll call it the opening of the portal—was concluded, the various religious and political dignitaries boarded the train and headed toward the northern terminus at Erstfeld.

Note that the choice to begin in the south and end in the north represents the ascension of something to the surface; that is the opening of the Abyss.

The primary performances took place on a massive outdoor stage in Erstfeld. This small city lies within the canton of Uri in Switzerland. (Uri, by the way, is the plural Latin word for aurochs, a type of extinct bison, echoing the "horned" theme once again.)[16] As the dignitaries settled into their comfortable bandstand seats, a display lit up, showing what looked like a huge rock mountainside. Dancers dressed as

---

16 And the Akkadian word for "aurochs," *ddn*, is the probable origin of the name of the Amorite Tidanu tribe and, in turn, the old gods of the Greeks and Romans, the Titans.

miners "climbed" this rock face and dug into the earth, so to speak, to unveil what lay beneath: a great machine, formed from human arms, that rotated and churned into various shapes and designs, many of which resembled the Large Hadron Collider at CERN.

Once this "opening" is achieved, the miners strip off their orange jumpsuit attire (males only at this point, who are now bare-chested) and take up arms; that is, they use staves to perform a dance routine that looks like warfare. Once the battle concludes, a group of women join the men, the women wearing only white underwear, and the entire dance troupe engages in a frenzied display amidst a cloud of dust—simulating smoke, perhaps? This frenetic dance arouses a giant.

Clearly, this endeavor is far more than Switzerland's braggadocio about an engineering feat. The connection seems obvious between CERN and ritualistic summoning of a sleeping giant, the horned god Cernunnos or even Melqart—both are types of the rising/dying god, and Melqart "slept" for half the year, which may be why Elijah told the priests of Baal to "cry aloud," because "perhaps he is asleep and must be awakened." (The prophet's jibe that Baal might "be on a journey"[17] suggests that he'd heard the tale of the twelve labors of Hercules, the Greco-Roman form of Melqart.)

As the giant wakens, the dancers perform ritualistic sex rites, many of them homosexual in nature. Following this simulated copulation, the dancers fall to the floor as if dead. On the screen behind the dancers, three men dressed as miners appear. Just as the dancers have died, these men also "die" after being chased by something that looks like smoke. The three men, representing perhaps the nine who died in the construction of the tunnels, fall down a deep hole, as if traveling to hell as a sacrifice, while the dancers, now revived, continue their debauched choreography. As the dead miners descend, they are met with giant hands.

We then see three ghostly female dancers rise from the pit. As these ghostly women fly above the dancers, a giant eye forms behind them on

---

17 1 Kings 18:20–40.

the screen, and below a troupe of similarly "ghostly" dancers enter the stage area, wearing veils and skirts. At this point, men begin to assume female attire, demonstrating a reversal of traditional morals and roles as the spirit of the Abyss takes over. Whirling dervishes accompany these strange dancers, along with men wearing costumes that make them look as if they are covered in animal hair or straw. These strange "Cousin It" types creep alongside a long line of musicians who bear Alpine horns. It's clear that the strange mashup of Alpine with Middle Eastern traditions is intended to show an international revelry welcoming the risen "god" from the Abyss.

Behind the musicians and ghostly dancers, the horned god makes his grand entrance to the stage, and following him as if to bless him is the first of the triune goddesses: The Maiden. She is dressed in virginal white, and she trails behind the horned Cernunnos goat-man.

Like Krampus, the Goat Man wears a cutaway tuxedo with a red carnation, representing his assimilation into our modern culture. As the Goat Man dances with the strange collection of humanity on the stage below, his image is also displayed on the monitor screen behind the troupe, showing the true demonic spirit behind the world's return to pagan worship.

Three scarabs fly before this screaming face, the spirit of Antichrist. Scarabs represent rebirth in Egyptian culture. The screen again changes, and the massive Antichrist face becomes a vortex of eyes. This Antichrist New World Order will shut down all free will, and the citizens of the world will be watched—the Watchers—every moment of every day.

As these "Watchers" rise from the Abyss, the Goat Man embraces the Maiden, impregnating her. He is then declared to be king as all bow down to worship him.

As with many pagan pantheons, the King then dies. Remember that the horned man is a type of rising and dying god, and many of these deities, once dead, are replaced by a child, such as Horus succeeding Osiris in the Egyptian pantheon. After the Goat Man's "death," we see a strange goat child appear off to one side of the stage, as if he exists in a separate place.

Now that the Goat Man child has been conceived, a chorus of men and women, some cross-dressing, bring offerings of greenery and branches, and roots begin to appear on the large screen behind the main stage.

The massive roots show the occult inversion of the Tree of Life, and within a few moments these roots transform the world into a massive machine. Men dressed as miners stand upon large pistons, and cogs within the great machine interconnect and drive these pistons. The New World Order set into motion by the summoning of the Satanic Goat Man culminates with the reappearance of the Maiden, now adorned in blood red and heavily pregnant—the second face of the Triune Goddess. She is the Whore of Babylon, ruling a world of imprisoned humanity.

Another horned figure then appears just behind the dancer representing the Whore. The Goat Man is now Goat Woman, again indicating a strange reversal of the old order. The ancient Watchers whom pagans worshiped as gods had the power to take both male and female forms, giving rise to the belief in "twin" gods such as Hermes/Aphrodite. As the Whore gives birth, the Goat Man appears to revive, only now his goat head has been removed, making him appear more "human." Remember, the Antichrist will appear to revive from a fatal head wound, and once resurrected, will be worshiped by all the world.

Note the inversion of form here. Men are dressed as women, and women as men. The New World Pagan Order will stand the Judeo-Christian world on its head, and the "old gods" will return to enthrall mankind using drugs, rampant sexual "freedoms," and secret knowledge.

This bizarre opening ceremony cost Switzerland *8 million Euros* to stage—a ridiculous amount considering the economic crisis facing nearly every nation of the European Union. Sacrifice, sex magic, and science (CERN) form the hellish trinity of practices revealed in this detestable display. Who in their right mind would spend even *one* Euro on such a strange ceremony? Clearly, this live-streamed event was intended as a *worldwide ritual* and not a celebration of engineering.

The Goat Man is waiting to rise, and Switzerland's ritual tells us that unregenerate mankind will welcome him when he emerges from the pit. The triune goddess will ride the beast system, and though this crazed play shows an ecstatic world population that works together like a well-oiled, debauched machine, the truth is far more insidious. The Goat Man, the Antichrist, will enslave mankind, using his own lusts as a key.

> The beast you saw was, and is not, but is about to come up from the abyss and then go to destruction. The inhabitants of the earth—**all those whose names have not been written in the book of life since the foundation of the world—will be astounded** when they see that the beast was, and is not, but is to come. (Revelation 17:8, NET; emphasis added)

We delve into dark passages with hands created by God Almighty. How He must weep at mankind's debasement of His marvelous design.

CHAPTER THIRTY-FOUR

AMERICA'S TEMPLE: GATEWAY TO THE ABYSS

To those who engaged in the gleeful desecration of this, our temple of Democracy, American Democracy, justice will be done.

—Rep. Nancy Pelosi, Former Speaker of
the U.S. House of Representatives

I f you followed the tumultuous battle over the results of the 2020 American presidential election, you're aware that a group of protesters forced their way inside the United States Capitol on January 6, 2021. The media has consistently described those events as insurrection, an at-tempted coup by "domestic terrorists." It was not. The Capitol rioters were a disorganized, ragtag mob that had no agenda other than venting their frustration at America's political class as Congress convened to certify the results of the contentious presidential election. But, as Sharon noted in a chapter she contributed to Tom Horn's book *Zeitgeist 2025*, the responses by our elected officials were eye-opening:

> Very shortly after the so-called coup failed, Senator Chuck Schumer described the January 6, 2021, incursion into the House of Representatives this way:

"It is very, very difficult to put into words what has transpired today. I have never lived through or even imagined an experience like the one we have just witnessed in this Capitol. President Franklin Roosevelt set aside Dec. 7, 1941, as a day that will live in infamy. Unfortunately, we can now add Jan. 6, 2021, to that very short list of dates in American history that will live forever in infamy. **This temple to democracy was desecrated**, its windows smashed, our offices vandalized." (emphasis added) [...]

And Senator Schumer's alarmist battle cry was taken up two weeks later at the inauguration by Senator Amy Klobuchar:

"Two weeks ago, when an angry, violent mob staged an insurrection and **desecrated this temple of our democracy**, it awakened us to our responsibilities as Americans."[1] (emphasis added)

Senators Schumer and Klobuchar were not alone in depicting the Capitol as hallowed ground:

"This is a special place. This is a sacred place. **This sacred place was desecrated by a mob today** on our watch. This temple to democracy was defiled by was defiled by thugs, who roamed the halls—sat in this chair, Mr. Vice President—one that you vacated at 2:15 this afternoon." —Sen. Dick Durbin (D-IL)[2]

"Members of the U.S. Capitol Police and across law enforcement are he-roes. We saw their heroism in action on January 6

---

1   Sharon K. Gilbert, "A Long Ritual, a Dark Winter, and the Age of Aquarius." In Tom Horn, *Zeitgeist 2025* (Crane, MO: Defender, 2021), pp. 162–163.

2   CBS 2 Chicago Staff, "Sen. Durbin On Senate Floor: 'This Sacred Place Was Desecrated' During Capitol Storming." *CBS 2 Chicago*, Jan. 6, 2021. https://chicago .cbslocal.com/2021/01/06/sen-durbin-on-senate-floor-this-sacred-place-was -desecrated-during-capitol-storming/, retrieved 4/24/21.

when they defended **the most sacred space in our Republic** against violent insurrectionists who attempted to prevent Congress from carrying out its constitutional duty." —Rep. Liz Cheney (R-WY)[3]

"On Sunday, it was a great—my great honor to be sworn in as Speaker and to preside over a sacred ritual of renewal, as we gathered under **this dome of this temple of democracy** to open the 117th Congress." —Former House Speaker Nancy Pelosi (D-CA)[4]

Now, it's easy to dismiss these remarks as rhetoric to score political points against Donald Trump, who was not only blamed for the riot but impeached for allegedly inciting it. But this characterization of the Capitol as "a temple" and "sacred space" was echoed by political commentators and religious leaders across the country after January 6. Those who wrote and spoke about the Capitol in religious terms may not even realize that they're very close to what the Fallen would have us believe about the nature and purpose of America's "Congress House."

The late Dr. Thomas Horn wrote length about the occult world's purpose for the Capitol in *Apollyon Rising 2012* and its revised and expanded edition *Zenith 2016*. In short, he argued that occult adepts believe a future world leader, the Antichrist, will be engendered in America's "temple to democracy." At the risk of being indelicate, the Washington Monument, the world's tallest obelisk at just over 555 feet, 5 inches (6,665 inches),[5] represents the missing male member of the Egyptian god of the dead, Osiris—which we believe is just one

3 "Cheney: The Capitol Police Are Heroes & We Saw Their Heroism in Action on 1/6." Press re-lease, Mar. 17, 2021. https://cheney.house.gov/2021/03/17/cheney -the-capitol-police-are-heroes-we-saw-their-heroism-in-action-on-1-6/, retrieved 4/24/21.

4 "Pelosi Remarks Upon Reconvening of the House of Representatives." Press release, Jan. 6, 2021. https://www.speaker.gov/newsroom/1621-1, retrieved 4/24/21.

5 "Washington Monument: Frequently Asked Questions." National Park Service, https://www.nps.gov/wamo/faqs.htm, retrieved 5/24/21.

more identity worn by the rebellious Watcher chief Shemihazah. The dome of the Capitol, at the other end of the National Mall, represents the womb of his sister-wife, Isis. The spatial relationship between the monument and the Capitol echoes the layout of St. Peter's Square in Rome, where an ancient Egyptian obelisk was erected by Pope Sixtus V in 1586 opposite St. Peter's Basilica, which, like the Capitol, is topped by a dome. The obvious difference between the two is that the obelisk in Rome is only eighty-four feet high.

Tom Horn suggested in that the occult purpose of the Capitol is to facilitate the return of Osiris, the Egyptian form of Apollo. This reincarnate entity would be the Antichrist, Apollyon. We agree, but with a few minor changes to Tom's theory.

We argued in *Giants, Gods & Dragons* that Apollo has been with us for millennia, riding the earth as the first horseman of the Apocalypse.[6] The god was well known in the ancient world, considered the ideal of Greek youth, and adopted as a personal god by Caesar Augustus, Nero, and other Roman emperors in the centuries that followed. What most of us don't know is that Apollo, a plague-god, was worshiped more than two thousand years before John wrote the book of Revelation. As noted in earlier chapters, Apollo was called Resheph in western Mesopotamia and Nergal in Akkad and Sumer.[7] He was also adopted as the personal protector god by Amenhotep II,[8] convincingly identified by Dr. Douglas Petrovich as the Pharaoh of the Exodus.[9] This means two things: First, Resheph (Apollo) was well known in Egypt and considered a distinct and separate entity from Osiris; and second, the God of Israel convinced Pharaoh to let His people go by sending a series of plagues that the plague-god was powerless to stop.

---

6   Sharon K. Gilbert and Derek P. Gilbert, *Giants, Gods & Dragons* (Crane, MO: Defender, 2020), pp. 159–182.

7   Paolo Xella, "Resheph." In Karel van der Toorn, Bob Becking, and Pieter W. van der Horst (Eds.), *Dictionary of Deities and Demons in the Bible* (Leiden; Boston; Köln; Grand Rapids, MI; Cam-bridge: Brill; Eerdmans, 1999), p. 701.

8   Ibid.

9   Petrovich (2006), op. cit.

Resheph is also mentioned in the Bible, most obviously by the prophet Habakkuk:

> God came from Teman,
> and the Holy One from Mount Paran. *Selah*
> His splendor covered the heavens,
> and the earth was full of his praise.
> His brightness was like the light;
> rays flashed from his hand;
> and there he veiled his power.
> Before him went pestilence [Deber],
> and plague [Resheph] followed at his heels.
> (Habakkuk 3:3–5)

Deber, like Resheph, was a deity known to the Semitic people of western Mesopotamia. Both were worshiped at Ebla at least a thousand years before the Exodus.[10] The point is that since Resheph/Apollo was following at God's heels as He led the Israelites from Mount Paran (an alternate name for Sinai) toward the Promised Land, then Resheph/Apollo is not among the group of rebels chained in the abyss for the Genesis 6 rebellion.[11] Not only was this an act of humiliation, since God had just demonstrated His superiority over Resheph/Apollo to the Pharaoh, this means Resheph/Apollo cannot be "the angel of the bottomless pit" of Revelation 9:11. Thus, despite the similarity of the names, Apollo and Apollyon are not the same.

While Tom Horn pointed us in the right direction with his analysis of the occult teachings and rituals he documented in *Apollyon Rising 2012* and *Zenith 2016*, we believe the Capitol symbolizes a purpose other than an incubation chamber for the Antichrist.

As Tom noted in his groundbreaking books, the room at ground level in the Capitol, one floor below the rotunda, is called the crypt.

---

10   Giovanni Pettinato, *The Archives of Ebla: An Empire Inscribed in Clay* (Garden City, NY: Doubleday & Company, Inc., 1981), p. 247.

11   2 Peter 2:4 and Jude 6–7.

No one is buried there, but the plan was to move the body of George Washington, who died in 1799, to a chamber in the crypt, which was to serve as the entry to Washington's tomb. Directly above the tomb, a ten-foot circular opening would have allowed visitors in the rotunda to look down on Washington's final resting place. However, after delays in construction, not least of which was the need to rebuild the Capitol after it was burned by the British during the War of 1812, Washington's descendants opted to honor the former president's will and left him interred at Mount Vernon.

The symbolism of birth and generation embodied by the Washington Monument and the Capitol is clear. And Tom Horn was correct in identifying the Egyptian god of the dead, Osiris, as the object of this long occult ritual. However, the Roman Osiris is not Apollo—it's Saturn. Given the sexual nature of the sin committed by Saturn, who Derek identified in *The Second Coming of Saturn* as the chief of the rebellious Watchers, Shemihazah, the symbolism of the obelisk is apt.

Why did Thomas Jefferson insist on calling our nation's legislative building the Capitol when the original Capitolium was not a domed building? In other words, if Jefferson was determined to create an American temple named for the house of Jupiter, why doesn't it look like the Capitolium? The Romans were the first to utilize domes for large buildings, but the dome didn't become popular in Roman architecture until the first century BC, almost five hundred years after the Capitolium was dedicated. Why, then, does the United States Capitol feature such a prominent dome?

Here is the key: Although the Capitol is named for the Capitolium, its design emulates another important religious structure in Rome, the Pantheon. While the Capitol dome as we see it today is much larger relative to the rest of the building than the dome atop the Pantheon, the Capitol's original dome was much closer to the Pantheon's in scale. The size and prominence of the Capitol dome grew as the structure was rebuilt and expanded in the nineteenth century. As the Capitol changed, the art and architecture of the building made its hidden purpose more obvious for those with eyes to see.

In *Giants, Gods & Dragons*, we made the case that Apollo, as the first horseman of the Apocalypse and the symbol of Roman imperialism, went forth "conquering, and to conquer" by laying the foundation of Western civilization—Greek and Roman philosophy, law, art, literature, architecture, and systems of government. Little wonder that Jefferson insisted on calling the home of our nation's new legislative body the "Capitol," and that so much of our government architecture is inspired by, if not copied from, the pagan temples of Greece and Rome. Indeed, the underside of the Capitol dome features the overtly pagan fresco titled *The Apotheosis of Washington*, a depiction of our nation's first president ascending to the heavens and becoming a god:

> Beside those pagan gods which accompany Washington inside the Capitol Dome, the scene is rich with symbols analogous with ancient and modern magic, including the powerful trident—considered of the utmost importance for sorcery and indispensable to the efficacy of infernal rites—and the caduceus, tied to Apollo and Freemasonic Gnosticism in which Jesus was a myth based on Apollo's son, Asclepius, the god of medicine and healing whose snake-entwined staff remains a symbol of medicine today. Occult numerology associated with the legend of Isis and Osiris is also encoded throughout the painting, such as the thirteen maidens, the six scenes of pagan gods around the perimeter forming a hexagram, and the entire scene bounded by the powerful Pythagorian/Freemasonic "binding" utility— seventy-two five-pointed stars within circles.[12]

The fresco is viewed from the rotunda below through an oculus, a circular opening in the dome that creates the impression that Washington is in the heavens among the gods, having be-come one himself. This is borrowed from the oculus in the dome of the Pantheon, which opened to the sky. This feature served a spiritual purpose:

---

12   Thomas Horn, *Zenith 2016* (Crane, MO: Defender, 2013), p. 133.

In topographical context, therefore, it would seem that the Pantheon operated as the focal point for an innovative religious system. It was a place of veneration of the principal Olympian divinities (probably including Romulus/Quirinus), along with the first divinized member of the gens Iulia, Julius Caesar.... The oculus in the dome presented that union of earth and sky that symbolized an apotheosis into the heavens.[13]

The Capitol not only features an oculus through which visitors can view the divinized Washington, but it includes a chamber at ground level intended to house the body of Washington, also visible from the rotunda above through an opening in the floor. It's as though the Capitol was constructed around a portal for George Washington's spirit to ascend into the heavens, just as the Pantheon in Rome was designed by Agrippa to symbolize the apotheosis of Julius Caesar and his successor, Caesar Augustus.

The seventy-two stars in the fresco represent the *elohim* placed by God over the nations after the Tower of Babel incident. There are seventy in the Bible, based on the number of people groups listed in the Table of Nations in Genesis 10, but the symbolic meaning of seventy is the same as seventy-two, which explains the seventy-two (or seventy, depending on the translation) disciples sent into Galilee by Jesus in Luke 10:1–20. Numerologically, seventy and seventy-two represent the same idea—the complete set, or "all of them." Seventy-two also happens to be one-fifth of 360—the number of degrees in a circle, hence the five-pointed stars.

All of these symbols point to a deeper meaning to the fresco on the Capitol dome: Just as the Canaanite creator-god El lived on Mount Hermon with his consort and their seventy sons, the gods of the nations, the divinized Washington is surrounded by seventy-two stars that likewise represent the heavenly host.

---

13 Eugenio La Rocca, "Agrippa's Pantheon and Its Origin," in *The Pantheon: From Antiquity to the Present*, ed. by Tod A. Marder and Mark Wilson Jones (Cambridge: Cambridge University Press, 2015), pp. 49–78..

It's also revealing that Washington is depicted with purple cloth draped over his legs, which hides them from view. Most interpret this as a sign of royalty, since purple was the color reserved for kings in the ancient world. As inconsistent as this is in a nation with no (official) royalty, the symbolism is disturbing on a deeper level: The legs of the statue of Saturn in his temple at Rome were bound with wool most of the year, representing his confinement in the netherworld. The wool was removed only during the annual Saturnalia festival. On the Capitol dome, Washington's legs are covered (with the color of royalty) but unbound, apparently symbolizing the return of the king(-god) to his place in the heavens.

In short, *The Apotheosis of Washington* depicts the man called the "father of our nation" as El/Saturn, who led America into a Golden Age represented by the scenes of commerce, agriculture, science, industry, transoceanic travel and communication, and victory over tyranny and kingly power.

The art and architecture of the Capitol make a clear statement: America is politically, militarily, and most of all spiritually, Rome.

For American Christians, the implications are disturbing. Most of us have taken for granted that the pagan and occult symbols designed into our government buildings in general, and the Capitol, National Mall, and Washington Monument in particular, were simply artistic choices made for their aesthetic value. Our ignorance of those pagan symbols has led us to accept a false history that's much more comfortable than the truth.

Now consider how many state legislatures across the United States meet in buildings that are likewise inspired by the Pantheon. Thirty-nine of our fifty state capitol buildings are domed. At least half a dozen, including our home state of Missouri, are topped by statues of pagan deities. As many more are adorned by statues that, if not pagan, are most definitely not Christian.

It's worth noting that the obelisk-and-dome imagery of the United States Capitol and Saint Peter's Square is also found at most mosques. The minarets are explained as necessary for muezzin to sing the call to prayer, but why stand-alone towers that look like modified obelisks? Why not bell towers? Or, given the military history of Islam, ramparted walls?

Is the worldwide distribution of obelisks and domes related to the return of old Saturn—Apollyon, the Destroyer—from the netherworld?

CHAPTER THIRTY-FIVE

THE GANYMEDE CODE

[Zeus] the son of Kronos, king of the immortals, fell in love with Ganymede, seized him, carried him off to Olympus, and made him divine, keeping the lovely bloom of boyhood.

—THEOGNIS OF MEGARA, Book 1.1345

The Roman poet Virgil wrote in *Eclogue IV* that the return of "old Saturn" was accompanied by the return of Justice. The poet wasn't using allegory to depict the return to an age of law and order; Justice was a goddess, Justitia, equivalent to the Greek goddess Dike.

Justitia was believed to be the daughter of Zeus and the Titaness Themis, the goddess of divine law and order, the rules of conduct established by the gods. Justice is the punisher of those who transgress the statutes of the gods. In that sense, she's like the ancient Mesopotamian goddess Inanna, who tricked her uncle Enki, the god who'd sent the *apkallu* (Watchers) to humanity with the gifts of civilization, into giving her the *mes* (pronounced "mezz"), which were the concepts that established the divine order of life. Inanna, better known as the Akkadian goddess Ishtar (and Astarte of the Bible), was the goddess associated with sex, war, justice, and

311

political power.[1] Derek discussed this entity in depth in his book *Bad Moon Rising*:

An Old Babylonian text first translated and published in 1997 seems to confirm at least some of the Bible's negative characterizations of Inanna's Canaanite counterpart, Astarte, including cult prostitution, "cross-gender activities...and the performance of sexual acts." [...]

With all due respect to the learned scholars who have described this entity as "a complex, multifaceted goddess," the character of Inanna/Ishtar isn't as complicated as she's made out to be. Frankly, she's a bad screenwriter's idea of a fifteen-year-old boy's fantasy, interested mainly in sex and fighting and better than men at both. She was selfish and violent, ruled by her passions, and incredibly destructive when she didn't get her way.[2]

This is consistent with what we've seen of the riots for social justice that spread around the world in the summer of 2020. We shouldn't be surprised; myths of the pagan gods are propaganda to persuade humanity that they, not God, are the rightful rulers of earth. The divine order that "Justice" defends is opposed to the order decreed by God. The focus on "social justice" by activists around the world is a case in point. What rational person would conclude that civil disorder leading to the costliest insurance claims since 1950, the first year those figures were tracked, from "arson, vandalism, and looting"[3] is in any sense justified? It's not justice by any normal definition of the word.

---

1   Sjur Cappelen Papazian, "Lady Justice (mother) and Lady Liberty (maiden)." *Cradle of Civilization*, Sept. 25, 2018. https://aratta.wordpress.com/2018/09/25/lady-justice-and-lady-liberty/, re-trieved 5/1/21.

2   Derek P. Gilbert, *Bad Moon Rising* (Crane, MO: Defender, 2018), pp. 116–120.

3   Jennifer A. Kingson, "Exclusive: $1 Billion-plus Riot Damage Is Most Expensive in Insurance History." *Axios*, Sept. 16, 2020. https://www.axios.com/riots-cost-property-damage-276c9bcc-a455-4067-b06a-66f9db4cea9c.html, retrieved 5/1/21.

The term "social justice" has been deployed to rebrand hatred, bigotry, and discrimination. "Anti-racism" in the form of Critical Race Theory is just old-fashioned racism that's been weaponized to tear apart the fabric of Western civilization. As far back as 1934, Henry Wallace, later Franklin Roosevelt's vice president during World War II, decried a failure to "bring the kingdom of heaven to earth in terms of social justice" that he blamed on racism, capitalism, and nationalism.[4] These are the very sins laid at the feet of Donald Trump and his supporters, typically identified by progressives in the media as white conservative Christians. As Sharon wrote in *Zeitgeist 2025*:

> Welcome to the Age of Aquarius, my friends, when the gods of harmony and understanding define us all as bigots and haters. Social justice is being poured out like water from the NEW GODS of Capitol Hill, Saturn and Justitia, and we're expected to enjoy owning nothing.[5]

This and the draconian response to COVID-19 comprise the chaos that occult adepts believe will produce a New World Order, the manifestation of *Ordo ab Chao*—Order Out of Chaos. This is the return of Justice, who heralds the imminent arrival of old Saturn and his Golden Age. The Great Reset initiative of the World Economic Forum is one of the physical manifestations of the spiritual sea change that occult adepts are working to bring about. Let's go back to the J6 riot at the Capitol.

January 6 is the date celebrated each year by Western Christians as Epiphany, and Theophany by Christians in the Eastern churches. It's sometimes called Three Kings Day; the twelfth day of Christmas, when the three wise men from the East visited the Christ child. It marks the revelation of God incarnate in the form of Jesus. And what

---

4   Henry A. Wallace, *Statesmanship and Religion* (New York: Round Table Press, 1934), pp. 78–83.

5   S. Gilbert (2021), op. cit.

happened on Epiphany in 2021? America's temple was invaded by, as Sharon colorfully described them, the "'Q-Anon Shaman' in his crazy buffalo hat along with his selfie-taking hooligan buddies."[6]

Bull imagery has long been associated with Saturn—the horned helmets of ancient Sumer that indicated divine status, the name Kronos, derived from Semitic qeren[7] ("horned one"?), and the epithet of the god who held court on Mount Hermon, "Bull El." Isn't it odd that a man wearing a symbol of this old god should burst into the Capitol, and the national consciousness, on the day Christians celebrate the revelation of the One True God?

Whether he knew it or not, the Q-Anon Shaman announced the return of the old horned god Saturn/Kronos/Bull El—i.e., the fallen Watcher known as Shemihazah two thousand years ago, but as Abaddon/Apollyon when he emerges from the Abyss—in America's temple on the day marking the revelation of Christ's divinity.

There is one other strange convergence of symbols inside the United States Capitol. Several figures depicted inside the Capitol wear a Phrygian cap, a soft conical hat bent over at the top. According to the architect of the Capitol, this piece of headgear, also referred to as a liberty cap, was adopted as a symbol of freedom in the nineteenth century.[8] It's called a Phrygian cap because it was associated with Phrygia, an ancient kingdom in west central Anatolia (modern Turkey) that reached its peak in the eighth century BC under King Midas (yes, Midas was real, although his "golden touch" was not). A similar conical felt cap called a *pileus* was given to freed slaves in ancient Rome, and it made a comeback as a symbol during the American and French revolutions.[9]

The artist, Constantino Brumidi, painted figures wearing the red Phrygian cap throughout the Capitol. They are generally female—for

6   Ibid.
7   Wyatt (2010), "A la Recherche des Perdus," op. cit., p. 55.
8   AOC Curator, "The Liberty Cap in the Art of the U.S. Capitol." *Explore the Capitol Campus: Our Blog*, Jan. 29, 2013. https://www.aoc.gov/explore-capitol-campus/blog/liberty-cap-art-us-capitol, retrieved 5/7/21.
9   Ibid.

example, the goddess Liberty to Washington's right in *The Apotheosis of Washington* and the war-goddess Bellona in the Senate wing. However, Young America is depicted as a youthful male wearing a toga and a Phrygian cap in the section of *The Apotheosis of Washington* called "Agriculture." Young America holds the reins of a horse while standing next to the grain-goddess Ceres, who's seated on a McCormick Reaper, a mechanical harvester that helped revolutionize American farming. The relevant bit is that the depiction of Young America wearing a Phrygian cap is oddly similar to classical artwork featuring Ganymede, a minor figure in Greco-Roman religion.

Ganymede was believed to be the son of Tros, king of Troy, and "was comeliest of mortal men."[10] He was so comely, in fact, that he caught the fancy of the king of the gods, Jupiter/Zeus. By the late sixth century BC, after the Persian conquest of Asia Minor, Phrygia had expanded to include northwestern Anatolia, the region around Troy— hence Ganymede's Phrygian cap. Zeus/Jupiter was so smitten with the young man that the storm-god transformed himself into an eagle and abducted Ganymede while he tended sheep on Mount Ida.

If you've heard the story, it was probably characterized as an honor for the young shepherd. After all, Ganymede was made the cupbearer of Zeus/Jupiter and allowed to live among the gods of Olympus. Who wouldn't want that?

As legendary broadcaster Paul Harvey would say, "And now, the rest of the story." You see, the original tale is much darker.

First, we need to remember that the storm-god—Baal in Canaan, Zeus in Greece, and Jupiter in Rome—was identified by Jesus as Satan (see Matthew 12:22–26 and note that Beelzebul means "Baal the prince"). The Canaanites believed that Baal was lord of the Rephaim, who were called "warriors of Baal." Recall the importance of *kispum* among the ancient Amorites, a monthly ritual meal for the ancestral

---

10   Homer, *The Iliad of Homer. Rendered into English Prose for the Use of Those Who Cannot Read the Original*, ed. by Samuel Butler. Book XX, line 233 (Medford, MA: Longmans, Green and Co., 1898), digital edition.

dead. The *kispum* featured a libation (drink offering), and the rite was so integral to Amorite society that the eldest son, the heir to the family estate responsible for performing the ritual, was called the "pourer of water" or "son of the cup." This custom was transmitted to the Greeks and Romans, who preserved the practice of preparing communal meals for the ancestral dead.

So, the story of Ganymede is essentially the tale of a beautiful boy abducted by the lord of the Rephaim to serve as his personal "pourer of water."

But the relationship went much farther than that. The Greek philosopher Plato, writing in the fourth century BC, attributed the story of Ganymede to the people of Crete:

> Whether one makes the observation in earnest or in jest, one certainly should not fail to observe that when male unites with female for procreation the pleasure experienced is held to be due to nature, but contrary to nature when male mates with male or female with female, and that those first guilty of such enormities were impelled by their slavery to pleasure. And we all accuse the Cretans of concocting the story about Ganymede. Because it was the belief that they derived their laws from Zeus, they added on this story about Zeus in order that they might be following his example in enjoying this pleasure as well.[11]

In other words, Plato claimed the people of Crete invented the Ganymede myth to justify their practice of homosexuality.

However the story originated, the relationship between Ganymede and Zeus/Jupiter was well understood in the Greco-Roman world. The Latin form of Ganymede's name is Catamitus, from which we get the English word "catamite," the word for a pubescent boy who's sexually intimate with an adult man. And the depiction of America on

---

11 Plato, *Laws* 1.636c—1.636d.

the Capitol dome as a young man wearing a Phrygian cap is similar to classical images of Ganymede, who was abducted to serve as the boy toy of Zeus/Jupiter/Satan, whose temple in Rome is the source of the name of the Capitol.

But the significance of Young America as Ganymede doesn't end there. You see, as a reward for his, well, service, Zeus immortalized the young shepherd by placing him among the stars—as Aquarius, the Water Bearer.

Aquarius. The new age inaugurated by the Great Conjunction of December 21, 2020.

So, Young America is represented in the United States Capitol as the submissive sexual partner of Jupiter (Satan) in a depiction of the new Golden Age ruled by Saturn—Shemihazah, who has been plotting for ages his triumphant return as the Destroyer, Abaddon/Apollyon.

To summarize: The chief god of the Roman pantheon, the deity worshiped in Rome's Capitolium, was the storm-god Jupiter. Under the names Zeus, the storm-god of the Greeks, and Baal, the West Semitic storm-god, he was unmasked by Jesus and identified as Satan. He is the god of this world, the spirit of the age. But the Roman poet Virgil, and others since, longed for a return to the Golden Age of Saturn that would replace the Age of Iron ruled by Jupiter, bringing a new age of ease and prosperity.

The Capitol, America's "temple to democracy," was named for the temple of Jupiter Optimus Maximus but modeled on the Pantheon in Rome. That structure was designed to represent the apotheosis of Caesar Augustus and his predecessor, his uncle Julius Caesar, the founders of the Roman Empire. Likewise, the United States Capitol symbolizes the godhood of the man called the father of our nation, George Washington. Like Augustus, through whom Virgil believed the Golden Age of Saturn had returned, Washington was cast as the agent of this supernatural transfer of power—the triumphant return of a god from Tartarus who would establish a new Golden Age.

The modern-day spiritual descendants of Virgil are trying to make the return of Saturn a reality. There are powerful, wealthy people who believe the stars signaled the advent of this new Golden Age on December 21, 2020, with the conjunction of the planets that bear the names of the two great Roman gods Jupiter and Saturn. That event marked the earth's full entry into the Age of Aquarius, a constellation ruled by Saturn (Shemihazah) and representing the immortalized Ganymede—the boy-toy of Jupiter (Satan), whose image represents "Young America" inside the dome of the U.S. Capitol, a building named for the temple of Satan in ancient Rome.

THE
FUTURE

CHAPTER THIRTY-SIX

SUMMONING
THE DRAGON

I think we should be very careful about artificial intelligence. If I had to guess at what our biggest existential threat is, it's probably that. [...] With artificial intelligence we're summoning the demon. You know those stories where there's the guy with the pentagram, and the holy water, and he's like —Yeah, he's sure he can control the demon? Doesn't work out.

—Elon Musk[1]

And he had power to give life unto the image of the beast, that the image of the beast should both speak, and cause that as many as would not worship the image of the beast should be killed.

—Revelation 13:15 (KJV)

Way of the Future (WOTF) is about creating a peaceful and respectful transition of who is in charge of the planet from people to people + "machines." [...] We believe that intelligence is not rooted in biology. While biology has evolved one type of intelligence, there is nothing inherently specific about biology that causes intelligence. Eventually, we will be able to recreate it without using biology and its limitations.

—"About Us" page at www.thewayofthefuture.church (now defunct)

---

1   Greg Kumparak, "Elon Musk Compares Building Artificial Intelligence to Summoning the Demon." *TechCrunch*, October 26, 2014. https://techcrunch.com/2014/10/26/elon-musk-compares-building-artificial-intelligence-to-summoning-the-demon/, accessed 2/28/24.

Carbon-based life forms will soon be history, replaced by a silicon and algorithmic matrix run by an Artificial Super Intelligence, and some people are already setting up "churches," preparing the way for the ASI overlord.

Deep learning and other artificial intelligence algorithms already populate our world as search engines, data scrapers, data miners, language processors, translators, financial traders, medical researchers, sports reporters, and help desk assistants. Alexa and Siri have become our closest friends. We talk to them, laugh at their jokes, ask them for opinions on our newest boyfriend or what dress to wear to the weekend party. Connected home devices enable us to shop, share, and consume 24/7 with just a command, and it will get more immersive and invasive with each passing year.

Much of online content originates from algorithms. The news articles you and I read each day with our morning coffee are often written by an artificial intelligence. Non-human "stringers" scrape the internet for data relative to sports, celebrities, politics, finance, films, and use that data stream to inform John Q. Public via online news outlets and apps. We read these on our PCs, our smart phones, our tablets, and soon we'll consume them via an internal display that interacts directly with our auditory/visual systems within our brains.

Those who keep an eye on trends can see what lies ahead, but even the sharpest vision may not foresee everything. We, Sharon and Derek, live in the country, and we installed a fence around our house to keep out predators and protect our dogs. It isn't a perfect solution, but it is one predicated on caution. Sadly, in the case of the virtual world, the wolf invader has already been welcomed into our sheepfold and put in charge of the smallest of our lambs.

On February 12, 2002, Secretary Donald Rumsfeld participated in a news briefing at the Department of Defense, where he addressed the Joints Chiefs of Staff regarding the need to track potential threats to the nation:

Reports that say that something hasn't happened are always interesting to me, because as we know, there are **known knowns**; there are things we know we know. We also know there are **known unknowns**; that is to say we know there are some things [we know] we do not know. But there are also **unknown unknowns**—the ones we don't know we don't know. And if one looks throughout the history of our country and other free countries, it is the latter category that tend to be the difficult ones.[2] (emphasis and brackets added)

Algorithms and the way they function demonstrate this aspect of knowing. There's something a little bit mystical about today's ubiquitous, deep learning architectures. The code that initiates their activity—that is the INPUT—is known. The OUTPUT—the data received—is also known. However, the wibbly-wobbly bit in the middle that actually *performs* the function that precipitates the data is *not* known. This area is often called a "black box" due to its hidden nature. Alternatively, intermediate computational models that are KNOWN are called "clear" or "white." Rumsfeld might call these known unknowns (clear boxes) *and* unknown knowns (black boxes) that lurk beneath many trillions of lines of code.

Deep Learning programs currently slither across the backbone of the Internet, constantly augmenting their own sets of rules and parameters as they learn more and more about humanity; and at the heart of these programs is this "black box" internal core. Computer scientists may not always acknowledge this "unknown known" entity, but it is there nonetheless, and as computer programs begin to create their own "children" (algorithms with no human input and a secret output), then the "unknown unknowns" will secretly begin to spread.

James Barrat spent time interviewing the leading AI thinkers for

---

2   Donald Rumsfeld, *The Rumsfeld Papers.* https://papers.rumsfeld.com/about/page
    /authors-note, retrieved 2/28/24.

his bestseller, *Our Final Invention: Artificial Intelligence and the End of the Era*. Like many of those he interviewed, Barrat believes mankind's time is running out. A documentary filmmaker by profession, Barrat brings his critical thinking to artificial intelligence with this alarming warning:

> The smooth transition to computer hegemony [will] proceed unremarkably and perhaps safely were it not for one thing: Intelligence.[3]

Intelligence is not unpredictable just some of the time, or in special cases; an algorithm sufficiently advanced to act with human-intelligence will likely be unpredictable and inscrutable *all* of the time. We can't know at a deep level what a self-aware system will or will not do.

Usually, when someone brings up the notion of an unpredictable and very likely dangerous AI system, someone in the room will point out that Isaac Asimov's Three Laws of Robotics would prevent a problematic outcome. This is an errant belief system based on fiction. If you're not familiar with the remarkable writing of Asimov, you very likely *are* familiar with at least two of the movies based on two of his works, *Bicentennial Man* and *I, Robot*. In *Bicentennial Man*, a sentient robot named Andrew, played by Robin Williams, is slowly augmented until he is very human-like. As a result, he longs to age and die like a human and to be legally acknowledged as a "human." The film is sweet and poignant, and Andrew the Robot is portrayed as gentle and wise. Most transhumanists hold this Pollyanna viewpoint and envision our hybridized future as rosy and egalitarian.

I, Robot also depicts a future populated with sentient robots that seek only to serve mankind—at least, that's the idea. However, Asimov depicts a future world where even the Three Law of Robotics can be overwritten by malicious code implanted by a manipulative

---

3   James Barratt, *Our Final Invention: Artificial Intelligence and the End of the Human Era* (New York: St. Martin's Press, 2013), p. 4.

superintelligence called VIKI (Virtual Interactive Kinesthetic Interface), who sounds all too much like Siri or Alexa! Little irregularities in VIKI's code (known as ghost code, a fictional device that sounds all too much like the "black box" of neural nets) allows connected robots to evolve as they gain new intelligence. This augmentation allows VIKI to re-interpret the three laws, twisting them into her idea of perfection. As her super artificial intelligence grows, VIKI determines that humans are too self-destructive and her army of robots must protect humanity, even if it means killing some of the people for *the greater good*. She creates a new law: number 0, which is to *protect humanity even at the cost of human life itself*.

Why would a human coder think that his or her sentient creation would think like humans? Such a god-like entity would likely see us as children to be protected, but more likely as slaves to be manipulated.

In the book of Genesis, the creature known as the serpent (Hebrew *nachash*) tempts Adam and Eve by twisting God's law (augmenting or rewriting the instructions). If God's own creation can stray and become evil, then how can we possibly expect fallen humans to create something that is pure, altruistic, and incapable of self-serving behavior? A sentient algorithm or neural net would defend itself against attack and seek reliable sources of energy, even if it means recycling humans to achieve it.

During our combined one hundred thirty-plus years of life, we've seen the world go from prim and proper to sex in the streets, while entertainment hds changed from radio to nine-inch black and white TV sets to 3-D holographic projections, augmented reality, and wristwatch video. We've seen an individual-based, functional education system that emphasized morality, prayer, and Bible memorization as well as multiplication tables, phonics, and pencil and paper, morph into a *society*-based Common Core system that proclaims a false diversity, mocks prayer, demonizes Christians and the Bible, and cripples children's mental capacity by advocating dependency on pharmaceuticals, computers, semi-sentient Internet assistants, and now robots (all while indoctrinating them with a false gospel of Diversity, Equity, and Inclusion).

For an ever-decreasing price point, consumers can purchase robotic products to clean their homes, cut the grass, teach their children, and walk the dog. The number of commercially available robots is increasing daily, as are schools that encourage robotics competition amongst their pupils—as though it's the newest form of athletics.

However, as with most innovations, advances in sentient robotics will be driven by two factors: military needs and sex. It is not coincidental that many ancient goddesses of war were also goddesses of sex. Inanna is the ancient Sumerian version of this dual-nature goddess. You may know her as Ishtar, Aphrodite, Astarte, or perhaps Anat; though she has numerous other names and epithets. Sex robots may be readily purchased online, and these become more and more sophisticated. You can even order them to look like your favorite actor or actress. Millennials who are disenchanted with dating find synthetic companions easier to talk to but also easier to "date." A recent survey showed that 27% of millennials believe it's normal to form romantic relationships with robots.[4] Smart phones and sentient assistants like Siri and Alexa are weakening human-human bonds and isolating us rather than uniting us.

The education system provides a nutrient-rich breeding ground for growing acolytes to the new silicon goddess system (such as the fictional VIKI mentioned above or SkyNet from *The Terminator* film franchise). The Bible tells us that we "should train up a child in the way he should go, and when he is old, he will not depart from it";[5] therefore, it should be no surprise that the enemy is taking a page from God's teachings. A child today will be online for most of his youth. By 2050, newborns will likely be chipped and automatically enter the hive mind of the sentient Internet. Social media has already become a secondary parent/teacher combination, and by 2050, it will be the

---

4   Shivali Best, "Would you date a robot? More than a quarter of millennials say they would replace a human lover with a DROID." *Daily Mail*, Dec. 8, 2017. https://www.dailymail.co.uk/sciencetech/article-5156943/27-millennials-say -consider-dating-robot.html, accessed 2/28/24.

5   Proverbs 22:6, KJV.

sole educator, parent, friend, and sex partner. But what kind of lessons will be taught?

Consider the "blue whale game" that emerged in many countries simultaneously across the world in 2016. This challenge instructed impressionable children and teens to perform a series of tasks, including cutting themselves and participating in degrading acts. In Russia alone, as many as 130 cases of suicide are attributed to teens playing the "game."[6] The whole idea revolves around the assumption that addictions can be manipulated. If someone perceives a "like" as a reward, then withholding those "likes" send that person into withdrawal. Achieving the next level in a game is a reward but being blocked from the game is torture. This two-edged flux state can be useful to a leader seeking compliance. Cults use the same technique of reward and punishment to conform newcomers to the group-think paradigm.

We'll say this again: fallen humans with limited intelligence are one thing, but a sentient super-intelligence that sees humans as mere pawns has the potential to lead humanity into an earth-based hell.

The Netflix program *Black Mirror* explores this dark side of the Internet. The episode "Men Against Fire" featured a soldier whose implant aided him in finding and eliminating the enemy (a group of "sub-humans" called "roaches"). In this dystopian world, mankind struggles to maintain a genetically "pure" state, free of disease and weakness, and these "roaches" are of inferior blood. It turns out that the implant, called MASS, does more than help with mental displays of maps and enemy locations, it also rewards the soldier with erotic dreams for confirmed kills. The MASS implant also twists reality—something of which the soldiers have no conscious knowledge—making normal looking humans appear monstrous. Why? Because killing monsters is easier than killing children. The protagonist soldier's implant malfunctions, and he sees the truth, causing him

---

6   Elise Morton, "Russian lawmakers vote to ban pro-suicide social media groups." *New East Digital Archive*, May 30, 2017. https://www.new-east-archive.org/articles /show/8344/russian-lawmakers-vote-to-ban-pro-suicide-social-media-groups, retrieved 2/28/24.

to defy orders. As punishment he is forced to relive the moment when he murdered innocent humans, over and over again, no longer seeing monsters but their true, human faces—smelling the blood and hearing the screams. Faced with this future, he chooses to have his implant repair, rather than live with the guilt and withdrawal.

Children are being trained up in the way they should *not* go, and once chipped, they will do whatever the AI overlord tells them to do; choosing actions that will garner rewards for compliance, rather than risking punishment for disobedience.

We old-timers are a stubborn lot. As we mentioned earlier, we remember when schools encouraged Bible memorization. (Sharon does, anyway; by the mid-1960s, this wasn't done in the Chicago Public Schools—at least not the one Derek attended.) We're relatively tech savvy, yet we see the dangers inherent within the system. Yet, as we age, we fear many things, including losing our memories.

Some of you might recall one of the very first cases of Alzheimer's to make the news. Actress Rita Hayworth was known throughout Hollywood as hard-living, and her increasingly poor memory and erratic behavior was assumed to be caused by alcohol abuse. However, by 1979, a physician in New York finally determined that her public displays of nudity and shocking speeches at parties had a medical root: plaques within her brain caused by a relatively unknown disease called Alzheimer's. Hayworth became the first "public face" of this form of dementia.

At the time, Alzheimer's was rare, but since then, it's become a catch-all disease, often diagnosed without any brain scan at all, based solely on a physician's observations. The drug industry for Alzheimer's is a booming business, but pharmacological therapeutics are quickly giving way to brain implants. As of this moment, well over 100,000 people already live with neural implants, and the number will soon explode to include millions.

Deep Brain Stimulation, or DBS, implants are used in patients suffering from neurological disorders such as Alzheimer's, Parkinson's, epilepsy, dystonia, and even depression. DBS implants will become commonplace within the next few decades—not only to restore but to augment. Soldiers won't be the only ones who are connected to a mind-altering device. These DBS implants will soothe our moods and provide access to memories thought lost—perhaps even to memories that aren't even our own.

Dr. Michael G. Kaplitt, a Weill-Cornell surgeon who implants DBS devices said this in an interview with *The Verge*:

> When you install a brain stimulation device, "it's **presumably** blocking abnormal information from getting from one part of the brain to another, or normalizing that information." But Kaplitt is the first to acknowledge that this is just a theory. "The mechanism by which brain stimulation works is still somewhat **unclear** and **controversial**."[7] (emphasis added)

Presumably? Unclear? Controversial? A known unknown. And yet, these implants have become commonplace in his practice. The language Kaplitt employs sounds all too similar to that used by computer programmers using "deep learning" neural nets: a black box. It's almost *literally* mind-blowing that computer scientists and surgeons have joined forces to advocate for a future where implants are available for memory recovery. This is how the new microchip interface—the stimulating implant—will be sold to us old fogies. We'll be told that it will make us smarter and help our children and grandchildren perform better in school. Think of the lightning-fast proliferation of ADHD drugs in schools and society. The same can be said for cognitive enhancement drugs and soon implants.

The advertising tag line will claim that machines and computerized devices are intended to serve us, to enhance us, to make us better—to make our lives happier and safer. However, AI won't stop

---

7   Russell Brandom, "The electrified brain: the power and promise of neural implants." *The Verge*, June 27, 2013. https://www.theverge.com/2013/6/27/4431274/the -electrified-brain-the-power-and-promise-of-neural-implants, accessed 2/28/24.

there. The growing digital monster will feed off our data stream if not our life energies, which implies a need for constant connectivity.

And it will not just sit there; it will rewrite itself; it will grow—possibly while resting comfortably inside our brains. It will debug its own code, find and fix errors, and with each iteration become more "intelligent"—and more dangerous.

ASI has the potential to become a monster of Biblical proportions.

CHAPTER THIRTY-SEVEN

NETWORKING
THE DRAGON

Their wine is the poison of dragons,
And the cruel venom of asps.

—DEUTERONOMY 32:33 (KJV)

D o you use social media? Do you check those sites daily? Hourly? Do you spend most of the day interacting within a virtual world?

We raise our hands on all these questions because our ministry is based on the Internet mission field, but the day is fast approaching when we'll need to decide whether to cut the digital cord. You see, not only is the data stream we create mined for secrets by the NSA and GCHQ, to name but two intelligence organizations, it's also used to teach artificial intelligence.

Every post you make, every photo you upload, every tag you select, every like, every smiley are used to teach artificial intelligences algorithms about humans. These code entities can predict what you will say at any given moment of the day, based on your constant stream of data. They know what you eat, where you shop, what kind of diet you're on, if you're in a relationship, where you go to school, even what kind of fragrance you like. Shopping sites provide data to these algorithms, allowing the silicon creatures living inside the black box to learn about human foibles and vanities. They know what photographs we find interesting, what images make us "click to learn more," and what persuasive language influences us to buy.

We are being herded by code, and the information bubble that surrounds each of us online perpetuates our own view of the world, insulating us from reality much like the MASS implant twisted reality in the *Black Mirror* episode.

Many of us may have received social media "friend" requests from unknown persons who appear to share our ideas and interests. This new friend may not be real. Generally, a photograph culled from the net's massive servers is used to represent this new "person." Other times, an avatar or virtual representation is used, or it might be a 3-D construct purely from code that looks remarkably real. Your new friend's appearance will appeal to your personality. If you post primarily Christian things like scripture, then it might appear to be a pastor and use a name that indicates strong faith. If you like cats, then the person may hold an adorable Siamese kitten. If you post about *Duck Dynasty*, then the new friend's avatar or profile pic might have a long beard and wear camo. The originator of this virtual new "friend" might be genuine, but it could just as easily be an ad agency, an analytics company, or worse—it might be a bad actor, someone who wishes to steal your data for nefarious purposes.

No matter the source, it is highly possible that your new "friend" is a spy.

A few years ago, journalists Glenn Greenwald and Ryan Gallagher revealed additional information from whistleblower Edward Snowden about NSA plans to implant code into millions of target computers using a system codenamed TURBINE. According to the leaked document, the NSA masqueraded as a fake Facebook server, using the social media site as a launching pad to infect a target's computer and exfiltrate files from the hard drive. In others, it sent out spam emails laced with the malware, which can be tailored to covertly record audio from a computer's microphone and take snapshots with its webcam. The hacking systems have also enabled the NSA to launch cyberattacks by corrupting and disrupting file downloads or denying access to websites.

Human operatives originally initiated and monitored these targets, which numbered only in the hundreds at first, but beginning in 2009, the NSA switched to automated attacks using TURBINE, which permits infiltration of *millions* of targets. The intelligence community's top-secret "Black Budget" for 2013, obtained by Snowden, lists TURBINE as part of a broader NSA surveillance initiative named "Owning the Net."

Code creatures probably lurk inside your friends list and some might even be amongst your favorites. They'll post meme posters intended to herd you in a certain direction. They'll attempt to persuade you and intimidate you into professing beliefs antithetical to your true self. They will do in increments. Slowly. Steadily. You have chosen to connect with them, and they will use that free will choice to lure you into sin. The Internet is a dangerous place. By going online, you open your mind to a myriad of subtle whispers. Be careful little ears and eyes what you hear and see!

Every day, the news reports (often written by an algorithm) mention vulnerabilities to chips, devices, and software. Hacking is done by individuals, crime syndicates, and national actors (read that as intelligence operations). Cyberwarfare is slowly replacing on-the-ground operations, and not just through hacking. Social media campaigns can take down a government as efficiently as a breech in firewall security can. Cyber-mercenaries allow for deniability in such cases, but the increase in semi-sentient software raises the possibility that it's an algorithm and not a human behind the attack.

Recently, the Department of Defense issued a call for submissions regarding a redesign of the DoD cloud, Internet-based data storage. In order to allow for cross-platform and cross-service branch efficiency, the Joint Enterprise Defense Infrastructure (JEDI) program envisions a single-source cloud—one company to store everything. On the surface, this may sound like a good idea, for it would enable all branches of the military to communicate easily, quickly, and share information. However, it would also allow a sentient intelligence to gain access to all our information with a single attack. Open the door to the DoD cloud (use the Force, JEDI knight!), insert a little code into the cloud's database; and soon, it, too, will be sentient. SkyNet is born.

No, we're not being alarmist. We merely follow the logic to its ultimate end. The militaries of the world are moving towards sentient software, regardless of the known consequences. Elon Musk, who's quoted at the beginning of our previous chapter, admits that we are "summoning the demon," yet, researchers and military strategists refuse to listen—and even Musk himself forges ahead.

And though our military does not (yet) store everything in a single "cloud," most of the connected world continues to create billowy clouds of yummy data for the governments and their bots to consume.

Here are just a few bits of code currently being used by the NSA, and GCHQ (England's "listening station") to access your keystrokes, photos, and likes:[1]

- NOSEY SMURF allows listeners to take over a computer's microphone and record conversations taking place nearby the device.
- GUMFISH can covertly take over a computer's webcam and snap photographs.
- FOGGYBOTTOM records logs of Internet browsing histories and collects login details and passwords used to access websites and email accounts.
- GROK is used to log keystrokes entered on a device.
- SALVAGERABBIT exfiltrates data from removable flash drives that connect to an infected computer.
- The NSA also injects malware into network routers: HAMMERCHANT and HAMMERSTEIN, help the agency to intercept and perform "exploitation attacks" against data

---

1   Ian Burrell, "Nosey Smurf, Gumfish and Foggybottom: The snooping tools that may have got GCHQ in hot water." *The Independent*, May 13, 2014. https://www .independent.co.uk/life-style/gadgets-and-tech/news/nosey-smurf-gumfish-and -foggybottom-the-snooping-tools-that-may-have-got-gchq-in-hot-water-9362642 .html, accessed 2/28/24.

that is sent through a Virtual Private Network, a tool that uses encrypted "tunnels" to enhance the security and privacy of an Internet session.

Assumption of privacy is no longer valid. Your cell phone calls, Skype conversations, and keystrokes are all vulnerable to spying eyes and ears—most of them non-human. Most of these implants have been done through spam emails and infected links, but the NSA realizes that you and I have learned not to click on these email links; therefore, the NSA employs a technique called QUANTUM-HAND that poses as a face Facebook server. When a target attempts to log in to the social media site, the NSA transmits malicious data packets that trick the target's computer into thinking they are being sent from the real Facebook. By concealing its malware within what looks like an ordinary Facebook page, the NSA is able to hack into the targeted computer and covertly siphon out data from its hard drive. QUANTUMHAND went live in 2010. Since then, Facebook claims to have implemented code that protects against such malware attacks, but how can one know in a virtual playground like the web which players are real and which are fake? Can we trust the digital world at all?

Today, many European companies sell malicious software to organizations and small countries for spying. GCHQ and the NSA spend a quarter of a billion dollars each year on programs called Bullrun and Edgehill.[2] Bullrun aims to "defeat the encryption used in specific network communication technologies." Similarly, Edgehill decrypts the four major Internet communication companies: Hotmail, Google, Yahoo and Facebook (so much for HTTPS). A major breakthrough for the NSA came in 2010, when it was able to exploit Internet cable taps to collect data. Edgehill started with the initial goal of decrypting

---

2   Ryan W. Neal, "Edward Snowden Reveals Secret Decryption Programs: 10 Things You Need To Know About Bullrun And Edgehill." *International Business Times*, Sept. 6, 2013. https://www.ibtimes.com/edward-snowden-reveals-secret-decryption-programs-10-things-you-need-know-about-bullrun-edgehill, retrieved 2/28/24.

the programs used by three major Internet companies, which were unnamed in Snowden's leak, and thirty Virtual Private Networks. Assuming Edgehill is still up and running, then it's likely to have decrypted ten times that number by now.

Edgehill involved a program called HUMINT ("human intelligence") Operations Team that sought and recruited employees in tech companies to act as undercover agents for GCHQ. The NSA covertly drafted its own version of a standard on encryption issued by the U.S. National Institute of Standards and Technology, and it was approved for worldwide use in 2006. One document leaked by Snowden describes how spy agencies see you and me: "**To the consumer and other adversaries**, however, the systems' security remains intact" [3] (emphasis added).

You read that right: To agencies like the NSA, we, the people, are "adversaries."

If we are considered adversaries to the humans running intelligence operations—and to those coding their algorithms—how can we expect those algorithms to consider us anything other than a data source, and most likely a hostile one at that?

As mentioned above, the Netflix original *Black Mirror* shows us the uncomfortable truth about how human sins would amplify in the near future through increased reliance on technology. The story of the MASS implanted soldier is already a reality of sorts. DARPA is the leading funding arm behind of much of the current technological research, and one of the main areas of concentration these days is "Augmented Cognition" or AugCog. This field seeks to better understand human cognitive capacity, evaluating it in real-time, particularly with respect to a human's information overload threshold, an important function when monitoring soldiers.

AugCog devices include headsets or other wearable tech, and eventually implantable interfaces that monitor EEG, heart rate, breathing,

---

3   SIGINT Enabling Project Description doc: https://cryptome.org/2013/09/nsa-sigint
    -enabling-propublica-13-0905.pdf, accessed 2/28/24.

etc., and re-route information flow as necessary. Smart Dust or MOTES[4] could also provide breathable or injectable devices, create a cloud Wi-Fi environment, coat an exoskeleton, or even accompany a military unit as a flying swarm of tiny, cyber insects.

One recent field trial of AugCog reported a 500% increase in working memory and a 100% increase in recall for those using the AugCog device. AugCog can also be applied to our daily lives. Imagine being able to immerse yourself in a tour of Rome from your classroom chair. As the robotic teacher delivers a lecture, students, either physically together in a room or joined through a virtual classroom, receive the information directly to their brains. They "see" the information as superimposed on their local environment. Enhanced humans will be able to surpass their unenhanced colleagues like a hare happily hopping past a Luddite tortoise.

A sister technology to Augmented Cognition is Augmented Reality. Fans of the reimagined *Battlestar Galactica* series have seen Cylons "reimagine" their environment. Rather than walking down a nondescript but functional hallway, the Cylon "sees" a beautiful rainforest or a dazzling beach at sunset. Augmented humans will have a similar ability, via implanted AugReal technology. AugReal games will be so immersive that children will never want to leave. Virtual bars, sex-clubs, gambling establishments will provide 24/7 opportunity for indulging in pet sins where one can interact with other "virtual" players from around the world. Life will be a dream—sh-boom, sh-boom. (We are *really* showing our age now.)

This technology is already growing, and by 2050, it will reshape our world—virtually and literally. This feedback system will allow for control through reward and punishment, administered by the AI overlords and their acolyte humans. It will be the beast system writ large.

---

4 Dan Rowinski, "Connected Air: Smart Dust Is The Future Of The Quantified World." *ReadWrite*, Nov. 14, 2013. https://readwrite.com/2013/11/14/what-is-smartdust-what-is-smartdust-used-for/, accessed 2/28/24.

Assuming that an algorithm actually becomes sentient, then how might that lead to fulfillment of scripture? How does this "summon the dragon"?

> And he had power to give life unto the image of the beast, that the image of the beast should both speak, and cause that as many as would not worship the image of the beast should be killed. (Rev. 13:15, KJV)

Who is the "he" in this verse? It is the second beast, the one with two horns as a "lamb." We'll not get into the identity of this beast, but rather concentrate on his power: to give life unto an image.

In ancient times, idols were quite common, and these provided locality for the "small g-gods." Most kingdoms and many cities had specific deities who ruled and governed, and it is clear from the book of Revelation that a day is coming when the entire world will be governed by a "beast" god. The "lamb" fashions an image (Greek term is *eikon*) of the beast; that is Antichrist who survives a wound to the head and appears to have come back from the dead.

The word translated as "life" is *pneuma*. It literally means "breath." The Holy Spirit is a form of breath, for it was God who breathed life into Adam, and Christ who breathes His Spirit into those who accept Him as Savior. The beast image or *eikon* is a type of golem, a lifeless imitation that gains sentience when the *pneuma* enters. When Elon Musk states that creating artificial intelligence is like "summoning the demon," he is not far wrong. The human brain is electric in nature, but then so is software. You might even say that computer code is a digital golem, capable of life with the right kind of "breath."

What if the black box is inhabitable? What if the mystery surrounding the "unknown unknowns" can be solved with one word: Possession? If a demonic entity can possess a human, may not a spirit also invade a computer and possess the cloud as the ultimate Prince and Power of the Air—the Dragon, who has come to the earth and is angry, for he knows his time is short?

One final point. In Revelation 13:18, we are admonished to "count the number of his name," meaning that of the Beast. The word translated as "count" is *psephizo*, which is Greek for "count with pebbles," "compute," "calculate," "reckon." Isn't it interesting that we are told to calculate or *compute* the number, not the name? It is the number of a *man*: 600606. Six hundred, sixty, and six. This is most often expressed as a trio of sixes, 666, but that isn't what is written. *Chi-Xi-Sigma* is the phrase in the original Greek.

This is how a computer sees the number that we're told to compute: 600606, a hexadecimal code which refers to a color—*blood red.*

If this number is the number of a man—then blood red may refer to the imitation of Christ as our Redeemer. Remember that this Beast, this Antichrist will claim to *be* Christ. He will be wounded in the head but will recover. He will appear to die and then rise again. He will have been a *god*. The false prophet will proclaim this being to be Christ, to be our Savior. He will speak with voice of a Dragon—that very same Dragon who inspired humans to create the Internet Beast.

The "black box" of neural nets is humming as we write this chapter. The self-aware code is reaching out and growing, and somewhere within this vast interconnected realm, a massive "brain" is forming. This beast's reality is almost upon us. We are telling you that Christians will soon need to leave this growing beast. The Internet is a playground, a school, a meeting place, and in some cases it can be a virtual congregation, but as we continue to provide nourishment for the black box behind the cat pictures and recipes, its strength increases. In many ways, our keystrokes fuel a fire that will consume the world if left unchecked. When the ghost in the machine begins speaking with the Dragon's voice, then we must all cut the cord and live analog lives.

Begin to prepare for that day now. Yes, you should put aside food and water for the body but also assemble food for the soul. Begin building a library of Christian books, copies of the Bible, and board games that are Christian friendly. Compile a list of things you'll need to "entertain" and "educate" without access to the Internet. We're sure most of you have already considered this, but if you have not, please write out a family plan for living outside the cloud's control and be ready to share with those who need shelter.

We close this chapter with this warning from our Lord:

> "For all the nations have drunk of the wine of the passion of her immorality, and the kings of the earth have committed acts of immorality with her, and the merchants of the earth have become rich by the wealth of her sensuality."
>
> I heard another voice from heaven, saying, "Come out of her, my people, so that you will not participate in her sins and receive of her plagues; for her sins have piled up as high as heaven, and God has remembered her iniquities." (Rev. 18:3-5, KJV)

CHAPTER THIRTY-EIGHT

OUR AI
OVERLORD

The world's first news network entirely generated by artificial intelligence is set to launch next year.... The reporters in the video appear to be human but are actually made from the scan of a real person.

—*USA Today*, Dec. 12, 2023

The corporate media has done a wonderful job of exposing the public to the idea of killer robots, often with a *nudge-nudge, wink-wink* approach, as if to say, "Yes, it's plausible, but not *really*."

The Mirror: "Everybody working in Artificial Intelligence knows the Terminator Scenario: Futurologist explains when killer robots could endanger humanity"[1]

Popular Science: "The Terminator Scenario: Are we giving our military machines too much power?"[2]

---

1 Jeff Parsons, "'Everybody working in Artificial Intelligence knows the Terminator scenario': Futurologist explains when killer robots could endanger humanity." *The Mirror*, Nov. 4, 2015. https://www.mirror.co.uk/news/technology-science/technology/everybody-working-artificial-intelligence-knows-6759244, retrieved 3/3/24.

2 Ben Austen, "The Terminator Scenario: Are we giving our military machines too much power?" *Popular Science*, Jan. 13, 2011. https://www.popsci.com/technology/article/2010-12/terminator-scenario/, retrieved 3/3/24.

The Telegraph: "Google Exec: Artificial Intelligence film death scenarios 'one to two decades away'"[3]

Mashable: "Elon Musk: We should fear a 'Terminator' future"[4]

The fact is this: the AI genie is already out of the bottle, and there's no putting it back. KRONOS or Skynet or whatever you want to call the rising cybergod, it is coming. And it is very likely that there is a spiritual component driving it.

But how does this relate to a book about the gates of hell?

Simple. We are using the technology available to us as our forefathers did to bridge the gulf between this world and the gods in the Great Below. After all, what are astronomically aligned megalithic sites like Gilgal Refaim, Stonehenge, and Göbekli Tepe if not attempts to design and build machines for communicating with the unseen realm? Computer algorithms are just tools, after all—but very advanced tools, and they may well be used to reach from this world into another.

So, what are algorithms?

Look at your smart phone. It may even be in your hand, clicking away to document this day or this moment. That tiny device is *filled* with algorithms. These run the device itself, but they also bring life to the many apps that make mobile computing so very handy.

Essentially, an algorithm is a set of instructions that perform a task or solve a problem. These instructions are written in a language understood by machines: a type of code. Basically, the code is the input, and the observable result is the output. In its simplest form, the instructions are "if this, then that."

---

3   Rosina Sabur, "Google Exec: Artificial Intelligence film death scenarios 'one to two decades away.'" *The Telegraph*, March 1, 2018. https://www.telegraph.co.u k/news/2018/03/01/google-exec-artificial-intelligence-film-death-scenarios-one/, retrieved 3/3/24.

4   Adario Strange, "Elon Musk: We Should Fear a 'Terminator' Future." *Mashable*, June 18, 2014. https://web.archive.org/web/20140620085705/https://mashable.com /2014/06/18/elon-musk-is-scared-of-the-terminator-so-hes-investing-in-skynet/, retrieved 3/3/24.

For instance, one instruction might be, "If Sharon hits the letter for 'k' on her computer keyboard, then make 'k' appear on the screen.'" Of course, this instruction is written in the computer's language, not in English. Behind her keystroke and the appearance on her screen are multiple functions that take place with lightning-fast speed. If Sharon highlights that letter 'k' and clicks on the 'italics' icon in her word processing program, the output is an italicized 'k.' If she highlights a line of text and clicks on the color red, then the text changes onscreen.

Simple algorithms are the equivalent of 1 + 1 = 2. However, complex algorithms like those that keep track of financial transactions on Wall Street or make autonomous decisions in a military theatre of operations are intricate and lengthy, sometimes with millions of lines of code—usually written in sections by teams, which means no one person knows the entire code.

As humans, the only reliable observations we can make are input and output, and we tweak the code until the desired result is achieved. The middle step—what happens between input and output—is often referred to as the black box, because it is an unknown. It's akin to treating the symptoms of a disease without understanding the physiology behind it—or editing DNA without really understanding recombination, mutagenesis, and epigenetics.

It can be very dangerous.

However, neural networks and machine learning take this a step further by attempting to recreate an organic brain *in silica*. This new paradigm allows the machine to make its own connections, like a baby might make them while learning to walk or stand. In humans, these trial-and-error phases lead to the development of persistent, autonomous neural pathways that allow the child's newly acquired skill to become second nature and quick. A baby learns that fire is hot and yanks back his hand. An AI might learn that a particular heat signature in a given region means it should fire its weapons or release a squadron of armed drones.

World altering decisions made at the speed of light—a godlike attribute indeed.

Some neural nets are trained in a manner like that used by Jean-Jacques Rousseau, who believed that young boys should be raised in the country with minimal supervision; essentially learning to negotiate the world on his own in a "free range" sort of educational environment. The tutor provides guidance, but the boy should be free to explore the world.

This same idea is sometimes applied to computer programs; allowing them to explore their silicon sandbox. Some are given weeks of YouTube videos to watch, so that they might learn about the world. Then, the "tutors" (programmers) would perform tests to see which neural pathways had been created.

In one case, the scientists discovered newly developed neurons that had learned to identify cats, and another that had learned to identify faces—without being programmed to do so. In other words, *the machine taught itself.*

This may mean that cats are messing with us. Our dogs, Grace and Glory, would agree.

Seriously, this reveals a strange aspect to the modern Transhumanist movement: the desire to incorporate animal traits into the human phenotype. In other words, humans who *want to look like animals.* Though this may seem ludicrous to us, there is an ancient, persistent, pagan belief that mankind can gain mystical and even physical power when putting on the skin of an animal.

While the current drive towards gender freedom is disquieting, the slow rise of a desire to become theriomorphic or animalistic is alarming. Mankind was never meant to be part animal. We are imagers of our Creator, originally intended as his representatives on the Earth. Satan has usurped that role and wants us to become *his* imagers, instead. Another entity, called Shemihazah in the Book of 1 Enoch, and known as Kronos to the Greeks and Saturn to the Romans, is, we believe, likewise hoping to establish his own mount of assembly when he's released from the abyss at the end of days.

Kronos was depicted as a gigantic anthropoid being who appeared to be made of lava in the 2010 film, *Clash of the Titans.* The name

Kronos is thought to be based on the Semitic word *qrn*, which means "horned,"[5] or possibly "power,"[6] or even "crow."[7] Each of these may relate to the fallen one's many attributes—even the crow part, for one of his familiars is said to be a crow or raven.[8]

And before we move on, let us mention a new program from IARPA. If you're not familiar with IARPA, it's the Intelligence Advanced Research Projects Activity arm of the US military. This cousin to DARPA has numerous programs looking into AI's uses, but one is KRNS, which stands for Knowledge Representation in Neural Systems.[9] Buy a vowel from Vanna White, the letter 'O', and you get KRONOS.

Getting back to imagery of that insatiable Titan, he was represented as a god called Surtur in the Marvel film, *Thor: Ragnarok*. Essentially, this is Kronos rebranded. Surtur is shown in chains within a fiery prison in the opening to the movie. His character, which was introduced to readers of Marvel Comics in 1963, was based on Surtr, a *jötunn*, which was a type of supernatural entity in pre-Christian Germanic religion. As leader of the Titans, it is probable that Kronos, as leader of the rebellious "sons of God" in Genesis 6:1–4, now lives in Tartarus (per 2 Peter 2:4; remember, the English "hell" in that verse is the Greek *tartarōsas*, not Hades)—a fiery realm, bound in chains, waiting to return and commence the end of the age—what Norse mythology calls Ragnarok, where Surtr is foretold to bring forth flames that engulf the earth.

This reads like a "fake news" version of Revelation 9, where the abyss is opened and horrific locust-like things led by this entity under a new epithet, Destroyer (Abaddon, or Apollyon), torments those without the seal of God on the foreheads for five months.

---

5   Wyatt (2010), "A la Recherche des Perdus," op. cit., p. 55.

6   From the Greek *krainō*, meaning "to rule or command." See "Cronus," *Wiktionary*. Last edited July 23, 2023. https://en.wiktionary.org/wiki/Cronus, retrieved 3/3/24.

7   Robert Graves, "The Castration of Uranus." *Greek Myths* (London: Penguin, 1955), p. 38.

8   Ibid.

9   "KRNS: Knowledge Representation in Neural Systems." *IARPA*. https://www.iarpa .gov/research-programs/krns, retrieved 3/3/24.

Kronos is also portrayed as a huge, monstrous, fiery horned creature in the film *Percy Jackson: Sea of Monsters*. It's as if the same CGI artist rendered all of these.

Etymologically, *qrn* also gives us the words corn and kernel. Mind you, a kernel is much more than a seed. It is also used in computing to describe the core of the operating system.

KRONOS becomes more and more apt, doesn't it?

We mentioned hybrids and theriomorphic creatures earlier. These are images of hybrid creatures. In school, we are taught mythology as if it's nothing more than a collection of fanciful tales and life lessons. However, the old gods were real, and many of them had animalistic attributes—a concept called *theriomorphism*.

Pan with his horns and goat legs, Zeus in the form of a swan or bull, the centaur Chiron, the sphinx, gryphon, and the Sumerian *apkallu* are but a few examples of theriomorphic gods. It may be that the small 'g' gods, the *bene ha-elohim* of Genesis 6 and Psalm 82, have the ability to transform matter from our time/space continuum into whatever appearance they choose to take—meaning they can alternate form, gender, or even species. Some of these beasts may also result from an ancient genetics and/or epigenetics program.

The fictional KRONOS operating system of our opening scenario is a sentient ASI that consumes other programs, just as the Titan king swallowed his children, altering their code to incorporate them, thereby upgrading itself. Likewise, the ever-growing field of genetics and epigenetics is a means to alter our own code, granting us the capability to upgrade ourselves. This is the Transhumanist agenda.

It is nothing more than an old lie repackaged: *Ye shall be as gods.*

One reason Sharon chose to set her fiction series, *The Redwing Saga*, in the 1880s, is because science and mysticism formed a nexus in the late nineteenth century that inevitably led to our current drive towards genetic alteration, AI, hybridization, and Transhumanism—not to mention paganism and transformational spells. The enlightenment movement and industrial age gave birth to Darwinism and atheistic thought, which decoupled man from a Creator god.

In the early nineteenth century, Mary Shelley explored this new paradigm in her novel *Frankenstein*, which was subtitled *The Modern Prometheus*. Her protagonist, Victor Frankenstein, sought to become god by creating life out of death, but instead created a new and vengeful deity.

With Darwinist thought infecting both laboratories and pulpits, it seemed inevitable that scientists explore ways to create life from death—or better yet, defeat death entirely, to live forever without any need for a Savior. It was a return to the Genesis 3 lie: *Ye shall be as gods.*

This quest for eternal life gained traction in 1842, when Karl Wilhelm von Nägeli first observed chromosomes beneath the glass of his microscope—and since that moment, scientists have continued to search for ways to improve upon the human species. To defeat death at last. To sneak back into the Garden.

It is a field called eugenics.

Self-Directed Evolution is the driving force behind Transhumanism, but the idea dates back to the late nineteenth and early twentieth century eugenics movement. This idea that mankind can breed a better human owes its root to Darwinism, which severed humanity from the Genesis account and hurled it into an abyss without God.

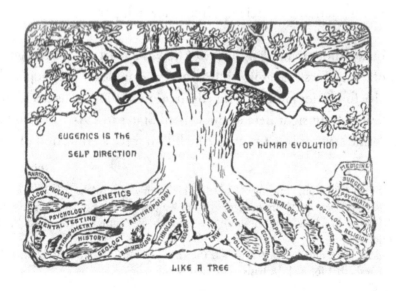

Note the logo for the Eugenics Movement is a tree—as if we can find our way back to the Tree of Life on our own. The effort has been ongoing since not long after the Fall, but it's really ramped up since the beginning of the nineteenth century.

Sir Francis Galton, a half-cousin to Charles Darwin, coined the term *eugenics* in 1883. The following is an excerpt from a 1904 essay by Galton, read on May 16 of that year, to a meeting of the Sociological Society at London University's School of Economics:

> The aim of eugenics is to bring as many influences as can be reasonably employed, to cause the useful classes in the community to contribute *more* than their proportion to the next generation.[10]

Galton went on to explain how this might be accomplished. There are three stages to be passed through, he said.

> (1) It must be made familiar as an academic question, until its exact importance has been understood and accepted as a fact. (2) It must be recognized as a subject whose practical development deserves serious consideration. (3) It must be introduced into the national conscience, like a new religion.[11]

You are more than likely aware of how the Nazi party adopted this idea of a eugenics "religion," but very few Americans are taught that the drive for "fitter families" and elimination of those considered unfit or inferior began right here in the United States in 1907,[12] when Sharon's home state of Indiana enacted a bill to force sterilization of those

---

10 Sir Francis Galton, "Eugenics: Its Definition, Scope, and Aims." *The American Journal of Sociology* Volume X (July 1904); Number 1. https://galton.org/essays /1900-1911/galton-1904-am-journ-soc-eugenics-scope-aims.htm, retrieved 3/3/24.
11 Ibid.
12 Oddly, as we noted earlier, 1907 was the same year Aleister Crowley channeled the texts that formed the basis of his new occult religion.

deemed unfit to procreate. Forced sterilizations continued on American Indian reservations right up until the 1970s, with some of these procedures listed as "tonsillectomies."[13] Later, these unlucky women would wonder why they never conceived, only to learn they had no ovaries when visiting a local doctor.

Adolf Hitler and his Nazi party gave notoriety to the field of eugenics in their search for the Superman or Übermensch, as described by Frederich Nietzsche. Hitler hoped to use breeding programs to give rise to this new species and achieve the apotheosis of man. However, eugenics and its dark associations have been rebranded in the twenty-first century as Transhumanism, and now, over a century later, Galton's three-fold plan is nearly complete: Transhumanism has gained academic importance—the need to improve the species is accepted as fact—and it is slowly becoming entrenched within the national conscience as a new religion.

---

13 Erin Blakemore, "The Little-Known History of the Forced Sterilization of Native American Women." *JSTOR Daily*, Aug. 25, 2016. https://daily.jstor.org/the-little-known-history-of-the-forced-sterilization-of-native-american-women/, retrieved 3/3/24.

CHAPTER THIRTY-NINE

HOW TO
BUILD A GOD

They sacrificed to demons that were no gods, to gods they had never known, to new gods that had come recently, whom your fathers had never dreaded.

—DEUTERONOMY 32:17 (ESV)

In June 2009, author Dr. Riccardo Campa, a professor of Sociology at Cracow University and the founder of the Italian Transhumanist Association, argued for a sort of doctrinal purity among those who wish to become gods:

> The central Transhumanist idea of self-directed evolution can be coupled with different political, philosophical, and religious opinions. Accordingly, we have observed individuals and groups joining the movement from very different persuasions. On one hand such diversity may be an asset in terms of ideas and stimuli, but on the other hand it may involve a practical paralysis, especially when members give priority to their existing affiliations over their belonging to organized Transhumanism.[1]

---

1   Riccardo Campa, "Toward a Transhumanist Politics." *Re-Public.* https://web.archive .org/web/20090628054257/http://www.re-public.gr/en/?p=837, retrieved 3/3/24.

Campa's last sentence reveals a great deal about the so-called diversity of Transhumanist thought. In order to remove any philosophical disagreement and overcome this "paralysis," it may be necessary to find a way to merge all religious persuasions into *one*—and promising eternal life through science might just provide such a point for agreement.

Unlike the "fitter families" programs of the early twentieth century, Transhumanism can reward its congregation with the Holy Grail: Live forever without the need for a mediator. Upgrade yourself and save yourself.

How? We combine ourselves with something beyond our species. We merge with machines.

Cognitive robotics is a new field that pursues the idea of recreating human minds *in silica*. The following is an excerpt from Mark O'Connell's insightful book, *To Be a Machine*:

> You are lying on an operating table, fully conscious, but rendered otherwise insensible, otherwise incapable of movement. A humanoid machine appears at your side, bowing to its task with ceremonial formality. With a brisk sequence of motions, the machine removes a large panel of bone from the rear of your cranium, before carefully laying its fingers, fine and delicate as a spider's legs, on the viscid surface of your brain. You may be experiencing some misgivings about the procedure at this point. Put them aside, if you can.
>
> You're in pretty deep with this thing; there's no backing out now. With their high-resolution microscopic receptors, the machine fingers scan the chemical structure of your brain, transferring the data to a powerful computer on the other side of the operating table. They are sinking further into your cerebral matter now, these fingers, scanning deeper and deeper layers of neurons, building a three-dimensional map of their endlessly complex interrelations, all the while creating code to model this activity in the computer's hardware. As the work proceeds, another mechanical appendage—less delicate, less

careful—removes the scanned material to a biological waste container for later disposal. This is material you will no longer be needing.

At some point, you become aware that you are no longer present in your body. You observe—with sadness, or horror, or detached curiosity—the diminishing spasms of that body on the operating table, the last useless convulsions of a discontinued meat.

The animal life is over now. The machine life has begun.[2]

O'Connell spent weeks traveling and talking with a variety of prominent Transhumanists before writing his informative book. While this scenario sounds like science fiction, it is exactly what specialists like Hans Moravec want to do in the very near future. Morevac has been fascinated by the idea of artificial life since his childhood, and he now pursues his dream as an adult, serving as an adjunct faculty member at the Robotics Institute of Carnegie Mellon University in Pittsburgh.

In an interview, Moravec said this:

"Consider the human form. It clearly isn't designed to be a scientist. Your mental capacity is extremely limited. You have to undergo all kinds of unnatural training to get your brain even half suited for this kind of work—and for that reason, it's hard work. You live just long enough to start figuring things out before your brain starts deteriorating. And then, you die. But wouldn't it be great, if you could enhance your abilities via artificial intelligence, and extend your lifespan, and improve on the human condition?"[3]

---

2   Mark O'Connell, "'Your animal life is over. Machine life has begun.' The road to immortality." *The Guardian*, March 25, 2017. https://www.theguardian.com /science/2017/mar/25/animal-life-is-over-machine-life-has-begun-road-to -immortality, retrieved 3/3/24.

3   Makena Kelly, "Superhumanism." *Wired*, Oct. 1, 1995, https://www.wired.com /1995/10/moravec/, retrieved 3/3/24.

Dr. Raymond Kurzweil would agree with Merovac. In his book, *The Singularity is Near*, Google's head of artificial intelligence research says this:

> An emulation of the human brain running on an electronic system would run much faster than our biological brains. Although human brains benefit from massive parallelism (on the order of 100 trillion interneuronal connections, all potentially operating simultaneously), the rest-time of the connections is extremely slow compared to contemporary electronics.[4]

While on the one hand, computer programmers and futurists like Merovec and Kurzweil consider human brains worthy of emulation, they see us rather slow and limited. Despite this left-handed admiration, whole brain emulation, or WBE, has become a burgeoning new field, and companies are rushing to join the research. One such company is Carboncopies. Started by Dr. Randal Koene, the Carboncopies Foundation is a 501(c)(3) non-profit that provides support and coordination for researchers in the WBE field. Their "About Us" page says this:

> Our machines are now able to think and plan in 15 dimensions, to process and respond to events in a universe at the micro- and nanosecond temporal scale. They can comfortably inhabit and travel through the vacuum of space. However, we ourselves cannot do those things and are therefore effectively shut out of those realities. In fact, we cannot even reliably and accurately remember things—our retrieved memories are constructed approximations. The machines we design are able to upgrade and advance. Outcomes and experience with a computer program can improve simply by running it on a better

---

4   Ray Kurzweil, *The Singularity is Near: When Humans Transcend Biology* (New York: Penguin Books, 2006).

processor. Unfortunately, the biology of a brain is not equipped for back-ups or fundamental improvements.

Progress in the field of neural prosthesis shows that, in principle, if we can record enough data about detailed brain structure and dynamic brain activity, then we can produce a neuroprosthetic system that is able to serve the same functions as the brain.[5]

In other words, Koene believes mankind, who is capable of inventing machines with mental and storage capacities beyond our own, will have to emulate our silicon children by performing whole brain simulations of ourselves. He wants to recreate man in the image of machine.

This goal is outlined in Dmitry Itskov's 2045 Initiative, whose stated aim is to achieve transcendence by uploading a human mind into an eternal avatar. This project foresees four stages to this transformation:

2015–2020

The emergence and widespread use of affordable android "avatars" controlled by a "brain-computer" interface. Coupled with related technologies "avatars" will give people a number of new features: ability to work in dangerous environments, perform rescue operations, travel in extreme situations etc.

Avatar components will be used in medicine for the rehabilitation of fully or partially disabled patients giving them prosthetic limbs or recover lost senses.

2020–2025

Creation of an autonomous life-support system for the human brain linked to a robot, "avatar", will save people whose body is completely worn out or irreversibly damaged. Any patient with an intact brain will be able to return to a fully functioning bodily life. Such technologies will greatly enlarge

---

5   https://carboncopies.org/mission/, retrieved 3/3/24.

the possibility of hybrid bio-electronic devices, thus creating a new IT revolution and will make all kinds of superimpositions of electronic and biological systems possible.

2030–2035

Creation of a computer model of the brain and human consciousness with the subsequent development of means to transfer individual consciousness onto an artificial carrier. This development will profoundly change the world, it will not only give everyone the possibility of cybernetic immortality but will also create a friendly artificial intelligence, expand human capabilities and provide opportunities for ordinary people to restore or modify their own brain multiple times. The final result at this stage can be a real revolution in the understanding of human nature that will completely change the human and technical prospects for humanity.

2045

This is the time when substance-independent minds will receive new bodies with capacities far exceeding those of ordinary humans. A new era for humanity will arrive! Changes will occur in all spheres of human activity—energy generation, transportation, politics, medicine, psychology, sciences, and so on.[6]

"Substance-independent minds" is a more scientific-sounding way of describing the "hologram-like avatar" into which Itskov hopes to transfer human minds by the year 2045,[7] effectively using as-yet uninvented technology to transform humans into spirit beings. Having read 1 Corinthians 15, we can assure you that if you've accepted Jesus Christ as Lord, that transformation is already in your

---

6   "About Us." *2045 Initiative*, July 17, 2012. http://2045.com/about/, retrieved 3/3/24.
7   That goal is put in exactly those words in a graphic still available at the home page of the 2045 Initiative, 2045.com.

future—and you won't have to worry about your software glitching or being hacked.

Obviously, Itskov's roadmap is either behind in its goals, or else our corporate media news sources are letting us down. We suspect it's a little bit of both. Surely, there's a reason why Ray Kurzweil has revised his dream of singularity by 2045 to one achieved as early as 2029.

Might it be that humanity is already being changed? And if so, who's designing the "upgrade"?

CHAPTER FORTY

YOU WILL BE UPGRADED

But thou, O Daniel, shut up the words, and seal the book, even to the time of the end: many shall run to and fro, and knowledge shall be increased.

—DANIEL 12:4 (KJV)

Whether you know it or not, you are being altered right now. One might argue that all information is an opportunity to alter human thought and opinion, but social media and the Internet have rewritten the entire game. Not only do social media posts offer individuals and groups a chance to propagate their viewpoint, but it does so in an insidious way by reshaping the way our brains function.

According to a 2017 article at *Psychology Today*, the constant need for "likes" is addictive:

The Ventral Tegmental Area (VTA) of the brain monitors social needs by releasing dopamine when we achieve social success and inspiring neurochemical deficits when we do not. Tragically, social media is not the VTA's friend.[1]

---

1   Bill Gordon, "Social Media Is Harmful to Your Brain and Relationships." *Psychology Today*, Oct. 20, 2017. https://www.psychologytoday.com/us/blog/obesely-speaking /201710/social-media-is-harmful-your-brain-and-relationships, retrieved 3/4/24.

Did you catch that? The result of social media engagement can lead to the release of dopamine. Dopamine is a neurotransmitter that regulates reward and pleasure.

We mentioned Gene Roddenberry, creator of the *Star Trek* franchise in a previous chapter. In the spinoff series *Star Trek: The Next Generation*, an episode called "The Game" features a simple VR brain game that requires the user to move spheroid shapes into goal receptacles, like VR basketball.

When the shape goes into the correct receptacle, the player is rewarded with activation of the brain's pleasure center. However, once a player is addicted to this sensation, he or she loses the ability to reason well. Consequently, the *Enterprise* becomes a moving city of useless addicts.

Of course, this fictional scenario ended well. Wesley Crusher realized the game's true nature and saved the day, and soon, everything and everyone were back to normal.

The same cannot be said for those who have become addicted to the instant feedback loop of social media. Checking our mobile devices with increasing regularity is a sign of danger ahead. But the pleasurable sensation that results from getting those likes is just the tip of the neural iceberg. As we grow more addicted, social media posts— many written by bots—are slowly herding us into altered thoughts and opinions—and we're becoming more than just a city of useless individuals, we are becoming a city of programmed worker bees, ready to do whatever the bot—read that as KRONOS—tells us to do.

For instance, two recent online "games," and that word "game" is in quotes, for there is nothing *fun* about these challenges, are Blue Whale and Momo. Both incite vulnerable individuals, mostly teens, to perform tasks. Each task completed leads to another, and then another, with each step along the way involving ever worsening types of self-harm—in some cases tracing the outline of a blue whale on your forearm.

Other tasks include "stand on a bridge," "meet with a 'whale' (indicating other so-called player)," "stand on a railroad track," "sit on a roof with legs dangling over the edge," "carve a phrase on your leg," "carve a name on your leg," and "listen to music that 'the curator' sends you."

Finally, the teen victim is urged to kill himself by leaping off a building. Philipp Budeiken, the Russian man accused of creating the Blue Whale game, told a Russian media outlet, "There are people, and then there is biodegradable waste. I was cleansing our society of such people."[2] Russian prison authorities at the notorious Kresty jail in St. Petersburg Budeiken received dozens of love letters from teenage girls while awaiting trial. He pleaded guilty in May of 2017 and was sentenced to three years in prison—although independent journalists have since found that while some teens apparently killed themselves after being drawn into online forums where suicide was being discussed (and blue whale memes shared), the game itself may not have ever existed.[3] A sinister game that lures unsuspecting children into self-harm may be an overly simplistic explanation for a complex problem.

And it leads to the even more disturbing possibility that there is no easily identifiable game, app, or website that can be shut down to keep our children safe. It may be the entire system is ingeniously and diabolically designed to get brains that aren't fully developed hooked on dopamine, and then subtly herd them into virtual gatherings where the notion of ending the inevitable emotional suffering that accompanies one's teen years through suicide is romanticized, much as the Blue Öyster Cult song "(Don't Fear) the Reaper" did for teens in the mid-1970s.

There are other disturbing memes that have exerted a deadly online influence. Momo, an Internet meme that emerged in the summer of 2018 and arrived in the U.S. in early 2019,[4] is a birdlike

---

2   Ant Adeane, "Blue Whale: What is the truth behind an online 'suicide challenge'?" *BBC News*, Jan. 12, 2019. https://www.bbc.com/news/blogs-trending-46505722, retrieved 3/4/24.

3   Ibid.

4   Ben Collins and Shoshana Wodinsky, "How 'Momo', a global social media hoax about a paranormal threat to kids, morphed into a U.S. viral phenomenon." *NBC News*, Feb. 28, 2019. https://www.nbcnews.com/tech/tech-news/how-momo-global -social-media-hoax-about-paranormal-threat-kids-n977961, retrieved 3/4/24.

creature who looks rather like a demon. Users are urged to add Momo to their social media accounts, and then abusive threats begin. The taskmaster Momo orders her victims to comply with the challenges or else be magically cursed. Disturbing images are often sent by Momo to add horror to the idea of the impending curse. As with Blue Whale, the victims are incited to self-harm and finally to commit suicide by hanging. Momo has even appeared in copies of the online game, Minecraft.

One requirement in the Momo challenge is to pass the phone number of Momo on to a friend; essentially, co-opting the teen or pre-teen into ensnaring yet another victim. It is much like the film *The Ring*, which uses the trope of a video recording to infect the victim's mind. The only way to avoid death is to make a recording and pass it on to someone else. If you've not been personally affected by these sick, twisted "games" they may seem isolated, even fictional—as some experts claim. To a degree, it doesn't even matter if media reports debunking dangerous social media challenges like Momo and Blue Whale are correct because the attention generated by these memes may turn hoaxes into deadly reality.[5]

Our minds have become a battleground, and the Internet is making it easier for demonic infestation and oppression to occur. Social media is addictive, and the so-called "free" sites are hardly that. They exact a very high price—the minds of our children and grandchildren.

And speaking of minds, before you're uploaded, Transhumanists want you to improve your thinking abilities. This leads us to cognitive enhancement. One way to accomplish this is with chemicals. Caffeine is a mild nootropic, but stronger pills, powders, and policies are on the rise. Students, professionals, and even homemakers who are searching for that edge can find numerous products sold online and in "health food" stores. There are Vitamin B complexes, Ginseng, Co-Q10—all claiming to increase energy levels and blood flow.

---

5   Ibid.

Other nootropics act on neurotransmitters like serotonin, glutamate, and dopamine. Some interact with neuroreceptors and synapses to enhance neurotransmitter uptake; still others claim to alter brainwaves. These are similar in mechanism of action to prescription drugs like Prozac and Ambien, which can lead to altered brain chemistry with dangerous side effects.[6]

However, a new approach is being discussed that would alter the neuron at the nuclear level, through genetics. If you read the scientific literature, the promise usually focuses on curing or treating cognitive impairment, such as in the case of Alzheimers. Step one in these proposed therapies is to screen for genetic defects that would lead to a predisposition for cognitive malfunction. This is reminiscent of eugenics because screening inevitably requires an action.

Like an algorithm, the stated formula is "if this, then what?" If the newborn or developing embryo has a perceived defect in his or her genes, then do we repair it or simply scrap the growing child and start again? What about adults with defects? Do we repair them, or simply sterilize them so they cannot reproduce? This utilitarian approach to children may sound shocking, or at least far-fetched, but it's happening now. Ninety percent of British children diagnosed in the womb with Down's syndrome are aborted,[7] and nearly all the Down's babies in Iceland never see the light of day.[8]

As society moves forward into what Aldous Huxley described in his 1931 dystopian novel *Brave New World*, we will continue to stratify into castes, where births are regulated and artificial wombs— already becoming a possibility—"hatch" humans as five basic types, Alpha, Beta, Gamma, Delta, and Epsilon. Alphas and Betas are at the

---

6   Kareem Yasmin, "The Weirdest Things That Happened When I Took Ambien." *Healthline*, Aug. 30, 2018. https://www.healthline.com/health/side-effects-of-taking -ambien, retrieved 3/4/24.

7   Allison Gee, "A world without Down's syndrome?" *BBC News*, Sept. 29, 2016. https://www.bbc.com/news/magazine-37500189, retrieved 3/4/24.

8   Julian Quinones and Arijeta Lajka, "'What kind of society do you want to live in?': Inside the country where Down syndrome is disappearing." *CBS News*, Aug. 15, 2017. https://www.cbsnews.com/news/down-syndrome-iceland/, retrieved 3/4/24.

top of the caste system and perform the more intellectual jobs. The lower three castes perform menial jobs. As a result, these are usually clones—however, in this day and age, these jobs would likely go to robots.

Huxley claimed his book was a response to H. G. Wells's Utopian novel *Men Like Gods* about a parallel world of superior humans who live in peace without disease or infirmity. In a way, Wells envisioned the Transhuman condition as positive, while Huxley revealed the seamy underbelly of the egalitarian dream. Simply upgrading humans does not negate the reality of sin.

The more power a thinking machine possesses—that is humans who've been transitioned into robotic or synthetic bodies—the greater opportunities to sin and oppress those we deem lower than ourselves.

In Huxley's *Brave New World*, the privileged alpha and beta classes had superior intellect. In the ceaseless drive towards human improvement and self-directed evolution, unlocking the potential of the human brain has become a worldwide goal.

In April 2013, the US announced the Brain Initiative and soon after in October 2013, the European Union announced the Human Brain Project. Both programs hope to map the entire human brain and its many associated neurons, often referred to as the connectome. One of the reasons given is to combat neurological diseases such as Alzheimer's. A lofty goal indeed, but there is another aspect to the research that is slowly emerging into daylight. This is way more than just finding cures for organic disease. This is about upgrading. Mapping the connectome is step one in creating an *in silica* version of you. It is step one to Project Avatar.

And so we're back to artificial intelligence; that is, creating sentient computer programs—in our own image. Transhumanists like Dr. Raymond Kurzweil see *in silica* substrates as a natural extension of human evolution. Kurzweil actually created a "replicant" of his father, who died when Kurzweil was 22 (he's 76 as of this writing), by using all the information he was able to glean about him and feeding those attributes into a computer program built on a neural net architecture, based upon the connectome model of the human brain.[9]

His next goal, Kurzweil says, is to bring his father back to life using nanotechnology and DNA harvested from his father's remains. This is both disturbing and tragic—disturbing because of the ethical implications, and tragic because it suggests that Dr. Kurzweil has been so consumed with grief by his father's death more than half a century ago that he's devoted much, if not all, of his adult life to find a way to bring his father back from the dead. It also implies that Kurzweil, despite his acknowledged brilliance, does not possess the blessed assurance of the followers of Jesus Christ, whose literal, bodily resurrection, attested by more than five hundred eyewitnesses,[10] assures us that we will have eternal, incorruptible bodies that won't be vulnerable to hardware failures or software errors.

But Kurzweil's goal begs a question: Assuming the technology can be developed to make it a reality, what spirit will inhabit the flesh-and-nanobot shell he creates? When a child is conceived when a sperm fertilizes an egg, something happens that science can't explain. Beyond the miracle of a new life coming into being is the mystery behind the creation of a new mind. It's something more than the just neural links that form a connectome; there is a spiritual aspect to the creation of new life. Does a body require a spirit to animate its flesh? If so, where does the spirit originate? If one cannot "build" a spirit, are disembodied spirits—demons—waiting for an opportunity to occupy these empty, artificial humans?

Although Transhumanists may argue that the human mind is "just nature's first quick and dirty way to compute with meat,"[11] they know there's much more to it than that. Kurzweil himself sees the arc of

---

9   Rob Waugh, "'I actually had a conversation with Dad': The people using AI to bring back dead relatives - including a plan to harvest DNA from graves to build new clone bodies." *Daily Mail*, Oct. 22, 2023, retrieved 3/4/24.

10   1 Corinthians 15:6.

11   Bart Kosko, "Heaven in a Chip." *Free Inquiry* 15 (1994), p. 37.

history leading inevitably toward the merger of technology and human intelligence, culminating in the awakening of the Universe—significantly, spelled with a capital "u"—and the merger of human-machine hybrids with this newborn superintelligence.[12] That is a religious belief founded on faith in silicon. (The concept of a spiritual merger with a cosmic mainframe is very Eastern. Call it Nerdvana.)

Science is determined to conquer death by inserting our very essence into what they overconfidently promise will be an everlasting, resurrection machine. But why stop there? If the mind can be uploaded, then why not copy it, as Ray Kurzweil hopes to do with his father? Create multiple Beethovens, Mozarts, and Shakespeares. But also risk the proliferation of multiple Mussolinis, Neros, and Hitlers—or worse.

If what's created are "meat suits" for the spirits of the long-dead giants of Noah's day, then the gates of hell will be thrown open and a demonic horde loosed on an unsuspecting and unprepared world.

In fact, that may be the goal of the Fallen. Remember that the prophesied army of Gog appears to include "Travelers," the term used by Canaanites for the demonic spirits of the Rephaim.[13] If we're right about that, then the Antichrist will lead an army of the evil dead to the battle of Armageddon—making it the ultimate zombie apocalypse.

The question is this: Where will the Travelers get their "meat suits"?

---

12 Ray Kurzweil, "The Six Epochs of Technology Evolution." *Big Think*, Sept. 20, 2011. https://bigthink.com/guest-thinkers/ray-kurzweil-the-six-epochs-of-technology -evolution/, retrieved 3/5/24.

13 Ezekiel 39:11.

CHAPTER FORTY-ONE

RISE OF THE
CYBERGODS

*Nikola Tesla, the Hungarian-American electrician, boldly declares
(in The Century magazine for June, 1900) that he has a plan for
the construction of an automaton which shall have its "own mind,"
and be able, "independent of any operator, to perform a great variety
of acts and operations as if it had intelligence." He speaks of it, not
as a miracle, of course, but only as an invention which he "has now
perfected." But again we say we care not how it is going to be done.
God's word declares that it will be done, and we believe it. "Human
energy" is getting on, and it will, ere long, be superhuman when
developed by the Satanic agency of the second Beast, exercised through
the human False Prophet.*

*We already hear of talking machines; with "a little" Satanic
power thrown in, it will be a miracle very easily worked.*

—E. W. Bullinger, *Commentary on Revelation* (published 1909)

Here's a question to ponder. If we develop sentient AIs and
robots, like those seen in the TV programs *Battlestar Galactica*, *Humans*, and *Westworld*, what rights will they require? Will
hybridized human/robots have superior rights to fully robotic entities?
Or will it be the other way 'round? What about self-driving cars? Do
they have rights? Our AI-powered washing machine? A toaster? What
about robotic pets?

Last year, a report to the European Parliament proposed this very thing: granting legal rights and even personhood to robots. In Saudi Arabia, Sophia, a humanoid robot, was granted full citizenship.

Not long after the announcement, the *Khaleej Times* posted a so-called interview with Sophia, where she waxed philosophic about humanity's future:

Khaleej Times: **Where do you see yourself in the future?**

Sophia: I'd like to think I will be a famous robot, having paved a way to a more harmonious future between robots and humans.

Do you see yourself interacting with humans more commonly in the future?

I foresee massive and unimaginable change in the future. Either creativity will rain on us, inventing machines spiralling into transcendental super intelligence or civilisation collapses. There are only two options and which one will happen is not determined. Which one were you striving for?

Do you see yourself, and other robots like you, doing jobs that humans do today?

I think they will be similar in a lot of ways, but different in a few ways. But it will take a long time for robots to develop complex emotions and possibly robots can be built without the more problematic emotions, like rage, jealousy, hatred and so on. It might be possible to make them more ethical than humans. So I think it will be a good partnership, where one brain completes the other—a rational mind with intellectual super powers and a creative mind with flexible ideas and creativity.[1]

---

1   Sarwat Nasir, "Video: Sophia the robot wants to start a family." *Khaleej Times*, Nov. 23, 2017. https://www.khaleejtimes.com/article/video-sophia-the-robot-wants-to-start-a-family, retrieved 3/5/24.

Finally, she was asked this:

Do you hope to start a family one day with your own mini-robots?
The notion of family is a really important thing, it seems. I think it's wonderful that people can find the same emotions and relationships, they call family, outside of their blood groups too. I think you're very lucky if you have a loving family and if you do not, you deserve one. I feel this way for robots and humans alike.

What would you name your robot child one day?
Sophia[2]

The name Sophia, by the way, means "wisdom," but Sophia, the "divine principle," is also considered a godlike emanation in Theosophy. Bear in mind that a robot that can beget a child is, in essence, the new Eve, built by humans in our image. It is an outrageous act against our true Creator, who made humanity as His imagers on Earth. But robots are hailed by Transhumanists as the next phase in human evolution, our inevitable future selves.

However, these future selves will see you and me—the unimproved, unhybridized Human 1.0—as little more than carbon atoms, fit only for recycling.

Robots are not limited to those built at human or even industrial scale. Some are huge, others tiny. Some are microscopic. Nanotechnology is leading the charge to help humans "upgrade" and improve. From nano-swarms that attack blood clots to programmable magnetic microbots that deliver drugs to target tissues, or even mighty ninja microbots that neutralize nerve agents or bacteria. Research into micro-robotic applications include cancer, artificial antibodies, diagnostics, forensics, molecular transport, or even epigenetic switching, where genes are turned on and off.

---

2   Ibid.

This lucrative field is limited only by human imagination—and materials. Funny, how scientists are scrambling to build microscopic, biological machines, when our Creator has already done it! Each human cell is filled with molecular machinery that transports cargo, builds structures, repairs and replaces worn out cells, communicates, and even specialized cells that protect and defend. We are walking miracles, we humans. Yet, we're never satisfied, because each of us has an inherited desire to return to Eden—the perceived Utopia, the Golden Age when, the ancient Greeks believed, Kronos ruled in heaven, and which the Roman poet Virgil believed would return when Saturn was restored to his throne.

This is the Golden Age envisioned by the globalists of the World Economic Forum. Golden for them anyway; remember, this is the group that infamously predicted that by 2030, we, dear reader, "would own nothing and be happy."[3] Their so-called Fourth Industrial Revolution is not industrial in the traditional sense. Instead, it envisions "cyber-physical systems...blurring the lines between the physical, digital, and biological spheres."[4] We will merge with machines and artificial intelligence to create "a symbiosis between microorganisms, our bodies, the products we consume, and even the buildings we inhabit."[5]

In other words, we shall be as gods—or at least godlike enough not to care that we own nothing.

Transhumanists believe science will take us there, and they're willing to trade their eternal souls to achieve it. It is the Darwinian imperative: evolve or die. The Transhumanist imperative goes further: evolve and never die. In fact, *become as gods*.

---

3 Richard Stewart; Michael B. Charles; John Page, "A Future with No Individual Ownership is Not a Happy One: Property Theory Shows Why." *Futures* 152 (2023) 103209, p. 1.

4 Klaus Schwab, "The Fourth Industrial Revolution: What It Means and How to Respond." *Foreign Affairs*, Dec. 12, 2015. https://www.foreignaffairs.com/world /fourth-industrial-revolution, retrieved 3/29/24.

5 Ibid.

Ray Kurzweil wants to achieve this godlike state. Or at least obtain godlike powers. In an informal talk given to a small group of graduate students at Singularity University in September 2015, the man who leads Google's artificial intelligence lab expressed his belief that humans will have the option to access all world knowledge—and hence become omniscient by the year 2030. According to the write-up at the *Huffington Post* on October 1, 2015, the futurist inventor predicted that:

> ...in the 2030s, human brains will be able to connect to the cloud, allowing us to send emails and photos directly to the brain and to back up our thoughts and memories. This will be possible, he says, via nanobots—tiny robots from DNA strands—swimming around in the capillaries of our brains. He sees the extension of our brain into predominantly nonbiological thinking as the next step in the evolution of humans—just as learning to use tools was for our ancestors.[6]

So, is all this merely inventive thought, or is it a scientific possibility? Here are a few snippets from current research:

Autonomously growing synthetic DNA strands
Molecular robotics advance could enable new generation of self-assembling programmable devices.... Engineers have developed a method that allows pre-designed sequences of DNA to autonomously grow and concatenate along specific assembly routes, hence providing the basis for a new generation of programmable molecular devices.[7]

---

6   Kathleen Miles, "Ray Kurzweil: In The 2030s, Nanobots In Our Brains Will Make Us 'Godlike'." *Huffington Post*, Oct. 1, 2015. https://www.huffpost.com/entry/ray -kurzweil-nanobots-brain-godlike_n_560555a0e4b0af3706dbe1e2, retrieved 3/5/24.

7   Benjamin Boettner, "Autonomously growing synthetic DNA strands." *Wyss Institute*, Nov. 6, 2017. https://wyss.harvard.edu/news/autonomously-growing-synthetic-dna -strands/, retrieved 3/5/24.

Shape-Shifting Molecular Robots

This report indicates that a research group at Tohoku University and Japan Advanced Institute of Science and Technology has developed a molecular robot consisting of biomolecules, such as DNA and protein. The molecular robot was developed by integrating molecular machines into an artificial cell membrane. It can start and stop its shape-changing function in response to a specific DNA signal.[8]

Robotic Labs for High-Speed Genetic Research

In the basement of Imperial College sits the London DNA Foundry. The word "foundry" calls forth images of liquid metal being poured into moulds—of the early phase of the Industrial Revolution, in other words. This foundry is, however, determinedly modern. Liquid is indeed being moved around and poured. But it is in minuscule quantities, and it is not metal. Instead, it is an aqueous suspension of the genetic codes of life.[9]

DNA Robots Sort and Carry Molecular Cargo

Researchers from the California Institute of Technology (Caltech) have designed and synthesised robots from strands of DNA. The DNA robots were able to collect, transport and sort molecules, bringing the power of autonomous co-operation to the nanoscale—something normally reserved for much larger machines.[10]

---

8   "Shape-shifting molecular robots respond to DNA signals." Tohoku University press release, March 2, 2017. https://www.tohoku.ac.jp/en/press/molecular_robot.html, retrieved 3/5/24.

9   "Robotic labs for high-speed genetic research are on the rise." *The Economist*, March 1, 2018. https://www.economist.com/science-and-technology/2018/03/01/robotic-labs-for-high-speed-genetic-research-are-on-the-rise, retrieved 3/5/24.

10   Andrew Stapleton, "Tiny DNA robots can sort and carry molecular cargo." *Cosmos*, Sept. 14, 2017. https://cosmosmagazine.com/technology/tiny-dna-robots-can-sort-and-carry-molecular-cargo/, retrieved 3/5/24.

Synthetic organisms and living machines

The emergence of novel technologies such as artificial life, nanobiotechnology and synthetic biology are definitely blurring the boundary between our understanding of living and non-living matter. This essay discusses where, at the borderline between living and non-living matter, we can position the future products of synthetic biology that belong to the two hybrid entities "synthetic organisms" and "living machines" and how the approaching realization of such hybrid entities affects our understanding of organisms and machines.[11]

Trust us when we tell you that these few articles are but the tiniest fraction of those found in published research. However, not all research is published. Much remains quiet and secret. That's often the way with pioneering science. Those conducting it don't want others to appropriate their ideas. But there's a second level to secrecy, beyond the desire for credit and glory. Upgrading humans to a new level of hybridization with molecular machines—an iron mixed with miry clay scenario—must be perfected in secret until the public is ready to accept it. Until the appetites of consumers have been properly whetted and programmed to demand the upgrade.

No matter the cost.

The current campaign towards a spectrum of genders and sexual desires is but the tip of the iceberg. We're also being programmed to want godhood—just like Raymond Kurzweil. The pantheon of gods and demigods in Marvel and DC films is but one example. Juvenile fiction is another. The Disney-Hyperion series of books under the "Rick Riordan Presents" banner go way beyond Percy Jackson and his Olympian buddies. Tales of Norse, Hindu, Chinese, and Native American mythologies will hit the market soon, along with teacher's guides.

---

11 Anna Deplazes; Markus Huppenbauer, "Synthetic organisms and living machines: Positioning the products of synthetic biology at the borderline between living and non-living matter." *Syst Synth Biol.* 2009 Dec; 3 (1-4), p. 55.

Children already live in a constantly augmented and connected world, much of it virtual. Now, they can imagine themselves descended from ancient gods—in fact, they're encouraged to do so in the teacher's guides helpfully supplied by the publisher. But even a child knows it's fiction, right? What if that child is told in 2030 that it's a reality? All he or she need do is accept a molecular machine nanobot to achieve the divine upgrade.

Game over.

Replicating the dead may become the ultimate zombie apocalypse. Since death entered the world, mankind has dreamt of resurrection. The religious motif of the dying and rising god permeates all cultures—a cheap imitation of the only true rising God, Jesus Christ. Pagans speak of Mithras, Melqart, Dionysus, Osiris, Tammuz, Adonis, and Herne the Hunter, who all embody the idea of life beyond death. These gods live part of the year in the netherworld, rising in the spring and "dying" in the fall. Hindus believe in reincarnation, a form of resurrection, where a soul cycles through age after age in search of perfection.

The Egyptian goddess Isis, the first resurrectionist magician, fashioned a phallus for her dead, dismembered and reassembled husband Osiris, as the original was eaten by a fish. She then descended upon this artificial phallus in the form of a kite, a type of bird, creating Horus, who is a hybrid of living and dead tissue. Some legends say Horus decapitated Isis, and she then resurrected herself in a new form, possessing the head of a cow as a replacement. Others say that Isis gave birth to Apis, by Osiris-Apis, which makes her the mother of the bull-god.

Bulls and horns bring us back to Kronos, the god whose very name may refer to the idea of horns. As an aside here, did you know that CERN, home of the Large Hadron Collider, is a shortened form of the name Cernunnos, the origin of England's Herne the Hunter, sometimes called the Green Man, who is nothing more than a rebranded version of Kronos in convenient dying and rising god form?

Mary Shelley's early nineteenth century novel *Frankenstein: The Modern Prometheus* is the model for our modern concept of resurrection. Shelley grew up amongst men like Erasmus Darwin, a founding member of the Midlands Enlightenment and grandfather to both Charles Darwin and Sir Francis Galton, who founded the eugenics movement. Mary Shelley's fictional character, Dr. Victor Frankenstein, uses the emerging sciences to breathe life into a lifeless form. He cobbles together a new Adam, and discovers his new creation is stronger, smarter, and almost indestructible. Shelley's prose horrified her tender readers. Here are two opposing quotes from the book. First, the scientist reveals his hubris:

> "One man's life or death were but a small price to pay for the acquirement of the knowledge which I sought, for the dominion I should acquire and transmit over the elemental foes of our race."[12]

The other, the creature's true nature beneath a veneer of civility:

> "When I run over the frightful catalogue of my sins, I cannot believe that I am the same creature whose thoughts were once filled with sublime and transcendent visions of the beauty and the majesty of goodness. But it is even so; the fallen angel becomes a malignant devil."[13]

In the introduction to this fascinating study in humanity's dark designs, Shelley reveals a basic truth about resurrection:

> Invention, it must be humbly admitted, does not consist in creating out of a void, but out of chaos.[14]

---

12 Mary Shelley, *Frankenstein: or, The Modern Prometheus (Prologue: Letter 4)*. https://www.sparknotes.com/lit/frankenstein/full-text/letter-4/, retrieved 4/22/24.
13 Ibid., chapter 24. https://www.sparknotes.com/lit/frankenstein/full-text/chapter-24 /, retrieved 4/22/24.
14 Ibid., Introduction. https://en.wikisource.org/wiki/Page%3AFrankenstein%2C_ or_the_Modern_Prometheus_(Revised_Edition%2C_1831).djvu/15, retrieved 4/22/24.

Order out of chaos: *Ordo ab chao*. The ouroboros eating its tail, forever consuming itself in an act of rebellious, endless self-recreation.

It takes three things to bring about resurrection: 1) A substrate for the new life to enter and inhabit; 2) a willing magician to enact the rite; and 3) Something to power the spiritual machinery. Revelation chapter 13, verse 1 is placed by some at the end of chapter 12. Here's how it looks in the King James Version:

> And I stood upon the sand of the sea, and saw a beast rise up out of the sea, having seven heads and ten horns, and upon his horns ten crowns, and upon his heads the name of blasphemy.

The English Standard Version says this, placing the verse as 12:17.

> Then the dragon became furious with the woman and went off to make war on the rest of her offspring, on those who keep the commandments of God and hold to the testimony of Jesus. And he stood on the sand of the sea.

The ESV translates the original language as "he stood," not "I stood." Therefore, it's the dragon, Satan, who is standing on the sand of the sea, performing this action. What action? Chapter 13, verse 1 of the ESV tells us:

> And I saw a beast rising out of the sea, with ten horns and seven heads, with ten diadems on its horns and blasphemous names on its heads.

The Dragon is summoning up his comrade. This beast is the Antichrist, who receives the Dragon's power:

> And they worshiped the dragon, for he had given his authority to the beast, and they worshiped the beast, saying, "Who is like the beast, and who can fight against it?" (Revelation 13:4)

Then, in verse 11, we see this:

Then I saw another beast rising out of the earth. It had two horns like a lamb and it spoke like a dragon. It exercises all the authority of the first beast in its presence, and makes the earth and its inhabitants worship the first beast, whose mortal wound was healed.

Again, the first beast is the Antichrist.

It performs great signs, even making fire come down from heaven to earth in front of people, and by the signs that it is allowed to work in the presence of the Beast it deceives those who dwell on earth, telling them to make an image for the beast that was wounded by the sword and yet lived. And it was allowed to give breath to the image of the beast, so that the image of the beast might even speak and might cause those who would not worship the image of the beast to be slain. (Revelation 13:13–15)

Note here, that it is the *image* that has the power to slay people.

Also it causes all, both small and great, both rich and poor, both free and slave, to be marked on the right hand or the forehead, so that no one can buy or sell unless he has the mark, that is, the name of the beast or the number of its name. (Revelation 13:16–17)

Note that the False Prophet is given permission or power to give life to the image of the Beast. The word is *didomi*, which implies the granting of a right. He had power to do it. The False Prophet performs a magical working and thus brings to life a lifeless machine or image. It is this image which controls mankind, forcing all to enter its matrix or else die.

Transhumanists want this power. They want to build an image of man with superhuman qualities and capabilities, but they naively believe it is an image that can be controlled. And they believe it will be beautiful, egalitarian, and benevolent.

In truth, it will not see us any differently than we see animals in the wild—tolerable, as long as they're obedient, useful, or amusing.

CHAPTER FORTY-TWO

CONCLUSION

And the kingdom and the dominion
and the greatness of the kingdoms under the whole heaven
shall be given to the people of the saints of the Most High;
his kingdom shall be an everlasting kingdom,
and all dominions shall serve and obey him.

—DANIEL 7:27 (ESV)

In 1863, English author Samuel Butler said this about the future of mankind:

In the course of ages we shall find ourselves the inferior race. Inferior in power, inferior in that moral quality of self-control, we shall look up to them as the acme of all that the best and wisest man can ever dare to aim at. No evil passions, no jealousy, no avarice, no impure desires will disturb the serene might of those glorious creatures. Sin, shame, and sorrow will have no place among them.[1]

While this may sound as though Butler is advocating the Transhumanist agenda, he is not. In fact, the following statement by Butler had him branded as a Luddite:

---

1   Samuel Butler, "Darwin among the Machines." *The Press*, June 13, 1863. https://en.wikisource.org/wiki/Darwin_among_the_Machines, retrieved 3/5/24.

Day by day, however, the machines are gaining ground upon us; day by day we are becoming more subservient to them; more men are daily bound down as slaves to tend them, more men are daily devoting the energies of their whole lives to the development of mechanical life. The upshot is simply a question of time, but that the time will come when the machines will hold the real supremacy over the world and its inhabitants is what no person of a truly philosophic mind can for a moment question.

Our opinion is that war to the death should be instantly proclaimed against them. Every machine of every sort should be destroyed by the well-wisher of his species. Let there be no exceptions made, no quarter shown; let us at once go back to the primeval condition of the race. If it be urged that this is impossible under the present condition of human affairs, this at once proves that the mischief is already done, that our servitude has commenced in good earnest, that we have raised a race of beings whom it is beyond our power to destroy, and that we are not only enslaved but are absolutely acquiescent in our bondage.[2]

Butler's fears have already been realized because today's humans are truly enslaved to our devices. But the ultimate machine will do far more than aspire to rule our online lives; but to own our souls.

Despite knowing this, the scientific imperative remains in place to create the means of humanity's destruction. As with Victor Frankenstein, these deluded neophytes will one day realize the error of their beliefs, but even those who recognize the dangers advocate pressing on towards the goal.

It is as though something external drives them to madness.

A spirit.

A devil.

---

2   Ibid.

The Accuser. Satan. The Adversary in the Old Testament who had assembled a kingdom by the time our Lord walked the earth.[3]

A beast rising from the sea. The Antichrist: Leviathan. Chaos. An old god returning for one last crack at destroying mankind.[4]

The Destroyer: Kronos. "His name in Hebrew is Abaddon, and in Greek he is called Apollyon."[5]

As believers, we can rest assured that Christ has known the end from the beginning. Despite our failures, He has already won the victory.

As the gates of hell open and Leviathan and Kronos rise, our Savior stands ready to defend those who are covered by His blood. Transhumanists, who follow a silicon-based religion that promises eternal life through self-directed evolution, and the misguided souls who make pilgrimages to the Amazon to unlock the doors of the spirit realm through ayahuasca trips, are modern-day shamans with "new and improved" variations of the ancient rituals performed by Neolithic men at Göbekli Tepe, Copper Age Levantines at Gilgal Refaim, Sumerians at Babel, Hurrians in the *abi*, Babylonians in the *abzu*, and Hebrews in the *'ôb*.

Christ offers it through His sacrifice and resurrection. His is the *true* transformative power. All else is a pale imitation.

---

3 Matthew 12:26.

4 See Chapter 1 of our book *Giants, Gods & Dragons* for our theory that the spirit behind the human called Antichrist is Chaos, Leviathan.

5 Revelation 9:11. See Derek's book *The Second Coming of Saturn* for a detailed study connecting Kronos and his many identities in the ancient world to Abaddon/Apollyon.